Marxism
In
United States History
Before the Russian Revolution

(1876-1917)

AIMS HISTORICAL SERIES NO. 9

The American Institute for Marxist Studies (AIMS) is a non-profit educational, research and bibliographical institute. Its purposes are to encourage Marxist and radical scholarship in the United States and to help bring Marxist thought into the forum of reasonable debate to produce a meaningful dialogue among Marxist and non-Marxist scholars and writers. Its policy is to avoid sectarian and dogmatic thinking. It engages in no political activity and takes no stand on political questions. It grinds no axe for any group, party, sect, organization.

To these ends it invites the support and participation of all scholars and public-spirited individuals.

Marxism
In
United States History
Before the Russian Revolution

(1876-1917)

Oakley C. Johnson

Published for A.I.M.S. by
HUMANITIES PRESS
New York, 1974

© Copyright 1974 by
Oakley C. Johnson

Library of Congress Cataloging in Publication Data

Johnson, Oakley C   1890-
    Marxism in United States history before the Russian
Revolution (1876-1917)

    (AIMS historical series, no. 9)
    Bibliography: p.
    1. Socialism in the United States—History.
I. Title.   II. Series: American Institute for
Marxist Studies. AIMS historical series, no. 9.
HX83.J64   335.4'0973   73-13902
ISBN 0-391-00326-7

Printed in the United States of America

To Mary O. & Mary Lea

ACKNOWLEDGEMENTS

The more than twelve years of work I have put in on this book might have ended in nothing, had not Herbert Aptheker taken over the labor of editing. What seems likely to be my final illness—centering in a damaged heart—prevents further active library research. Dr. Aptheker not only undertook editing, but also suggested the re-writing of one chapter, the expansion of another, and caught various errors. Without his encouragement and supervision, I would have been helpless.

Previously, most of my research was done at three libraries, and I want to thank each one by name: First, the Tamiment Library, now owned by New York University, but originally the library founded by Alexander Trachtenberg at the Rand School of Social Science, and still located at Seven East Fifteenth Street, New York City. Its chief librarian, Dorothy Swanson, knew everything and unearthed everything that I asked for. Second, the Labadie Collection, founded by my old friend, Jo Labadie, the "gentle anarchist," through his gift of books and papers to the University of Michigan Library, Ann Arbor, Michigan, while I was still a student there. Its curator, Edward Weber, helped me immeasurably, not only while I worked there in the Summer of 1966, but by mail in the intervening years. Third, the New York Public Library, which has an astonishing accumulation of pamphlets and papers, a considerable number of which were gifts, years ago, from Friedrich Adolph Sorge, last secretary of the First International. The Library also has, to serve its vast public, a staff of kindly and efficient workers.

The entire list of people to whom I am grateful is far too long to insert here, but I must mention Gibby Needleman, my lawyer in these days; and, most of all, my wife, Mary Lea Johnson, and my daughters, Nancy and Priscilla, for faithful and—I fear—unrequited backing throughout.

Oakley C. Johnson
December, 1972

PREFACE

In this book I seek to answer the question: What was the role of Marxism in this country before any socialist state existed, when Socialism was only a theory and a hope?

I do not want to exaggerate, for it is obvious that Marxism was not dominant here, otherwise we would already have socialism. Rather, my thesis is that Marxism, although a minor factor in our history, was nonetheless a significant one, worth studying and evaluating. Furthermore, it was in every instance an influence on the side of progress.

I am using a compartmentalized approach, trying to measure the impact of Marxism on our politics, trade unions, art and literature, on such movements as that for woman suffrage and for full Negro freedom, on the churches, on reform legislation, on general culture and social ideals. I am also attempting to indicate the extent of Marxist influence on various segments of the population and in the farthest stretches of United States territory.

The introductory chapter on Karl Marx pictures his important personal influence here before, during and after the Civil War, and the writings by him which first received publication in the United States. From then on, the book traces the organized socialist movement. It deals with the achievements and aspirations of the Workingmen's Party of the United States, which became the Socialist Labor Party, from 1876 onwards, of the Socialist Party from 1900 onwards, of the many trade unions with socialist leadership. The chapter on legislation indicates how Marxist influence was important in securing labor and social reforms and political freedoms. The chapter on the church takes up the fascinating story of Christian ministers like George D. Herron, Charles H. Vail, Bouck White, Bishop Franklin Spencer Spalding, Bishop William Montgomery Brown, and Albert Rhys Williams. In literature and art, similarly. And so with the other sections; documented.

The impact of Marxism upon immigrant groups, prior to 1917, was considerable. This was notably true among Spanish-speaking, Slavic, Finnish, Germanic and Jewish peoples. Some indication of this appears in the pages that follow; actually, however, this is a story that requires and merits—though it does not yet have—a book all its own.

At the close I have a brief epilogue on the growth of these Marxist roots into the international Marxism-Leninism that followed.

CONTENTS

I

Karl Marx
and the United States

Karl Marx died in 1883, and his friend and collaborator Frederick Engels spoke the farewell words at his grave: "On the afternoon of the 14th of March at a quarter to three," Engels began, "the greatest living thinker ceased to think."

In this address, Engels summed up what Marx meant for mankind. It contained high praise for the founder of scientific socialism, but not too high for that time, nor for ours. Two billion people today revere Marx's name, and honor his achievements.

Three times in this brief speech Engels connected Marx with the United States. He said the death of Marx was a loss to "the fighting European and American proletariat"—and we recall, as we read, that the workers of this country were indeed fighting in the 1880's for the eight-hour day. Engels referred next to Marx's great journalistic contributions, beginning with "the first *Rheinische Zeitung* in 1842" and ending with "the New York *Tribune* from 1852 to 1861." In his conclusion Engels again spoke of the workers' loss: Marx, he said, was "loved and mourned by millions of revolutionary workers from the Siberian mines over Europe and America to the coasts of California."

Marx did take an active interest in the United States. It is not too much to say that, next to Germany, where he was born, and England, in which he lived most of his life and where he is buried, his greatest attention all his adult life was given to this country.

When he was twenty-six years old, and still defining and developing his philosophic views and methods, he made a notable statement in a polemic about social questions against a now-forgotten writer named Karl Heinzen. The subject of the polemic is not important here, but the heart of it was that Heinzen thought Communists were narrow-minded for continuing their struggle against the bourgeoisie even after the overthrow of the monarchy, as in France. Why, he asked, in effect, did Marx and Engels attack the kind German *capitalists!*

Writing in *Vorwarts* (1844), a German paper published in Paris, Marx stated in the course of his remarks: "Socialism and Communism did not originate in Germany, but in England, France and North America. The first appearance of a really active Communist Party may be placed within the period of the bourgeois revolution, at the moment when constitutional monarchy *was abolished.*"

What did Marx mean by listing "North America" as a place where communism "originated"? This was four years before he and Engels wrote the *Communist Manifesto*. It is clear that Marx was not yet thinking of modern or scientific socialism. He was thinking of the communism of the Utopians, who did in fact originate the idea of socialization of property in the hope of solving the problems of poverty and crime. Claude St. Simon, philosopher, and Francois Fourier, sociologist, in France and Robert Owen, manufacturer and philanthropist, in England, were the originators of this early socialist theory, and the plans outlined by both Fourier and Owen were extensively tried out in the United States. Marx was right in thus singling out the three countries, including our own, as the homelands of elementary socialist theory.

It is important to go more deeply into the American contribution.

Robert Owen himself came to the United States during the administration of James Monroe to launch his experiment at New Harmony, Indiana. He was greeted with respect and even acclaim. He twice addressed a joint session of the United States Congress on the subject of socialism, which he called a "New System of Society." The first speech was on February 25, 1825, and the second, March 7.

"It is therefore, no light duty that is about to devolve on those who are to direct the affairs of this extensive empire," Owen told the senators and representatives, and the president and his cabinet who were assembled with the Congress. "For the time is come, when they will have to decide, whether ignorance and poverty, and disunion, and counteraction, and deception, and imbecility, shall continue to inflict their miseries upon its subjects, or whether affluence, and intelligence, and union and good feeling, and the most open sincerity, in all things, shall change the condition of this population, and give continually increasing prosperity to all the states, and secure happiness to every individual within them."

The first of these two lectures by Owen was arranged by Henry Clay, Speaker of the House; the second by President-Elect John Quincy Adams. Shortly afterward Owen visited Thomas Jefferson at Monticello, and James Madison at Montpelier and was cordially received by both. It is significant that Owen let it be known that he wanted to extend his "New System," eventually, "to the blacks and the Indians."

As he spoke, Owen's settlement at New Harmony was already under way, and it managed to survive a few years despite its inner faults and its outer capitalist encirclement. Its achievements in advancing educational techniques and ideals were particularly notable.

Engels described Owen as "a man of almost sublime, childlike simplicity of character, and at the same time one of the few born leaders of men." He had already, before coming to America, tried out his socialist plans in Manchester, England, and New Lanark, Scotland. He was able to improve the character of thousands of the town's population, Engels adds, "simply by placing the people in conditions worthy of human beings." Owen was the founder of "infant schools," as then called, predecessors of our modern nursery schools and kindergartens. His educational plans were carried out still more extensively at New Harmony. Our country can be proud that it supplied opportunity for Owen's project.

Some fifteen years later the utopian socialism of Fourier, the French thinker, found powerful advocates in the United States. Albert Brisbane, noted newspaper man, became a follower of Fourier and introduced the latter's ideas into the United States in 1840 through his essay, *Social Destiny of Man.* In 1842 Brisbane also published a socialist column in the New York *Tribune,* with Horace Greeley's blessing—in the same paper that ten years later was to carry articles by Marx.

"We assert, and will prove," Brisbane declared in *Social Destiny Of Man,* "that Labor, which is now monotonous, repugnant and degrading, can be ennobled, elevated and made honorable;—or in other words, that Industry can be rendered attractive." He challenged the reader: "Have not the human race some higher Social Destiny to attain than the state in which they now vegetate? Are not some great ameliorations possible? . . . The present is doubt, and the future is blank." In short, he contended, the social structure under which the people lived was "a miserable system of waste and poverty."

In the same year Orestes Brownson, editor of the Boston *Quarterly Review,* and an advocate of the ideas of the other French utopian, St. Simon, started to write a review of Carlyle's *Essay on Chartism,* and ended up with a veritable manifesto on *The Laboring Classes.* He urged: " . . . we must destroy the power of the Banks over the government, and place the government in the hands of the laboring classes themselves, or in the hands of those, if such there be, who have an identity of interest with them."

In 1844, Parke Godwin, son-in-law and biographer of William Cullen Bryant and a writer on Bryant's paper, the New York *Evening Post*—and, like Brisbane, a Fourierist—produced the notable work, *Democracy, Constructive and Pacific*. Godwin ably criticized the shortcomings of American society. One of the chapter headings was: "The Revolutionary Work Finished, the Democratic Work Hardly Begun." He denounced the "Division of Society into Classes—One, Possessing All, the Other Nothing."

Alongside this intellectual ferment went the organizing activities of George Ripley, radical Congregational pastor, co-editor with Charles A. Dana of the *New American Cyclopedia* (to which Marx later was a contributor), who founded Brook Farm in 1841. Brook Farm was a utopian socialist venture along the line of the Fourierism advocated by Brisbane and Godwin. It won the admiration and to some extent the support of most of the intelligentsia of the period. Among its more than one hundred members were Charles A. Dana, who later became an editor of the New York *Tribune* and visited Karl Marx in Europe. Another member was Nathaniel Hawthorne; others who were friendly but not actual members of the community were Margaret Fuller, editor of *The Dial,* Horace Greeley, editor of the New York *Tribune,* and Ralph Waldo Emerson, chief intellectual leader of his time.

These sketchy references are enough to show how socialism and communism "originated" in part—as the younger Marx said—in "North America." There were scores of other communistic communities in the United States in the first half of the 19th Century, including one in Texas led by the ex-Jacobin, Etienne Cabet. They were a part of the broad fight-back against capitalism, a fight-back which included the organization of labor unions and of strikes for a living wage. Viewed historically, they were a preparation for scientific socialism, that is, for Marxism.

But—what is Marxism?

Marxism is, first of all, the teaching of Karl Marx; but it is more than that, for Engels collaborated with Marx, and his independently written works are a part of the body of teaching that we call Marxism, along with Marx's works and those written jointly by the two men. But here, too, we must note that Marxism is a teaching that is not theory alone, but a merging of theory and practice: Marx's teaching has to do with changing the world, and the Marxist must act as well as understand. And yet again we must correct ourselves: Marxism is a growing science, and as it is studied and applied in different times and circumstances, its content expands; great leaders like Lenin come, and others arise in Asia, the United States, Africa, Latin America and elsewhere, who interpret Marxism anew and bring it to bear under ever varying conditions and places.

Marxism is not, and has never been claimed to be, the invention of Marx alone. Lenin, who has given the best short summary of it, describes it as the continuation and union of "the three ideological currents of the nineteenth century, represented by the three most advanced countries of humanity: classical German philosophy, classical English political economy, and French socialism combined with French revolutionary doctrine."

The first was Hegel's method of dialectics, which Marx combined with materialism, then illustrated from history and used to study society and to organize social improvement. Marx called this dialectical materialism.

The second was the study of capitalist industry and the capitalist market, such as Adam Smith and David Ricardo carried on in their work on political economy, along with the labor theory of value that they elaborated, all of which Marx examined thoroughly in his *Critique of Political Economy* and in his three-volume *Capital,* and in so doing added to the labor theory the concept of *surplus value* which reveals where profits come from and how the rich exploit the poor who work for them.

The third consisted of the strong democratic currents in French history, beginning with the Encyclopedists such as Diderot, nonconformists such as Voltaire, and leaders of the French Revolution such as Robespierre, culminating in the great utopian socialist thinkers, St. Simon and Fourier.

French bourgeois historians—notably Francois Guizot and Augustine Thierry—held that class struggles were the dominant sources of change in their country. Marx, using a dialectical approach to the interpretation of all history, incorporated this concept of class struggle as a corner-stone of his teaching. Thus "class struggle" was originally a matter of capitalist, rather than socialist, theory.

As a matter of fact, Marx could (but apparently didn't) have gotten the class struggle idea from our own James Madison, who, like Guizot and Thierry, was well aware of it. As American radicals have often noted, Madison wrote in *The Federalist*—long before the *Communist Manifesto* appeared—that "those who hold and those who are without property have ever formed distinct interests in society." Incidentally, the first one to call attention to Madison's statement—so far as I know—was Daniel De Leon, in the *Nationalist* of August, 1889.

We cannot leave the theme of sources of Marxism without reference to the American anthropologist, Lewis H. Morgan, and his book, *Ancient Society, or Researches in the Lines of Human Progress from Savagery through Barbarism to Civilization,* published in New York and London by Macmillan in 1877. Engels tells us that Marx "had made it one of his future tasks to present the results of Morgan's researches in the light of the conclusions of his own—within certain limits, I may say *our*—materialistic examination of history, and thus to make clear their full significance." Marx never got around to doing this book, but he left notes of his plan for it. Using these, Engels wrote his notable *Origin of the Family,*

Private Property and the State in the Light of the Researches of Lewis H. Morgan, published in 1884.

In acknowledging all these sources, however, it would be wrong not to point out that Marx and Engels immeasurably enriched the ideas thus provided by other thinkers.

Finally, Marxism from the very first meant the organizing of the working class, internationally in the First International, and nationally in political parties. This follows from the essential union of theory with practice that Marxism insists upon; it holds that it is the mission of the organized working class to establish socialism, which will then evolve into full communism.

Marx began writing about the United States while still in Germany, and did still more of it during his successive exiles in France, Belgium, and England. In working out his theory of the state and private property, he took account—among other things—of the right to vote, and of abolition of a property qualification for that right, "in many cases of the North American States," as Franz Mehring's biography of Marx reports.

In the *Communist Manifesto,* Marx and Engels indicate that Communists would support other working class political movements "for the attainment of immediate aims," naming among others the "Young Agrarians in America." The latter was a movement of New York State farmers who struggled against high rents and for agrarian reform.

An English translation of the *Communist Manifesto,* as Engels observes in a prefatory note, appeared in the United States in 1872 in *Woodhull and Claflin's Weekly,* a New York paper.

In the same year (1848) that first saw publication of the *Communist Manifesto,* while Marx was leading the democratic associations in Cologne, Germany, he was visited by the two outstanding American journalists referred to above, Albert Brisbane and Charles A. Dana. Brisbane reported afterward: "I saw Karl Marx, the leader of the people's movement . . . He was a man in the thirties with a squat powerful body, a fine face and thick black hair. His features indicated great energy and behind his moderation and reserve one could detect the passionate fire of a daring spirit."

What Dana thought may be judged from the fact that later—while Marx lived in exile in London—he invited Marx to be a regular contributor to Horace Greeley's New York *Tribune,* and Marx accepted—an agreement that continued for nearly a decade. A pamphlet by Marx entitled *Herr Vogt,* in which he defended himself against now forgotten slanders spread by this Vogt, contained, as it happens, a copy of a letter from Dana complimenting Marx on his contribution to the *Tribune.*

Marx's *Tribune* articles began in 1852. In the preceding autumn one of his close friends and followers, Joseph Wedemeyer, emigrated to the United States, and among other activities served as Marx's literary agent. Weydemeyer himself set up a German-language monthly, *Die Revolution,* and to it Marx contributed one of his most important historical writings, *The Eighteenth Brumaire* (1852), which thus received its first publication in the United States. (This work, written in German, also made its English premiere in this country, more than four decades later, when Daniel De Leon published it serially in *The People,* Socialist Labor Party periodical.)

Marx also published in other German-American papers in the 1850's: The *New England Zeitung,* Boston, in which appeared his account of the trial of the Cologne Communists; the *New-Yorker Belletristiche Journal und Criminal-Zeitung;* and the New York *Turn-Zeitung,* in which Weydemeyer republished Engels' *Peasant War in Germany.* Besides the New York *Tribune,* Marx's ideas also became known through other English-language papers, such as the New York *Democrat* and the Washington *National Workingmen's Advocate.* "For months," says Karl Obermann, biographer of Weydemeyer, "the two men [Marx and Engels] wrote only for America."

When eleven German Communists were put on trial at Cologne, Germany, in 1852 (this was after Marx had gone to London), Marx—though ill and overworked—was obliged from a distance to carry on their defense. The evidence against them had been fabricated by the police. This is how Marx's wife described the situation in a letter to a friend in New York:

> All the proofs of the forgery have had to be provided from here and my husband has had to work all day and even far into the night. And then we have had to copy everything six or seven times and send it to Germany by various ways, over Frankfort, Paris, etc., because all letters to my husband and all his letters to Germany are opened and confiscated. The whole affair has now been reduced to a struggle between the police on the one hand and my husband on the other, and my husband is being made responsible for everything, even the conduct of the trial.

But "Marx won the victory," his biographer, Franz Mehring, declares, and exposed the forgery, though seven of the Communists received prison sentences anyhow. Part of the success of the expose was due to the publication in the Boston *New-England Zeitung* of Marx's revelations about the German police shenanigans. Engels got 450 copies from the United States for distribution in Germany, where the press was muzzled.

During the political struggles here that preceded the election of Abraham Lincoln, and the Civil War that followed, Marx's interest in the United States was intense and his contribution to its progress was considerable. Joseph Weydemeyer and others devoted to Marx's teachings played an important role in mobilizing thousands of newly naturalized Germans behind Lincoln's Republican Party in the presidential election campaign of 1860. In New York, Philadelphia, St. Louis and Chicago, especially, the German population voted for Lincoln and free labor. The researches of Herman Schlueter, labor historian, and F. J. Herriott, author of the noted study, "The Conference of the Deutsches Haus" in Chicago on the eve of Lincoln's nomination, as well as other authorities, show that the German vote was a decisive factor that helped tip the balance toward Lincoln and guarantee his election. Leading and educating those German-Americans, and a considerable section of organized labor also, were the Communist Clubs of New York, Chicago and St. Louis, and their mentors in London, Marx and Engels.

As for the Civil War itself, one need only look at the correspondence of Marx and Engels as given in *The Civil War in the United States,* brought out by International Publishers in 1937, to see how the two men followed and analyzed its progress for the entire four years. Not only their private thinking is revealed here, for some of it seeped through into the conduct of the War. Marx urged the arming of the slaves, the issuing of an emancipation proclamation, the strategy of marching through Georgia to the Atlantic to cut off the Confederate Army from its base of supplies. One can't claim that Lincoln followed the direct advice, or even that he was precisely aware that it had been given: but it was published (some of it in the *Tribune*), and it got around. Other keen minds came to similar conclusions (Frederick Douglass, for one), and Lincoln eventually acted.

Lincoln certainly knew of the help he got from the newly organized First International, for he received and answered their greeting, sent on November 29, 1864, through the American ambassador in London, Charles Francis Adams, congratulating him on his re-election to the presidency. This message, which was the first public statement of the International, said in part:

> The workingmen of Europe feel sure that, as the American War of Independence initiated a new era of ascendancy for the Middle Class, so the American anti-slavery war will do for the working classes. They consider it an earnest of the epoch to come that it fell to the lot of Abraham Lincoln, the single-minded son of the working class, to lead the country through the matchless struggle for the rescue of an enchained race and the reconstruction of a social world.

It was Marx who proposed to the General Council of the International the sending of this congratulatory message; it was Marx who wrote it, and Marx's signature, with others of the Central Council, was on it.

In his reply, Lincoln agreed that the conflict "with slavery-maintaining insurgents" was indeed "the cause of human nature." He said the North felt "new encouragement" from the message of "the workingmen of Europe." He was glad, he said, to receive "their enlightened approval and earnest sympathies."

Lincoln also knew of the demonstrations by British workers in protest against the British government's contemplated intervention in the Civil War on the side of the South—and of their success in helping to prevent that particular barbarity. Marx and the International had a good deal to do with this action of the British working class.

The overall relationship of Marx and Lincoln cannot be adequately judged without taking into account Lincoln's famous statement: " . . . that labor is prior to, and independent of capital; that, in fact, capital is the fruit of labor, and could never have existed if labor had not first existed; that labor can exist without capital, but that capital could never have existed without labor. Hence . . . labor is the superior . . . greatly the superior to capital."

After Lincoln's assassination, Marx again wrote on behalf of the International, this time to President Andrew Johnson, expressing condolence at the untimely death of "one of the rare men who succeed in becoming great, without ceasing to be good"—and at the same time urging strict fulfillment of the "stern duties" left by the Civil War. But there was no reply. The new chief executive proved unable to carry out the "political reconstruction and social regeneration" that Marx spoke of.

It is not well-known that a third official communication to our country was issued by the First International, congratulating the American people on the successful ending of the Civil War. This was the address, *To the People of the United States,* and it declared: "No more shall the salesman's hammer barter human flesh and blood in your market places, causing humanity to shudder at its barbarity."

The third letter was written in the same spirit as the *Address to President Lincoln* and the *Address to President Johnson,* both of which were composed by Marx, but its author, according to the recently published *Minutes of the General Council,* was the International's general secretary, William R. Cremer, an Englishman. Though the letter was not Marx's, its content was certainly Marxist. It was adopted at a meeting (Sept. 28, 1865) at which Marx was present, and the next day the General Council's important Standing Committee, of which Marx was a Member, approved it and ordered copies sent to all sections of the International, including that in New York.

It is important to recall this Address today because of the following passage, which elaborated a point stressed over and over again by Marx:

> Since we have had the honour of expressing sympathy with your sufferings, a word of encouragement for your efforts, and of congratulations for the results, permit us also to add a word of counsel for the future.
>
> As injustice to a section of your people has produced such direful results, let that cease. Let your citizens of to-day be declared free and equal, without reserve.
>
> If you fail to give them citizens' rights, while you demand citizens' duties there will yet remain a struggle for the future which may again stain your country with your people's blood . . .
>
> We warn you then, as brothers in the common cause, to remove every shackle from freedom's limbs, and your victory will be complete.

We cannot leave the subject of the Civil War without mention of the followers of Marx who, with his blessing, joined Lincoln's northern armies to battle against the Confederacy. Of these, chief are Joseph Weydemeyer, who became a brigadier general and August Willich, another member of the Communist League, who also became a brigadier general in the Union Army. These Communists were latter-day Lafayettes who not only fought for freedom here but became citizens and builders of our country.

Nor can we omit mention of Marx's articles in the Vienna paper, *Die Presse,* through which he popularized in Europe the cause of Lincoln and the war against slavery. He praised, for example, William Lloyd Garrison, Gerrit Smith, and Wendell Phillips for their leadership of the Abolitionists before and during the War. Speaking of Wendell Phillips, Marx wrote on one occasion: "For 30 years he has without intermission and at the risk of his life proclaimed emancipation of the slaves as his battle-cry, regardless alike of the persiflage of the press, the enraged howls of paid rowdies and the conciliatory representations of solicitous friends."

Just as the first public statement of the International's General Council was to an American president, so the first message of the International's 1st Congress—at Geneva, 1866—was to an American labor union. Marx congratulated the National Labor Union then meeting in Baltimore for demanding, as did the Geneva Congress, that the workday be limited to eight hours.

Some of Marx's pithy advice to American workers is as relevant today as it was in his lifetime. Labor in a white skin cannot be free so long as labor in a black skin is branded, he told them.

The first International held five historic congresses in different European cities, and some of the delegates in 1868 and 1872 were from the United States. At the Fourth Congress, held in Basle, Switzerland, there was one American delegate; at the Fifth Congress, at the Hague, Holland, there were four Americans. It was this Fifth Congress which voted, at the suggestion of Marx and Engels, to transfer the head office to the United States.

The International was moved to New York in 1872, where it functioned with an American governing council headed by F. A. Sorge, friend of Marx, as general secretary, for nearly five years before it was finally dissolved. The International was in constant touch with Marx, who advised on innumerable problems, as described in that excellent work, *The First International in America,* by Samuel Bernstein. (Augustus M. Kelley, New York, 1962) During its life in this country, the International was an important initiating and guiding force for American labor, and its teachings formed the direct foundation for the socialist movement that followed.

If one examines the work of the International in New York, one realizes how splendid that foundation was. During the "long depression," of 1873-1877 demands were formulated for relief and for public works; it sent petitions to New York City's mayor and to the Congress in Washington for action on behalf of the jobless; it called on President Grant to summon a special session of Congress in order to sanction broad internal improvement programs. It issued a "Manifesto to the Working People of North America" which insisted on a moratorium on rent, work for all at regular rates, and an eight-hour day. It organized unions (such as the Furniture Workers' Association in 1873); it supported strikes and raised money for the strikers; and it set up (as in Newark, N.J.) labor defense councils on behalf of arrested workers. And not only on the Atlantic seaboard: "The hand of the International," says Bernstein, "was as plain in Chicago as in Philadelphia or Newark." But never was the lesson omitted that Socialism was the ultimate solution for economic woes.

Marx himself gave the best analysis of the achievement and significance of the International, and at the same time, as Mehring writes, refuted the assertion that it had been a failure.

> "In reality," Marx said, "the social-democratic workers' parties in Germany, Switzerland, Denmark, Portugal, Italy, Belgium, Holland and North America, organized more or less within national frontiers, represent just as many international groups. They no longer represent isolated sections, sparsely distributed over various countries and held together by a General Council on the periphery, but the working class itself in constant, active and direct connection, held together by the exchange of ideas, mutual assistance and joint aims. . . . Thus, far from dying out, the International has developed from one stage to another and higher one in which many of its

original tendencies have already been fulfilled. During the course of this constant development it will experience many changes before the final chapter in its history can be written."

Reference has been made to Marx's correspondence with Weydemeyer, and to his exchange of messages with F.A. Sorge, general secretary of the International while it was located in New York. He also corresponded with many other Americans, and so did Engels.

Among the Americans Marx wrote to were his old-time Chartist friend, G.J. Harney, then assistant secretary of state of Massachusetts; Moncure D. Conway, a prominent social thinker and philanthropist; and John Swinton, noted editor who had visited him the year before, and to whom he sent a copy of the French edition of *Capital*. In his letter to Swinton, Marx described Henry George's *Progress and Poverty* as "a last attempt— to save the capitalistic regime."

Among those Engels wrote to—after Marx's death—were Philip Van Patten, an early national secretary of the Socialist Labor Party; Hermann Schlueter, the labor historian; and Florence Kelley, noted social worker who had earlier translated and had published Marx's lecture on *Free Trade* (Boston, 1888), and also Engels' *Condition of the Working Class in England in 1844* (N.Y. 1887). The latter book about England did not appear in England until five years after it came out in the United States.

In his letter to Schlueter, Engels made the oft-quoted statement: "Once the Americans get started, it will be with an energy and impetuousness compared with which we in Europe shall be mere children." In his letter to Florence Kelley, Engels made that other oft-mentioned observation: "I consider that many of the Germans there have made a grievous mistake when they tried, in the face of a mighty and glorious movement [the Knights of Labor] not of their own creation, to make of their imported and not always understood theory a kind of . . . dogma, and to keep aloof from any movement which did not accept that dogma. Our theory is not a dogma but the exposition of a process of evolution, and that process involves successive phases."

In writing to Conway, Marx spoke of the plight of the Communards fleeing from the bloody vengeance of French reaction after the fall of the Paris Commune in 1871. Marx encloses, he says, a list of some 80-90 refugees, whose condition is "truly deplorable," and urges formation of "a special committee, if possible, to take over the job of finding work for the refugees, most of whom are skilled workers and professional men." Marx himself probably did more for them than anyone else. Mehring says that Marx's house was a refuge for the fugitive Communards "who were always certain of receiving advice and finding assistance there."

Marx was equally concerned about the Irish victims of British oppression, and concerning them Mehring tells a delightful incident involving Marx's daughter Jenny:

> The English press obstinately remained silent about the barbarities committed against the imprisoned Fenians, so Jenny Marx sent a number of articles to Rochefort's *Marseillaise* under the pseudonym of Williams, a name which her father had used quite a lot in the fifties. In these articles she described passionately how democratic England treated its political prisoners, and these revelations in a paper which was probably more read than any other on the continent were too much for Gladstone. A few weeks later most of the imprisoned Fenians were free and on their way to America.

Another daughter, Eleanor Marx Aveling, translator and writer, made a lecture trip through the United States with her writer-husband, Edward Aveling, and reported on conditions she saw. Engels, too, made a month-long trip to this country, and rather enjoyed himself. "Everything in America has to be new," he wrote in his notes, "everything has to be rational, everything has to be practical, consequently, everything is different from what it is with us."

It is worth noting, briefly, that two typically American objections to Communist and Socialist organizations were handled effectively by Marx.

One was the charge of *conspiracy,* of *secrecy.* "Our Statutes," said Marx, speaking for the International, "make it the duty of all sections of our association to act openly, and even if the statutes were not clear on the point, the character of an association which identifies itself with the working class excludes any possibility of such an association taking on the form of a secret society."

The other was the charge of *violence,* of advocating *forcible overthrow* of a government as a matter of principle, regardless of conditions. Marx dealt with this at a First International meeting in Amsterdam, the Netherlands, as follows:

> Some day, the workers must conquer political supremacy, in order to establish the new organization of labor: they must overthrow the old political system whereby the old institutions are sustained. If they fail to do this, they will suffer the fate of the early Christians, who neglected to overthrow the old system, and who, for that reason, never had a kingdom in this world. Of course, I must not be supposed to imply that the means to this end will be everywhere the same. We know that special regard must be paid to the institutions, customs, and traditions of various lands; and we do not deny that there are certain countries, such as the United States and England, in which the workers may hope to secure their ends by peaceful means. If I mistake not, Holland belongs to the same

category. Even so, we have to recognize that in most continental countries, force will have to be the lever of revolution. It is to force that in due time the workers will have to appeal if the dominion of labor is at long last to be established.

It was Marx's insistence on this rational approach that led finally to a break between the International and the followers of Auguste Blanqui. The latter advocated the seizure of power through a daring coup carried out by a small minority, that is, by a putsch. Marx would have none of it. Marx wanted the whole working class informed and organized, having faith that they would take the power in their own time and in their way. Among Marx's reasons for moving the International to New York was that of getting free from the Blanquist tendency which, because of the despondency following the fall of the Paris Commune, was temporarily strong in some parts of Europe. Another reason was to avoid the anti-political Bakuninist influence which was then dominant in Spain and Italy. The Bakuninists wanted, it was said, "to destroy political power, not to conquer it" (Mehring). Marx was determined that the International, while it lasted, should have a chance to give the world's workers a correct general line to improve their lot and win eventual control over their destiny.

Marx himself felt keenly the frustrations of poverty. Referring to his fiftieth birthday, he exclaimed, "Half a century on my back and still a pauper!" But he never surrendered. To Engels he wrote, when his only son died at the age of nine: "In all the terrible anxiety of suffering I have gone through, I have been sustained by the thought of you and your friendship, and by the hope that we have still something worthwhile to do together in the world."

John Swinton, the correspondent referred to above, a distinguished American journalist, who during the Civil War was managing editor of the New York *Times,* visited Marx in 1880, less than three years before Marx died. In an article in the New York *Sun,* on which he worked after leaving the Times, Swinton wrote:

> One of the most remarkable men of the day who played an inscrutable but puissant part in the revolutionary politics of the past forty years is Karl Marx. A man without desire for show or fame, caring nothing for the fanfaronade of life or the pretense of power, without haste and without rest, a strong, broad, elevated mind, full of far-reaching projects, logical methods, and practical aims, he has stood and yet stands behind more of the earthquakes which have convulsed nations and destroyed thrones, and do now menace and appall crowned heads and established frauds, than any other man in Europe. . . .

He was at Ramsgate, the great seashore of the Londoners, while I was in London, and there I found him in his cottage with his family of two generations. The saintly faced, sweet-voiced, graceful woman of suavity who welcomed me at the door was evidently the mistress of the house and wife of Karl Marx. And is this massive-headed, generous-featured, courtly, kindly man of 60, with the bushy masses of long revelling gray hair, Karl Marx? His dialogue reminded me of that of Socrates—so free, so sweeping, so creative, so incisive, so genuine—with its sardonic touches, its gleams of humor, and its sportive merriment. He spoke of the political forces and popular movements of the various countries of Europe—the vast current of spirit of Russia, the motions of the German mind, the action of France, the immobility of England. He spoke hopefully of Russia, philosophically of Germany, cheerfully of France, and somberly of England—referring contemptuously to the atomistic reforms over which the Liberals of the British Parliament spend their time. Surveying the European world, country after country, indicating the features and developments and the personages of the surface and under the surface, he showed that things were working toward ends which will assuredly be realized.

Swinton spoke of Marx's *Capital* (he meant the first volume, since the second and third had not yet appeared), which had been published in German and in a Russian and a French translation, but not yet at that time in an English one. Marx told him, he said, of the volumes to come, saying that the third—on "Credit"—would be largely illustrated from the United States, "where credit had such an amazing development." Swinton continued, in the closing words of his interview:

The afternoon is waning toward the long twilight of an English summer evening as Mr. Marx discourses, and he proposes a walk through the seaside town and along the shore to the beach, upon which we see many thousand people, largely children, disporting themselves. Here we find on the sand his family party—the wife, who had already welcomed me, his two daughters with their children, and his two sons-in-law, one of whom (Charles Longuet) is a professor in King's College, London, and the other, I believe, is a man of letters (Paul Lafargue). It was a delightful party—about ten in all—the father and the two young wives, who were happy with their children, and the grandmother of the children, rich in the joysomeness and serenity of her wifely nature. Not less fine than Victor Hugo himself does Karl Marx understand the art of being a grandfather; but more fortunate than Hugo, the married children of Marx live to cheer his years. . . . And the talk was of the world, and of man, and of time, and of ideas, as our glasses tinkled over the sea.

That was 1880, and the first English translation of *Capital,* by a third son-in-law, Edward Aveling, and Samuel Moore, and edited by Frederick Engels, did appear in 1887, four years after Marx's death. But it was known and quoted long before that, in Marx's own lifetime, on both sides of the Atlantic. As a matter of fact, says Paul Lafargue, in a memoir of the Marx family, "in America, during a big strike in New York passages from the work were published in the form of leaflets in order to urge the strikers to see it through and prove to them the justice of their demands."

The complete English text of *Capital,* including Volumes II and III, translated by Ernest Untermann, was first published by Charles H. Kerr and Company in Chicago—Volume II in 1906 and Volume III in 1909.

II

Marxism in Yankee Politics

"In a Yankee country," Marx wrote to an American friend, half-jokingly, it was necessary "to consider the Yankees first of all."

He had in mind the historical Yankee propensities, characteristics, and traditions in matters political, as well as the special problems American workers had to face.

The story of Marxist political action in the United States, both in its successes and its failures, illustrate Marx's adroit and somewhat cryptic wisecrack.

The start here was propitious, positive, and early. The United States was the world's second country to have a functioning Marxist political party. The Workingmen's Party of the United States was organized on July 19-23, 1876, in Philadelphia, one hundred years (almost to the day) after the Declaration of Independence.

The dates emphasized are those on which the Marxist impress was unmistakable, even though limited. The first country to have a Marxist party was Germany, in 1875, through unity between the followers of Ferdinand Lassalle, on the one hand, and those associated with the Marxists, Wilhelm Liebknecht and August Bebel. This is not to deny that it was Lassalle who founded the Social Democratic Party of Germany in 1869; nor is it to deny that Marx in his *Critique of the Gotha Programme* severely took to task the program of the united Social Democratic Party of 1876. The latter party was indeed a Lassallean-Marxist compromise, but it was Marxist in large part, and, more important, the Marxist influence was destined to expand and take control.

Let us outline the rise of Marxist parties during the 1870's:

  1875: The German Social-Democratic Party.

1876: The Workingmen's Party of the United States.

1876: The Portuguese Socialist Party (a very small group).

1877: The Austrian Socialist Party (which was quickly crushed by the government: a new one had to be organized in the '80's).

1878: The Danish Social Democratic Federation.

1878: The Dutch Social Democratic Union (later re-organized as a party in the '90's).

1879: The Spanish Socialist Workers Party (small, and obstructed by anarchist influence in the working class).

France did not have a Socialist Party until 1880, at which time Jules Guesde and Gabriel Deville, assisted by Marx's sons-in-law, Jean Longuet and Paul Lafargue, organized it on a platform written by Marx himself. Belgium formed her Socialist Party that same year. A year later, Great Britain's Social Democratic Federation was established under Henry M. Hyndman's leadership. Tsarist Russia's first Marxist organization, led by G.V. Plekhanov, was set up in 1883. Then came Norway's in 1887, Austria's second try in 1888, and Sweden's in 1889.

It was not until the 1890's that Italy acquired a Marxist party (1892), and after her came Poland (1893) and Holland (her second try, 1894). In tsarist Russia, Lenin's League of Struggle for the Emancipation of the Working Class—which followed Plekhanov's earlier group—began to function in 1895. In Ireland, the first Marxist party was organized in 1896 by James Connolly, who had lived and worked for some years here in the United States.

With the exception of Argentina (1896), all parties of Marxist socialism in South America and Asia were formed after 1900.

The First International officially ended its existence July 18th, 1876; the next day, the ten representatives of the International, who had just dissolved that historic body, joined representatives of other groups to begin establishing the Workingmen's Party of the United States.[1]

Some essentials of the story resemble the formation of the German Social Democratic Party the year before. The Lassalleans in this country had already, as in Germany, formed Social Democratic Organizations. The chief ones were the Social Democratic Workingmen's Party of North

---

1. It is sometimes said that the "Social Party," formed by Sorge and other members of the New York Communist Club in 1868, was the first Marxist party in the United States, which may be true in a verbal sense. But this "party" was set up before the International was moved from London to New York; it never functioned as a party; and it lasted only a few months, soon merging with the National Labor Union in early 1869, and becoming Section I of the First International in New York in 1872.

America, and the Workingmen's Party of Illinois, both set up in 1874. The new party—the Marxist Workingmen's Party of the United States— was thus a merger of the two Lassallean parties and the sections of the First International.

This new party represented the entire country, with membership in New York, Philadelphia, Pittsburgh, Newark, N.J., Paterson, N.J., Chicago, St. Louis, New Orleans, Grand Rapids, Mich., San Francisco, Lawrence, Mass., Milwaukee, Baltimore, Cincinnati, and New Haven, Conn. Leading individuals included F.A. Sorge, a musician, the International's general secretary; Karl Speyer, a cabinet-maker, a close associate of Sorge; Otto Weydemeyer, son of Marx's old friend, Joseph Weydemeyer; J.P. McDonnell, an Internationalist and trade-union organizer, who was made editor of the new party's paper, *The Labor Standard;* Adolph Strasser, a Lassallean and cigar-maker; P.J. McGuire, a Lassallean; and Adolph Douai, editor of the German paper, *Die Arbeiter-Union.* The first national secretary was native-born Phillip Van Patten, who later carried on a correspondence with Engels.

The difference between Marxists and Lassalleans expressed itself practically in disagreement about entering candidates, for public office. A year or so before the Workingmen's Party was formed, the Marxists stated that it would be advisable to postpone political activity "until the organization of the working classes has progressed far enough, until the laborers in the organizations are sufficiently disciplined, that they can come forward as a distinctly separate party, diametrically opposed to the old political middle class parties, that they can pursue and carry out their own objects." And in the compromise agreement made when the Party was formed, it was stated that all sections of the party were "earnestly invited to abstain from all political movements for the present and to turn their back on the ballot box."

But in little more than a year the party began to run candidates for local office, and perhaps this was in line—remembering Marx's phrase— with "considering the Yankees."

So it was that the new party in the next couple of years ran local candidates in New York, New Haven, St. Louis, Milwaukee, Cleveland, Cincinnati, Chicago, Detroit, New Orleans, Boston and Denver, and some were elected. In Chicago, one of its candidates for alderman was Albert R. Parsons, who about a decade afterward, led the fight for the 8-hour day and was hanged as a result of the Haymarket frame-up.

Note should be taken of the question of Lassalleanism. Ferdinand Lassalle was, like Marx, a German of Jewish descent and a brilliant pioneer socialist. His theory differed from Marx's in at least two important respects: he regarded socialism and the socialist movement as merely national, and paid no attention to international aspects; and he put his whole faith in political action and disregarded trade unions. With Marx, of course, internationalism was a cardinal principle, and working-class political action was to be based on a unionized working class. The Lassallean and Marxist trends competed for a few years, but within a generation the Marxist view pushed ahead in all socialist parties, including the American. One reason for this was the all-round and all-encompassing theory set forth in *Capital, Anti-Dühring,* and other classic works, against which Lassalleanism turned out to be mere unavailing demagogy. As Wilhelm Liebknecht said in a telegram on the occasion of Marx's death: "Marx changed Social-Democracy from a *sect* . . . into a *party.*"

The year after the Workingmen's Party was formed, its name was changed to Socialist Labor Party, and that is the name by which it is known in history.[2]

Socialist Labor Party

Many talented and prominent people became members of the Socialist Labor Party in the succeeding quarter of a century. One of these was C. Osborne Ward, a brother of the well-known sociologist Lester F. Ward. C. Osborne Ward twice visited the General Council of the First International in London and met Marx, and he afterward belonged to the First International in New York, though he was not always fully in line with its policies. After 1876, he lectured occasionally under Socialist Labor Party auspices. Most important, he was the author of the monumental work, *The Ancient Lowly,* privately published in 1888 and re-published by Charles H. Kerr & Co., in 1907. (A copy of it, marked "Gift of F.A. Sorge," may be found in the New York Public Library.) Ten years before this (1878) Ward had produced his *Labor Catechism of Political Economy: A Study for the People,* which was a thoughtful and sometimes scintillating but erratic hodgepodge of dialogues in which he discussed "scientific socialism," "monopoly," the principles of the Socialist Labor Party, political economy, government ownership of utilities, and so on.

Also notable among Socialist Labor Party leaders was German-born Dr. Adolph Douai, whose fine pamphlet "Better Times!" was first published in 1866, and re-published by the Socialist Labor Party in 1884. Unlike Weydemeyer and Sorge, Dr. Douai became a Marxist after he came to the United States.

Another pioneer socialist of the time—his name almost forgotten

---

2. *"Socialistic* Labor Party" was the official designation, as shown in the records of 1879 and 1881. Shortly afterward the term became *Socialist* Labor Party.

now—was P.A. Lofgreen, who published *The Coming Revolution: Its Principles,* in 1878 in St. Louis.[3] "My object," he said, on the title page, "is not to make people read, but to make them think." (This book, too, was in the private library of F.A. Sorge, and is now in the New York Public Library.) The content is, like Osborne Ward's *Labor Catechism,* a set of dialogues, with the aim of answering current objections to socialism.

Another Socialist Labor Party member was the brilliant Florence Kelley, who in 1888 translated into English, Marx's lecture on "Free Trade," which he had delivered in Brussels in 1848. She also translated Engels' classic, *Condition of the Working Class in England in 1844.* Both works were published in the United States. She corresponded extensively with Engels.

Still another propagandist for the S.L.P. was Laurence Gronlund, an immigrant from Denmark, who wrote a significant exposition of socialism in 1884 called *The Cooperative Commonwealth.* He used this term, he said, to show "that Socialism is no importation, but a home-growth wherever found." This work is an important native Marx-influenced work on Socialism though as Engels noted, Gronlund-Lofgreen did a lot of borrowing of ideas without giving credit.

Edward Bellamy's *Looking Backward,* published in 1888, is a work of fiction describing an imaginary socialist civilization. Thousands of readers of this romance became converts to socialism. Bellamy did not belong to the Socialist Labor Party, but he surely helped to build it. He disclaimed indebtedness to previous thinkers, but it is obvious that he absorbed a good deal of Marxism from the intellectual atmosphere of his time.

So great was Bellamy's influence through this novel that a kind of political party grew up around him based on "Nationalism"—from the *nationalizing* of railroads, mines, monopolies, utilities—a kind of utopian socialist party. But, as with Lassalleanism, so with Nationalism: there was no real basic theory, and many of Bellamy's adherents gradually went over to Marx. Here, for example is a news item from the *Workmen's Advocate,* November 22, 1890, page 1, column 3, which tells of the organizing of a local of the Socialist Labor Party in Brooklyn the week before. In the story is this sentence: " . . . Mr. C.H. Matchett of Nationalist Club No. 1 of Brooklyn and Organizer of the City Hall Section of the S.L.P. delivered an excellent lecture, in which he depicted the new conditions of industry and life under the Co-operative Commonwealth which it is the aim of Nationalism and Socialism to establish." The

---

3. It appears that "P.A. Lofgreen" was a pseudonym used by Lawrence Gronlund during an early sojourn in St. Louis. See Robert V. Bruce, *1877: Year of Violence.*

concluding sentence was: "The name of this Section will be: 'The South Brooklyn American Section No. —— of the Socialist Labor Party.' "

The C.H. Matchett referred to (who was both a Nationalist and a member of the S.L.P.) became in 1892, the first Socialist candidate for vice president of the United States.

Around 1890 appeared the Curacao-born Daniel De Leon, a lecturer at Columbia University on International Law. He had joined the Nationalists around the mid-1880's, and worked his way toward the Marxists. De Leon was a man of exceptional ability. His chief contribution to this country was to center the attention of the socialist-minded on Marx and Marxism. In the course of this he attended international congresses of the newly formed Second International. Furthermore, he helped to place Socialist ideas more definitely into national politics. He translated works by Marx, Engels, Bebel. And at the turn of the Century he established the first daily Socialist newspaper in English in the United States.[4]

One of De Leon's original writings was his *Two Pages from Roman History* (1903), the "two pages" being two lectures, one on plebs leaders and the other on the Gracchi brothers, famed tribunes of the Roman populace. Other early writings by De Leon included *Reform or Revolution,* a lecture at Boston in 1896, and *What Means This Strike?*, an address at Bedford, Massachusetts, in 1898.

In 1892, Simon Wing, of Boston, Massachusetts, a photographer, inventor of the "tin type" and of other photographic devices, and a manufacturer of cameras, was nominated for president, the first candidate for president of the first Marx-led party in the United States. Wing (1826-1910), a descendant of English settlers to Massachusetts in 1632, was an independent, original thinker. He began his voting career as an anti-slavery man, and after joining the Marxists continued as a Socialist his whole life till his death at the age of 84.

With Wing, as already stated, was the vice-presidential candidate, Brooklyn-born Charles H. Matchett, an electrician and an active member of the Knights of Labor. In 1892, Wing and Matchett won a vote of 21,512.

At the next presidential election, in 1896, Matchett was the S.L.P. candidate for president, and his running mate was Matthew Maguire, a New York-born machinist of Irish descent. Maguire was founder of the Machinists and Blacksmiths' Union and a leader in the 8-hour movement.

Matchett and Maguire won a vote of 36,275 for Socialism in 1896.

4. Exception must be made for the St. Louis *Star,* an English Marxist daily set up in 1877, which lasted about a year, according to Morris Hillquit's *History of Socialism in the United States.*

Meanwhile De Leon's positive contributions to Marxist history were beginning to run out. His insistence on Marxist principles, while it helped scientific socialism get on its feet, began after a while to solidify into dogma. Without intending it, De Leon was strait-jacketing the Marxist party into a sect.

Engels once said he wished that socialists would not pick quotations from Marx or himself, but "would think as Marx would have thought in their place." This is where De Leon failed.

His sectarianism in socialist theory spread over into labor and political tactics. As he grew older, he rejected all "immediate demands" as reformist; and he thought out a wholly unworkable trade union scheme, the results of which still plague American advocates of industrial unionism and of Marxism. Brilliant younger men were attracted to the Socialist movement—Hermann Schlueter, historian and friend of Engels; Morris Hillquit, lawyer and author of *History of Socialism in the United States;* James F. Carey of Massachusetts; Caleb Harrison of Illinois; Benjamin Hanford, Ohio-born printer; Algernon Lee, school teacher, originally of Ohio; Job Harriman, lawyer of California—all of them names to conjure with in socialist history, and all had originally joined the Socialist Labor Party. But they were cramped by De Leon's doctrinairism. In addition, independent socialists arose outside the party—W.J. Ghent, Illinois printer and author; John Spargo, Vermont journalist; Charles Edward Russell, journalist and muckraker; A.M. Simons, historian; Gustavus Myers, historian and muckraker; and others. Victor L. Berger in Milwaukee was leading his own Social Democratic constituents, among whom was Frederic Heath, editor and writer. And Eugene V. Debs, leader of the American Railway Union, but outside the Socialist Labor Party, was reading Marx and thinking.

Hillquit, backed by Max Hayes and Job Harriman, led a revolt against De Leon, who, unfortunately, seemed not to understand what was happening, or why. They joined Berger's Milwaukee Social Democrats, and the supporters of Debs, to found a new Socialist party.

Out of the Socialist Labor Party and into the new Socialist Party marched the cream of the cadres educated, but frustrated, by De Leon. Around the year 1900 (between 1898 and 1901 to be exact) old and new Socialists realigned themselves. These included not only all those named above but also the first Socialist candidates for high office: Simon Wing, Charles H. Matchett, and Matthew Maguire. Among them, were three magnificent women who left the Socialist Labor Party for the Socialist Party: Florence Kelley, the brilliant friend of Engels; Kate Richards O'Hare, later editor of the *National Rip Saw;* and the devoted young Ella

Reeve Bloor. Also included eventually, was Solon De Leon, De Leon's talented son.[5]

The turn of the century thus saw the split finalized, the first ideological division within the Marxist movement in this country. De Leon lived fourteen years longer, and the Socialist Labor Party still has a formal existence, but in reality (except for two incidents to be noted later) the story of the Socialist Labor Party ends here.

The Socialist Party

The birth of the Socialist Party of America was as interesting as that of the Workingmen's Party of the United States, but it had a different pattern. The new party had greater successes, and carried Socialist progress to a higher stage; but it had its own problems that were just as difficult as those of the older party, and potential inner divisions that turned out to be equally unbridgeable.

First of all, there was the division between itself and the Socialist Labor Party, for always there were efforts to unite the two parties of socialism. One of those who sought unity was Socialist Labor Party member Boris Reinstein, who, years later, became librarian of the Third International. But unity of these two organizations was a chimera. It never had a chance.

The Socialist Party started in several parts of the country before 1900; it ran candidates in the 1900 presidential election before it was actually organized; and finally, after much travail, it did become an organized party, with elected officers, a headquarters, and real existence in 1901. The events, the actors, and the successive staging of the scenes constitute an evolving drama that must be sorted out and described before any analysis of its later history will be understandable.

While in the '90's unrest was beginning within the Socialist Labor Party, there were developing throughout the country other forces which also helped to build the new Socialist Party.

The Christian Socialist movement, starting in Boston in 1889, declared that "the aim of socialism is embraced in the aim of Christianity," and insisted that "the Church has a definite duty" in regard to it. The movement lasted only a few years, but one of its graduates was Professor George D. Herron, who taught Applied Christianity at Iowa College, and eventually became a leader of the Socialist Party. Herron and his followers were the second acquisition (after those who withdrew from the Socialist Labor Party) of cadres to join the new party.

5. Italian-born Louis C. Fraina, New York journalist, did not leave the Socialist Labor Party until 1914.

In the first decade of the twentieth century a new kind of Christian Socialism developed, which was different from the earlier one. The earlier kind held itself aloof from the Socialist party of its time, and disapproved of the class struggle. Not so the newer kind of Christian Socialists. The interdenominational Christian Socialist Fellowship, organized in 1909, explicitly supported the candidates, the Marxist program, and the activities of the Socialist Party, and even sent delegates to the congresses of the Second International. Much the same could be said of another such organization, functioning, however, only within the Episcopal Church: the Church Socialist League, set up in 1911. These two socially militant Marx-influenced groups of Christian Socialists numbered in their ranks younger colleagues, so to speak, of Professor Herron, including the Rev. Edward Ellis Carr, head of the Christian Socialist Fellowship, and the Rev. Eliot White, a vice-president of the Church Socialist League, along with such lay Socialists as Prof. Vida D. Scudder and social worker, Ellen Gates Starr.

Simultaneously with the Christian Socialists should be considered the Populists—"People's Party"—which was, in a way, the last genuine non-Marxist revolt of the exploited in this country. It was based on the poor farmers of the west and south, and had a reform program. Its beginning was in 1890 in Kansas, and its first candidates for president and vice-president won a million votes in 1892, the same year that saw the first Marxist presidential candidates. But the Populists endorsed Bryan in 1896, and their separate place in political history came to an end. However, Eugene V. Debs himself at this time supported the Populists; so did Henry Demarest Lloyd, author of *Wealth Against Commonwealth* (1894); and J.A. Wayland, founder of the *Appeal to Reason*. Indeed by 1909 some fifteen per cent of the Socialist Party were old Populists. They had moved toward Marxism. Thus, the Populists served as the third source of cadres for the Socialist Party.

The historic Pullman strike of 1894, centering in Chicago and fought by Eugene V. Debs' American Railway Union, was the culmination of a series of great strikes of the period; it was a definite time of learning for American workers. The strike was defeated by government troops and court injunctions, and for this reason Debs turned his attention to political action. Two years later he began to think of socialism, but he thought at first of "colonization"—a plan to capture some western state and then spread socialism from there, which meant a queer marriage of community utopianism and local socialist politics. But the marriage went on the rocks. The colonizing Social Democracy of America, which was formed in 1897, and which Debs joined, split in 1898. The political contingent—that is, the Marxist-influenced group, led by Debs and Victor

Berger—separated themselves from the colonizers and formed the Social Democratic Party of America, with headquarters in Chicago. Thus, Debs and Berger—the American Railway Union and the Milwaukee Social Democrats—constitute the fourth and fifth acquisitions, respectively, for the Socialist Party.[6]

Most important, however, in a chronological sense, was the split within the Socialist Labor Party, and the setting up of a new "Socialist Labor Party." This took place in July, 1899, when Section New York recalled the members of the National Committee (as it had the nominal power to do under the S.L.P. Constitution). The insurgents then elected Henry L. Slobodin, a New York Socialist Lawyer, as the new national secretary (they hoped) of the Socialist Labor Party. The intention of the party rebels was to oust De Leon and the then national secretary Henry Kuhn.

But, as Hillquit recorded later in his *History,* "The war within the Socialist Labor Party was now on in earnest." The De Leon faction, through court action, was able to hold on to the party name, the party organ (*The People*), and the party property. The insurgent group was at last obliged for the time being to name itself the Social Democratic Party (a sort of standard term), and its organ *The Worker*. This group, led by Morris Hillquit of New York, Job Harriman of California, and Max Hayes of Ohio, then called a convention (1899) at Rochester, N.Y., and took two important actions: they invited unity between themselves and the newly formed Social Democratic Party of Debs and Berger; and they nominated national candidates for office for the 1900 elections: Job Harriman for president and Max Hayes for vice president.

Now came the crucial negotiations for unity between the "Rochester faction" of the S.L.P. (unwillingly registered as the Social Democratic Party) and the Debs-Berger Social Democratic Party located in Chicago. A committee of nine from each side carried on the unity discussions. Hillquit, Harriman, Max Hayes, J. Mahlon Barnes and others represented the "Rochester" S.L.P. faction, while Victor Berger, Frederick Heath, James F. Carey, Margaret Haile and others represented the Debs-Berger organization.

"To seal the treaty of peace," as Hillquit puts it, it was agreed at the outset that the top candidates in 1900 would be Eugene V. Debs for president and Job Harriman for vice-president, and in this way there was a guarantee of socialist candidates on the ballot. (The Rochester nomination of Harriman was downgraded to second place, and that of Max

6. Some S.L.P. members went over to the Debs-Berger Social Democracy in 1897-8, without waiting for the S.L.P. insurgents led by Hillquit, to organize at Rochester in 1899. One of them was New York lawyer Isaac A. Hourwich, father of Nicholas I. Hourwich, who years later was a leader of the Socialist Party left wing.

Hayes for vice-president was dropped, in the interest of unity.) In addition, the two sides also agreed to accept as a campaign platform the "Rochester S.L.P." program plus the Debs-Berger Social Democratic "immediate demands."

But the two could not agree on a name for the party, nor on a party headquarters, nor on national officers. While the election campaign was on there was a "tacit truce" between the unity-seeking groups, and Debs and Harriman won a vote of 87,814 in 1900, the highest socialist vote recorded in the United States up to that time.

The Socialist Labor Party, now a purely De Leon-led group, also ran candidates in 1900, who received a vote of 34,191—less than half the vote of the new party, and even less than its own vote in 1896. But observers were not slow to note that the combined vote of the two socialist organizations indicated a fairly strong voter interest throughout the country in Marxist political ideas, at this beginning of the twentieth century.

With the election past and considerable success achieved for the "new" socialist party, a convention was called to meet at Indianapolis in 1901. There were 124 delegates, of whom three were Negro and one was Puerto Rican. Eighty per cent of the delegates were nativeborn. Leon Greenbaum was elected the first national secretary; the headquarters were established at St. Louis, Mo.; the agreed name of the organization was the Socialist Party of America.

"The Socialist Party of America, in national convention assembled," said the first paragraph of the Platform, "reaffirms its adherence to the principles of international socialism, and declares its aim to be the organization of the working class and those in sympathy with it into a political party, with the object of conquering the powers of government and using them for the purpose of transforming the present system of private ownership of the means of production and distribution into collective ownership by the entire people."

Immediate demands, which were opposed by De Leon, were defended: "we recognize that the time and manner of the transition to socialism also depend upon the stage of development reached by the proletariat." The Party, therefore, would "support all active efforts of the working class to better its condition." The Party supported "reduction of the hours of labor," higher pay, "state or national insurance" against unemployment, "equal civil and political rights for men and women," and other reforms, including public ownership of the means of transportation, communication and utilities. The platform warned, however, against "so-called public-ownership" in which capitalists sought control "for the purpose of obtaining greater security in the exploitation of other indus-

tries and not for the amelioration of the conditions of the working class."
From 1901 on, the Socialist Party grew rapidly. The following table from the *American Labor Yearbook* for 1917-18, outlines the story:

Year	Candidate	S.P. Presidential Vote
1900	Eugene V. Debs & Job Harriman	87,814
1904	Eugene V. Debs & Benjamin Hanford	402,283
1908	Eugene V. Debs & Benjamin Hanford	420,713
1912	Eugene V. Debs & Emil Seidel	897,011
1916	Allan L. Benson & George R. Kirkpatrick	590,297

Deb's running mate in 1904 and 1903 was Benjamin Hanford, Cleveland-born union printer and Socialist, a popular agitator in the press and on the soapbox. His articles were collected from the New York *Call* and published in 1909 in the pamphlet, *Fight for Your Life,* which included a story creating the legendary "Jimmy Higgins," the type of indefatigable rank and file Socialist who made every party activity succeed.

In 1912, when nearly a million votes were won by the Socialist Party, Debs' running mate was Emil Seidel, the mayor of Milwaukee, most important city to be headed by a Socialist.

In 1916, as the table shows, the Socialist vote declined to half a million, partly because Debs was not this time the Party's candidate, and partly because of the confusion and uncertainty arising out of the First World War. (Woodrow Wilson, Democrat, was campaigning to "keep us out of war.") The Socialist candidate for president was Allan L. Benson, the well-known journalist and muckraker, and for vice-president another writer, George R. Kirkpatrick, author of *War—What For?*

A further and more significant indication of Marxist influence in politics was the election of many local officials throughout the country. In 1912, according to James Weinstein in *Studies on the Left* (Winter, 1960), 1200 electoral offices in "340 municipalities from coast to coast" were filled by Socialists, "among them 79 mayors in 24 states." There were in that year 22 Socialists in state legislatures. Victor Berger was elected congressman from Wisconsin in 1910 and Meyer London from New York in 1914. Emil Seidel became mayor of Milwaukee in 1910 and Thomas Van Lear the mayor of Minneapolis in 1916. Other fairly large cities that elected Socialist mayors were Flint and Kalamazoo in Michigan, Butte in Montana, and Schenectady in New York. In 1911 Ohio elected seventeen socialist mayors; Minnesota, Illinois, and Pennsylvania elected six each; and Michigan and Utah, five each. In 1912 Socialist mayors were chosen in Gulfport, Florida, and Winnfield, Louisiana.

Theodore Roosevelt was worried, it is said, by the rise in Socialist strength. Already in 1908, when Debs campaigned across the country on the "Red Special" (consisting of an engine and one coach) there was, wrote Ray Ginger in *The Bending Cross,* a desperate campaign by the old party politicians to "Stop Debs."

Important is the fact that in 1916, despite the slump shown in the Table, there was a recorded Socialist vote in 47 of the 48 states.[7] (*American Labor Yearbook,* 1917-18.) In seventeen of them the vote was more than 10,000: California, Illinois, Indiana, Iowa, Kansas, Massachusetts, Michigan, Minnesota, Missouri, New Jersey, New York, North Dakota, Oklahoma, Pennsylvania, Texas, Washington, Wisconsin. Others that were just under 10,000 but more than 9,000 were Colorado, Idaho, Montana, and Oregon.

A further instance of Marxist influence is the steady and gradual adoption of Socialist "immediate demands," not only in legislation but in the platforms of other parties. The "Bull Moose" Progressive Party in 1912, for example, took over quite a few planks from the Socialist platform. Among them were direct election of U.S. Senators, equal suffrage for men and women, prohibition of injunctions in labor disputes (with a little hedging), the abolition of child labor, the eight-hour day (not completely), the abolition of convict contract labor, a department of labor in the Cabinet, and so on.

In the Weinstein article cited above there is a table of Socialist periodicals in twenty-eight states, showing that some 140 such papers were in existence during the years 1913-1916 (omitting those founded in 1917) of which more than a hundred were English-language papers. These included the Alaska *Socialist,* of Fairbanks, Alaska; the Oakland, California, *World;* the *Eye Opener,* Chicago; the *International Socialist Review* (Chicago); the *Appeal to Reason,* Girard, Kansas; the *National Rip Saw,* St. Louis, Missouri; the *Melting Pot,* St. Louis, Missouri; the New York *Call;* the *Intercollegiate Socialist* (New York); the *Masses* (New York); the *Iconoclast,* Minot, North Dakota; the *Citizen,* Cleveland; *Justice,* Pittsburgh; and the Milwaukee *Leader.* In those years Oklahoma had 19

---

7. In the 48th state, Utah, there was a Socialist Party state secretary, C. T. Stoney, whose office was at 713 First Avenue in Salt Lake City; and there had been a vote of 9,023 for Debs in 1912. Apparently the 1916 vote was simply not reported.

Socialist papers in English; New York, 10; Ohio, 10; Minnesota, 8; Pennsylvania, 8; Kansas, 7; Missouri, 6; and California, 5.

Two socialist publications that were no longer extant in 1913, when Weinstein's list starts, were nonetheless important: the *Coming Nation* (1893) and *Wilshire's Monthly* (1900), both of which lasted many years.

Almost all of these papers were privately owned, and most showed the aberrations and pet emphases of their publishers; but all supported the Socialist Party, its candidates and its program. All of them advertised and sold works on scientific socialism, including basic works by Marx and Engels: the *Communist Manifesto; Wage-labor and Capital; Socialism, Utopian and Scientific;* and *Capital* itself.

The private ownership of these papers was not calculated to emphasize party discipline or a unified concept of theory, but, under the conditions of the time, it did produce a varied approach to the public, aroused interest in Marxist ideas, and stimulated socialist thought among widely differing sections of the population.

In 1903, when his *History of Socialism in the United States* was published, Hillquit was already able to observe that the Socialist Party differed from the reform parties in being national rather than sectional. The Populists had their strength in the West, the Greenbackers in the Middle West, and the Henry George movement in the East. "The Socialist vote, however," he said, "is pretty well distributed all over the country."

There ought indeed to be a history of the Socialist Party in each of the states, but very few have been produced. The Socialist history of New York and California is generally available; William Z. Foster included in his work some treatment of Washington State, where Dr. Herman F. Titus edited the Seattle *Socialist;* studies of the Non-Partisan League of North Dakota have incidentally revealed previous Socialist history there; Meridel Le Sueur's *Crusaders* has given us much of the Socialist background of Minnesota; and my biography of Charles E. Ruthenberg, *The Day Is Coming,* contains a good deal of data on Ohio.

In addition, some university graduate theses of uneven quality have been done on the Socialist history of Oklahoma, North Dakota, California, Louisiana and a few other states. One of these, Donald Kenneth Pickens' master's thesis in 1957, was entitled *The Program and Principles of Oklahoma Socialism* (University of Oklahoma, Norman, Oklahoma). In his dedication he says it was "written in memory of Grandfather Pickens, an Oklahoma Socialist." Dr. Ruth A. Allen, Emeritus Professor of Economics of the University of Texas, has done some research in the labor history of her state, including data on Thomas A. Hickey, old-time Socialist leader, who was a member of both the Socialist Labor Party and the Socialist Party.

There is need for much further work. Thus, why not a history of the Alabama Socialist movement? In Bessemer, Alabama, the *Southern Socialist* was published early in the 1900's, edited by G. W. Price. He said in the September, 1903, issue: "We print 1000 copies of this number, and expect to issue 1500 copies of the next number. How many do you want?" The paper referred to the "world's greatest philosopher in political economy, Karl Marx." On the front cover of this number was a portrait of "Comrade F.X. Waldhurst," a 35-year old cabinet worker, who was "State Secretary of the Socialist Party of Alabama." It was announced that C.H. Spencer would be the Party's candidate for mayor of Bessemer. The State of Alabama, it said, already had twenty-eight local branches, and intended to have more. And a few years later, in 1912, Alabama gave Debs 3,029 votes.

Or why not a socialist history of Missouri, where Marx's friend, Joseph Weydemeyer, and the latter's son Otto, settled down? In St. Louis there used to be a branch of the First International. After the Civil War, according to biographer Karl Obermann, Joseph Weydemeyer was elected county auditor in St. Louis, taking office on January 1, 1866. By 1910, the *Coming Nation,* published in St. Louis, was saying "Socialism is the next stage in human progress." In 1911, Missouri elected socialist mayors in four cities: Buffalo, Cardwell, Gibson, and Minden Mines. By 1912 Missouri was able to give Debs 14,612 votes.

Louisiana is notable in that it had the highest Socialist vote in 1912 of any southern state: 5,240. In earlier and later years its vote was much lower. The key to the 1912 vote was the great lumber workers' struggle in which Bill Haywood personally took a hand, a struggle in which Louisiana Socialists cooperated with the I.W.W., and in which white and Negro workers were united in splendid solidarity. Covington Hall, Louisiana's Socialist poet, wrote a leaflet for this "long, hard bitter three-year (1910-13) 'lumber war'." In an article in the *International Socialist Review,* Covington Hall said the timber workers, white and black, "had grown tired of the 'white supremacy' and 'social equality' flim-flam, and set out to organize One Big Union of *all* the workers and overthrow peonage forever in the mills and forests of the South."

A thesis (1951) at Louisiana State University, *The Socialist Vote in Louisiana, 1912: An Historical Interpretation of Radical Sources,* by H. Grady McWhiney, states: "What is even more remarkable is that a considerable number of men were voting for a party supposedly dedicated to destroying the Southern way of life." He notes that in Winn parish, in the cypress belt of Louisiana, the Socialists "elected a school board member and a police juror, as well as an entire slate of municipal officers in the town of Winnfield." In West Carroll Parish another Socialist was elected a police juror. In one town in Beauregard Parish, "Debs received more votes than Roosevelt and Taft combined."

But the timber workers' strike was beaten down by the lumber companies, and this promising united front died.

Michigan was early on the scene in the world of Socialist thought. In the Labadie Collection at the University of Michigan Library is a copy of the "Platform, Constitution and Resolutions" of the "Socialist Labor Party," published by the "National Executive Committee" in Detroit, Michigan, under date of April, 1880. On the back cover of the document are announcements of pamphlets by A. Douai, Laurence Gronlund, Osborne Ward, Karl Marx, and P.J. McGuire, for sale by the Party's national secretary, Philip Van Patten, in Detroit. Also announced are "Socialist Tracts"—*What is Socialism?, What Socialism Means, What Socialism Offers,* and so on—authored and published by Judson Grenell of Detroit.

In the Socialist Labor Party days, wrote Frederic Heath in *Socialism in America,* published at the turn of the century, there were 358 Socialist votes in a local Detroit election in 1895; in 1897, in a statewide Michigan election, there were 2,166. A study of this period by Sidney Glazer, *Labor and Agrarian Movements in Michigan, 1876-1896* (Ph.D. dissertation University of Michigan, 1932) shows that there existed a weekly paper, the Detroit *Socialist,* in 1877-78. Another periodical, a monthly, known as the *Three Star,* was set up in 1880 by Joseph Labadie and Judson Grenell to function as the "semi-official organ of the Socialistic Labor Party."

In 1900 Michigan gave 2,826 votes to Debs in his first campaign, and increased this to 23,211 in 1912; in 1916, for Benson, it was 16,120. Besides Flint and Kalamazoo, Michigan chose Socialist mayors in three other cities in 1911; Greenville, South Frankfort, and Wilson. Later, in 1916, a Socialist mayor was chosen in Traverse City. In the years just preceding the Russian Revolution, from 1912 to 1916, the Party's state secretaries were cigar-maker Ben Blumberg of Grand Rapids, shoe merchant Joseph Warnock of Harbor Springs, and shoemaker, John Keracher of Detroit. The Michigan press in the Socialist Party period included a Finnish paper in Hancock, *Tyomes* (1903); the *Progressive Worker,* Holland, (1911); *Peo's Paper,* Kalamazoo (1911); and the *Michigan Socialist,* Detroit (1916).

Some significant theoretical contributions by leaders of the Socialist Party were written between 1900 and 1917. Here is a selected list, chronologically arranged:

> 1902: W.J. Ghent, *Our Benevolent Feudalism,* Macmillan, New York. Lawrence Goldman says in *Studies on the Left* (#3,

1963) that this book gave Jack London the basis for his novel, *The Iron Heel.*

1903: A.M. Simons, *Class Struggles in America,* C. H. Kerr & Co., Chicago. This pamphlet is significant as the first examination of United States history from a more or less Marx-oriented point of view. Completely re-written and expanded, it was published in 1911 by Macmillan as *Social Forces in American History.*

1903: Morris Hillquit, *The History of Socialism in the United States,* Funk & Wagnalls, New York. This classic work helped to launch the new Marxist organization, the party of Debs.

1904: W.J. Ghent, *Mass and Class,* Macmillan, New York.

1906: Joseph Dietzgen, *Philosophical Essays,* C.H. Kerr & Co, Chicago.

1906: Joseph Dietzgen, *Positive Outcome of Philosophy,* C.H. Kerr & Co., Chicago. Note: In 1886, before publication of these essays, Dietzgen was an editor of a Socialist Labor Party German-Language paper, and at that time he defended the Haymarket martyrs despite the surrounding reactionary hysteria.

1907: Louis B. Boudin, *The Theoretical System of Karl Marx,* C.H. Kerr & Co., Chicago. With this book, American labor began to show its grasp of scientific socialism. "Its limpidity and clarity of style," says William J. Blake, in *An American Looks at Karl Marx,* "alone would make it noteworthy."

1908: Jack London, *Revolution,* a lecture. *Contemporary Review,* New York. Other essays of social comment by Jack London, such as are collected in *Jack London: American Rebel,* edited by Philip S. Foner, might be put alongside *Revolution.*

1910: Herman Schlueter, *The Brewery Industry and the Brewery Workers Movement in America,* Union of Brewery Workers, Cincinnati, Ohio. This, a Marxist work, was the first history of a labor union in this country.

1910: James Oneal, *The Workers in American History,* National Rip-Saw Publishing Company, St. Louis, Missouri. A militant exposé of class forces in early American history.

1911: Gustavus Myers, *History of Great American Fortunes,* in three volumes, C. H. Kerr & Co., Chicago. This influential work has inspired several successors by other authors in recent years.

1913: Herman Schlueter, *Lincoln, Labor and Slavery,* Socialist Literature Company, New York. In his Preface, Schlueter writes: "The author's standpoint in the treatment of this subject is that of historical materialism, first brought into the science of history by Karl Marx and Frederick Engels."

1915: Scott Nearing, *Anthracite: An Instance of Natural Resource Monopoly.* The John C. Winston Company, Philadelphia. "Dedicated to an order of life in which the chief aim will be happy and noble human beings."

To these might be added some memorable propaganda titles—Marxism-on-the-soapbox:

1905: John M. Work, *What's So and What Isn't.* National office of the Socialist Party: Chicago. Clear, simple, admirable. (In 1918 the same author wrote *Why Things Happen to Happen,* a popular exposition of historical materialism.)

1909: Ben Hanford, *Fight for Your Life.* (Stories and sketches that first appeared in the New York *Call.*) Wilshire Publishing Co., New York.

1909: Oscar Ameringer, *Life and Deeds of Uncle Sam.* Reprint in 1912 by Political Action Company: Milwaukee. Packed with humor and quite a bit of grim truth.

III

Marxism and American Trade Unions

A remarkable debate took place on April 4, 1865, at a session of the General Council of the First International, between Karl Marx and John Weston. The debate was to settle once and for all whether a raise in wages was really worth fighting for, and whether trade unions, which struggled to get such raises, brought harm or benefit to working people.

John Weston, a carpenter and a leading Internationalist, brought up the question, going against his own union in saying that a raise in wages was of no use at all, and that labor unions were also useless, or worse. Back of Weston was the noted economist, John Stuart Mill, one of the formulators of the "wages fund" theory.

The question is academic now, and serves only to underscore one of the services Marx performed for trade unions in general. He demolished the Weston-Mill argument, provided an unassailable theory for the economic struggles of the workers, and justified the existence of unions.

The "wages fund" idea was that at any given time there was a definitely limited amount of money for the payment of wages, an amount that could not be increased. If a strike did by chance win a raise in pay, the capitalists would raise prices, and the workers would win nothing. This "wages fund" idea was really identical with the so-called "iron law of wages" believed in by Ferdinand Lassalle, which in turn explains why the Lassalleans had no faith in trade unions, relying solely on "political" activities. The Marxists also used political action, but preferred to have strong unions as a foundation.

Marx began his counter-argument by praising Weston's "moral courage" in taking a stand unpopular among workers. He added, with the courtesy he always showed to fellow workers: "I hope that, despite the unvarnished style of my paper, at its conclusion he will find me agreeing

35

with what appears to me the just idea lying at the bottom of his theses, which, however, in their present form, I cannot but consider theoretically false and practically dangerous."

The debate was easily won by Marx, but the paper he read was never published until his daughter Eleanor Aveling found it long after his death and gave it to the world as *Value, Price and Profit*.

The very next year after this debate, at the first congress of the First International, in Geneva, Marx went further. "The immediate task of the trade unions," he said, in a report, "is restricted to the needs of the daily struggle between labor and capital—in a word, to questions of wages and working hours." But that was not all, and could not be all, for "the trade unions involuntarily become organizing centers for the working class." While they are "indispensable in the daily struggle," he said, "still more important is their other aspect as instruments for transforming the system of wage labor and for overthrowing the dictatorship of capital."

This was in truth but a re-statement of the advice he had already given trade unions in the second part of the debate with Weston: "Instead of the conservative motto: *'A fair day's wages for a fair day's work!'* they ought to inscribe on their banner the revolutionary watchward: *'Abolition of the wages system!'* "

How to bring about this higher consciousness in trade unions and among trade unionists has for a century been the thorniest problem for Marxists, but there have been successes as well as failures.

Higher wages and shorter hours were the two general tasks Marx gave to unions in the day-to-day struggle. The matter of wages was handled in *Value, Price and Profit*. The question of hours was dealt with in Chapter X of *Capital:* "The Working Day."

Marx began by asking, "What *is* a working day?" The answer, so far as capitalist ideas went—as American workers have confirmed a thousand times over—was a day of "very elastic nature," days of "8, 10, 12, 14, 16, 18 hours, i.e., of the most different lengths." What this meant was that the workers *had* to fight for shorter hours. Said Marx: "In place of the pompous catalogue of the 'inalienable rights of man' comes the modest Magna Carta of a *legally limited working-day*, which shall make clear 'when the time which the worker sells is ended, and when his own begins.' "

Marx, expressed pleasure at the decision of the National Labor Union of the United States to fight for an 8-hour day. The two Congresses—the First International in Geneva and the first national federation of American workers in Baltimore—were meeting at about the same time (1866), and both adopted resolutions on the subject. Said the American labor body—"Eight hours shall be the normal working day in all states of the

American Union." Said the International, speaking for the workers of all the world—"Eight hours should be the legal limit of the working day."

The *Manifesto* was primarily a political document, but it recognized the necessity of forming "combinations [trade unions] against the bourgeoisie," and it indicated the general attitude that a Marxist party should take toward trade unions. Marx and Engels told the various socialist parties that they had "no interests separate and apart" from the proletariat, and that therefore, while they kept an eye on, and worked for, "the future" of the workers, i.e., socialism, they should not neglect the fight for immediate aims, the workers' "momentary interests."

After the transfer of the First International to New York, its American leaders, such as F.A. Sorge, continued to emphasize, as Marx had done, the importance of organized labor. In 1874, writes Samuel Bernstein in *First International in America,* they pointed out, in a discussion with Chicago Lassalleans, that "the trade unions provide the first troops in the class struggle, for their members combine as wage earners against their exploiters." And, they went on, this combining leads to politics. Economic conditions, they explained, were "pushing the trade unions on to the correct path, from the economic to the political struggle against the propertied classes." Unionists were obliged, as time went on, to use more than the strike weapon: they were compelled to demand laws in their favor, and to elect political representatives who would adopt and enforce those laws.

The First International in the United States did a great deal more, however, than defend the mere *existence* of trade unions: it raised money for strikes conducted by unions, and, in some instances, went to the trouble of directly *organizing* unions. Bernstein gives the example of the Furniture Workers Association, "set up by the First International," a union which, he said, "stoutly protected the interests of workers."

The same author cites numerous examples of assistance to striking trade unionists. "American workers' groups had already learned of the International's spreading influence and were asking its help," he writes. The striking horse-car conductors of New York City requested the General Council to publicize their appeal, 'To the Impartial, Intelligent and Sympathizing People of the City of New York.' " The conductors were protesting a 106-hour work week! Their appeal was promptly printed in both English and German socialist newspapers.

Among these pros and cons it should not be forgotten that the American leaders of the International were themselves workers and active trade unionists. It was an accepted rule that each one join the union of his trade. Fred Bolte was a cigarmaker; Carl Speyer, a cabinet maker and secretary of the Furniture Workers' Union: F. A. Sorge, a musician; J. P.

McDonnell, journalist, who had been on the old General Council in London, became an organizer of Irish workers while in the First International in New York; Simon Dereure, veteran Communard, was a shoemaker; C. Osborne Ward, former machinist, was a journalist; Conrad Carl, a tailor; etc.

Another citation from Bernstein will serve as a summary of the International's direct help to trade unions: "The record of the Committee shows its dedication to the cause of the workers. It urged the sections to organize them; it sent aid to strikers; it argued the cause of labor, never failing to point out that its welfare was the concern of the International."

An examination of the chief trade unions that arose in the United States after the American Civil War shows how the Marxist influence expressed itself, through leadership, ideas, aims and activities, right up to 1917.

The National Labor Union, founded in 1866 by the leader of the Iron Molders, William H. Sylvis, was the first national federation of trade unions in this country, and, as said above, it was praised by Marx for its stand on behalf of the 8-hour day. In her monograph, *William H. Sylvis and the National Labor Union,* Charlotte Todes says there were 77 delegates from 13 states, ten of them officers of national unions, at its organizing convention in Baltimore, showing the real importance of this union in the history of American organized labor.

This Union is also important for the progressive precedents it set for all future American labor. These included its valiant struggle for the 8-hour day (which won concessions from President Grant); its alert recognition of inter-national opportunities and responsibilities; its welcome to Negro labor and to women labor, and its opposition to the military and to monopoly.

Sylvis, the leading spirit of the National Labor Union, and his co-worker, William J. Jessup, head of the New York State Workingman's Assembly, were fully aware of the work of the First International abroad, and kept in close touch with it. Sylvis often declared that "the interests of labor are identical throughout the world." In a speech before his own Molders' Union he argued for "an alliance with trade organizations throughout the world." Again, as recorded by Herman Schlueter in *Lincoln, Labor and Slavery,* Sylvis told the International in 1869: "We have a common cause. It is the war of poverty against wealth. In all parts of the world labor occupies the same lowly position, capital is everywhere the same tyrant." And Jessup, acting for the New York Ship Joiners, contacted the London Society of Carpenters and Joiners, of which R. Applegarth was the head, to propose that the two organizations, located on opposite shores of the Atlantic, be amalgamated. Applegarth was one of those who helped establish the First International.

At the same time, the leading labor journals of this country, the *National Workman* of New York and the *Workingmen's Advocate* of Chicago, regularly printed news about the First International. The latter paper published the *Address* of the International Working Men's Association, drafted by Marx, and ran Marx's *Civil War in France* (a discussion of the Paris Commune) serially in its columns. It also published many articles by William Liebknecht, the leading Marxist of Germany. The *National Workman* similarly gave American workers full information about European labor affairs, including the decisions and proclamations of the International.

Marx himself wrote, in a letter to an American friend, Siegfried Meyer, July 4, 1868: "We are in direct communication with Whaley, Sylvis, and Jessup." This "Whaley" was J. C. C. Whaley, first president of the National Labor Union and a member of the First International.

Furthermore, the First International was to some degree organizationally intertwined with the National Labor Union. "Section 1 of New York was the most active body of the First International in the United States," wrote James S. Allen in *Reconstruction: The Battle for Democracy,* and added: "The Section was also affiliated to the National Labor Union as Labor Union No. 5." This constituted a direct Marxist voice within organized labor in this country. F. A. Sorge, soon-to-be secretary of the First International when it located in New York, was a member of Labor Union No. 5, in 1869.

Thus, it was natural for Sylvis to respond warmly to greetings from the First International, and to its invitation to the N.L.U. to send a delegate to Europe. There was not time at this first gathering to send such a representative, but the reply of the N.L.U. to the men of the International bade them "Godspeed in their glorious work." At the second N.L.U. congress, in 1867, President Jessup moved to affiliate with the International, and Sylvis supported the motion—which, however, was voted down. Nevertheless, while backing away from direct affiliation, the congress chose a delegate to attend the International's next congress. The man chosen was Richard F. Trevellick, head of the Detroit Trades Assembly—but he could not collect money enough to make the trip. Finally, in 1869, the N.L.U. elected A.C. Cameron, editor of the *Workingmen's Advocate,* as delegate to the International Congress at Basle, and he did attend and take part in the discussions.

In 1870, in Washington, D.C., the *National Colored Labor Union,* which had broken away from the National Labor Union, also elected a delegate to the Congress of the International scheduled to meet in Paris.

His name was Sella Martin, a Negro unionist from Massachusetts, but he—like Trevellick earlier—could not raise the money to go.

It was in 1869 that Sylvis died suddenly at the age of forty-one, an event that saddened American labor and brought from the International Marx's letter of condolence, describing Sylvis as "a loyal, perservering and indefatigable worker in the good cause."

In 1870, after Sylvis' death, the N.L.U. adopted a resolution which read as follows: "The National Labor Union declares its adherence to the principles of the International Working Men's Association, and expects to join the said Association in a short time."

Unfortunately, the expectation was never realized. The N.L.U.'s membership, and its leadership, too, during its brief but important four-year rise, were simultaneously looking at Greenbackism as well as Marxism. Greenbackism or a policy of inflation seemed attractive at the time, and the Union collapsed.

Nevertheless, the first nation-wide labor federation, the National Labor Union, supplied the progressive traditions that, in every economic crisis of our history, have sustained American working men. These traditions of struggle were in large measure sparked by Marxism. "It can be claimed with confidence," wrote Samuel Bernstein, "that American labor leaders who had passed through the school of the International were the best protagonists of the American trade union movement."

The magnificent but brief career of the Marx-influenced National Labor Union (1866-1871) was followed by two other broad leagues of labor: The Knights of Labor, organized in 1869; and the International Labor Union, in 1877.

Although the Knights of Labor was founded earlier, it started out as a secret order, and did not become dominant until several years had passed; but the second organization, the International Labor Union, was in many ways a direct successor of the National Labor Union, in aim, principles, and personnel.

The International Labor Union was a merger of the former members of the old International with followers of Ira Steward's Eight-Hour movement. Its founders included the Marxists, F.A. Sorge, who had been general secretary of the First International; J.P. McDonnell, editor of the Socialist Labor Party paper, *The Labor Standard;* Dr. Adolph Douai, co-editor of the *New-Yorker Volkszeitung;* and Otto Weydemeyer, son of Joseph Weydemeyer; and the non-Marxists, Ira Steward and George Gunton; George E. McNeill, a Christian socialist; Albert R. Parsons, syndicalist-inclined socialist; and others. Karl Speyer, an old Internationalist and associate of Sorge, was elected secretary of the International Labor Union.

The I.L.U.'s Declaration of Principles said "the wage system is a despotism" and called for "final abolition of the wage system". It argued that the "first step towards the emancipation of labor" would be a shorter workday. To win shorter hours the I.L.U. called for creation of unions "where none exist", and the "amalgamation of all Labor Unions", along with the establishment of "a general fund for benefit and protective purposes."

The I.L.U., even more that the N.L.U., was friendly to Negroes and women. It carried on many historic labor battles. The I.L.U. led the Fall River textile strike in 1878-79, which Philip Foner described as "one of the greatest in American history."

But the Union's resources were insufficient, and the times were not ripe. The I.L.U., like the N.L.U. before it, lasted only about five years. Its thousands of members, wrote Foner, "were to carry their labor solidarity and class consciousness into the organization of the Knights of Labor."

The Knights of Labor did not have the organizational Marxist ties that the other two unions had. To be sure, it is said that its founder, Uriah S. Stephens, a tailor, had read a copy of the *Communist Manifesto* given him by a fellow tailor, George Eccarius, who was the first general secretary of the London International. Stephens was in part guided by the *Manifesto* when he organized the Knights, the story claims. As a matter of fact the Order did stress labor solidarity, and aimed to achieve "the complete emancipation of the wealth producers from the thraldom and loss of wage slavery." The Knights of Labor admitted all men and women to membership, "of every craft, creed and color."

Stephens' successor, Terence V. Powderly, wrote in his autobiography, *Thirty Years of Labor:* "In 1880, Osborne Ward, a socialist, lectured in Scranton [of which Powderly was then the Mayor] to an outdoor audience, and I presided at the meeting. . . . I wished to hear all sides, and . . . was well pleased with his exposition of the principles of the party he represented." In another place Powderly wrote, "The aim of socialism, in a word, is to make the world better."

However, the Knights of Labor was a ritualistic secret Order; its spokesmen did not oppose capitalism as an economic system, nor indicate any wish to abolish it; and in general it held aloof from the socialist movement. Neither Stephens, who was Grand Master until 1879, nor his successor, Powderly, were really socialistic.

Powderly did, to be sure, join the Socialist Labor Party at one time; but he soon left, and later denied he had ever joined! On the other hand—however we regard Stephens and Powderly as individuals—it is nevertheless a fact that a good many Marxists joined the organization that they headed, and were active and influential members of it.

German-born Theodore F. Cuno, engineer, journalist, member of the First International, and a friend and correspondent of Frederick Engels, joined the Knights of Labor in the 1870's and became a respected leader in it.

Phillip Van Patten, first general secretary of the Socialist Labor Party and also Secretary of the Socialist-organized and socialist-controlled Central Labor Union of New York, joined the Knights of Labor in 1881. In New York, says Morris Hillquit in his *History of Socialism,* "one Local Assembly, known as the 'Excelsior Club,' was composed almost exclusively of socialists," and many other K. of L. local assemblies were sympathetic to socialism.

The activity of Socialists in the K. of L. is instanced by the Jay Gould railroad strike of 1885. The Knights Local Assembly 3218, which had been organized by the socialist editor, Joseph R. Buchanan, threw itself into support of the strike. Buchanan's influential socialist paper, *The Labor Inquirer* of Denver, publicized the demands of the railroad workers. Only needless surrender by Powderly himself prevented a great strike victory.

Another instance is that of Martin Irons, socialist chairman of District Assembly 101, who led the K. of L. strike in the Texas & Pacific railroad shops in 1886—only to be defeated by Powderly's betrayal. Such well-known Socialist Labor Party members and propagandists as Jo Labadie and Judson Grennell of Michigan were at the same time members and critics of the Knights of Labor.

Half a decade after the Buchanan-Irons achievements, when Daniel De Leon became Socialist Labor Party leader, the entire New York K. of L. District Assembly, known as "D.A. 49," came for a time under the leadership of the Socialists (until De Leon himself organized a dual union). During this period Lucian Sanial was the S.L.P. candidate for editor of the Knights of Labor's journal, and so strong was the Socialist sector in the Union that the Knights' leadership was obliged to promise him the job—but reneged on it afterward.

Oscar Ameringer, Socialist editor and historian, was a member of the K. of L. in his younger days. So was John Mahlon Barnes, who years later originated the Debs "Red Special".

Socialists were active in other unions besides the giant Knights of Labor. Foner cites the following: The Jewish Workingmen's Union of New York was formed under Socialist Leadership in 1885. In its organ, the weekly *Jewish Volkszeitung,* it published Marx's *Wage-Labor and Capital,* as well as other Socialist material deemed important to the Union. Another and larger Socialist-led New York union, the United Hebrew Trades, was organized in 1888, and is notable for the fact the future Socialist Party leader, Morris Hillquit, a shirt-maker, was its corresponding secretary. This Union adopted an advanced Marxist constitution and program. Socialists in Philadelphia, Chicago, and Boston organized affiliates of the United Hebrew Trades. Still another New York socialist-organized union about this time was the United German Trades, which supported Socialist Labor Party candidates for office and circulated Socialist papers and pamphlets.

It was not only Jewish and German trade unions that were influenced by the Socialists. The *Bulletin of the Socialist Labor Party* stated in 1880 that the establishment of city central labor bodies all over the country was "accomplished mainly by the efforts of Socialists who influence and in some places control these assemblies, and are respected in all of them."

In Chicago, Albert R. Parsons, a printer, was both a leading Socialist and a leader of organized labor. His story is told in Alan Calmer's *Labor Agitator*. Parsons helped organize the Amalgamated Trade and Labor Unions in 1878, and was elected its president.

"The role of the Socialist Labor Party," wrote Foner in an apt summary, "in founding national unions, in organizing city central bodies, and in building local unions . . . was an outstanding contribution to the developing American labor movement."

The successor to the Knights of Labor, with respect to size and influence, was the American Federation of Labor, founded in 1881. Its organizers were led to act by an editorial in a Socialist paper, the Newark *Home-Journal,* which urged the convening of a "Congress of labor" which should undertake "the organization of the unorganized."

The resulting call that was sent throughout the country by a group of unions added to "organization of the unorganized" the amalgamation of existing unions "so as to more successfully cope with concentrated capital." One hundred seven delegates in the organizing body in Pittsburgh represented the Molders (Sylvis' old union); the Carpenters (organized by Peter J. McGuire, who had been a founder of the Socialist Labor Party); the Printers; the Amalgamated Association of Iron and Steel Workers; the Glass Workers; the Cigar Makers (led by Samuel Gompers and Adolf Strasser); and a number of local assemblies of the Knights of Labor.

The Preamble adopted unanimously by the convention declared that "a struggle is going on in the nations of the civilized world between the oppressors and the oppressed of all countries, a struggle between capital and labor," and for that reason "a union founded upon a basis as broad as the land we live in, is our only hope."

Three years later the secretary of the Federation, Frank K. Foster, added a stronger note to the internationalism of the Preamble in an official communication to the French Socialist unions: "Labor knows no country," he wrote, "and the laborers of the world should clasp hands for their common weal." To his own people—the Fourth Congress of the Federation—Foster said, in an address: "A federation of the workers of the world has long been the dream of idealists; it remains with you to make it a reality."

Among those who from the first took a prominent part in the Federation was Samuel Gompers of the Cigar Makers, who tells in his autobiography, *Seventy Years of Life and Labor,* of his friendship and admiration for the men of the First International, naming especially F. A. Sorge, Konrad Carl, Karl Speyer, Fred Bolte, and J. P. McDonnell.

"I became much interested in the International, for its principles appealed to me as solid and practical," Gompers writes, but adds: "I never joined." Nevertheless he describes these Marxists thus: "Brainy men who reveled in life as a test of ability, men who dared as a matter of course." He sums up his views in the following words, as quoted by J.R. Commons: "I believe with the most advanced thinkers as to ultimate ends, including the abolition of the wage-system."

The four men spoken of here—Samuel Gompers, Peter J. McGuire, Adolf Strasser and W. H. Foster—were leaders of the American Federation of Labor for a generation. Of these, McGuire (a Lassallean) had been a member of the Socialist Labor Party, and Strasser (also a Lassallean) likewise. But Strasser and McGuire, and Foster too, like Gompers, became pure-and-simple trade unionists in their pursuit of business-style unionism.

It is clear, then, that Marxist ideas favorably influenced the Federation and its leaders in some of their basic programs and policies. It can also be affirmed that individual Marxists contributed—as they did earlier to the Knights of Labor—a great part of the Federation's organizing enthusiasm and working-class consciousness.

The presence of individual Marxists as Federation members, and the contributions they made, are especially noteworthy.

A. C. Cameron, one of the founders of the old National Labor Union, and that union's delegate to the Basle Congress of the First International—not strictly a Marxist, but Marx-influenced—was a delegate to the Federation's 1884 convention. He voted *Yes* on the historic call to make the 8-hour day start on May 1st, 1886.

This action of the A.F.L. demanding a workday of no more than eight hours was the origin of May Day as an international workers' holiday. The A.F.L. repeated this demand twice more: in 1887 and 1888. In 1889 the organizing congress of the Second International in Paris received a message from Gompers urging that May Day be made "an International

Labor Day," and the Paris Congress agreed. Its resolution called for world-wide demonstrations on May 1st for the 8-hour day, "Since a similar demonstration has already been decided upon . . . by the American Federation of Labor." May Day, the only world-wide holiday, was American-born.

Max Hayes, printer and longtime editor of the Cleveland *Citizen,* was both a national leader of the Socialist movement and a national leader of the Federation. His paper, the *Citizen,* was simultaneously an official organ of the American Federation of Labor and of the Socialist Party. In 1899, Hayes introduced into an A.F.L. convention a resolution which was adopted, urging study of trusts and monopolies, "with the view to nationalizing the same." In 1912, Hayes ran for president of the A.F.L. against Gompers, getting 5,073 votes against 11,974 for Gompers.

In that same election, another Socialist head of a union, William H. Johnston, ran for 3rd vice president, and received 6,171 votes, against his successful opponent who got 10,858.

These votes indicate the significant strength of the Socialists in the A.F.L. The constituent unions supporting the Socialists are stated in a 1960 Master's thesis at Duke University written by Alice Joyner Irby: "Backing the Socialists were such powerful unions as the Brewery Workers, the Typographical Union, the Hat & Cap Makers, the Bakery Workers, the Machinists, the Mine Workers (except Mitchell), the Western Federation of Miners, the Painters, the Glass Workers, the Boilermakers, and the Iron Shipbuilders."

The Typographical Union here mentioned had Max Hayes himself in its leadership. In 1902, says *Labor's Untold Story* (Richard O. Boyer and Herbert M. Morais), the W.F.M. adopted this resolution: "We . . . do advise and recommend the adoption of the platform of the Socialist Party by the locals of the Federation . . . " The Brewery Workers had already by 1912 had their history written by the Marxist, Herman Schlueter. Among the Cigar-Workers (not listed by Miss Irby) have been numbered scores and hundreds of Socialists, including British-born John J. Ballam and American-born Ben Blumberg, old-time propagandists.

In 1901 the Socialist Party organizing convention at Indianapolis adopted a resolution saying, "We consider it the duty of Socialists to join the unions of their respective trade and labor organizations." At every convention and congress thereafter it was routine practice to issue statistics on the proportion of Socialist Party members who were trade-union members, showing that a majority were bona fide organized workers. The Socialist Party Convention of 1912, in its Resolution on Labor Organizations, reaffirmed the duty of the members "who are eligible to membership in the unions to join and be active." The resolution also said it was the "duty of the party to give moral and material support to the labor organizations in all their defensive or aggressive struggles against capitalist oppression and exploitation." In that year, wrote William Z. Foster in his *History of the Communist Party of the United States:* "The [Socialist] party had a powerful base in the trade unions."

The Socialist Party regularly sent lecturers to address union members, gave financial aid to workers on strike, and publicized workers' grievances and demands. Socialist Party members walked on picket lines with strikers, distributed leaflets, solicited signatures on petitions, and helped in the defense of arrested unionists.

Any study of the great defense campaigns, as the successful Moyer-Pettibone-Haywood struggle, or the long fight for Tom Mooney's release, or the martyrdom of the McNamara brothers, bears out the above statement. All three cases concerned members of A.F.L. affiliates.

In 1905, Charles H. Moyer, president of the Western Federation of Miners, William D. Haywood, secretary-treasurer, and George A. Pettibone, a miner, were kidnapped in Colorado by boss hirelings and taken to Idaho to be falsely charged with the murder of former Governor Frank Steunenberg. Eugene V. Debs, head of the Socialist Party, wrote his celebrated editorial, "Arouse Ye Slaves," in defense of the three men. They were finally freed. Thomas J. Mooney, a member of the Molders Union and organizer of the Street Car Men of San Francisco, was convicted through bribery and perjury in a bomb-throwing case in 1916 and, after many years in San Quentin prison, was finally set free. James and John McNamara, leaders of the Structural Iron Workers, were convicted through trickery of a dynamiting charge in 1911 and sentenced to life terms. Haywood and Mooney were both for some years leading Socialists. The Socialist Party fought valiantly on behalf of all of these men, and on behalf of many similar cases.

Noteworthy were three outstanding examples of Marxist-trade unionist interaction: The American Railway Union; the Amalgamated Wood Workers International Union; and the Industrial Workers of the World.

The American Railway Union was organized and headed by Eugene V. Debs, in 1894, before he became a socialist. The story of the celebrated Pullman strike, the intervention of the Government on the side of the railway companies, the imprisonment of Debs, and Debs' gradual acceptance of Marxist socialism constitute a well-known chapter in our industrial history. The American Railway Union itself—what was left of it—also joined the Marxist-led movement as one of the groups which merged to found the Socialist Party in 1900-1901.

The history of the Amalgamated Woodworkers International Union of America goes back to 1873, when the First International set up the

Furniture Workers Association. The later history of the woodworkers is given in fair detail by Frederick Shipp Deibler in a doctor's dissertation in 1912 at the University of Wisconsin. "The Amalgamated Union," wrote Deibler, "inherited its political attitude as well as its social philosophy from the Furniture Workers' Union." This attitude and philosophy Deibler accurately described as "socialistic."

In 1885 the *Furniture Workers Journal* stated that the evils of capitalism could be overcome: "By placing machinery, like all other means of labor, within the reach and into the possession of *those who are using them;* or, better, into the *collective possession of all,* in order to enable the workman to participate in the blessings produced by labor-saving machinery and increased commodities of every kind."

In the year before (1894), the Furniture Workers had already adopted formally the following resolution:

> Whereas, a permanent transformation of this social system, which exists for the benefit of a few and the detriment of the many, can only be brought about by independent political action of the wage working class, therefore be it
>
> Resolved, That the 9th Convention of the International Furniture Workers of America call upon its members to turn their backs upon all capitalist boodle parties, and wherever possible to attach themselves to an independent labor party, based upon the platform of the Socialist Labor party, and to be active in this direction.

This provision was retained in 1904 in the Constitution of the Amalgamated Wood Workers International Union, which was a merger of the Furniture Workers and the Machine Woodworkers.

Finally comes the Industrial Workers of the World, organized in 1905 by the leading socialists in the country: Daniel De Leon of the Socialist Labor Party, and Eugene V. Debs and William D. Haywood of the Socialist Party. Associated with them were Charles H. Moyer, Mother Jones, and Lucy Parsons (Mrs. Albert R. Parsons). Not long afterward other Marxist-minded militants were associated with the Wobblies: Elizabeth Gurley Flynn, John Reed, and Joe Hill, to name but three.

Aside from the people involved, the Preamble of the I.W.W., written by Daniel De Leon, shows its Marxist ideological basis:

> There can be no peace so long as hunger and want are found among millions of working people and the few, who make up the employing class, have all the good things of life. The working class and the employing class have nothing in common. Between these two classes a struggle must go on until all the toilers come together on the political, as well as on the industrial field, and take and hold

that which they produce by their labor through an economic organization of the working class without affiliation with any political party.

The final clause gives an opening for syndicalism, somewhat altering the Marxist conception of workers' seizure of power, and a few years later the syndicalists did indeed dominate the I.W.W.*

*For additional data, see appendix C.

IV

Marxism
and Reform Legislation

When Samuel Gompers and Morris Hillquit confronted each other in New York, in May 1914, as witnesses before the Commission on Industrial Relations, an argument developed. Gompers claimed the American Federation of Labor was first to fight for legislation favorable to workers, and that the Socialist Party had stuck labor demands in its platform later, just as "vote catchers." In his autobiography, *Loose Leaves from a Busy Life,* written years later, Hillquit returns to the argument and expands on his reply to Gompers. "Historically, Mr. Gompers was quite wrong. The principal planks I enumerated in my examination had been formulated by the Socialist movement in the days of the First International, i.e., in the seventies of the last century and long before the organization of the American Federation of Labor." Historical records confirm Hillquit's statement.

In 1848, in the *Communist Manifesto,* Marx and Engels insisted on political action by the workers. This was one respect in which they differentiated themselves from the Utopians, Owen and Fourier. Owen actually opposed the Chartists of England, who had advanced their "People's Charter" of government reform. Fourier likewise opposed the *Reformistes* of France. The *Manifesto* gives a ten-point program of measures suggested as "pretty generally applicable" when workers in any country take over political control. This included the income tax (on the rich), abolition of the right of inheritance (of big property), control of credit through a national bank, cultivation of waste lands, improvement of the soil, "free education for all children in public schools," and "abolition of child factory labor." These, combined with the eight-hour day and a bigger wage, as advocated in *Value, Price and Profit,* provided a general basis for a working-class political platform, short-term as well as

49

long-term. In fact the *Manifesto* (in another section) indicates as much in speaking of the "fight for the attainment of the immediate aims" of the workers.

In 1850, in the *Address of the General Council to the Communist League,* Marx gave advice to the revolutionary workers' movement in Germany, urging them to pressure the petty bourgeois political party toward more and more reforms. The workers could not yet "propose any directly communist measures," but the petty bourgeoisie would be "compelled to propose more or less socialist measures."

We may recall that Joseph Weydemeyer, Marx's best known representative in the United States, was active in the Republican Party campaign for the election of Lincoln in 1860. He worked through the Chicago Workers' Society, which, says Weydemeyer's biographer, Karl Obermann, "asked every Republican candidate to state his position on . . . better labor legislation." Weydemeyer was applying Marxist thinking to the American conditions of that time.

In 1865, when the First International was established in London, Marx, in his *Inaugural Address,* discussed the insufficient diet of the British poor, the employment and oppression of British children, and the revelation in the Government's reported tax returns of deepening class division in British society. He praised the Ten Hour Bill as an important beginning of reform, and denounced British industry, "which, vampire-like, could but live by sucking blood, and children's blood, too."

The *Address* also advised workers to delve into foreign policy—"to master themselves the mysteries of international politics." In doing this they must, he said, "watch the diplomatic acts of their respective governments," and if they couldn't prevent barbarous encroachments, at least they could denounce them, and thus "vindicate the simple laws of morals and justice, which ought to govern . . . the intercourse of nations."

In sum, as the *Address* adds *(Provisional Rules),* it is *"the duty of a man to claim the rights of a man and a citizen."*

In the United States, these principles were applied in more specific detail by American members of the First International, as shown by the work of the American branches of the International up to 1872.

The Central Committee of the American sections, according to Samuel Bernstein, in his *First International in America,* praised the American workers' resolve to press for labor legislation. Noteworthy is the parade of workers in New York on September 13, 1971, in which the American branches of the International had a large contingent carrying the red flag. The demonstration concluded with resolutions for the eight-hour day, against convict labor, against the spread of monopolies, and for the administration of public utilities. It was at this demonstration that a leaflet quoting an excerpt from Marx's *Capital* on the "normal working day" was distributed "in thousands of copies."

A little later[1] the American Internationalists fought through to success what we may call the *first* "First Amendment case": a memorial demonstration honoring the Paris Commune and the murdered Communards. The police had issued a ban on the march down Fifth Avenue, but, says Bernstein, they "had to cancel the previous order." The Internationalists based their demand to march on the constitutional right of peaceful assembly.

Immediately after these events came the historically notable episode in which Congressman George F. Hoar of Massachusetts referred with approval to the First International. He had himself introduced a bill providing for appointment of a wages and hours commission, and, in the words of Bernstein, "he had the clerk of the House read [the International's] resolution that called for a statistical survey of the workers' situation in Europe and America."

A few months after this action by Congressman Hoar, the International itself was transferred to New York by decision of the Hague Congress. Here, wrote Bernstein, "One of the first plans to cope with the problem of unemployment" was presented to the government by the International. The plan, offered in 1873, demanded: (1) Work for the unemployed at usual wages; (2) enough food in advance to feed needy families for a week; and (3) a six-months' moratorium on rent.

In 1874 the First International, in New York, announced that its political action for the time being would be confined to "the endeavor of obtaining legislative acts in the interest of the working class proper." The program called for a working day of not more than eight hours, employers' liability for accidents, a lien law to guarantee payment of workers' wages, abolition of child labor, sanitary inspection of factories, bureaus of labor statistics, and prohibition of indirect taxes.

The above list includes the establishment of bureaus of labor statistics as a beneficial measure for the working class. This is in accord with the "statistical survey" which pleased Congressman Hoar. It is fascinating to note how detailed was the plan devised for such a survey, as given in the *Papers of the International Workingmen's Association,* edited and commented on by Samuel Bernstein. The plan called for Name, Trade, Age, Sex of Workers, Hours of labor, Time for meals, Number unemployed, Number in family, et cetera. It asked questions, as, Are the children in school? It inquired about "peculiar diseases of trade."

It is important to note the ways in which the followers of Marx strove

1. December 10 and December 17, 1871.

to get legal concessions from the federal and state governments to benefit the workers. First, they sought new laws, such as an eight-hour day; second, they struggled to maintain those constitutional rights which employers and politicians disregarded, as the right of peaceful assembly; third, they tried by the widest publicity to bring about a more humane political climate for changed laws, as in the arguments against child labor.

The First International is to be credited with a share in two partial successes: the eight-hour day was legally established for most government workers in President U. S. Grant's Administration (1868-1869), through pressure by the National Labor Union[2] supported by the International; and state bureaus of labor statistics began to be set up about that time in Massachusetts and Pennsylvania, and slowly spread to other states.

But even more weight will be given the International's achievements in the field of social legislation if we consider that the struggle continued under its Marxist successors (the Socialist Labor and Socialist Parties), that its cogent arguments proved their validity to more and more people, and that more and more of its proposals for immediate relief were taken over by capitalist parties and enacted into law (however limited such laws often were in practice).

The Workingmen's Party of the United States, founded in 1876, included in its Declaration of Principles not only its aim of emancipation of workers from capitalism, and its consequent independence of all capitalist parties, but also a platform of immediate measures "to improve the condition of the working classes." These included the eight-hour day in private industry (as well as government employment), sanitary inspection of mines and factories, a federal bureau of labor statistics, prohibition of prison contract labor, prohibition of child labor under the age of fourteen, free public schools, free administration of justice, "strict laws making employers liable for all accidents to the injury of their employees," and abolition of antiunion conspiracy laws.

When in 1878 the organization's name was changed to the Socialist Labor Party, the party constitution was altered, but these immediate demands were substantially retained. By 1879 there were some additions. One new demand was "political equality before the law, of all citizens, without regard to creed, race, or sex." Another was "the establishment of a national ministry of labor."

2. The National Labor Union sent Richard Trevellick—the one who had been unable to go to the Lausanne Congress of the First International in 1867—to Washington in 1868 to urge an eight-hour law for government employees. The law was enacted, but the pay was reduced. Finally, "moved by a storm of protest from the working people, led by Sylvis, Cameron, Trevellick and Jessup" (Commons), President Grant issued a proclamation on May 19, 1869, stating there would be no cut in wages for the shorter day for government workers.

Phillip Van Patten, general secretary, made an important report to the second Socialist Labor Party convention, which began December 26, 1879, in Allegheny, Pennsylvania, and referred proudly to some of the three-year-old Party's successes. Three Illinois state representatives and one Illinois state senator had been elected the previous year,[3] he said, and continued: "During their first term they introduced bills to enforce the payment of wages in cash, prohibiting children's labor and the employment of convict labor by private individuals, a bill to license locomotive engineers, to enforce the eight-hour law already on the statute books, to create a bureau of labor statistics [in Illinois], to secure proper ventilation in the mines, to make employers responsible for injuries to employees while at work, and a number of other important measures. Most of these were killed either by direct vote or by amendments which destroyed their efficiency. The bureau of labor statistics was however established, and good results [were] hoped for."

In the city of Chicago the Party had done well too, he said. The candidate for mayor was Dr. Ernest Schmidt, "an old associate of Karl Marx," and, although defeated, he had gotten 12,000 votes. One of Dr. Schmidt's co-workers, "Comrade Fred Stauber," was elected alderman from the 14th ward, and he "did good service in the city council, by exposing frauds and corrupt jobs dating back a number of years." According to Alan Calmer's *Labor Agitator: The Story of Albert R. Parsons,* Stauber "initiated many practical benefits, such as public baths, for the workers in his ward," and was reelected the next year.

In this convention report Van Patten also briefly surveyed some half-dozen state bureaus of labor statistics, calling them "valuable institutions." Some—like that of Massachusetts—were "too timid," but others—like that of Ohio—were truthful and thorough. In the state of Missouri, he noted, the new bureau of labor statistics was "under the management of Comrades Hilkene and P. J. McGuire."[4] It was anticipated, Van Patten said, that the coming 1880 census would reflect data from these newly established bureaus.

Scarcely three years after this historic convention, a hearing on "Relations between Labor and Capital" was held before the Blair Committee of the United States Senate, and some new legislative ideas were brought to public notice by the Socialists. Dr. Adolf Douai was the spokesman of the

3. The representatives were C. Ehrhardt, C. Meier, and Leo Meilbeck; the senator was Sylvester Artley.
4. One of the pamphlets for sale by the S.L.P. National Office, and advertised in the leaflet containing the minutes of the convention, was "Why the State Should Create a Bureau of Labor Statistics," by P. J. McGuire. As for Hilkene, the Missouri Historical Society reports (in a letter to me, Nov. 21, 1963) that in 1880-81 William H. Hilkene was State Labor Commissioner of Missouri.

Socialist Labor Party before the Committee,[5] September 20, 1883. His testimony, according to Charles R. Martin's *Handbook of the Independent Order of the Knights of Labor* "contains the first elaboration of the idea of the Initiative and Referendum made in the United States."

In his testimony, Dr. Douai also made an interesting comment on the S.L.P. demand for prohibition of the labor of children under the age of fourteen. "You know," he told the Committee chairman, Senator H. W. Blair of New Hampshire, "that this has been secured in the State of New Jersey, chiefly through the action of our party."

In 1889, another convention of the S.L.P. took place, this time in Chicago, at which a new campaign platform was drawn up by the Communard, Lucien Sanial. Hillquit praised it, saying it "was given a national coloring by basing its arguments on the Declaration of Independence."

Adopted as a "state platform," this document began:

> When a body of citizens separate themselves from existing political organizations of age, respectability and historic achievement and form a party pledged to measures inconsistent with societary institutions of long standing and of widely accepted worth, it is incumbent upon them to justify their conduct by evidence of such weight and character as shall satisfy the impartial judgment of thoughtful men of the rectitude of their purposes and of the public need of the reforms they advocate.

After a brief socialist analysis of United States' economic history, a program is given which follows previous ones but expands and particularizes some demands: Make members of Congress "subject to recall"; "give the people the right to propose laws"; "confer universal and equal right of suffrage . . . and secret ballot"; "abolish capital punishment"; "prohibition of night work for women"; "scientific management of forests and waterways"; "compulsory education of all children . . . to be gratuitous."

When Daniel De Leon joined the S.L.P. in 1890, the Party still put forward "immediate demands," as shown by the 1892 platform on which Simon Wing and Charles H. Matchett were the first presidential and vice presidential candidates to campaign for the Cooperative Commonwealth. It repeated the 1889 proposals, and also asked that "inventors . . . be remunerated by the nation," that a "progressive income tax" be imposed, also a "tax on inheritances," "repeal of all pauper, tramp, conspiracy and

5. United States Senate, "Report upon the Relations between Labor and Capital," *Blair Committee Report*, Vol. II (Washington, D.C.: U.S. Government Printing Office, 1885), pp. 702-743.

sumptuary laws," "equalization of women's wages with those of men where equal service is performed," "an efficient employers' liability law," people's right to propose laws by Referendum, right to recall elected officials, "universal and equal suffrage, without regard to color, creed, or sex," and "the principle of minority representation."

The S.L.P.'s 1896 platform has these same demands, but by 1900 they were all dropped, and were no longer supported by the Party. De Leon regarded all advocacy of reforms as mere reformism. From 1896 onward the S.L.P. ceased to be an aggressive influence on American law making. This does not, however, contravene the fact that the first two decades of the first Marxist party in the United States indisputably exerted notable pressure in the direction of progressive legislation, materially assisting the parallel pressure of the Populists and organized labor, and surpassing these other influences in systematic propaganda year after year.

The Socialist Party from 1900 on continued and expanded Marxist working class pressure on law makers and administrators. The result was the growth of a body of citizens with an intellectual and critical attitude toward law and politics, armed with a scientific analysis of current social and economic problems. Both the socialist attitude and the socialist analysis were infused with sympathy and humanism in the face of poverty, unemployment, and hunger.

In 1900 the not-yet-united Socialist Party, coalescing with some difficulty while actively participating in a national election, put forward a program which clearly related its revolutionary Marxist objective to the workers' immediate needs. The founders considered it "of the utmost importance for the Socialist Party to support all active efforts of the working class to better its condition."

Then followed the immediate demands, which included the main points previously expressed in the Socialist Labor Party programs. There is no need to repeat them, except to call attention to the wording of some of them. Point Number Three asked for "state or national insurance of working people in case of accidents, lack of employment, sickness, and want in old age," thus anticipating the later provisions for Unemployment Insurance, Workmen's Compensation, Medicare, and Social Security. Another called for "the initiative and referendum, proportional representation, and the right of recall of representatives by their constituents."

One prominent example of socialist influence on legislation—or on planned legislation—is the rise of the short-lived "Bull Moose" Progressive Party led by Theodore Roosevelt. Although Roosevelt feared and hated the Socialists, he was impressed by their voter appeal, as shown by his theft in 1912 of a considerable part of the Socialist's "demands" and their insertion in the "Bull Moose" platform.[6] Anyone who picks up *National Party Platforms, 1840-1956,* compiled by Kirk H. Porter and D. B. Johnson, and compares the respective 1912 programs of the Socialist and Progressive Parties, can confirm this. The Bull Moose platform says "the *old parties* have turned aside" from their proper task, thus snatching even this half-century-old socialist phrase, *the old parties*. It, too, calls for "direct primaries," "direct election of U.S. senators," "equal suffrage to men and women alike," prohibition of injunctions in labor disputes, "prohibition of child labor," "abolition of convict contract labor system," "a department of labor with a seat in the Cabinet," "a graduated inheritance tax," and "government power to levy an income tax." Some of the phrasing by this capitalist party has the appearance of hedging, such as "an eight-hour day for working women and young persons" (not for workers in general), "a system of social insurance adapted to American use," and "standards of compensation for death by industrial accident and injury and trade disease."

The effectiveness of socialist advocacy may be gauged by noting the number of these reforms that have been adopted since 1912, such as a department of labor, the income tax, social insurance, and other limited but useful provisions in the law.

Another example of a quite different kind is the Non-Partisan League and its legislation on behalf of the working farmer. The connection here is that the Non-Partisan League was the creation of members of the Socialist Party, and started as a kind of united front farmers' organization. But the officialdom of the Socialist Party was unbending in its sectarianism: "No compromise. No political trading." The Party refused to approve the League.

Andy Omholt and Otto Anstrom, life-long Socialists and long-time residents of North Dakota, both told this writer: "It was the Socialists who built the Non-Partisan League. A. C. Townley was on the North Dakota Socialist Party State Committee. There were thirty-two Socialist locals in North Dakota in 1916, and most of them went into the Non-Partisan League. The League was sparked by the Socialists. That's definite!"

If we go back three years before the Non-Partisan League was formed, and look at the program of the Socialist Party of North Dakota, we can see that the Party did indeed have its eye on the struggling farmers. Its eight demands in 1912 included state ownership and control of "grain elevators, packing houses, and cold storage plants" Also included were "state life, fire, hail, pest and animal insurance." Reduction of freight

---

6. Among many such comments in Socialist periodical literature, see for example, "Stealing Planks," *International Socialist Review* (November 1912), p. 399.

rates was demanded "on native coal shipments within the state." Also, "state lands [were] to be leased, not sold," and the rent charged was to be no more than the tax paid on similar land by private owners.

The League was in fact a Socialist activity in 1915 and 1916, until John Spargo (who himself later became a Republican) reported its activities unfavorably to the National Committee. Spargo said the League had succeeded in several Western states because of "the activity and organizing genius of a farmer named Townley, a Socialist, for many years active in the Socialist Party and a member at the time of forming the League, I believe." Spargo concluded that the League's "course of action is quite incompatible with . . . the organic law of the Socialist Party."

Most of Townley's army of League organizers were also Socialists; as Robert L. Morlan's *Political Prairie Fire* says, "[they were] members of the Socialist Party, and they did not abandon their beliefs."

It is interesting to note that, while A. C. Townley, a Socialist, was the League's organizer, Dr. Walter Thomas Mills, an old Socialist lecturer, was its philosopher. In *Document 101,* published by the League after it broke with the Socialist Party, Mills wrote that the League aimed "to build a fighting machine with which successfully to oppose and to destroy the autocratic political machinery of the private monopolists."

The Non-Partisan League fell short of Mills's hopes, but it did succeed in bringing about legislation beneficial to dirt farmers: "state credit facilities, state insurance systems, public ownership of certain means of distribution, and the like" (Morlan). Its achievements are a part of socialist-influenced legislation.

One may begin a study of the effectiveness of socialist influence on legislation with a citation from the Party's own estimate of its accomplishment. The Socialist *Congressional Handbook* of 1914, just two years after the big Debs vote of 1912, gives a fairly objective summary of legislative successes and limitations. This *Handbook* was prepared by Carl D. Thompson, director of the Party's Information Department, and his special assistant, Ralph Korngold, who later became a well-known biographer.

Under the heading, "What Socialists Have Done," the *Handbook* states:

> The Socialists in the state legislatures of this country have accomplished three things: *First:* They have actually succeeded in putting into the statute books of the various states some 141 different laws. *Second:* They have been indirectly instrumental and [have] assisted in putting on many more. *Third:* They have prepared with great care and completeness the definite, concrete legislative measures that make up the [short-range] Socialist program.

Thus the specific measures by which the principles of Socialism may be applied have been reduced to the cold letter of the law and deposited in the official records of a dozen different states, and, we may add, in the Congress of the United States as well.

These 141 legislative enactments in one or another state are classified under several heads: (1) *labor* measures, such as requiring blowers on emery wheels used in metal polishing, keeping factory doors unlocked during working hours, ordering safety appliances on corn shredders, requiring the keeping of records of injuries to employees, forbidding the use of injunctions in labor disputes; (2) *political* measures, such as making election day a half-holiday, and providing for recall of elected officials in municipalities; (3) *municipal* measures, such as giving cities the right to build ice plants and erect comfort stations, and providing for abatement of smoke nuisance; (4) *educational* measures, including a minimum wage for teachers, school lunches for children, and free night schools; and (5) *miscellaneous* measures, such as a mothers' pension law and various resolutions or petitions to Congress.

The latter item merits some emphasis, even though actual enactment of laws did not result: (a) for example, the Kansas Legislature adopted a Socialist-sponsored memorial to Congress petitioning for old age pensions, and the Wisconsin Legislature asked Congress for an investigation of the possibility of old age pensions; (b) the Wisconsin legislature in a joint action petitioned Congress to permit loans to farmers from funds in postal savings deposits; and (c) the Illinois State Assembly adopted a resolution "expressing sympathy for the Belgian suffrage strike" (that is, a strike of Belgian workers for the simple right to vote).

Concerning socialist legislation in the Congress, the *Handbook* tells of Victor Berger's lone battle against the opposition of 391 fellow congressmen and all 96 senators. Despite obstacles, Berger proposed, unsuccessfully, an eight-hour day for all government employed labor, a general old age pension, the right for postal employees to organize in a union, a bill to protect women workers in the District of Columbia, a resolution to investigate the McNamara case, another resolution to investigate the strike on the Harriman railroad lines, a bill to lend federal money to city governments to provide work for the unemployed at union rates, and a resolution asking the President to withdraw troops from the Mexican border. (This was April 5, 1911; at the time "President Taft massed troops on the frontier and seemed to be preparing to go to the rescue of Diaz," against whom the Mexican people were rebelling.)[7]

In a resolution calling for investigation of the Lawrence, Massachu-

7. *The American Labor Year Book, 1917-18*, p. 299.

setts, textile strike, Berger exploded a widely circulated Republican myth. "The American Woolen Company," he said, "has for years been the recipient of a government subsidy in the form of a high tariff. The claim has been made that this high tariff is levied in order to protect labor. Yet in spite of this claim it is generally conceded that these operatives [i.e., the workers on strike] are among the lowest paid of those of any industry in America."

In 1901, A. M. Simons, editor of the *International Socialist Review,* published a little pamphlet, *What the Socialists Would Do If They Won in This Election.* Dealing with the City of Chicago, in order to base his discourse on a concrete situation, he started out by explaining that many "interrelated and mutually correlated changes" would be going on at the same time, but he would begin with the schools. "Every child of school age in the city would be registered, and the record of the school attendance of every child on that register would constitute a proof of the absence of child labor."

But this was just a start. Socialists would not attempt "to stuff the brain that was carried above a shivering, half-clad body and hungry stomach." There would have to be school lunches, and clothing for all children. And still more: The health of the parents was necessary, and there would have to be inspection of food sold, and of working conditions. And not just this, but the parents had to have jobs. Among various other changes, certain structures would be moved or cleared away, so that the lake front could be used by the people for summer bathing. Simons concludes:

> "Where will all the money come from with which to do these things?" some little shop-keeping bourgeois is asking. Well, where did all the wealth that is now in the world come from? Did not the laborers create it, and is there anything to make one believe that they forget how to create more?

Simons spoke officially for the young Socialist Party. An outstanding individual Socialist, Florence Kelley, devoted her long life in large part on behalf of children. Her record goes back before our century, with an article, "Our Toiling Children," published in 1889, and another, "The Working Child," published in 1896.[8]

"There are two ways of dealing with the problem of the working child," Miss Kelley began, in the second publication referred to:

---

8. *The Working Child* is in the New York Public Library, and, interestingly, is stamped, "Gift of F. A. Sorge." Sorge was general secretary of the First International in New York.

One is to prohibit outright the employment of children under 16 years of age . . . the other is the method adopted by all manufacturing countries, including our own, and consists in legislating to keep in the market an abundant supply of child labor while restricting to some extent some of the most flagrant abuses which accompany it.

In another paper, published in 1903, Miss Kelley discussed "An Effective Child-Labor Law." She began by saying the topic assigned her was "An *ideal* Child-Labor Law"—but declared there could be no such thing: only "a sweeping prohibition of all labor for all children."

In view of the great progressive influence exerted by the National Child-Labor Committee, take note of its personnel. In 1906, for example, Florence Kelley was, as always, on the Board of Trustees. In that year Scott Nearing, a Socialist, was secretary of the Pennsylvania Child Labor Committee, and J. G. Phelps Stokes (a Socialist, and husband of Rose Pastor Stokes) was on the New York Child Labor Committee. In 1908 Robert Hunter, a Socialist, was on the National Child-Labor Committee.

All the time the Socialist Party, like the Socialist Labor Party before it, was agitating against child labor and for more and better schools. A Socialist campaign leaflet in 1904 carried the slogan, "Vote for more schools! Up with the Arm and Torch!" It cited statistics showing that in 1901 there were 58,000 New York children in part-time classes, while in 1904 things were worse: there were more than 70,000 children in part-time classes.

In 1912, the Socialist New York *Call,* as was its custom, publicized the report of Owen Lovejoy, general secretary of the National Child Labor Committee. This report enumerated the states where improved child labor laws had been enacted, and implied some praise for them. But Louisiana, the report said, was "moving backward": it had just rejected a child labor bill.

The point of this is that the progress made against child labor—such as it was and is—has been due in considerable measure to the work of individual Socialists and of the Socialist Party.

One must admit that when a political movement of labor which aims to abolish capitalism tries to make laws *about* labor *under* capitalism—it is attempting something difficult. Some would regard it as also inconsistent; Marxists regard it as necessary.

A step-by-step look at some of the measures actually won should be useful.

From 1899 to 1903, the first Socialist law makers, James F. Carey and F. O. MacGartney, had minor successes in the Massachusetts legislature. One of their bills "shortened the hours of state and county employees," according to Ethelwyn Mills's summary of Socialist legislation.[9] A second shifted the burden of proof from the employee to the railroad company in suits to recover damages for injury or death.

From 1905 to 1911, out of a dozen elected Socialist legislators in Wisconsin, there were Fred Brockhausen, secretary of the State Federation of Labor, and Frank Weber, its general organizer, along with Carl D. Thompson, head of the Socialist Party's information department. This group fought through into law fifteen bills (out of 72 introduced). They included:

1. A bill providing for the erection of guards and railings over dangerous machinery in factories.

2. A bill providing that metal polishing machines be equipped with blowers and enough draft to remove metallic dust.

3. A bill requiring railway companies to equip trains with enough men to handle the work without overburdening the train men ("the Full Crew Bill").

4. An eight-hour telegraphers' law.

In 1913 there were four Socialists in the Illinois Legislature, including the lawyer, Seymour Stedman, and the founder of the Chicago Workers' School of Government, Christian M. Madsen. The Illinois Socialists privately took credit, by the way, for an important but not always observed part of law making: the defeat of obnoxious bills backed by special interests, simply because even non-Socialist legislators did not care to "go on record in favor of measures that [were] too brazen." As for direct positive action, they got a bill through—but not their own—providing for "semi-monthly payment of wages," to help hard-pressed workers whose corporation employers held back their money for a whole month. Representatives of railroad companies lobbied against the Socialist proposal and defeated it. But a similar bill introduced by an old Party man won majority backing and was passed.

In another instance the Illinois Socialists brought about the *union label* on all state printing—by a kind of trick. Their bill to do this failed of passage, but when their stationery was delivered, the four Socialist representatives refused to accept it, explaining that they could not correspond with constituents on nonunion paper. The printers then put the union label on all their work, to save themselves trouble, and no member of the legislative body, old Party or not, dared protest against it!

9. Published by the Socialist Party, 1914, as *Bulletin No. 1* of the Information Department.

In 1911 the Socialist and trade unionist, James H. Maurer, introduced into the Pennsylvania Legislature a bill "to repeal the law creating the army of mounted policemen which the capitalists call the State Constabulary." It did not pass, but it called attention to the repression practiced against striking coal miners. The Congressional Commission on Industrial Relations held hearings in this period, at which representatives of the Socialist Party and the I.W.W. testified, revealing that in such communities as Paterson, New Jersey, Los Angeles, California, Lead, South Dakota, and Ludlow, Colorado, "the right of collective bargaining on the part of employees [was] denied" (Ethelwyn Mills). The gradual recognition of this right later on can be credited in some degree to the persistent protests of Socialist legislators.

Workmen's Compensation was referred to earlier as a Massachusetts partial victory. W. J. Ghent, Socialist theoretician, said in a leaflet published in 1912, "the most advanced measure so far projected" for Workmen's Compensation had been prepared by the Joint Conference of the Central Labor Bodies and the Socialist Party of New York, and brought before Governor Charles Evans Hughes's State Commission in 1910—even though there were no Socialists then in the State Legislature. It was passed in a modified form, as Gompers boasted, with A.F.L. backing, but only, Hillquit explained, "after the New York State A.F.L. had received a good deal of valuable instruction on the subject from the Socialists."[10]

In Kansas, in 1913, Socialists won passage of a law requiring that bath houses be provided for miners.

In 1916 William Coleman, a Socialist alderman-at-large in Milwaukee, introduced a resolution which—we are told in *American Labor Who's Who*—"resulted in the present system of state employment offices."

One can agree that such legislation is far from socialism, but one can also say that labor would not surrender a single item.

"Minot [North Dakota] . . . is the town on the Great Northern road, where, fourteen years ago, Jim Hill fired the station agent because he was a subscriber to the *Appeal to Reason.*" So wrote Ida Crouch-Hazlett in Minot's socialist paper, *The Iconoclast,* in May 1912.

The station agent's firing is just one example in just one locality of the obstacles met by Socialists in the United States. The Socialists fought back by exposing the facts and insisting on the Bill of Rights: freedom of thought, of speech, of the press, of assembly.

In Fitchburg, Massachusetts, in January 1906, City officials devised an

10. *The Double Edge of Labor's Sword* (New York: Socialist Literature Co., 1914). (Pamphlet.)

anti-red flag regulation to harass Socialist parades, which at that time used the international symbol as a matter of course. In Philadelphia and Denver free speech fights were carried on simultaneously in September of the same year. *The Worker* reported thirteen Socialists arrested in Philadelphia, including Ella Reeve Bloor and Joseph O'Brien, "in the area of the Baldwin Locomotive Works . . . for obstructing highway." In Denver, Socialist soapboxers campaigning for William D. Haywood for governor were dragged off in the patrol wagon as fast as they got up to speak. A little later Horace Traubel, editor of *The Conservator,* wrote: "I Know Just How You Feel About It, Dear Comrade," and urged the Socialists to keep on going. In Boston, the local Socialists met in historic Faneuil Hall to pay tribute to the "Great Agitator," Wendell Phillips.

In 1909 Fred D. Warren of the *Appeal to Reason* was convicted of offering a kidnap bribe through the mails. George H. Shoaf, labor journalist, told the story in the *Appeal.* The legendary Clarence Darrow was Warren's attorney. Debs charged the trial was an attack on the liberty of the press. Upton Sinclair said the outrageous verdict had "set my blood to boiling." Warren's speech in his own defense in the Fort Scott, Kansas, courtroom was, Shoaf said, an "Indictment of Capitalism and Its Despotic Institutions." In this speech Warren exposed the actual kidnapping of Haywood, Moyer, and Pettibone of the Western Federation of Miners at the instigation of the mine owners' association in Colorado and Idaho.[11]

The New York *Call,* in 1910, reported the free speech fight in Spokane, Washington, in which Elizabeth Gurley Flynn and others were arrested "for speaking in the streets." When the Spokane Women's Club heard Miss Flynn afterward describe the conditions in the City jail, they took a hand in civic affairs: they insisted that matrons be employed there, to supervise arrested women. In New York, Mary Dreier, head of the Women's Trade Union League, was arrested for picketing the Triangle Waist Company. At a Socialist women's meeting in Carnegie Hall, chaired by Anita Block, women's editor of the New York *Call,* a resolution was unanimously adopted protesting police interference with free speech.

In 1912 the long free speech fight in San Diego, California, was reported by Vincent St. John, a leader of the Industrial Workers of the World (IWW), in the *International Socialist Review.* At the time he wrote, 210 men and women were still jailed for the crime of speech. A defense organization, including the I.W.W., the Socialist Party, Single Taxers, and the trade unions, was formed to defend the soapboxers.

11. For the case of William D. Haywood, Charles H. Moyer, and George Pettibone, see Richard O. Boyer and Herbert M. Morais, *Labor's Untold Story* (New York: Cameron and Kahn, 1955), pp. 166 ff.

The New York *Call,* September 29, 1912, said of a local struggle what could have been said of many others: "The battle for the sustenance of the constitutional right of free speech is on between the Socialists of Kings County and the local authorities. The battle . . . will be to decide the important question as to whether or not a judge has the right to forbid the speakers of the Socialist Party from exercising their constitutional right of speaking on the street."

In Manhattan this same year occurred another type of free speech fight. A meeting was advertised to take place in early October in a public school near First Avenue and East 4th Street, similar to others held in various school auditoriums. The speakers were to be S. John Block, Socialist candidate for the State Supreme Court, and Marie B. MacDonald, Socialist candidate for Congress. At the last moment the Board of Education closed the school doors and prevented the meeting from going forward. After an exchange of letters, the authorities offered a second date for the circumvented meeting, and the Socialists accepted this offer—October 31, just a few days before the elections.

The strike at Little Falls, New York, in late 1912, contains within its history the characteristics of a struggle for basic constitutional rights, and illustrates the role of the Socialists in winning, or hoping at a later time to win, what the Constitution guarantees.

Some 1,500 workers—Polish, Austrian, Slavic, Italian (mostly women)—were on strike against the Phoenix and Gilbert Knitting Mills, with Benjamin J. Legere, a Socialist, as chairman of the strike committee. Police Chief James ("Dusty") Long was out to break the strike, and he jailed not only Legere and leading strikers but also Socialist Mayor George Lunn and his wife of nearby Schenectady, the Rev. Robert A. Bakeman, Miss Helen Schloss, Socialist tenement investigator from New York, Miss Jessie Ashley, Socialist attorney, and others—for street speaking or picketing. Chief Long closed down the strike relief kitchen. He drew up typed instructions to guide the testimony of the police witnesses at the resulting trial—which the defense got hold of and promptly published. Helen Keller sent a check for help to "the brave girls who are striving so courageously to bring about the emancipation of the workers at Little Falls."

In some cases of this kind officials backed down, as in 1916, at Troy, New York, where the Mayor withdrew the order forbidding Socialists to speak at street corners. Many strikes were lost, as at Little Falls, with the free speech cases to be fought out afterward in court. Sometimes, repeal of repressive legislation was secured.

Principles were asserted and fought for which had their impact on court interpretations in later years, and helped to establish more firmly (at least in our traditions, if not in practice) the freedoms embodied in the Bill of Rights.

Many old Socialist proposals, which once were considered "subversive," are now—as Lillian Symes remarks in *Rebel America*—regarded as "intrinsically American."

As far back as 1897, for instance, Debs' Social Democracy had planks in its platform which now seem matter-of-course. One was "the establishment of postal savings banks"—but bankers in those days took a dim view of them. Another was public works to employ the unemployed—a device which many think Franklin D. Roosevelt invented.

In 1898 the Social Democracy became the Social Democratic Party, and its new program included the idea, "Labor legislation to be made *national,* instead of *local*"—and today the antiunion state "Right-to-Work" laws are opposed not only by organized labor but by many politicians.

In 1903 the Socialist Party's representative in the Massachusetts Legislature, Frederic O. MacCartney, introduced a bill to enable cities and towns to establish municipal coal and wood yards, so as to ease the price to needy working families—but the State Supreme Court ruled such laws unconstitutional.

In 1911 the Socialists in the Wisconsin Legislature secured home rule for the City of Milwaukee, enabling it to engage in activities forbidden to Massachusetts towns—"the right to secure land and property with which to begin the building of workingmen's homes." This was followed by other measures affecting public utilities: "legalizing bonds . . . for an electric lighting plant and declaring invalid certain injunctions brought against the city to restrain it from erecting the plant"; and "authorizing cities operating heating plants to install and operate pipes and mains in the same way as for water works."

Incidentally, it was the Socialists of Wisconsin who demanded and won a half-holiday on election days, a measure which today seems but ordinary "good business."

Still another point about Milwaukee: The City Administration was just as corrupt in 1911, says Oscar Ameringer in *If You Don't Weaken,* as any city described by Lincoln Steffens in *The Shame of the Cities.* "Gold coast and red-light district, gangster and blackmailer, pickpocket and parson, during the campaign all of them were united in the holy crusade against the 'godless Socialists.' " Under the Socialist administration corruption was dealt heavy blows—but capitalism, to be sure, remained.

In 1912 James H. Maurer, Socialist trade unionist in the Pennsylvania

Legislature, led a desperate protest against the treatment of the aged poor in almshouses, and nationally the Socialists were working for an Old Age Pension. In a folder written by W. J. Ghent and issued by the Socialist Party, we read this: "It would seem—would it not?—that if we can pay pensions to men who, as soldiers, have destroyed lives, we might also pay pensions to men who, as toilers, have protected and sustained lives." Said Victor L. Berger, offering an old age pension bill in Congress: "Society owes a debt to its aged workers."

About the same time, in Williams County, North Dakota, a Socialist farmer named D. I. Todd was protesting the cruel tactics used against the wheat farmers. Todd wrote in *The Iconoclast* (October 11, 1912, p. 4):

> There are on file in each of the elevators in this county the names of hundreds of honest, upright farmers who through stress of poverty have given crop mortgages or liens upon their crops. In practically all cases these lists of names are posted where the public has access to them and in most cases the amount of the indebtedness is shown, as well as their address. In one elevator we counted over 930 such mortgages and liens, running as high as $4,000 in some cases. In another case was a list of a corporation in Minneapolis who posted 25 mortgages ranging from $10 to $875. The aim is to show that it has a plaster on these men's crops and warning the public that if these men present any grain for sale, the money must be withheld and turned over to this foreign corporation.

At this time Todd was a candidate on the Socialist ticket for Public Administrator of Williams County.

In 1914, as I learn from this same D. I. Todd, the little Socialist local in Hebron Township, Williams County, got up a draft of a bill providing for hail insurance, and sent it to the State Convention of the Socialist Party meeting in Minot. It was a call for a law "whereby the State would insure crops against hail loss for all formers who signed agreements to pay their pro-rata share of losses during the growing season, such share to be added to their next taxes." And to the astonishment of everybody the legislature passed the bill, "the first such law in the U.S.A., but most states (in the West) have one now."[12]

In any discussion of the effect of Marxism upon American law making, the question is bound to come up: If beneficial legislation can be brought about gradually under capitalism, through normal causes which include pressures from the Socialist movement, why work particularly for socialism?

12. Letter to me from D. I. Todd, May 11, 1960.

The answer is twofold: First, reforms under capitalism, whatever their nature, seem never to be complete, and in fact must always be limited by capitalism's need for profit. Second, human striving for freedom cannot for long tolerate the private ownership of those things that control the lives of all. The ultimate goal is always greater than any or all immediate triumphs.

V

Marxism and the
Negro People's Freedom Struggle

Back in 1912 the Negro Socialist, Hubert H. Harrison, taking issue with Rudyard Kipling, wrote in the *International Socialist Review* about "The Black Man's Burden." It is the black man, he argued, who bears the worst burden of toil and deprivation, of exploitation and oppression.

"Now," he wrote, "the essence of citizenship is the exercise of political rights"—but in sixteen southern states millions of Negroes are denied such rights. The economic position of Negroes he called "this second slavery." He gave facts and figures on the virtual denial of education to Negro children. "When a group has been reduced to serfdom, political and economic," he declared, "its social status becomes fixed by the fact."

Later that year, writing in the same magazine on "Socialism and the Negro," Harrison said: " . . . the mission of the Socialist Party is to free the working class from exploitation, and since the Negro is the most ruthlessly exploited working class group in America, the duty of the party to champion his cause is as clear as day." But, he added, in a rebuke that should have gotten more attention at the time, "no particular effort" had been made to do so.

The respect that Harrison deserved is evident in the words of J.A. Rogers from his book, *World's Great Men of Color:*

> Harrison . . . was not only perhaps the foremost Aframerican intellect of his time, but one of America's greatest minds. No one worked more seriously and indefatigably to enlighten his fellowmen; none of the Aframerican leaders of his time had a saner and more effective program—but others, unquestionably his inferiors, received the recognition that was his due. Even today but a very small proportion of the Negro intelligentsia has ever heard of him.

Harrison was for many years a lecturer, soap-boxer, writer, and organizer for the Socialist party. "With Elizabeth Gurley Flynn, Bill Haywood, Morris Hillquit, and other party leaders," Rogers says, "he labored for the emancipation of the workingman." His passionate devotion to both socialism and the advancement of his people was supported by one teaching of Karl Marx: "Labor cannot emancipate itself in the white skin where in the black it is branded." Marx said this in the days before the Civil War. During that conflict he and Frederick Engels exerted every effort to get the Lincoln administration to issue an early Emancipation Proclamation, thus making slavery in name the central issue of the war, as it already was in fact. They made every effort, also (and not without effect), to prevent the British Government from siding with the Confederacy. Through the agency of the International, from the time it was organized in 1864, they sought to educate the American working class about the evil and the dangers of slavery. As the Civil War ended, they urged full citizenship rights to the freed Negro people: "Remove every shackle from freedom's limbs," their message warned; "Let your citizens . . . be free and equal, without reserve."[1]

This attitude was carried forward by the members of the First International who resided in the United States. When the New York Communist Club joined with German trade unionists in 1868 to form the short-lived Social Party of New York and Vicinity, one of its planks, says James S. Allen in *Reconstruction: The Battle for Democracy,* "demanded the repeal of all discriminatory laws"; another "favored the eligibility of all citizens . . . for office."

On September 13, 1871, a contingent of Negro workers took part in the great mass demonstration for the eight-hour day in New York, marching with the First International sections behind the red flag, and was greeted with applause.

There was a section of the First International also in Washington, D.C. (as in St. Louis, Chicago, and other cities), and it is interesting to note that Richard J. Hinton, "who had taken part in John Brown's uprising at Harper's Ferry, was among the most active members" of the Washington group, according to Allen.

Marxist influence reached the National Colored Labor Union headed by Isaac Myers; this union chose a member, the Reverend Sella Martin, to represent it at a Congress of the International—the same Sella Martin who

---

1. In his letters to Abraham Lincoln, Karl Marx spoke of the Civil War as "the matchless struggle for the rescue of an enchained race and the reconstruction of a social world" in *The Civil War in the United States* (New York: International Publishers, 1937), p. 281.

in 1870 was editor of *The New Era,* of which Frederick Douglass was corresponding editor. Frederick Douglass himself succeeded Myers in 1870 as president of the National Colored Labor Union. One of the delegates present with Douglass at the Union convention was Peter H. Clark, of the Colored Teacher's Cooperative Association of Cincinnati, Ohio, who later was a leader in the Socialist Labor party. At a meeting of the Union called by Frederick Douglass in Columbia, South Carolina, in 1871, a newspaperman quoted by Charles H. Wesley (*Negro Labor in the United States*), "wanted to know if this Union was another name for Communism, or if it was a colored offshoot of the International."

There is no definite proof that Douglass, one of the two greatest Aframericans (with W. E. B. Du Bois) in United States history, was favorably interested in Marxism, or directly influenced by it; but there is circumstantial evidence. He lived during the period that the First International was active in New York, and during the most productive years of the Socialist Labor Party. In England he met leading Chartists and liked their ideas. He was clearly acquainted with equalitarian philosophy, and open-minded toward all progressive reform movements.[2] Douglass was a long-time friend of Wendell Phillips, Christian Socialist, who is said to have joined the First International.

It has been said that Douglass—whether Marxist or not—was *dialectical* in his thinking. An example of this is his change in attitude toward the United States Constitution: William Lloyd Garrison thought it a covenant with Hell, but Douglass came to regard it as basically antislavery and libertarian, as have the Socialist Labor Party and the Socialist Party through the years.[3] Another example is his transfer of activity from the Radical Abolitionists to the Republican party, where the mass of the antislavery people were, using arguments and explanations similar to those of Marx's friend, Joseph Weydemeyer, who also supported the Republicans and Lincoln.

One wonders, to be sure, at this point, whether Douglass was even aware of the existence of Joseph Weydemeyer, who fought militarily and politically against slavery, and died a year after the Civil War ended. Did he know of Weydemeyer's friend, Hermann Meyer, a Marxist who before the Civil War had been an Abolitionist in Montgomery, Alabama? Did he know of still another contemporary, Dr. Adolph Douai, who edited an anti-slavery paper in San Antonio, Texas, before the Civil War, and

2. Philip S. Foner calls Douglass "the universal reformer" in *Life and Writings of Frederick Douglass* (New York: International Publishers, 1950-55), Vol. II, p. 13.
3. See speech by Frederick Douglass, July 6, 1863, in Philadelphia: "Abolish slavery tomorrow, and not a sentence or syllable of the Constitution need be altered."

became a Socialist Labor Party editor and leader in New York in the 1880's? It is hard to believe that so alert a man as Douglass would not know something about these men and their ideas, but there is no precise evidence that he did.

Douglass said on one occasion that "the American people must stand *each for all and all for each,* without respect to color or race." In another place he said, with the eight-hour day in mind: "Our sympathies, as far as the *elimination of work* is concerned, are naturally enlisted on the side of the laborers." In still another place he stated that the "poor laboring white man" was "almost as much a slave as the black slave himself," explaining in this way: "The white slave had taken from him by indirection what the black slave had taken from him directly and without ceremony. Both were plundered and by the same plunderers."[4] These ideas might have been derived from the Socialist Labor party platform of 1879. Thus the historical tie-up of the current of Marxism with the Negro people's struggle is strongly suggested, straight through from John Brown to Frederick Douglass, from the Abolitionists to the Socialist Labor Party.

How did it happen that the Marxist support to the Negroes' struggle became diluted and perfunctory in Hubert Harrison's day? To what extent, nonetheless, did Marxism help that struggle in the days from the 1870's to 1917?

The 1879 platform of the Socialist Labor party declared for political equality "without regard to creed, race or sex," and appealed to working people of the South, "regardless of color," to unite with their brothers of the North against the southern landlords and the northern capitalists.

Philip Van Patten, Socialist Labor Party general secretary, told the convention that adopted this platform that in Cincinnati, Ohio, "Peter H. Clark, a colored man," had been a candidate of the Party for Congress the preceding autumn, along with Solomon Ruthenberg of the same state. The very first Socialist congressional nominations were thus one Negro and one white.

Incidentally, this Negro Socialist, Peter H. Clark, a co-worker of Frederick Douglass, had been a prominent leader of the working class in St. Louis during the great railroad strike of 1877. This is what he told the striking workers:

> Let us finally not forget that we are American citizens: that the right of free speech and a free press is enjoyed by us. We are exercising today the right to assemble and complain of grievances.

4. Philip S. Foner (ed.), *Frederick Douglass: Selections from His Writings* (New York: International Publishers, 1945).

The courts of the land are open to us, and we hold in our hands the all-compelling ballot. There is no need for violent counsels or violent deeds. If we are patient and wise, the future is ours.[5]

Another outstanding Negro leader within the Socialist Labor party was Frank J. Ferrell, a machinist. Philip S. Foner, in his *History of the Labor Movement in the United States,* Vol. II, describes him as "the most famous Negro in the Knights of Labor." Ferrell represented New York's District 49 at the Knights of Labor convention at Richmond, Virginia, in 1886. Here, supported by his fellow unionists, he was the center of successful, if temporary, efforts to oppose segregation in that city.

There were also Negroes outside of the Socialist Labor party who were influenced by Marxist ideas, as shown in Dr. Herbert Aptheker's *A Documentary History of the Negro People in the United States.* He cites Thomas Fortune's *Black and White: Land, Labor and Politics in the South,* published in 1884. "Let us see if the cause of the laboring man is not the same in all sections . . . as it is in all the world. If . . . I can incontestably demonstrate that the *condition of the black and white laborer is the same, and that consequently their cause is common;* that they should unite under the one banner and work upon the same platform of principles for . . . the more equal distribution of the products of labor and capital, I shall not have written this book in vain . . . "

We can include the Reverend Reverdy C. Ransom among the nonparty Socialists. "As early as 1896," according to August Meier's dissertation, *Negro Racial Thought in the Age of Booker T. Washington,* "Reverdy Ransom favored Socialism in an article in the A.M.E. Church *Review.*" Ransom's article was entitled "The Negro and Socialism," and appeared in October, 1896. He predicted, says Meier, that when the Negro "comes to realize that Socialism offers him freedom of opportunity to cooperate with all men upon terms of equality in every avenue of life, he will not be slow to accept his social emancipation."

Somewhere along the line, unfortunately, under the leadership of Daniel De Leon, the Socialists became doctrinaire. "De Leon would invariably remind his listeners," says Arnold Petersen, Socialist Labor party national secretary, in *Daniel De Leon: Social Architect,* "that there was no such thing as a race or 'Negro question' . . . that there was only a *social,* a *labor* question, and no racial or religious question so far as the Socialist and labor movements were concerned."

This denial of reality does not mean that De Leon did not give some sympathetic thought to the condition of Negroes. Indeed, in his *Flash-*

5. Robert V. Bruce, *1877: Year of Violence* (Indianapolis and New York: The Bobbs-Merrill Company, Inc., 1959), p. 231.

lights of the Amsterdam Congress (1906), De Leon quotes (questionably) Frederick Douglass as saying that "the present condition of the Negro is tangibly worse than when he was a chattel slave." But De Leon uses this alleged quote from Douglass as the text for a sermon on capitalism as the *shadow of death* through which the workers must pass to socialism. De Leon's argument was that even though wage slavery was (supposedly) worse than chattel slavery, it was a progressive step forward. "It is progress," he said, "because the present condition, the wage slave status, is the necessary precursor and key with which to open the gates of the Socialist Republic."

As theory, this is only half correct. If De Leon had followed Marx a little further and had taught that lynching, denial of civil rights, and job discrimination against Negroes were things that workers in the white skin must fight against *en route to the Socialist Republic,* he would have been a true Marxist. But this would have required him to admit that there was after all a "Negro question." It would have required the Socialist Labor party to take a militant stand against the special oppression—political, economical, and social—that Negroes suffered.

While at the Amsterdam Congress, De Leon indignantly and properly opposed a proposition by Van Koll of Holland to restrict the immigration of "inferior" races. "Socialism knows not," De Leon wrote in scorn, "such insulting, iniquitous distinctions as 'inferior' and 'superior' races among the proletariat. It is for capitalism to fan the fires of such sentiments in its scheme to keep the proletariat divided."

De Leon was a thousand times right in this statement. But if capitalism has already divided the proletariat, what must the Marxist vanguard do? It is not enough to say *there is no Negro question,* meaning that workers do not draw the color line, when the color line already exists, drawn by others. Back in 1869 Isaac Myers, of the National Colored Union, said that Negro workers were eager for unity with white workers, but "the doors of workshops in North, East, and West were bolted against them."

Here, clearly, De Leon was trapped by his own doctrinairism. Though correctly denying the assertion that Negroes were inferior, he allowed himself to forget that white workers have a duty and a necessity to fight here and now for equal rights for their black brothers.

Born as it was at the turn of the century, the new Socialist party (which rebelled against De Leon) seemed destined to make a new start toward a genuine Marxist position on the Negro question. The Indianapolis founding convention (1901) adopted a resolution that acknowledged that Negroes, "because of their long training in slavery and but recent emancipation therefrom, occupy a peculiar position in the working class." In this situation, the capitalist class sought "to foster and increase color prejudice and race hatred between the white worker and the black." The Negro was betrayed by the old parties and even by religious and educational institutions "in his present helpless struggle against disfranchisement and violence."

"Therefore," the resolution stated, "we, the American Socialist Party, invite the Negro to membership and fellowship with us in the world movement for economic emancipation by which equal liberty and opportunity shall be secured to every man, and fraternity become the order of the world."

This resolution had a certain warmth that was lacking in the bare propagandistic call for membership "without distinction of color, race, sex or creed." Yet it, too, lacked something. Aside from the longstanding invitation to Negroes to join the Socialist movement, it stressed only sympathy with them in their oppression, not a pledge to fight against that oppression.

The warmth and meaning in the resolution were due almost solely to the insistence of the three Negro delegates at the 1901 convention: William E. Costley, a minister from San Francisco, and two coal miners, John W. Adams of Brazil, Indiana, and Edward D. McKay of Richmond, Indiana. According to the contemporary press, the original routine document submitted by the resolutions committee on the Negro question "was not satisfactory to these delegates," that is, to the three Negroes. Finally a special committee was set up that "with the assistance of the colored delegates" drafted the statement that has come down to us.

When Costley submitted his substitute for the first inadequate formulation, it contained a clause on lynching to which A. M. Simons, Socialist editor and historian, "took exception," while "Adams and Costley warmly defended it." Max Hayes, of the Printers Union, and the Reverend George H. Herron declared to their eternal credit that the Party "must not fail to meet the moral issue." But when the final wording was adopted, the clause that specifically condemned lynching did not appear.

Lacking in the resolution, therefore, was any forthright reference to either segregation or lynching. When the right of free press was involved, or free speech, the Socialists fought manfully against denial; if a working-class leader was kidnapped, as happened to William D. Haywood and his comrades in 1906, they rose to his defense. Why, then, was it thought un-Socialist to rise to the defense of the victimized Negro people? It can be explained theoretically only on the basis of De Leon's denial that there was a Negro question. De Leon was known as a "Marxist," and his narrow, doctrinaire limitation of theory—so contrary to Marx's own example as well as to his teaching—had its effect down the years on Socialist thought and action.

It even affected the thinking of Eugene Debs, a strong defender of equality of white and black workers. "Debs," says Ray Ginger in *The Bending Cross,* "always refused to speak before segregated audiences." At one time he declared, "I say that the Socialist Party would be false to its historic mission . . . if, on account of race considerations, it sought to exclude any human being from political equality and economic freedom." But he also hoped "the next convention (might) repeal the resolution on the Negro question," that is, the one adopted in 1901. Debs could say, on the one hand, "Of course the Negro will 'not be satisfied with equality with reservation. Why should he be? Would you?'" and then he would add, with no awareness of inconsistency: "We have nothing special to offer the Negro, and we cannot make separate appeals to all the races." He was hamstrung by the old misinterpretation of economic theory.

This is chiefly why the Socialist party never reaffirmed the 1901 resolution. Dr. W. E. B. Du Bois noted this in a *New Review* article in 1913, saying wryly that the Party had succeeded in at least not repealing its single straightforward declaration. Du Bois expressed the central truth when he asked, "Can the objects of Socialism be achieved so long as the Negro is neglected?" Whether intentionally or not, he was here echoing Marx's warning about the impossibility of freeing labor in the white skin "where in the black, it is branded."

There was an additional, and in fact, decisive factor at work, besides the misrepresentation of Marxist economics—race prejudice within the Party. Besides A. M. Simons, there were two other delegates at the 1901 convention—William L. Hamilton of Indiana and F. L. Robinson of Kentucky—who objected to the clause against lynching on the ground that it would lose votes in the South! Victor L. Berger, who was later elected to Congress, publicly described Negroes as rapists, according to Ira Kipnis in *The American Socialist Movement, 1897-1912.*

The most shameful passage in Socialist history occurred in 1902, only a year after the founding convention. The Second International, through its International Bureau, questioned the American party about its attitude toward lynching. The reply, as quoted by Kipnis, was as follows:

> The Socialist Party points out the fact that nothing less than the abolition of the capitalist system and the substitution of the Socialist system can provide conditions under which the hunger maniacs, kleptomaniacs, sexual maniacs and all other offensive and now-lynchable human degenerates will cease to be begotten or produced.

Another development came in 1904 when the Socialist party of Louisiana adopted a constitution providing for segregated locals. This was too brazen for the Socialist leadership, and the Louisiana application for a charter was turned down until the offending clause was deleted. But the resulting discussion in letters to the Socialist press showed how necessary was a campaign of instruction in Socialist humanism.

The Seattle Socialist, edited by Dr. Herman F. Titus, carried extensive reprints of opinion on both sides of the "segregated local" controversy. One of the antisegregation pieces was a featured letter from Turnersville, Texas, written by Edwin Arnold Brenholtz, who said, ironically, that segregated locals might increase the *numbers* in the Party, but he hoped that "each and every attempt to segregate a single human being will be promptly sat down on by the National Committee, and if not by them, then by the party at large, once and for all time." Then he added: "A local at this and every other place is greatly to be desired—but not at the cost of principle. What is now needed most of all is for every Socialist in the world to deliberately crush out of himself every vestige of race prejudice. . . . The work of the Socialist in the South in the immediate future lies not so much in making Socialist voters as in breaking down race prejudice."[6]

Important was the case of the Socialist attorney, Eraste Vidrine, himself a "Cajun" of New Orleans. He wrote an article for the *International Socialist Review* in January, 1905, again urging separate locals for Negroes, on the ground that comrades of the "gentler sex" would not be comfortable in a mixed local. He reported the actual existence of an all-Negro local in Lutcher, Louisiana, at that time. It is only fair to add, however, that Vidrine's views on the Negro question reportedly changed considerably as time went on.

Another Southerner, Covington Hall, a Socialist poet and a friend of Eraste Vidrine, took an opposing position. He helped Vidrine to correct his chauvinistic views. Covington Hall's articles in the *International Socialist Review* emphasize equality and comradeship of all workers, regardless of color, although in somewhat general terms.

Mixed with such efforts, however, were still such supposedly "correct" articles in *The Call* as that of the Socialist journalist Robert Hunter ("The Emancipation of the Negro"), calling on the Negro to "fight his own battles and win his own victories."[7]

Despite the doctrinairism, the white chauvinism, and the opportunism,

6. *The Seattle Socialist,* January 17, 1904, as shown by a photocopy supplied by the University of Washington Library (Seattle) through the courtesy of Robert D. Monroe, Head, Special Collections Division. It was evidently a page of correspondence on the controversial Louisiana proposal to organize segregated schools in the Socialist party.

7. *The Call* (New York), May 31, 1901; supplied on microfilm at the Tamiment Library, New York City, through the courtesy of Mrs. Louise Heinze, Librarian.

there continued to be voices raised within the Socialist party demanding a more forthright and positive stand on the Negro question. Dr. W. E. B. Du Bois and Hubert Harrison, the leading Negro Socialists, continued to thunder in their different ways. Mary White Ovington, white social worker, asked in *The Call* (New York) that the 1901 resolution be reaffirmed.

The most scholarly critique of Socialist practice in regard to Negroes was written in a series of some fifteen articles in the *International Socialist Review* (1909-1910) by Dr. I. M. Rubinow (under the pseudonym of I. M. Robbins). He took a sober Marxist position and buttressed his argument with statistics, analyses, and logic in a manner more like Marx's own than any other American Socialist theoretician.

In his conclusion he hoped, half-humorously, that his efforts had done some good, "for surely Comrade [Charles H.] Kerr would never have agreed to accept a series of fifteen articles about the foresaken Negro, for whom we have until now shown so very little concern." He ended with these words:

> The Socialist Party must take a definite attitude on the Negro problem, and must not be afraid to proclaim it. And this attitude must include something a good deal more tangible than the promise of "full products of one's labor in the cooperative commonwealth." It must include, if it is to be logical and honest, a clear, unmistakable demand for the entire abolition of all legal restriction of the rights of the Negro. . . . The attitude of the Socialist movement must not only be passively correct and decent, but actively aggressive. . . . Will we be wise enough to do it?

The Socialist movement, as things turned out, did not live up to the hopes of Rubinow, and certainly not to the ideals of Marx. But something was accomplished for all that. Marxism did indeed give some help to the struggle for the Negro people for full freedom, and furthermore, it kept alive the hope and the possibility of powerful white allies in that struggle. It did rather more through the Socialist party than had been done through the Socialist Labor party.

To begin with, one of the first candidates nominated for Congress by the Socialist party was the thirty-three-year-old Negro trade unionist James L. Bishop, of the Fifth District of Indiana, in the fall of 1902. "Bishop is an enthusiastic Socialist and an active worker in his union," declared *The Recorder,* a local Negro newspaper. It added that he was president of the local Central Labor Union of Clinton, Indiana.[8]

---

8. It is a coincidence that the first Negro nominee of the Socialist Labor party, Peter H. Clark, was also a candidate for Congress.

In 1904 one of the delegates to the Second National Socialist Party Convention, held in Chicago, was the Reverend George W. Woodbey, a Negro cleric from California and a Party member for many years.

Also in 1904, in the August issue of *The Comrade* appeared significant pro-Socialist quotations from two Negro periodicals, *The Broadax* of Chicago and *The Bee* of Washington, D. C. *The Comrade,* which is authority for the citations, was a Marxist art and literature magazine in the first decade of the century. It was the precursor of *The Masses.*

The Broadax, "published by and for Negroes," is quoted thus:

> Eugene V. Debs, who is making the race for President of the United States on the Socialist ticket, should receive the votes of two or three hundred thousand colored men, for he is one of the greatest champions of the civil and political rights of the Afro-American, and by doing so the Negro would show to the world of mankind that he is not the abject slave of either one of the great political parties.

The other publication, *The Bee,* said:

> The Socialist Party believes in the equality of man. Neither the Democratic nor the Republican party believes in human rights so far as the Negro is concerned. The Republican party has admitted its inability to protect the Negro in his vote. The Democratic party whenever it obtains power disfranchises the colored man. . . . In the coming contest what position will the colored voter assume? . . . Must the Negro in the coming campaign divide his vote? . . . The time has come for the colored man to act.

Further impressive evidence of the Negro's interest in and knowledge of Marxism is given in Herbert Aptheker's *Documentary History of the Negro People.* The newer Socialist Party, organized in 1900, was largely responsible for this renewed interest, but the social push came from the Negro people themselves. When George Edwin Taylor, first Black candidate for president, gave his acceptance speech to the National Liberty Party in St. Louis in 1904, he declared that Black workers were an important part of "the vast common working classes of this great republic." He added, in denouncing disenfranchisement laws against Black men: "The Negro of the United States is distinctively a factor in the great and grand army of American workingmen, and whatever enhances, strengthens, retards or impedes his progress, happiness, manhood, or citizenship rights, proportionately affects all the citizens of his class and standing." (cited work p. 854.)

But more pointed were the remarks of Jesse Max Barber, editor of the *Voice of the Negro,* published in Atlanta, Georgia, June, 1904;

The doctrine of Socialism is the doctrine of an Industrial State, directed by modern science, with government ownership and control of all public utilities, and based upon the equality of mankind. . . . Mr. Debs has said repeatedly that the Socialist party is the Black man's hope and friend. There are objections to Socialism in some of its aspects, but it is a splendid field for negotiations for the Negro in these days when the Republican party has forsook him to the persecutions of the Democrats. An examination of the field certainly could do no harm. We must affiliate with a party that will reward our endeavors with friendly co-operation. (*Ibid.* p. 856.)

Similarly, the *Georgia Baptist* of Augusta, Georgia, was quoted in the *New York Age* of September 6, 1906, as follows:

We are of the opinion that the colored voters of Georgia will find it to their interest to vote the Socialist state ticket in October. Nine-tenths of the white people who belong to the Socialist party are laboring people; they must live daily upon the sweat of their brow. Nine-tenths of the colored people are laboring people, who must eat bread daily in the sweat of their brow. The consolidation of wealth during the past score of years must admonish all laboring classes that their hope for the future devolves largely upon their coming together, and in one common cause, fighting the battle of labor against combinations of wealth. (*Ibid.* p. 857.)

At the National Negro Conference, New York City, May 31-June 1, 1909, the remarks of George Frazier Miller, a Brooklyn cleric, indicate not only his own knowledge of Marxism but his confident assumption that his hearers also were familiar with it.

Now, there is the great Socialistic party which stands for economic independence, which is the hope of the future today. I stand for rights. There are some people who say they want certain rights and do not want others. Some people say they are not looking for social equality. I want every kind of equality I can have. By that I do not mean that I want to force myself upon any man's presence, I never sought a man socially, and I don't expect to. I don't care whether he be rich as Carnegie, holy as St. John, wise as Socrates, or white as the Albanian fathers, but what I want is equality, and if I don't get equality, then I want superiority. Under Socialism we have economic independence. Everyone has the right to work and every man the full reward of his labors." (*Ibid.* p. 922.)

Continuing our attention to that same historic Black conference—from which evolved the N.A.A.C.P.—here is an excerpt from the speech delivered there by Dr. J. Milton Waldron, a Baptist minister of Washington, D. C., whose topic was "The Problem's Solution:"

In the second place, the Negro must make common cause with
the working class which today is organizing and struggling for better
social and economic conditions. The old slave oligarchy maintained
its ascendancy largely by fixing a gulf between the Negro slave and
the free white laborer, and the jealousies and animosities of the
slave period have survived to keep apart the Negro and the laboring
white man. Powerful influences are at work even today to impress
upon the Negro the fact that he must look to the business men of
the South alone for protection and recognition of his rights, while
at the same time these influences inflame the laboring white man
with fears of social equality and race fusion. The Negro, being a
laborer, must see that the cause of his labor is his cause, that his
elevation can be largely achieved by having the sympathy, support
and cooperation of that growing organization of working men the
world over which is working out the larger problems of human
freedom and economic opportunity. (*Ibid.* pp. 923-924.)

The ideas of Marx were clearly acceptable and inspiring to some Black
intellectuals throughout post-Civil War history. Only organized socialist
politics was at fault, as I have stressed elsewhere in this chapter.

Frank Crosswaith of New York was a young Black man in the Socialist
movement of 1906, as Elizabeth Gurley Flynn recalls in *I Speak My Own
Piece.* In 1909, the year that Hubert Harrison joined the Party, a Negro
preacher in Milford, Ohio, the Reverend Richard Euell, was already a
member. Writing for the *Ohio Socialist Bulletin,* he said that the Negro
"belongs to the working class and must be taught class consciousness."

In 1911, when Dr. W. E. B. Du Bois became a member of the Socialist
Party, he was put at once on the speakers' bureau. He left the Party a
year later, as he explains in *Dusk of Dawn,* to support Woodrow Wilson
for president, because the latter had assured "absolute fair dealing" to the
Negro people.

Just before joining the Party, Du Bois published a news item in *The
Crisis* (December, 1910) entitled "Socialists in Oklahoma." It was quoted
from *The Call* and described a convention of Negro organizations in
Chickasha, Oklahoma, that officially endorsed the Socialist platform and
"advised all the colored people of Oklahoma to vote the Socialist Ticket." The article hailed this event as "epoch-making," and went on to say:

It is a principle universally acknowledged by Socialists that although
Socialism is primarily the movement of the working class for the
overthrow of capitalist rule, it nevertheless must rush to the assistance of every oppressed class or race or nationality. The working
class cannot achieve its ultimate grand aim of freeing itself from

exploitation unless it frees all other elements of the community from exploitation. It cannot put an end to its own oppression unless it puts an end to all forms of oppression.

This was the genuine Marxist Socialist position. Odd that it had so little expression, even in words!

In the first five years of the second decade of the twentieth century, and especially when World War I got under way, there was a real Socialist upsurge in New York among Negro intellectuals. Outstanding among them was A. Philip Randolph, founder of *The Messenger,* which started publication under that name in early 1917 just before the Russian Revolution. (Actually, it had begun as *The Hotel Messenger,* a workers' union paper, in 1916, according to Richard B. Moore.) Associated with Randolph was Chandler Owen. Both Owen and Randolph were lecturers at the Rand School. Other contributors to *The Messenger* were W. A. Domingo, a fiery West Indian leader, and the scholarly Reverend George Frazier Miller of Brooklyn.

Still other New Yorkers were Richard B. Moore, orator and scholar, who had sat at the feet of Hubert Harrison. Moore read Morgan's *Ancient Society* in 1916, joined the Socialist party early in 1917, and left again when Algernon Lee, in a lecture to Harlem Socialists, declared that Negroes were sharecroppers, not industrial workers, and could not be organized. J.A. Rogers, the well-known Negro journalist, read a good deal of Marx, he says, around 1915 and afterward, and was especially influenced by Marx's materialist conception of history. Otto and Hermie Huiswoud were a West Indian husband and wife team of Socialist propagandists around 1912-1916.

Negro women also stepped forward, such as Helen Holman, described by those who heard her in 1916 as a brilliant and powerful public speaker; also Williana Burroughs and Grace Campbell, two talented and devoted public school teachers. A younger woman, Layle Lane, who later became a teacher, recalls belonging to a branch of the Intercollegiate Socialist Society at Howard University in 1916. Indeed, this branch sent a delegate named William Foster to the Society's 1916 national convention. The poet Claude McKay turned to socialism about this time, and was published in *The Masses.*

In Detroit there were four outstanding Socialist speakers who addressed huge crowds in Moose Temple early in 1917, only a few weeks before the first Russian Revolution, and one of them was a Negro. The list comprised Eugene V. Debs, the grand old leader; Louis B. Boudin, the lawyer and author; Charles M. O'Brien, of Canada, who had been a member of a provincial legislature there; and Ross D. Brown, of Muncie,

Indiana, described in the *Michigan Socialist* as "Colored Lecturer," "Able Exponent of Socialism," and author of a book, *The Real Cause of War.*

Another early prominent Negro Socialist was the late Benjamin Lowell Careathers, steel worker and trade-union organizer of Pittsburgh, and old-time friend of William Z. Foster. Careathers was a leader of the Socialist left wing.

The Industrial Workers of the World was another avenue through which Marxist thought reached some Negro leaders and through them the Negro people.

Most prominent of Negro wobblies was Benjamin F. Fletcher, longtime associate of William D. Haywood and Elizabeth Gurley Flynn. Fletcher lived in Philadelphia, was active in water-front organizational work, and was a leader among the longshoremen.

Owen Middleton, who years later was an artist and news correspondent at the United Nations, and, under the banner of Henry A. Wallace's Progressive Party, ran for legislative office in 1948, was in earlier days, as a young man, a member of the I.W.W. So was Lovett Fort-Whiteman, who later (1925) played a leading role as organizer of the American Negro Labor Congress. On the West Coast there was R. T. Sims, who came to the I.W.W. from the Socialist Party.

Newsman Cyril Briggs (died October 1966), who found the Socialist Party too dominated by its Right Wing, was favorably impressed by the non-discriminatory and militant policy of the I.W.W. before and during World War I. This can be said of other Marx-oriented radicals as well as Briggs: They demanded of their white comrades a forthright stand on the Negro question.[9]

While the I.W.W. practiced equality in relations of white and black workers, it tended to avoid theoretical discussion of black-white relations, or to over-simplify these relations. "Social equality" they simply laughed at, as a bourgeois theme unworthy of the attention of proletarians. To a degree, so far as theory was concerned, the I.W.W. rested its position on the old De Leon denial that a Negro question existed. (De Leon, of course, was one of the founders of the I.W.W. in 1905.) The I.W.W. solved it, one might say, by removing it from the agenda.

Socialists had a good deal to do with the founding of the National Association for the Advancement of Colored People (NAACP), by far the oldest civil rights organization—the organization that has stood for half a century as the backbone of Negro hopes and aspirations, and the symbol of Negro courage and culture.

9. A. P. Randolph and his co-workers on *The Messenger,* mentioned earlier, were also at first strongly influenced by the I. W. W.

In an article entitled "How the National Association for the Advancement of Colored People Began," Mary White Ovington, a Socialist, tells how the idea was suggested by William English Walling, another Socialist. In a magazine article Walling denounced the race riots of a few weeks earlier that had taken the lives of Negroes in Springfield, Illinois, Abraham Lincoln's city. He firmly states: " . . . We must come to treat the Negro on a plane of absolute political and social equality." With indignation and hope, he asked "what large and powerful body of citizens" was ready to come to the aid of the Negro people.[10]

Miss Ovington wrote to Walling, and after conferring with another friend, Dr. Henry Moskowitz, they issued "a call for a national conference on the Negro question," to be held in New York on February 12, Lincoln's birthday anniversary. Among the fifty-five signers, in addition to Dr. Du Bois, were such other Socialists as Charles Edward Russell, pioneer muckraker; Florence Kelley, friend of Frederick Engels; Mary E. Drier, suffragette and former president of the National Women's Trade Union League; and J. G. Phelps Stokes, later the husband of Rose Pastor Stokes. We may include also the names of others, especially William Dean Howells, utopian Socialist and contributor to Socialist campaigns; Leonora O'Reilly, utopian Socialist and suffragette; and Helen Olivia Phelps Stokes, who joined the Socialist party in 1911, the same year that Dr. Du Bois joined; George Frazier Miller, a Black minister from Brooklyn, N.Y.

The work of Marx provided the basis for a sound and effective working-class program on the Negro question, a program that the majority of Negroes might have supported. Inadequate use of this foundation was made, however, by the Socialist Labor and Socialist parties through their doctrinaire positions of unreality about particular racial discriminations and injustices. Something was nevertheless accomplished, in two ways: first, by making Marxist thought available to Negro leaders through some of the more advanced leaders directly allied with socialism; and second, a valuable and potentially powerful means of winning full Negro freedom—that of building real Black and white labor unity—was kept alive for the time that would certainly come.

As we have seen, Du Bois was justifiably impatient[11] in earlier days

10. *The Independent*, September 3, 1908, as quoted from William English Walling by Mary White Ovington in a brochure, "How the National Association for the Advancement of Colored People Began," published originally in 1914 by the NAACP, 20 West 40 Street, New York, N. Y. 10018.

11. Helen Alfred (ed.), *Toward a Socialist America: A Symposium of Essays by Fifteen Contemporary American Socialists* (New York: Peace Publications, 1958), pp. 179-91.

with the half-awareness of working-class socialism in this country, but his later thinking appears in these words:

> The footsteps of the long oppressed and staggering masses are not always straight and sure, but their mistakes can never cause the misery and distress which the factory caused in Europe, colonial imperialism caused in Asia and Africa, and which slavery, lynching, disfranchisement, and Jim-Crow legislation have caused in the United States.[12]

12. Ibid., p. 186.

VI

Marxism and the Battle for Woman Suffrage

The struggle for the ballot was a sector in the fight for various rights that women were and are deprived of, such as equal pay for the same work, trade union privileges, freedom from a raft of legal disabilities, and opportunity for consideration in leadership and popular esteem. The ballot has been a measuring-stick for progress of women's rights in general.

Those who write the conventional story of this progress have a tendency to omit the Marxist contribution. Forgotten by them are the hundreds of devoted Socialist women who consciously strove for the ballot.

This situation was recognized by Elizabeth Gurley Flynn, who published "Women in American Socialist Struggles" in *Political Affairs* back in 1960.[1]

The situation arises in part out of the production of books and studies which are in many ways models of scholarship, but which tend to make very slight reference—or none at all—to Socialist women suffragists. An example of this is *Century of Struggle* (1959), a generally fine book by Eleanor Flexner. It was praised by Grace Hutchins of Labor Research Association as "the first full, well-rounded story of the woman's suffrage movement."[2]

Yet this book has only one mention of the Socialist Party in the index. It speaks of very few Socialist women, and of the few mentioned, only one or two, such as Leonora O'Reilly, are referred to as Socialists. Even Florence Kelley, translator of some of the works of Marx and Engels, and member of both the Socialist Labor Party and the Socialist Party at

1. *Political Affairs*, April, 1960, pp. 33-39.
2. *The Worker*, Sept. 20, 1959, p. 10.

certain periods, is just a "passionate crusader" in this book.[3] Ellen Gates Starr, who was described in the *Christian Socialist* of April 1, 1914, as "a red card Socialist," is identified by Miss Flexner only as "of Hull House."[4] Charlotte Perkins Gilman, the poet, is described as "widely read," but there is no hint that she was a Socialist. The suffragette leader, Harriet Stanton Blatch, is of course highly praised, but no one would guess from this book that she ever wrote for the New York *Call*.[5]

This unfortunate trend among historians to bury the Marxists began years ago when the fight for the suffrage was hottest, and was recognized then, too, with surprise and dismay.

In 1910, for example, Lena Morrow Lewis, wife of Arthur Morrow Lewis, toured the country for suffrage on behalf of the Socialist Party, and was interviewed by a New York *Call* reporter.[6] She centered attention on the tendency of pure-and-simple suffragettes to shoulder all the glory, whenever a victory was won.

"At their recent celebration in Cooper Union over the victorious amendment in Washington state, which grants suffrage to all women," Miss Lewis said, "no credit whatever was given to the Socialist women who played such a large part in stirring up sentiment in Washington for the suffrage amendment. No mention was made of the fact that Gene Debs toured the state during the campaign, holding tremendous meetings, in which he devoted a considerable part of his every speech to the advocacy of the suffrage amendment. The fact was passed over that the Socialist party brought its machinery into action in aid of the women of Washington, and spread broadcast throughout Washington literature which called attention to the need for and the justice of the suffrage amendment. No attention was paid to the fact that the Socialist party sent a special organizer, Anna Maley, into Washington, where, in conjunction with the state organization, she worked hard for the amendment."

Victoria Woodhull was not only "a woman of beauty and wit," as Eleanor Flexner describes her,[8] but also in 1871-72 a leader of the Spring Street Council in New York, one of the main American divisions of the First International. She edited *Woodhull and Claflin's Weekly*, and pub-

---

3. *Century of Struggle*, p. 214.
4. *Century of Struggle*, p. 244.
5. See, for example, New York *Call*, May 1, 1909, p. 7, and Feb. 28, 1915, p. 9.
6. New York *Call*, Nov. 10, 1910, p. 4.
7. John M. Work, *What's So & What Isn't*, pamphlet, C. H. Kerr & Co., Chicago, 1905.
8. *Century of Struggle*, p. 153. See also Emanie Sachs, *The Terrible Siren* (About Victoria Woodhull), 1928, and Samuel Bernstein, *The First International in America*, 1962.

lished the first English translation of the *Communist Manifesto* in the United States. She organized the Equal Rights Party, was the candidate of this party for president, which suggested Frederick Douglass as her running mate. Miss Woodhull, backed by Susan B. Anthony and Elizabeth Cady Stantion, was the first woman in history to address a Congressional committee on the subject of votes for women.

Miss Woodhull was not a developed Marxist. Her group was later expelled from the International, not for advocating women's rights but for mixing spiritualism and bourgeois radicalism with working class thought, thus confusing and antagonizing the American public.

Miss Woodhull was not the only woman in the First International. There was a woman's section of the International in Milwaukee, as noted in Samuel Bernstein's *First International in America*.[9] Furthermore, as the same authority shows, women's organizations in New York cooperated with the International from the very first. The great Cooper Union anti-war meeting of Nov. 19, 1870, called in opposition to the Franco-Prussian War and specifically to the German annexation of Alsace-Lorraine, was addressed not only by spokesmen for the International, the trade unions, and the Free Thinkers, but also by "Mrs. L. D. Blake representing the women's societies."[10]

The resolution on women's rights adopted by the first Marxist party in the United States (1876) stated: "We acknowledge the perfect equality of rights of both sexes, and in the Workingmen's Party of the United States this equality of rights is a principle and is strictly observed."[11]

The Socialistic Labor Party (1879), which succeeded the Workingmen's Party, demanded full suffrage "without regard to creed, color, or sex."[12] So did the Socialist Labor Party in 1892, under Daniel De Leon's earlier leadership.[13]

The Socialist Party of Debs said the same thing in 1900, and in 1904 explicitly pledged "equal suffrage of men and women." It was in 1910 that the Socialist Party appointed a full-time woman's organizer, Marguerite Prevey of Ohio, to coordinate socialist work with advocacy of suffrage among women.

The capitalist parties avoided the issue. The Socialists could always

9. Samuel Bernstein, *First International in America*, Augustus M. Kelley, New York, 1962, pp. 265; 280.

10. *First International in America*, pp. 46-48.

11. *First International in America*, p. 287.

12. Photostatic Copy of "Platform, Constitution & Resolutions," Socialistic Labor Party, Dec. 26-31, 1879, and Jan. 1, 1880. Labadie Collection, University of Michigan Library, Ann Arbor, Mich.

13. Kirk H. Porter and D. B. Johnson, *National Party Platforms*, University of Illinois Press, 1956, p. 96 f.

point to the fact that theirs was the only political party which stood for equal suffrage.

This programmatic reality is augmented by the more important fact that Socialist women all along voted and held office within Socialist organizations from local to national level. They lectured, organized, served in positions of leadership, and, in the regular state and national campaigns, had their names on the ballot as candidates for public office. Socialist women had the ballot within the party many, many years before the 19th Amendment was passed.

This declared support for suffrage was not a mere "standing for" something, without positive action. Walter B. Rideout, now of the University of Wisconsin, takes note of "the valuable support that the Socialist Party gave to the movement for Woman Suffrage," and there is considerable evidence for this.[14]

On Jan. 16, 1911, Victor Berger—the first Socialist congressman—introduced a resolution into Congress for a constitutional amendment for woman's suffrage, and backed it up with a "monster petition of 109,582 people."[15]

Even earlier, on Feb. 22, 1908, the *Worker*—New York Socialist paper of half-a-century ago—reported Socialist testimony by Morris Hillquit and Meta L. Stern in Albany in favor of a constitutional amendment for equal suffrage. The Socialists demanded the franchise for women as a "social right."

In Illinois it was a Socialist member of the legislature, Seymour Stedman, who gave the principal speech on behalf of the state bill for woman suffrage.[16]

At the hearings before the joint committee on the Judiciary and the Committee on Woman Suffrage, United States Senate, April 23, 1912, testimony was given by all advocates of suffrage, and they included the Socialists, Miss Caroline A. Lowe of Kansas City and Miss Leonora O'Reilly of New York, spokesmen for working women.[17]

In addition, all through these years, thousands of leaflets were distributed throughout the country, like the one advertised in *The Progressive Woman*, a Socialist magazine, February, 1909: "Why the Socialist Woman Demands Universal Suffrage."

The Christian Socialist, a religious magazine which supported the

14. Walter B. Rideout, *The Radical Novel in the United States*, Harvard University Press, Cambridge, 1956, p. 75.

15. *Socialist Congressional Campaign Handbook*, 1914. p. 329.

16. Ethelwyn Mills, *Legislative Program of the Socialist Party, 1899-1913*. Bulletin No. 1, Information Dept. Chicago, 1914, pp. 45-46.

17. U. S. Senate, 62nd Congress, Second session, April 23, 1912.

Socialist Party program and candidates, reported, March 1, 1914, how all over the country "Women Run for Office on Socialist Ticket." In Illinois, for instance, Mrs. Mary Elliott was running for the collectorship in Edwardsville; Mrs. Grace Groetska, for school trustee of Glen Carbon; Mrs. Mary W. Busby, wife of a molder, for alderman in the Sixth Ward of Quincy; Mrs. Anna Tillquist, for assistant supervisor in that same ward; Mrs. Catherine Buss, for assistant supervisor in another township. And so on; no famous names. Just rank-and-file Socialist women showing they want the suffrage and are determined to use it for public benefit.

Among the few Socialists actually elected to office half a century ago, under local suffrage provisions, were some Socialist women. *The Progressive Woman* for January, 1910, reports, for example, that Olga Staps was elected to the schoolboard at Elmwood Place, Ohio, by 300 votes, a majority of 19. She was the only Socialist, along with five Republicans. Interviewed by the Cincinnati *Post,* she gave her 6-point program, which included small classes, the right of trial for a teacher when dismissed, "provision for the physical needs of children," and, above all, "Female teachers to be paid the same salary as male teachers for the same class of work."[18]

Literally hundreds of such varied examples could be given of direct Socialist work for woman suffrage.

The Socialists opposed limitations of the suffrage[19] as was first done in England, allowing the vote only to women of thirty or more; or, as some proposed, allowing only women *tax-payers* to vote; or limiting the vote to *white* women. For example, on Dec. 6, 1914, the New York *Call* carried an article, "Negro Women and the Suffrage," by Sarah Rush Parks, denouncing "cowardice and equivocation" on this question. "Women are *people*—Negroes are *people*—this is a government of the *people,*" she wrote.

Even more important, in some ways, was Socialist cooperation with the various suffrage organizations.

On Nov. 10, 1912, when a big suffrage demonstration took place in New York, the *Call* carried the page one banner headline, "35,000 Marchers for Suffrage heartily cheered by 100,000 Persons Watching Procession." This was followed by the sub-head, "Socialist Division in Mighty Parade for Equal Rights Shows Up 6,000 Strong and Gets Enthusiastic Greeting from Spectators." And finally, as the paraders wind up in

18. *The Progressive Woman,* January, 1910, p. 2.
19. "Restricted Woman Suffrage," by Bertha Howe, New York *Call,* Nov. 30, 1910, p. 4.

Union Square, working class speakers give "Plain Exposition of Why Women Should Have the Ballot in Every State."

In its "Woman's Day" number, the *Christian Socialist* two years later described the great suffrage parade that took place the preceding November, in Washington, D. C. All carried yellow banners, the suffrage color, and so did the Socialist section. But among the Socialist marchers— *"Suddenly the scene changed. The yellow was gone, and in its place was red—red sashes, red banners, red hat-bands, red dresses. . . . All was red, red, red. . . . On their banners the inscription: 'Every Socialist is a Suffragist.' "*[20]

A most vivid illustration of working together is given in a large advertisement of a Socialist meeting in the New York *Call* on Feb. 25, 1912, to be held in the Republic Theatre. The list of speakers and subjects tells the story: Alice Stone-Blackwell, suffragette, spoke on "The Emanicpation of Women"; May Wood Simons, Socialist, on "The Working Woman and Her Vote"; and Dr. George R. Lunn, Socialist mayor of Schenectady, on "The Woman in Her Politico-Economic Relation to Society." Rose Schneiderman of the Women's Trade Union League was chairman.

In the same issue of the *Call* in which this ad appeared there was a special article by the suffrage leader, Alice Stone-Blackwell, entitled "Woman's Enfranchisement and 'Big Business.' " She tells how the Boston and Maine Railroad fought against equal suffrage in New Hampshire. "North, South, East and West," she writes, "in one suffrage campaign after another, we have had a like experience. . . . We have found ourselves up against the open or secret opposition of 'Big Business.' "

One more example of this type: A leaflet announces "Labor Suffrage Mass Meeting" at Carnegie Hall, March 22, 1911, with Samuel Gompers of the A.F.L. and Mary Dreier and Helen Marot of the Women's Trade Union League as honorary vice-chairmen, and a mixed group of speakers, including the Socialist leader, Meyer London, and Socialist women, Clara Lemlich and Leonora O'Reilly.

Another type of cooperation was shown by the New York *Call* in issuing its "Special Woman Suffrage Edition," Feb. 27, 1909, and by the *Progressive Woman* in its "Special Suffrage Edition," March, 1909.

Still more pertinent is the reprinting in the *Socialist Party* Handbook of 1916 of the article, "Why We must Have an Amendment to the United States Constitution," by Mary Beard and Florence Kelley.[21] Similarly, the *Progressive Woman,* September, 1908, reprinted Susan B. Anthony's

20. *The Christian Socialist,* March 15, 1914, p. 3.
21. *Socialist Party Handbook,* 1916, p. 56 f.

reply to Theodore Roosevelt's argument about woman suffrage giving an opening to "race suicide."

Equally significant is the fact that Harriet Stanton Blatch contributed an article to the New York *Call,* May 1, 1909, entitled "The Working Woman and the Vote."[22]   She noted that there were then 5,000,000 working women in the United States. "Working women more than others need the vote," she wrote, "for they have not time to give to the indirect ways of getting laws passed."

A remarkable letter dated March 15, 1911, is extant at the Tamiment Library thanking Mrs. Blatch—who is addressed as "President, Women's Political Union"—for surrendering a date for a May Day parade to the Socialist Party. It appears that Mrs. Blatch had planned a suffrage parade, but at the request of William Mailly, Socialist secretary, she gave up the date.

The Comrade, socialist literary organ of a few years earlier, contains, "A Tribute to Elizabeth Cady Stanton" by Leonard D. Abbott, a member of the editorial staff, which among other things says the following: "In economics Mrs. Stanton was quite definitely a Socialist, and she contributed on occasion to the Socialist press. It is worth noting in this connection that her daughter, Mrs. Blatch, acted for some time on the executive committee of the London Fabian Society."[23]

There was friendship and cooperation between these leading suffragettes and the Socialist Party. That this joint relationship continued is shown by another special article by Mrs. Blatch in the New York *Call* some six years after the first on the subject, "How to Work for the Vote in New York State."[24]   Along with other suggestions she wrote: "If between now and November, there is any parade to be held, one section should be devoted by the women of the party to proclaiming pictorially the need of Votes for Women."

On Oct. 3, 1911, according to the Socialist Party records at the Tamiment Library, another letter to Local Socialist Party of New York— this one from the Women's Trade Union League—stated: "The League voted to endorse your demand for a City Charter Convention." The League's letter was signed by Helen Marot, secretary.

Similarly, the Consumers League of the City of New York, in a letter on Nov. 9, 1912 (Tamiment Library archives), invited the Woman's Committee of the Socialist Party to take part in a Conference on Minimum Wage Legislation in behalf of underpaid women workers. The

22. New York *Call,* May1, 1909, p. 7.
23. *The Comrade,* October, 1902, p. 58.
24. New York *Call,* Feb. 28, 1915, p. 9.

letter was signed by Belle L. Israels, chairman of a committee that included Frances Perkins as a member.

In Cleveland about this time (April, 1914) the Socialist Party of Ohio publicly endorsed the Woman's Suffrage Party's petition for the vote. [25]

In Socialist Party records is a letter from Lucy Burns, vice-chairman of the Congressional Committee of the National American Woman Suffrage Association at Washington, D.C., Sept. 13, 1913, asking Julius Gerber, Socialist Organizer of the New York Local, for "the names of foreign Socialists who have been admitted to this country after having suffered imprisonment for political offenses in their own country." Her question was precipitated by the fact that Mrs. Sylvia Pankhurst, who had been jailed in England for suffrage militancy, was coming to the United States to lecture, and it was thought advisable to have precedents that would help her get into this country. The organization that Miss Burns spoke for had Dr. Anna Howard Shaw as president, Jane Addams as first vice-president, and "C. Anita Whitney" (who later joined the Socialist Party and still later the Communist Party) as second vice-president. Other members of the committee included Alice Paul, Crystal Eastman Benedict (sister of Max Eastman), and Mrs. Mary Beard.

Gerber referred Miss Burns to the Socialists' attorney for refugees, Simon Pollock. When Mrs. Pankhurst arrived at Ellis Island, the old gimmick of "moral turpitude" was raised against her. But publicity in the *Call* and legal action in the courts won her freedom, and she spoke, as scheduled, at Madison Square Garden on Oct. 20, 1913, along with Charles Edward Russell, Socialist candidate for mayor of New York. [26]

Leading women Socialists were also suffragists, and helped to advance the suffrage cause. First among these is Florence Kelley. As translator of Marx's lecture, *Free Trade,* delivered in Brussels in 1848, and of Engels' *Condition of the Working Class in England in 1844,* she has a definite place in American socialist history. As mentioned earlier, she went into the Socialist Labor Party, but left because of the sectarianism which prevented fruitful social work. Later she joined the Socialist Party, and was for a long time active in the Intercollegiate Socialist Society. But perhaps it was her fight against child labor and in favor of shorter hours and safeguards for women workers, and her support of woman suffrage, that make her outstanding among American women. She was for years vice president of the National Woman Suffrage Association. [27] One of her

25. Oakley C. Johnson, *The Day Is Coming: Life and Work of Charles E. Ruthenberg,* International Publishers, New York, 1957, p. 84.

26. New York *Call,* Nov. 9, 1913, p. 15.

27. Dorothy Rose Blumberg, "Florence Kelley: Revolutionary Reformer," *Monthly Review,* November, 1959, pp. 234-242.

pamphlets was *What Women Might Do with the Ballot: the Abolition of Child Labor,* published by the National Woman Suffrage Association in 1912.[28] She was among the founders and builders of the N.A.A.C.P.

Kate Richards O'Hare, like Florence Kelley, joined the Socialist Labor Party first and then went to the Socialist Party. In the latter, Mrs. O'Hare became a member of the National Committee, and at one period was International Secretary. As editor of the *National Rip-Saw,* and as lecturer and pamphleteer, she had much influence among workers, especially women workers. She wrote the *Sorrows of Cupid* (1909), *Law and the White Slaver* (1911), and other pamphlets. She wrote a drama against war, and served in prison for opposition to war. She held the highest party posts of any woman, and probably gave more speeches for socialism than anyone else, except perhaps Eugene V. Debs. Mrs. O'Hare was a strong supporter of the votes-for-women movement. "All through the west and southwest," she told a Socialist conference in 1910, "I find it is not impossible at all for a Socialist to go in and take an active part in the woman suffrage movement without sacrificing her Socialist principles in the slightest degree."[29] Mrs. O'Hare, mother of four, was a member of the International Association of Machinists.[30]

Margaret Haile of Massachusetts tried to reform the Socialist Labor Party from within, then became associated with Debs in organizing the Social Democracy in 1897, and was a member of its platform committee. She withdrew from the Social Democracy—with Debs—when the Social Democratic Party (soon to be the Socialist Party) was set up in 1900. The seceding Social Democratic organizing committee of which she was a leading member met in Hull House when the turn was made toward real socialism. Margaret Haile had contributed a woman's column in 1894 to *Justice,* a Rhode Island paper, and to other papers. She was a teacher and journalist by profession, and a friend and co-worker of Antoinette Konikow, noted Socialist woman. Miss Haile has been almost forgotten, but in her day she was a power in social causes. Frederic Heath's *Socialism in America,* published in January, 1900, lists her, along with Corinne S. Brown and Eugene V. Debs, as among "One Hundred Well-known Social Democrats."[31]

Charlotte Perkins Gilman was founder in November, 1909, of *The Forerunner,* a remarkable one-woman 32-page publication in which she

---

28. Another of her pamphlets, *The Working Child,* published in Chicago back in 1896, is in the N. Y. Public Library, marked as "Gift of F. A. Sorge." Sorge was the secretary of the First International, 1872-1876.
29. *Proceedings,* National Congress of the Socialist Party, May 15-20, 1910.
30. *Progressive Woman,* August, 1910, p. 2.
31. Frederic Heath, *Socialism in America,* January, 1900, p. 127.

wrote all the copy. In the first issue she comments on the policy of her paper: "Is it a socialist magazine? It is a magazine for humanity, and humanity is social. It holds that Socialism, the economic theory, is part of our gradual Socialization, and that the duty of conscious humanity is to promote Socialization."[32] In the third number she wrote: "If you are a believer in women's voting, why don't you take the best equal suffrage paper in the country? Not the *Forerunner*—which is only a suffrage paper because of its interest in women, and only a woman's paper because of its interest in humanity, but this one: 'Vol. XL, *The Woman's Journal,* founded by Lucy Stone and Henry B. Blackwell.'" In the issue of October, 1910, Mrs. Gilman has a poem which for a time was quoted often: "The Socialist and The Suffragist," here are the first two stanzas and the final one:

> Said the Socialist to the Suffragist:
>   "My cause is greater than yours!
>   You only work for a Special Class,
>   We for the gain of the General Mass,
> Which every good ensures!"

> Said the Suffragist to the Socialist:
>   "You underrate my Cause!
>   While women remain a Subject Class,
>   You can never move the General Mass,
> With your Economic Laws!"

>   .   .   .

> The world awoke, and tartly spoke:
>   "Your work is all the same;
>   Work together or work apart,
>   Work, each of you, with all your heart—
> Just get into the game!"

Elizabeth Gurley Flynn said in the *Political Affairs* article referred to earlier: "Next to Bebel's *Women Under Socialism,* a book on my shelf I treasure is *Women and Economics,* published in 1898 by Charlotte Perkins Gilman." In a sense, Mrs. Gilman epitomizes the inseparable link between every Socialist woman and the fight for suffrage. Some Socialist women made suffrage their chief work, but all Socialists, men and women both, were by definition for it.

Ella Reeve Bloor, whose long Socialist career began in the 1890's in the Socialist Labor Party, continued after 1900 in the Socialist Party. Her two main interests were the defense of workers wherever they went on

32. *The Forerunner,* November, 1909, p. 32; January, 1910, p. 29; October, 1910, p. 25.

strike, and advocacy of woman suffrage. Mrs. Bloor was the first woman in Connecticut to run for public office. She was candidate for Secretary of State in 1910.[33] One of the high points of her early life was at the Socialist Party Convention, May 15-21, 1910, in Chicago, when she led the fight for a forthright official alignment of the Socialist Party with the equal suffrage organizations. It was objected by many Socialists that to join forces with non-Socialist organizations would blur class lines and obliterate working class consciousness. Mrs. Bloor argued, among other things: "While the Socialist Party should never merge its identity in any other movement, we should not place ourselves in a voluntary position of isolation, where the principles and aims of our party fully coincide with those of other organizations. We should heartily support the general movement of the women of America for their enfranchisement. In this case, as in many similar cases, Socialism must break through the narrow circle of our own organization and must penetrate into the masses of the people, as a living and vivifying social force." Caroline A. Lowe, another well-known Socialist woman leader, seconded the Bloor proposal, and Kate Richards O'Hare also supported it, but the sectarian forces at the Congress proved stronger. The position was taken that a Socialist can always work for equal suffrage wherever he or she happens to be, without the broad endorsement that the Bloor motion would have provided.[34]

Anita C. Block joined the Socialist Party in 1907 and started her memorable "Woman's Sphere" department in the New York *Call* in 1911, continuing it for about five years. Alongside the heading "Woman's Sphere," Mrs. Block was careful to place the explanatory subhead: "Today the Human Sphere, Unlimited, Unbounded." As a believer in the equality of men and women, she insisted that woman's "sphere" was the entire globe and everything in it. This "woman's" page was one of the most important features of the *Call*. It contained writings on birth-control by Margaret Sanger, the first such articles ever to appear in an American newspaper. It carried the polemic between Florence Kelley and the California Socialist, Agnes H. Downing, on how best to end child labor (in which Florence Kelley had rather the better of the argument). It also carried Agnes Downing's article on "What Socialists are Doing for the California Suffrage Amendment"; pieces by Jeannette D. Pearl on workers' education; "Musings of a Socialist Woman: Is *Motherhood* the Supreme Ideal of a Woman's Life?" by Antoinette Konikow; and "The Working Woman's Share in the American Woman Movement," by Meta L. Stern. It had poems by Daisy Sanial Gill (daughter of Lucien Sanial), and

---

33. *Progressive Woman*, September, 1910.
34. *Proceedings*, National Congress of the Socialist Party, Chicago, 1910.

by Charlotte Perkins Gilman, among others. It had book reviews; and of course Mrs. Block's own incisive and often ironic editorials, such as "Chivalry Once More," a comment on the Georgia Legislature's action in denying women the right to practice law in that state.[35]

The story of Margaret Sanger's work on the *Call* told in her *Autobiography*, 1938, merits notice. Anita Block called together a group of young mothers to ask questions of Margaret Sanger. The answers became a series of articles in "Woman's Sphere" under the title, *What Every Mother Should Know*. Then Mrs. Block asked for a second series on *What Every Girl Should Know*, and these were published, too—until the Post Office censor intervened.[36] Mrs. Sanger says her father was a Socialist and a friend of Debs, and "Therefore I joined the Socialist Party, Local Number Five," of which Anita Block and her husband, S. John Block, attorney, were members.

At least one of the New York *Call's* editorials, probably written by Mrs. Block, but not on the "Woman's Sphere" page, deserves special attention. Entitled "Woman and the Franchise," it was written with an acid pen. It called on the coming national convention of the Socialist Party to do more for suffrage than the Party had yet done. Let the Convention this year, the editorial said, "make the matter of the enfranchisement of women one of the things on which we fight a great and memorable campaign." In 1915, during the fight for the vote, Mrs. Block addressed the New York State Legislature as a representative of the Socialist Party, "the only political party," she said, "which unequivocally demands the suffrage for women."

The name of Louella Twining is selected to introduce a group of Socialist women who were especially active in suffrage work. Miss Twining was one of three delegates to the Second International in 1910, the others being May Wood Simons and Lena Morrow Lewis. It happened that Miss Twining got the floor and brought up the subject of the suffrage for women. Her speech was translated by Clara Zetkin, the leading advocate of women's rights in Europe and the one who proposed that the American Woman's Day be made International Woman's Day. *The Progressive Woman* reported that Clara Zetkin gave a "very spirited translation" of Miss Twining's speech.[37] In a later issue there is an article by Miss Twining entitled "At Monte Carlo with the Lafargues." She re-

---

35. New York *Call*, Jan. 21, 1912; Sept. 17, 1911; Feb. 25, 1912; March 12, March 21, April 21, 1912; Aug. 13, 1911; May 5, 1912.

36. *Margaret Sanger: An Autobiography*, W. W. Norton & Co., New York, 1938, p. 76.

37. *The Progressive Woman*, October, 1910, p. 2.

mained in Europe long enough to visit Paul and Laura Lafargue, and she gives a fascinating picture of this aging white-haired couple, the son-in-law and daughter, respectively, of Karl Marx. She writes that Paul Lafargue "reminds me of Eugene V. Debs in his gentleness," and adds "He reads *The Progressive Woman* every month." Louella Twining came naturally by her interest in women's rights. Her mother, Mrs. Florence Twining, was a Socialist and a suffragist, and they lived in Colorado where both were voters.

May Wood Simons, wife of A. M. Simons, also spoke at the international Congress, and her speech, the N. Y. *Call* reported, "was a credit to American Socialism and the women of America."

Lena Morrow Lewis, wife of Arthur Morrow Lewis, and the third American woman at the international gathering, was a newspaper woman and a long time lecturer and organizer for the Socialist Party. She was the first woman to be elected to the National Committee, preceding Kate Richards O'Hare, and, according to Elizabeth Gurley Flynn, she enlisted the support of Chicago trade unions for suffrage back in 1899.

Mrs. Marguerite Prevey, a distinguished professional woman of Cleveland, Ohio, was the first national woman's organizer to be chosen by the Socialist Party. This was in 1908, and her job was to "work for equal, civil and political rights among women and their organization in the Socialist Party." She may be taken as a type of balanced, sincere, far-seeing Socialist woman who over the years were Socialists and at the same time workers for suffrage.[38]

Anna A. Maley of New York, stenographer by profession, was the second national woman's organizer, chosen in 1909.[39] Two years later, Anita Block reported in Woman's Sphere—under the meaningful heading, "Anna A. Maley, Editor and Voter"—that this Socialist was editing *The Commonwealth,* a weekly paper published in Everett, Washington. "It is with envy," Mrs. Block said, "that we realize Anna Maley is working for Socialism in a state where she is a political factor." Women could vote in Washington.[40]

There was also Caroline A. Lowe, who in 1912 was general correspondent for the Woman's National Committee. Her articles in the N. Y. *Call,* in which she reviewed the reports made to the national office by local women's socialist organizations all over the country, are still interesting reading. They reveal, for one thing, that Socialist women had to re-

38. Oakley C. Johnson, *The Day Is Coming: Life & Work of Charles E. Ruthenberg,* International Publishers, New York, 1957, p. 29-30.
39. *Progressive Woman,* June, 1909, p. 5.
40. N. Y. *Call,* Oct. 8, 1911.

educate quite a proportion of Socialist men on the subject of women's participation in politics.[41]

Josephine Conger-Kaneko, whose husband, Kliichi Kaneko, was a Japanese, was founder and editor of the monthly *Progressive Woman* (for the first year it was called the *Socialist Woman*) in 1907, and kept it going for several years. During those years she centered attention on all active Socialist women, reported their doings, published their photos and their articles, and, as a regular feature, gave a biographical sketch of a Socialist woman each month. She always emphasized woman suffrage as a part of Socialist work. *The Progressive Woman* is a mine of information for the historian interested in the progress of American women.

May McDonald Strickland, wife of Frederick G. Strickland, and one of the magazine's featured women, was state secretary of the Socialist Party of Indiana.[42] Katharine M. Debs, identified as Mrs. Eugene V. Debs, is quoted prominently on "Right of Women to Vote." Mila Tupper Maynard is described as having been a Unitarian preacher for a while, then a reporter on the *Rocky Mountain News,* and then a Socialist lecturer and propagandist. May Walden—Mrs. Charles H. Kerr of the publishing firm— is quoted as saying "The Twentieth Century is Woman's." Winnie Branstetter, assistant state secretary of the Socialist Party of Oklahoma, argues, "Socialist Party Should Make a More Active Propaganda for Female Suffrage." Lida Parce Robinson, ex-president of the Arizona Equal Suffrage Association, has an article entitled "Victory and Defeat in Arizona," in which she describes how the women got the equal suffrage bill through both houses of the legislature by a two-thirds vote, only to have it vetoed by the governor; a bitter, sarcastic article. A biographic feature introduces us to Grace D. Brewer, a former schoolteacher, now a stenographer for the editor of the *Appeal to Reason,* and already a writer and speaker in her own right. "Socialism is unthinkable," she says, "without the full and unequivocal rights of women along with men." Only a taste is given here, but it indicates what this notable publication did. Ella Reeve Bloor, Rose Pastor Stokes, Kate Richards O'Hare, Elizabeth Gurley Flynn—these better-known women were also, of course, featured in *The Progressive Woman.*

Kate Sadler Greenhalgh has recently been rescued from near-oblivion by Harvey O'Connor in *Revolution in Seattle* (1964), who describes her as "the most extraordinary person in the Seattle radical movement." He adds: "In the Pacific Northwest Kate was the peerless socialist orator and among women was rivaled nationally only by Kate Richards O'Hare and

41. N. Y. *Call,* Jan. and Feb. 11, 1912.

42. *Progressive Woman,* Sept., 1918, p. 2; July, 1910, p. 2; Oct., 1910, cover; Vol. I, No. 9, p. 4; Dec., 1907, p. 5, etc.

Elizabeth Gurley Flynn." Mrs. Sadler devoted most attention to organizing workers and opposing war, but she was a Socialist, and her example inspired other women.[43]

Along with Kate Sadler we may recall other western and mid-western women, including Mrs. Corinne S. Brown rather slightingly referred to by Daniel De Leon in *Flashlights of the Amsterdam Congress.*[44] *The Progressive Woman,* however, speaks of her as follows: "If ever the history of the pioneers in the Socialist movement in America is written, the name of Corinne Stubs Brown will stand unchallenged for the most vital, courageous and brilliant woman in their ranks." She became widely known as president of the Illinois Woman's Alliance. Henry Demarest Lloyd once said of her, "Mrs. Brown is like a salt breeze blowing over pine woods." Eugene V. Debs called her "The Stormy Petrel." She was a Socialist Party delegate to the Amsterdam Congress in 1904 along with Herman Schlueter, labor historian, and that is where De Leon saw her. She was a determined worker for woman suffrage.

Another westerner was Mrs. Ida Crouch-Hazlett who was a newspaper woman in Denver, Colorado, one of the first states in which women could vote. She was a national organizer of the Woman Suffrage Association from 1896 to 1901, and from then to 1921 a lecturer for the Socialist Party. She was a candidate for Congress in 1902 on the Socialist ticket— "first woman parliamentary candidate in the world," according to Solon De Leon's *American Labor Who's Who.*[45]

Still another westerner was Charlotte Anita Whitney, who had a long record as a fighter for equal suffrage, being organizer of the National College Equal Suffrage League, 1911-13, and president of the California Equal Suffrage League, 1911-12. She joined the Socialist Party in 1914, according to her biographer, Al Richmond, in *Native Daughter.*[46]

Iowa-born Cynthia H. Van Names Leonard was so fiery a partisan of equal rights as to come under censure by Daniel De Leon more than half a century ago in his *Flashlights of the Amsterdam Congress.*[47] She had evidently been a delegate to an earlier Socialist Congress at Zurich. From the autobiography of A. Cahan, *Bletten Fun Mein Leben,*[48] and from *The Promised City* by Moses Rischin,[49] we learn that Synthia Leonard—a stately, white-haired lady—was a leading member of the Socialist Labor Party local they belonged to in the 80's. She was the mother of Lillian

43. Harvey O'Connor, *Revolution in Seattle,* Monthly Review Press, 1964, p. 43.
44. Daniel De Leon, *Flashlights of the Amsterdam Congress,* 1906, p. 44.
45. Solon De Leon, *American Labor Who's Who,* 1925, p. 51-2.
46. Al Richmond, *Native Daughter: The Story of Anita Whitney,* 1942, p. 249.
47. *Flashlights of the Amsterdam Congress,* p. 107.
48. A. Cahan, *Bletten fun Mein Leben,* Vol. II, pp. 307-308.
49. Moses Rischin, *The Promised City,* 1962, p. 225.

Russell. According to Lillian Russell's biographer—Parker Morell, *Lillian Russell: the Era of Plush*—the actress's mother, Cynthia Leonard, ran for mayor of New York in the election of 1884.[50]

A contemporary of Corinne S. Brown and Cynthia Leonard was Bertha Washburne Howe, who was also our recent contemporary. She died in Florida at the age of 104, active in social causes. Her life had been a blend of the Free Thought Society, the struggle for Negro equality, the movement for Woman Suffrage, and the Socialist cause. She read her first copy of the *Communist Manifesto* around the turn of the century and joined the Socialist Party about 1906. Among her contributions to the New York *Call,* were "Restricted Suffrage" and "Woman Suffrage and the Class Struggle."[51] [52]

Among prominent Socialists whom we might class as college women are Vida Dutton Scudder, Jessie Wallace Hughan, and Anna Rochester. All were interested in suffrage and peace. Professor Scudder was on the faculty of Wellesley College from 1910 for many years as a teacher of English literature. Her books, *Social Ideals in English Letters*(1898), and *Socialism and Character* (1912), were very influential among young women of her time.

Jessie Wallace Hughan earned her doctorate at Columbia University in 1910, and was a leader in the Young Peoples Socialist League from 1909 on. Her books, *American Socialism of the Present Day* (1910), *The Facts of Socialism* (1914), and *The Socialism of Today* (1916), were used as texts by a generation of young people. She contributed material to Alexander Trachtenberg's *American Labor Year Books.*

Anna Rochester, who studied at Bryn Mawr, joined the Socialist Party in 1910, and was later on the executive committee of the Young People's Socialist League (re-named afterward the League for Industrial Democracy). She was a research worker on the National Child Labor Committee, 1912-15, and for the U. S. Children's Bureau, 1915-21. Her activities during most of her life concerned the welfare of children, while her political interests were with the struggle for workers' and women's rights. Miss Rochester lived in New York, dying in 1966.

Rose Pastor Stokes, the beautiful Polish immigrant girl and strike leader, who married the millionaire J. G. Phelps Stokes, was not a college woman, but she was a poet, playwright, editor, journalist and lecturer, and a leader in the Intercollegiate Socialist Society. She was active also in the Woman's Trade Union League, and, from 1905 on, in the Socialist Party.

50. Parker Morell, *Lillian Russell: the Era of Plush,* 1940, p. 71.
51. N. Y. *Call,* Dec. 30, 1910, p. 4; June 10, 1910, editorial page.
52. Oakley C. Johnson, *An American Century: Recollections of Bertha W. Howe.* Humanities Press, New York. 1966.

With Charlotte Perkins Gilman, she exemplifies the propagandist who is also an artist.

Meta L. Stern, who made a new translation of Bebel's *Woman* to displace De Leon's, may serve to introduce a group of talented Socialist Leaders and equal rights advocates who include Mary E. Marcy, an editor of *International Socialist Review* and author of *Shop Talks on Economics* (1911); Theresa Serber Malkiel, author of *Woman and Freedom* (1911), member of the Socialist Suffrage Committee in 1915, polemicist against Ella Reeve Bloor earlier at the 1910 Socialist Party Congress, contending that working women should have their own separate equal rights campaign; Hortense Allison Wagenknecht of Oregon and Ohio, wife of Alfred Wagenknecht, and a militant member of the Socialist National Woman's Committee in 1912; Claire Strong Broms of Minnesota, school teacher, industrial unionist and admirer of William D. Haywood and Elizabeth Gurley Flynn; and Mother Jones, who in 1915, during the miners' strikes, warned suffragettes, "The women of Colorado have had the vote for two generations and the working men and women are in slavery."

A place must be made here for the un-groupables: Helen Keller, Socialist, who stood for all good causes and all oppressed people; Emma Lazarus of Jewish descent, author of the Statue of Liberty poem, "Mother of Exiles," who, according to her biographer, Eve Merriam, expressed pride to find "the fathers of modern socialism to be three Jews— Ferdinand Lassalle, Karl Marx, and Johann Jacoby . . .";[53] Maud Malone, shy and gentle New York librarian, who in 1905 started the Harlem Equal Rights League, in 1909 carried a "Votes for Women" placard down Broadway on St. Patrick's Day, in 1912, when presidential candidates Roosevelt and Wilson addressed election rallies, stood up and asked them, "Shall the Women Vote?" and in 1917 served sixty days in jail, along with other suffragettes, for picketing the White House;[54] and Helen Holman, Negro woman orator, friend of Kate Richards O'Hare and Elizabeth Gurley Flynn, who was listened to and admired by Richard B. Moore, himself a noted Black speaker.

Marxism had, and has an immeasurably larger and longer perspective than Woman Suffrage. It did not, to be sure, initiate the struggle for it, any more than it *initiated* the struggle for Negro emancipation or the eight-hour day or the Direct Election of United States Senators: but it took part in all these, and in many other struggles. It has been an important factor in American social reform movements, and a decisive one in some.

53. Eve Merriam, *Emma Lazarus: Woman With a Torch,* Citadel Press, New York, 1956, p. 101.
54. *Daily Worker,* Feb. 14 and Feb. 18, 1951.

VII

Marxism and the
American Christian Church

I joined the Congregational Church in a small town in Michigan in 1902, when I was twelve years old. I left about five years later because I read Unitarian tracts questioning the divinity of Christ and the authenticity of bible miracles.

Then in 1912, when I was 22, I joined the Socialist Party of Michigan, and cast my ballot for Eugene V. Debs for president.

I thus had an early experience in both Christianity and Marxism, and implicit in this was an urge to straighten out my own relationship to each of these bodies of thought.

Like everyone else—or *almost* everyone else!—I had heard of Marx's oft-quoted statement, "Religion is the opium of the people," and I had no reason to reject it. However, there soon came something of a logical crisis for me, which I wasn't really prepared to meet. It was in early 1919 that the Socialist Party of Michigan, under a rather sectarian Left Wing leadership which at that time I supported, declared in so many words that as a part of its political work it would "explain" and oppose religion. That in part is why the Michigan group became the first state organization to be formally expelled by the Socialist Party of America later that year, not long before the formation of the Communist Party.

Thus in my first seven years as a Marxist I was brought face to face with the subject I am now discussing, and I've given it quite a bit of study and thought in the half-century since.

First of all, let us look again at that quotation I spoke of, about the "opium of the people."

What Marx actually said, and its context, is this:

"Religious distress is at the same time the expression of *real distress* and the *protest against* real distress. Religion is the sigh of the oppressed

102

creature, the heart of a heartless world, just as it is the spirit of a spiritless situation. It is the opium of the people." Thus wrote Marx in 1844, when he was 26 years old. Humanist that he was, he regarded religion as a protest against distress and as a sigh of the oppressed, as well as, eventually, an opiate.[1]

This puts the religious question in a different light. As for the anti-religious stand by the Socialist Party of Michigan in 1919, I learned much later that Marxists do not approve of dividing workers politically on the basis of religion, any more than on the basis of language or color. Workers need to be united politically (as well as economically) on the basis of their common interests, and on nothing else.

Nevertheless, in trying to reach people with a new idea, old ideas continually pop up and must be answered. In their approach, therefore, the propagators of Socialism did not leave Christianity out of account. For example, the Socialist orator, Kate Richards O'Hare, an editor of the *National Rip-Saw,* argued directly with church people in her pamphlet, *The Church and the Social Problem,* published in 1911.[2]

> You say that the Socialists are un-Christian and atheistic," she begins. "That may be, according to your ideas; but this I know, irreligious as we may be, we are doing Christ's work, trying to make *your* religion live and livable, and doing our best to place as the four corner stones of our government the four fundamentals of Christ's law.
>
> If the Church won't do its duty, then the Socialist movement must do it, and I am with the force that does things.

The Socialists shamed the Church for ignoring social oppression, and some leaders of the Church responded—with good works.

The Socialists also used irony in confronting the Church. Paul Lafargue, one of Karl Marx's sons-in-law, wrote his celebrated squib on *The Religion of Capital,*[3] which contained this "Confession of Faith":

> I believe in Capital, the ruler of body and mind.
> I believe in Profit, His Right-hand Bower, and in Credit, His Left-hand Bower, both of which proceed from and are one with Him.

1. Selsam, Howard and Harry Martel, eds., *Reader in Marxist Philosophy,* N.Y., International Publishers, 1963, p. 227. On this whole question, see H. Aptheker, *The Urgency of the Marxist-Christian Dialogue,* N. Y., 1970, Harper & Row.
2. O'Hare, Kate Richards, *The Church and the Social Problem.* 1911. (Rip-Saw Series No. 2: 32-page pamphlet.)
3. Lafargue, Paul, *The Religion of Capital.* Socialist Co-operative Publishing Association, 184 William Street, New York. (Socialist Library, Published Monthly, Vol. II, No. 2, March 15, 1902.)

> I believe in Gold and Silver . . . .
> I believe in Dividends . . . .
> I believe in Private Property, the fruit of the labor of others; and
> I also believe in its existence from and for all time.
> I believe in the eternity of the Wage System . . . .

And so on.

This mockery was doubtless annoying to quite a few religious persons, but it was also difficult to argue against, because, after all, Christ said, "Ye can't serve God and Mammon."

One might think that neither the challenge of Kate Richards O'Hare nor that of Paul Lafargue would win converts to Socialism, but that would be a mistake. Here, however, are three examples of the kind that forced me to re-shape my opinions again and again.

In the Tamiment Library in New York (This is really the old Rand School Library of the Socialist Party of half a century ago), where a considerable quantity of old Socialist Party records are kept, I found a letter addressed to Julius Gerber, Organizer, Socialist Party, New York, dated June 15, 1911. It begins "Dear Comrade" and ends, "Thy Comrade, Annie Wright," of Brooklyn, New York. I knew there was a Quaker Socialist society in England, but this was the first sign I had found of Quaker Socialists in the United States.

Then, a California journalist, Reuben W. Borough,[4] told me in a letter that in Marshall, Michigan, where he went to high school in the early days of this century, the rector of the Episcopal Church gave him his first copy of *The Appeal to Reason,* the Socialist paper edited by J. A. Wayland.

A few years ago, Clarence Hathaway, former editor of the New York *Daily Worker,* told me that as a teen-ager he had been influenced in a leftward direction by a liberal pastor in his home town in Minnesota, the Reverend David Morgan.

To what extent, in fact, has Marxism influenced Christianity in the United States? And in what way has Christianity influenced the expression of Marxism in this country?

An answer may be approached by considering some Christian Socialist pastors who acknowledged Marxist influence and played an outstanding religio-political role.

Professor George Davis Herron (1862-1925)

Professor Herron was a Congregational pastor who began his radical career in 1891 when he delivered a sermon to the Minnesota State

---

4. Borough, Reuben W., contributor to Helen Alfred's *Toward a Socialist America* (1958), is writing his autobiography.

Association of Congregationalist Ministers entitled "The Message of Jesus Christ to Men of Wealth." In 1893 he became Professor of Applied Christianity at Grinnel College, Iowa, and held that position for six years. In 1900 he joined Eugene V. Debs in organizing the Socialist Party of America, and delivered the nomination speech for Debs as president.

Herron's wealthy mother-in-law, Mrs. Carrie Rand, established the endowment for the founding of the Rand School of Social Science in 1906, which was the center of Marxist activity in the United States for a generation.

When he nominated Debs for President, Herron delivered a hard-hitting campaign speech in which he revealed that he had already been voting the Socialist Labor Party ticket for eight years. He implied that now, with the new party headed by Debs, the Socialist movement might take "its coherent and conquering form in the politics of America."[5]

Explaining why he was supporting Socialism, he said: "Socialism comes not as a remedy for the evils of existing society, but as a program of principles for a new society; or rather, let us say, as the first proposition for social order that has ever been presented to the world."

Three years later, on the occasion of honoring the Paris Commune, when Herron gave his great lecture, "From Revolution to Revolution,"[6] he took the opportunity to defend the Marxist principle of class consciousness:

"I know," he said, "that the term 'class consciousness' is offensive to many, both without and within the socialist movement. I know that it is often used in a way that makes it seem like a tiresome and commonplace cant. Those who do not understand the term mistake class consciousness for class hatred. None the less, it remains true that until the working class becomes more vividly and intensely conscious of itself than it now is, until it realizes that it is the disinherited owner of the world that it has built on its own back, until it understands that there can be no possible identity of interest or reconciliation between itself and the employing or ruling class, its struggle toward emancipation will be blind and unintelligent, betrayed and baffled and compromised, and without that nobility of comprehension which should mark the greatest cause to which man has ever been summoned."

---

5. Herron, Prof. George Davis, "Why I Am a Socialist." Address at a Mass Meeting of the Social Democractic Party at Central Music Hall, Chicago, Sept. 29, 1900. (Pocket Library of Socialism, No. 20, Charles H. Kerr & Co., 153 E. Kinzie St., Chicago, Ill. Also published by the Headquarters of the Social Democratic Party, 126 Washington Ave., Chicago.)

6. Herron, Prof. George Davis, *From Revolution to Revolution.* An Address in Faneuil Hall, March 21, 1903. Published by the Comrade Co-operative Company.

The Reverend Charles Henry Vail (1866-1924):

The Rev. Charles H. Vail was, like Herron, a socialist in the days of the Socialist Labor Party, before the Socialist Party of Debs was organized. Vail wrote his *Modern Socialism* in 1897. It was published by the Commonwealth Company of New York which also published many other socialist titles, including *The Development of Socialism from Utopia to Science* by Frederick Engels, *The Right to Be Lazy* by Paul Lafargue, *Woman in the Past, Present and Future* by August Bebel, and *The Eighteenth Brumaire* by Karl Marx.

Vail produced a later and better book, *The Principles of Scientific Socialism,* in 1899, published by the Comrade Cooperative Publishing Company of New York, the first real Marxist textbook on Socialism in this country. It was re-published by the Charles H. Kerr Company of Chicago in 1908. I owned a copy of it about half a century ago, one of the first books on Socialism I ever read.

About 1900, Vail gave a lecture, "The Mission of the Working Class," in which he paid tribute to the Utopian socialists as forerunners, but added, "it was left for Karl Marx to clearly point out the genesis of surplus value and the evolutionary tendency in economics."

Vail was ordained in 1893, and belonged to the Universalist Church. His first pastorate was at the All Souls' Church, Albany, N.Y., 1893-1894. Then he went to First Church, Jersey City, New Jersey, 1894-1901, and during this period he became a Socialist. He continued in his church work for some years after that, while writing and lecturing on socialism.[7]

Bishop Franklin Spencer Spalding (1865-1914):

In the Tamiment Library in New York, is an obituary about the Right Reverend Franklin Spencer Spalding, Episcopal Bishop of Utah, killed in an automobile accident in 1914. He was known as "the Socialist Bishop," and every Party member in the United States mourned his passing.[8]

The full story of Bishop Spalding is told in the biography written by the Rev. John Howard Melish.[9] "Undoubtedly the most conspicuous fact in Bishop Spalding's life was his championship of the cause of the working man," says the biographer. "It was the passion of his life. He was an enthusiastic convert to the economic theories of Karl Marx and he saw

7. Vail, Rev. Charles Henry. *Who Was Who in America,* Vol. I, p. 1266.
8. New York *Call,* Sunday, Sept. 27, 1914, p. 7.
9. Melish, Rev. John Howard, *Franklin Spencer Spalding: Man and Bishop.* New York: Macmillan Co., 1917. (Pp. 236-256).

in Socialism the instrument by which, under God, the terrible wrongs and inequalities which mark the civilization of today were to be righted."

The author, Melish, an advanced liberal in his own right, was pastor of the Protestant Episcopal Church of the Holy Trinity in Brooklyn for many years.

Melish quotes Spalding as follows:

> Behind all the movement for social uplift outside the religious organizations today, is a philosophy which is as yet unappropriated by the Church, and yet which is, I believe, true. It is based upon the fact that environment has most to do with the making of the product, and that therefore the chief work of any organization desiring success must be to create right conditions. Karl Marx called it "Materialistic Conception of History," an expression his followers soften into the "economic interpretation of history," and to the hundreds of thousands of socialists who follow him, it means that a new form of society must be worked for, if need be, fought for, in which the fundamental business of the State shall be, to give to each human being a supply for its physical needs. Man may not be able to live by bread alone, but first of all he must have bread, and today there are millions even in this land who are hungry, and who have inadequate shelter and clothing.

Spalding cast his first ballot for Socialism in 1908, when he supported Debs on the latter's third try for the presidency.

I cannot refrain from citing one further passage from Bishop Spalding, as quoted by Melish from *The Christian Socialist* magazine (November, 1911), which had asked him for a statement. "The Christian," said the Bishop, "has the advantage over Karl Marx because he knows the name of the Truth which illuminated Marx's mind, of the Power which gave him his moral courage and of the Love which made him faithful unto death. The Socialist, on the other hand, possesses in the 'Materialistic Conception of History' and the 'Class Struggle,' two truths which the Christian must learn."

Bouck White (1874-1951)

Bouck White was educated at Harvard University, the Boston Theological Seminary, and the Union Theological Seminary in New York. His first job was as head for five years of the Men's Social Service department of Holy Trinity Church in Brooklyn.

But his fame began when he set up the Church of the Social Revolution in New York in the spring of 1914. It happened that the Ludlow Massacre took place about that time in John D. Rockefeller's Colorado coal and iron mines, and Bouck White led his poor ragged congregation to Rockefeller's plush First Baptist Church on Fifth Avenue (they were only a few blocks apart) so that both church groups might pray together for a righteous solution to the trouble at Ludlow.

But the Rockefeller church called the cops. White was arrested for "disturbing the peace" and sent to prison for as many months as the law allowed. Debs and other Socialists hailed him, and he was a cause celebre.

When White was asked, while in prison, "What is the relation of our Church to the Socialist Party?" he made a forthright reply. He agreed to the suggestion that the Church—that is, his Church of the Social Revolution—was "a sister movement to the Party." But he preferred, he said, to say: "The Church of the Revolution is destined to be the soul, of which the Socialist Party is the body."[10]

Bouck White wrote *The Call of the Carpenter* (1911) and *The Carpenter and the Rich Man* (1914), gradually evolving what may be described as a Marx-influenced interpretation of the New Testament.

Some of this is indicated in his re-writing of the Apostles' Creed, which goes like this:

> I believe in God, the Master most mighty, stirrer-up of Heaven and Earth, and in Jesus the Carpenter of Nazareth, who was born of proletarian Mary, toiled at the work bench, descended into labor's hell, suffered under Roman tyranny at the hands of Pontius Pilate, was crucified, dead and buried. . . ."[11]

And so on.

I'm not sure that Bouck White ever read Paul Lafargue's ironic creed, but we must see a degree of Marxist reaction in the efforts to re-do and improve the official religious credo.

The Rev. Edward Ellis Carr

The Rev. Edward Ellis Carr was in certain ways a phenomenon even among social-minded preachers. He was chief editor of the influential *Christian Socialist* magazine, published in Danville, Illinois, from the time of its founding in 1904-5 throughout its more than ten-year history. In 1907 he reported in its pages on his attendance as an official American delegate at the International Socialist Congress in Europe. *The Christian Socialist* always published the platforms and resolutions of the Socialist Party, and editorially supported Socialist candidates in the elections. Carr

---

10. White, Bouck, *Letters from Prison.* Introduction by Lucy Weeks Trimble. Boston: Richard G. Badger, 1915. Also, Toronto: The Copp Clark Co., Ltd., 1915. (P. 45)

11. White, Bouck, *Letters from Prison.* (p. 14).

himself praised the Charles H. Kerr publishing company for its services in making available the works of Marx and Engels (though he disapproved of Paul Lafargue and Arthur Morrow Lewis, who he said wrote not to make socialists, but "to make atheists out of socialists").

Over the years he listed hundreds of preachers who announced support for socialism. *The Christian Socialist* exulted on May 15, 1908, that ten of the 216 delegates to the Socialist Party national convention of that year were Christian clergymen. Carr published special editions of his paper for Baptists, for Roman Catholics, for Lutherans, and so on, trying to reach every denomination.

The Christian Socialist reported with pride in the issues of June 1 and June 15, 1909, that at the Fourth General Conference of the Christian Socialist Fellowship, held in Toledo, Ohio, there were 26 delegates from seven states, and that Mayor Brand Whitlock of the host city gave an official Address of Welcome.

The magazine was remarkably successful in securing and printing contributions of one sort or another from a wide variety of notables, including not only Socialist Party leaders but others: Edwin Markham, poet; Horace Mann, educator; Thomas Wentworth Higginson, author; as well as Clarence Darrow, Jack London, Upton Sinclair, Charlotte Perkins Gilman, and a long list of others.

Up to the time of World War I, *The Christian Socialist* could be described, I suppose, as a "party line" publication, but at that time patriotism intervened. The Socialist Party resisted United States entry into the war; *The Christian Socialist,* on the other hand, urged United States participation.

The Rev. Father Thomas McGrady (1863-1909):

There have been Roman Catholic Socialists, too, who paid honor to Karl Marx.

Father McGrady was rector of St. Anthony's Church, Bellevue, Kentucky, around the turn of the century, and when he died, in 1909, Eugene V. Debs wrote his obituary in *The Appeal to Reason,* which was reprinted in *The Christian Socialist.*[12]

Father McGrady wrote several socialist pamphlets, one of which was "A Plea for Social Democracy," published by Standard Publishing Company, Terre Haute, Indiana, in 1901.

"If our powers of productivity have been multiplied twenty-fold

12. *The Christian Socialist,* Vols. 5-6, Jan. 1, 1909. Debs' obituary on Father McGrady is on p. 2.

within the last half-century," he wrote, "then we should have twenty times the amount of comforts for the same application of labor in the days of our fathers. But such is not the case. Poverty has everywhere kept pace with the march of progress."

He asked: "Are your ears deaf to the lamentations that echo throughout this great land, from ocean to ocean, and from the Gulf to the Lakes? Are your hearts callous to the widow's wail and the orphan's cry?"

Going on, he analyzed the existing situation, and declared:

"The result of our economic system is seen in the growth of poverty among the toilers, and the amassment of great wealth by the idlers and parasites of society.

"Give the laboring man the full value of his labor, and there will be no hard times, no stagnation of industry, no strikes, no look outs, no crises, no failures, and, above all, the land will not be cursed with over-production, while millions are starving and in tatters."

Continuing, he said: "Socialism will give every man an opportunity. It will make all men free and equal. Under it there will be no privileged class, and *this* is why it has been so obstinately opposed."

An illuminating article was written by Father McGrady for *The Comrade* (predecessor of the *Masses*), Vol. II, No. 1, (1902), under the title, "How I Became a Socialist."

He wrote: "I perused the works of Laurence Gronlund, Bellamy, Vail, Sprague, and other Socialist writers, and became acquainted with the three great ideas of Karl Marx, and before the end of '99, I was firmly convinced that the collective ownership and administration of capital for the benefit of all the people was the only rational solution of the industrial problem. In the early part of 1900 I wrote to Father Hagerty, who was then rector of the Catholic Church at Cleburne, Texas, informing him that I was a disciple of Marx."

Father T. J. Hagerty, in replying, congratulated him.

Father Hagerty, was one of the organizers of the I. W. W. in 1905. He, Debs and Daniel De Leon brain-trusted that remarkable trade union effort. Hagerty designed the circular emblem, often called "Hagerty's Wheel."

In one of his pamphlets Hagerty quoted the Irish proverb: "We take our religion from Rome, but our politics from home."

Bishop William Montgomery Brown (1855-1937):

Bishop William Montgomery Brown was an old-fashioned fundamentalist cleric in Galion, Ohio, until 1911 when, while recuperating from an illness, he read Darwin's *Origin of Species* for the first time. Then, in the midst of World War I, he heard of "the economic causes of war" from a letter by Miss Ella Bronzelle in a local newspaper. He got in touch with her, and she advised him to read Socialist literature. He did. He subscribed to the *National Rip-Saw,* edited by Kate Richards O'Hare, and read dozens and hundreds of Socialist pamphlets, books and papers.

In later years, recalling his slow progress as a younger man, he said, candidly, "I was an ignoramus, but I was not a fool." He wanted the truth, he said, but only accidental events brought it near so that he could see it.

"Eventually," he said, in *My Belief: The Autobiography of an Idea,* "I read *Capital* by Karl Marx, a book and a writer of whom I had never heard before." His reading of *Capital* came after 1917, but his socialist beginnings, it seems clear, lay in the tumultuous months ending 1916 and starting 1917. He became a Socialist because he hated war.[13]

Bishop Brown's *Christianism and Communism* continued, in his unique and personal style, the battle for truth that his intellectual and moral awakening forced him—regardless of consequences—to take part in with all his might, even after the first half-century of his life had long since passed.

The Rev. Albert Rhys Williams (1883-1962):

The Rev. Mr. Williams died at his home in Ossining, New York, and perhaps I shouldn't at this time use the "Reverend" before his name. A year before his death he told me in a letter that his title had been "demitted," which is the term used when a clergyman, though not "unfrocked," voluntarily prefers to relinquish the title.

But he earned the title years before, for all that. Mr. Williams graduated from the Hartford Theological Seminary in 1907, and studied theology further at Cambridge, England, and at Marburg, Germany. He had a long career as a Congregational minister. According to *Who's Who in America,* he was "Minister and director Maverick Church and Forum," Boston, Massachusetts, from 1907 to 1914. Socialist solutions to social questions were discussed at the Forum, which was held in the church.

At this time, he made a radical change in his profession. He became a war correspondent, went to the Western Front, then to the Russian front, took an active part in the defense of Petrograd (he organized the Interna-

13. Wood, Charles W., "Is Bishop Brown Crazy?" Article in *Hearst's International,* December, 1923. (Quote: "How Bishop Brown arrived at his conclusion that there is no personal God is another story. Briefly, it was the war.")

tional Legion there), and eventually, returning to the United States, acted as a virtual spokesman for Lenin on questions of Soviet policy and of peace.

Williams' pamphlet, *The Bolsheviks and the Soviets,* was published by the Rand School of Social Science, New York, in 1919—and re-published the same year by both the People's Council, an anti-war committee in New York, and the National Office of the Socialist Party in Chicago. Later years he produced full-length books as well as pamphlets and lectures.

The foundation for Williams' long struggle for American-Soviet friendship was, however, laid in 1914, when he joined the Socialist Party.[14]

*   *   *

The above does not exhaust the subject, by any means. I have not discussed clergymen who were elected to office on the Socialist ticket, such as the Rev. George R. Lunn, a Presbyterian, who became mayor of Schenectady, N.Y., in 1911. (His secretary was the young Walter Lippmann.) Nor the Rev. J. Stitt Wilson, who a little later (1914) became mayor of Berkeley, California. There is also the Rev. Frederic O. MacCartney, a Congregationalist, elected as a Socialist to the Massachusetts legislature in 1900. Incidentally, after becoming a Socialist, MacCartney switched to Unitarianism and was appointed assistant pastor to the Second Unitarian Church of Boston.

Furthermore I have omitted such noteworthy personalities as the Rev. Eliot White, Episcopalian, who was a delegate to the national convention of the Socialist Party in 1908; and the Rt. Rev. Paul Jones, Bishop of Utah (successor to Bishop Spalding), who listed himself as a socialist in *American Labor Who's Who,* edited by Solon De Leon; and A. J. Muste, who voted for Debs in 1912; and the Rev. W. S. Harris, who wrote *Capital and Labor* in 1907; and the Rev. Walter Rauschenbusch, a Baptist minister, who in 1901 gave a friendly critique of Marxist and pseudo-Marxist socialism that is worth studying today. Nor have I referred to the Rev. Alexander Irvine of the Church of the Ascension, New York, who boasted that he could make socialists in his church faster than a trade union organizer could; nor to the Rev. John Haynes Holmes of the New York Community Church.

Note also a Negro cleric, the Rev. George W. Woodbey, of California, author of the *Bible and Socialism: A Dialogue Between Two Preachers,*

14. Letter from Mr. Williams to the writer, May 9, 1960. Also see Albert Rhys Williams, *Journey into Revolution. Petrograd,* 1917-18. Edited by Lucita Williams. Quadrangle Books, 1969.

published as a pamphlet in 1904. In this he speaks of Marx as "the great philosopher of modern times." Another Negro minister, the Rev. George Frazier Miller of Brooklyn, was a contributor to *The Messenger* which was founded in 1916-17 by A. Philip Randolph.

Usually Christians—at least those with a sense of history—speak of the Judeo-Christian heritage. Hence one should note forward-looking pro-Socialist thinkers like Rabbi Judah L. Magnes and Rabbi Stephen S. Wise.[15] Then, of course, there are the anti-religious Rationalists and Free Thinkers, like William Thurston Brown[16] and Hugh O. Pentecost,[17] who were both Socialist Party members.

As to the Christian Socialism of the utopian period, in the mid-19th Century, it bore no overt relation to Marxism. Alexander Trachtenberg was right in differentiating between that earlier non-Marxist Christian Socialism, led by W. D. T. Bliss and Professor John R. Commons, which was "unconnected with the Socialist Party of that time," and the later Christian Socialism I have in part described.

"Since 1900, however," Trachtenberg wrote, "Christian Socialism has stood for the movement within the Socialist Party of those who believe that only by means of the Socialist Commonwealth can Christian principles be applied in society."[18]

In an article in *The Christian Socialist,* June 1, 1908, Rufus E. Weeks makes the point even more positively. He insists that really there can't be two kinds of socialism—"a Christian Socialism and a non-Christian Socialism": There is just *Socialism*. But the Christians have "a special motive of their own—the Christian motive"—for supporting Socialism, And they all, he says, uphold the basic teaching, the Marxist doctrine.

There is, of course, the reciprocal influence of the Church on the Marxist movement.

It may be justly argued that the moral quality of Christian teachings helped to emphasize the strong humanist strain already present in Marxism, and served as a bridge across which a dialogue between Socialism and Religion could be begun.

At the same time, Church influence brought about an over-emphasis on the forms of ethics and a weakening, at times, of working class

15. Morris U. Schappes, in *Jewish Life,* November, 1955, p. 18.

16. Brown, William Thurston, of the Free Thought Society of New York. Letter to Julius Gerber, Socialist Organizer, at Tamiment Library, states he has been a member of the Socialist Party for fourteen years. Dec. 31, 1912.

17. *The Truth Seeker,* March 19, 1910. Address by Mrs. Bertha W. Howe at memorial meeting for Hugh O. Pentecost says he left the church of which he was pastor and had joined the Socialist Party.

18. *American Labor Year Book,* 1916, p. 157. Item: "The Christian Socialists."

militancy. Some of the clerical Socialists, as shown by the record, supported the Party's Right Wing faction, even to the extent of accentuating racist and militarist emanations.

The greatest obstacle to the spread of Christian Socialism was the spread of supposedly Christian Capitalism. It may be true that, as the Rev. George E. Littlefield said in 1904 in the *Arena* magazine, Christians should vote for Socialism because "Socialism will make religion real." But of course the established churches as a whole overwhelmingly supported the status quo.

VIII

Marxism
and Youth Organizations
Before 1917

Socialists in this country, perhaps more than in Europe, found that their capitalist opposition attacked them on every side, in the church and the school as well as on the job and in political combat. Adult Socialists, toughened by strikes and enlightened by Marxist explanations of the history of capitalism, were able to withstand these assaults. But their children, in both Sunday School and the public schools, were endlessly propagandized by anti-Socialism. Children of Socialists were dismayed at hearing their parents described as criminals or traitors. Professors in colleges scoffed at socialism, identified socialism with anarchism, and praised "free enterprise."

The Socialist movement around the turn of the Century had to fight back, and it did. *Socialist Sunday Schools* were set up for the very young; *Young People's Socialist Leagues* were organized for young workers; neighborhood classes, lectures, debates and lyceums of all kinds were held in hundreds of communities; socialist academies like the *Rand School* were established; and the *Intercollegiate Socialist Society* grew up in universities across the country.

When on December 29, 1906, Frances M. Gill, a New York stenographer, inserted an announcement in the New York *Call* signed "Secretary of the Socialist Sunday School Association," she unknowingly launched a bit of educational history. Miss Gill was a sister-in-law of Daisy Sanial Gill, poet daughter of Lucian Sanial, a Communard who had immigrated to the United States. The announcement was headed "Socialism and the Young," and called on those interested to contact the Secretary. There followed several years of intensive though intermittent organizing of those once-a-week Sunday Schools in large cities throughout the land.

The next notable step was the publication in Girard, Kansas, in 1908, of Nicholas Klein's *The Socialist Primer: First Lessons in Socialism for Children.* On the cover was a drawing of Karl Marx, with his name underneath. The lessons inside were illustrated by the wellknown *Appeal to Reason* cartoonist, Ryan Walker.

This textbook was described as "First Lessons for the Little Ones in Words of One Syllable." First came the alphabet, then drawings with captions: "Rat. O, see the Rat!" "Hog. See the fat hog!" A drawing of a man begging: "Man. Why does the man beg?" Drawing of a Top Hat: "Hat. See the big Hat!"

Pictures teach other words: *Fat, Box, Vote, Free, Slave.* (*Box* is labeled ballot box; *Free* is a man labeled Socialist; *Slave* is a worker with a pick ax.) Later lessons introduce the thought, "Man will not beg," "The box will be full," "The slave will be free." New words are similarly introduced: *Shop, child, house, work, shirk, world, wage,* and so on.

Among the three lessons we may notice Lesson XIX about *chattel slavery;* Lesson XXX about *oil wells;* Lesson XXXII about *Capital and Labor;* Lesson XXXIII about a *Strike.*

The book ends with a short story by Fred D. Warren, *The Boytown Railroad.* It tells how a boy concocted a playtime railroad and allowed other boys to ride on it—if they gave him all they had, or did his chores for him. The yarn ends with the exploited boys rebelling and building their own railroad, leaving the boy capitalist severely alone.

The author of this little text, Nicholas Klein, was a resident of Minnesota, and had been a delegate from that state to the second Socialist Party convention, held in May, 1904, in Chicago. Later that same year he had been one of the American delegates to the Paris Congress of the Second International, where he attracted the attention of an elderly socialist from a competing delegation—Daniel De Leon of the Socialist Labor Party.

The next event in this history was the publication of a periodical for the children of the Socialist Sunday Schools: *The Young Socialists' Magazine,* founded in 1908. A typical front cover design shows three workers of different countries shaking hands over the motto, "Workers of the World, Unite!" The editorial masthead says: "Organ of the American Socialist Sunday Schools."

The contents include articles, stories, and poems, some of them by such well-known socialists as Frances Willard, Ida Crouch Hazlett, Upton Sinclair (an extract from *The Jungle*), and Ella Reeve Bloor. There is a piece about "The Sun and Stars"; a series giving the "History of Our Country for Boys and Girls"; an exposition, "How Paintings Are Made"; an article, "Gravitation and Inertia"; a piece about "The Paris Commune"; short items about John Brown and Abraham Lincoln; a lesson in Esperanto; a "Talk on Evolution"; an editorial, "What Is Patriotism?"; a short article about the fate of the American Indian; cartoons, reproductions of paintings, photos of statues. Then there are, each month, lists of important historical anniversaries, such as the following:

Aug. 3, 1837—Eugene Sue, the great writer, died.

Aug. 5, 1895—Frederick Engels, the mental partner of Karl Marx, passed away.

Aug. 14, 1904—International Socialist Congress in Amsterdam.

Aug. 19, 1819—Death of James Watt, inventor of the steam engine.

Aug. 31, 71 B. C.—Spartacus was killed.

A new period was marked in December, 1911, with the publication in *The Call* of a polemical article by Jeannette D. Pearl (later the wife of Louis C. Fraina, who still later wrote under the pseudonym of Lewis Corey).[1] Miss Pearl opposed those idealists who wished to anticipate the education of a future Socialist society. "Our concern now," she wrote, "is not how we will do things under industrial democracy. What we are concerned with now is how to best educate for the overthrow of a rotten-ripe industrial autocracy."

The second effort at a textbook, or rather guidebook, David S. Greenberg's *Socialist Sunday School Curriculum*, published in 1913, followed to some extent the argument advanced by Miss Pearl. It was designed for teachers, to help them parallel the public school curriculum, enriching while correcting public school courses. Its aims, the Foreword stated, were "the teaching of the essence of Socialist philosophy and theory through the presentation of historical, industrial, economic and social phenomena: and the morality of a progressive society as opposed to the morality of custom."

This course of study covered six years, each year having 30 Sunday morning sessions, divided into four half-hour periods. There were Primary, Elementary, Intermediate and Advanced classes, using as texts, in the proper order, the Katherine E. Dopp stories about Cave Men and Lake Dwellers; data about the American Indian (H. R. Schoolcraft's writings); stories about John Ball and Wat Tyler in English History; selected chapters from Morgan's *Ancient Society;* stories from American colonial history; material from Kautsky's *The Class Struggle,* Bulfinch's *Age of Fable,* Marx's *Civil War in France,* James Oneal's *Workers in American History,* and Marx's *Capital.*

Along with this theoretical and historical material were intervals de-

1. "Converting the Children," N.Y. *Call,* Dec. 17, 1911, p. 11, Sunday Magazine Section.

voted to calisthenics, social hygiene, ethics and morals, music and dancing.

This ambitious effort continued into the middle of World War I. From 1912 on, Socialist Sunday Schools existed in New Jersey, Los Angeles, Cleveland, New York, and Rochester. Since then, some aspects of their work have merged into what is known as progressive education, a modicum of which has seeped into the public schools. The teachers in the Socialist Sunday Schools were unpaid volunteers, either public school teachers who were Socialists, or parents who had formerly been teachers. The War put an end to the movement.

One runs across an occasional adult today who attended these schools a generation ago. In Cleveland there was Helen, daughter of Socialist leader Alfred Wagenknecht, and now the wife of Carl Winter, editor of *The Daily World;* and Daniel, son of Socialist leader and eventual Communist Party founder, Charles E. Ruthenberg. In New York, social worker Vita Cunning recalls singing "The People's Flag is Deepest Red"; and newspaperman Erik Bert of the staff of the *Daily World* remembers the statuesque tableaux he took part in to commemorate historic working class events.

Outstanding among the teachers of the Sunday Schools, in addition to Jeannette D. Pearl, Nicholas Klein, and David S. Greenberg, were Fred Briehl, farmer, of upper New York State, and Professor P. Shedd of the University of Rochester. Professor Shedd, according to the New York *Call,* was fired in 1915 after 21 years in the University, at the demand of George Eastman of the Eastman Kodak Company.[2]

The Young People's Socialist League—whose consonantal initials (YPSL) resulted in the slang designation, "Yipsels"—consisted largely of young wage workers. The Marxism they learned could be illustrated from their own experience on the job.

The point was made that "modern industry does not train its juvenile employees but merely works them." Back in the 1890's Mrs. Hannah M. Morgan, wife of the Socialist trade unionist, Thomas H. Morgan, had organized women in the American Federation of Labor to lessen the horrible "sweat shop" conditions under which young people and children were employed. Young working people were not only exploited, often cruelly, but thwarted in development and education. When they united into a Socialist organization of their own, assisted by adult Socialists, they were fighting for themselves as well as for the children they might sometime have. Theirs was truly "the movement of the present," as well as, in a sense, "the future of that movement."

2. New York *Call,* January 11, 1915, p. 4.

The actual crystallizing of the Y.P.S.L. required several years, and the main beginnings were in two cities: New York and Chicago.

The New York beginning was as early as 1905, according to Ira Kipnis, *The American Socialist Movement, 1897-1912.* First there was a Junior Socialist Club, then (1907) a Young Friends Socialistic Literary Circle. By 1911, there were some eight hundred young Socialists "in various clubs throughout the country," but these groupings had no organizational connection with each other.

To provide some sort of unity, the clubs were tied together about October, 1911, in what was then called the Young People's Socialist Federation, with headquarters at 239 East 84th Street, New York. Its organ, *The Young Socialists' Magazine,* was published at 15 Spruce Street. The purpose of the Y.P.S.F., according to the magazine, was to conduct weekly meetings, with lectures and debates on economics, science and literature, followed by music and dancing. "The theories and philosophy of Socialism are discussed at the meetings," it was stated, editorially, "but there is no obligation on the part of a member to believe in Socialism. No matter what your personal beliefs or your race, color or creed may be, you are eligible for membership. . . . All that is required of you is to be sincere, to desire self-culture and to have a whole-hearted interest in the welfare of mankind."

A 4-page folder issued by the Y.P.S.F. was notable since the anti-war cartoon on the cover is by John Sloan, outstanding Socialist artist. The content shows that the Y.P.S.F. aimed mainly to counteract the militaristic Boy Scout movement sponsored by employers and the government. "Going to war should be no business of a civilized people," this leaflet said, three years before World War I.

The Young People's Socialist Federation was midway in its age-group appeal between the Socialist Sunday Schools and the later Young People's Socialist League. The Y.P.S.F. organized high school students rather than young workers. The real beginning of the Young People's Socialist League, as nationally organized and officially recognized in 1913, was in Chicago.

In that city groups of young people began to be constituted into Young People's Socialist Leagues by the State Secretary of the Socialist Party of Illinois, John C. Kennedy, in late 1907, and soon were made into a city-wide association. With it was merged another sizable young people's club called originally the "Workers' School of Government," organized, with the help of John C. Kennedy, by C. N. Madsen, the Socialist representative in the Illinois legislature. As the years went by, many speakers appeared before these Chicago youth groups, including

May Wood Simons, Seymour Stedman, Eugene V. Debs, J. O. Bentall, and other nationally known Socialist leaders.

Meanwhile, in May, 1913, according to Alexander Trachtenberg's *American Labor Year Book, 1916,* William F. Kruse was selected as national organizer of the Young People's Socialist League, and he proceeded to contact "all young Socialist organizations in the country" and to "federate them into a national organization." By 1916, he reported that "there were more than 4,000 members." He added: "The Y.P.S.L. members assist in propaganda and educational work, raise funds, and in general do a great deal to raise the standard of work and comradeship among even the older comrades."

An important point was made by the editor of the *Journal* of the Young People's Socialist League, at the time (May, 1913) when the work of national federation was under way. "A Young People's League," he warned, "is not a children's movement—at least not for children of a tender age. . . . Again, it is not true that a league should be organized exclusively for the propaganda of Socialism among young people. Of course, that is the basic principle upon which we build our organization, but there are other things to be considered. . . . To be a real success a Y.P.S.L. will be a combination of the propaganda, the social, and the educational; and will be controlled and directed by the youth of both sexes ranging from the age of 16 up to 30. . . . Youth demands that its politics be made lively and interesting. Youth craves for excitement, pleasure and recreation: and above all, youth demands that it associate with youth and not with fossils."

It was on the above "Chicago Plan" that the national Y.P.S.L. was founded in 1913 and soon became nation-wide with thousands of members. Hundreds of later Socialists trace the beginnings of their mental development back to the Y.P.S.L.

The International Socialist Society had an auspicious, almost a spectacular, origin in New York on September 12, 1905, and a notable country-wide growth over a period of nearly a dozen years. Its originators sought through this new organization to appeal to college youth, but they did more: they penetrated the American academic world, and reached some of the best faculty minds. The aim, to be sure, was to find out about Marxism, not necessarily to support it; but those who pushed such inquiry were mainly Marxists, and many who came to scoff remained to praise. The I.S.S. was formed, as it announced, "for the purpose of promoting an intelligent interest in Socialism among college men and women." It was "primarily a *study,* not a political propaganda organization." Nevertheless, the adjective "Socialist" which formed part of the name was not out of place. Those who set up the Society were Socialists;

those who took part in its advisory leadership were either Socialists or sympathizers; its officers made regular reports to the Socialist Party. Its subject matter was Marxism.

The I.S.S. had three main periods: 1905-1909, the organizational beginning, under Jack London, Upton Sinclair, William English Walling, Charlotte Perkins Gilman, and J. G. Phelps Stokes; 1910-12, the start of Harry W. Laidler's secretaryship, marked by Alexander Trachtenberg's student leadership at Yale and Walter Lippmann's at Harvard; and 1913-1916, the war years, marked by the founding of the *Intercollegiate Socialist*, by the rise of new Socialists and sympathizers in college faculties (Scott Nearing at Pennsylvania, Jessie Wallace Hughan at Barnard, Otto C. Marckwardt and Roy W. Sellars at Michigan, Vida D. Scudder at Wellesley), and by new student voices (Freda Kirchwey at Barnard, W. W. Denton at Illinois, Ammon A. Hennacy at Wisconsin, Will Weinstone at the College of the City of New York, Inez Milholland at Vassar, Paul H. Douglas and Randolph Bourne at Columbia.)

The attitude of leading academic thinkers toward Marxism in those years may be indicated by a sort of poll:

Prof. Richard T. Ely, Wisconsin: "It may be said, indeed, that nothing in the present day is likely to awaken the conscience of the ordinary man or woman, or to increase the sense of responsibility, as a thorough course in Socialism."

Prof. Ellen Hayes, Wellesley: "I frankly declare to you my belief that the Socialist ideal is the one ideal that redeems the human race and justifies its continuance on earth."

Prof. Charles A. Beard, historian: "In an age when Socialism is admittedly shaking the old foundations of politics the world over and penetrating our sciences, art and literature, it seems a work of supererogation to attempt to *prove* that men and women presumptively engaged in the pursuit of knowledge should take an intelligent interest in such an important matter."

Ernest Poole, novelist: "For you and me in the present life, the city as it is today, the present injustices, the present slums, the present grab for the dollar. For you and me the rough labor of ploughing, of clearing away, of breaking chains, of freeing ourselves from the bonds that enslave us so that our children's freer minds can go on with the mighty work of building."

Dr. Franklin H. Giddings, Department of Sociology, Columbia: "If I may venture an opinion as to the most important question in political economy before the American people, it is this: 'Shall the chief and controlling means of production in the United States, including mineral and forest resources, water power sites, railroads and means of communication, patent rights, and the enormous funds of loanable capital, be owned by a billionaire four hundred, who, by virtue of such ownership, will be able for all practical purposes to own a hundred or more millions of us ordinary human beings; or shall we ordinary human beings, in our collective capacity, own the means of production ourselves and proceed to work out the reality of a democratic republic?"[3]

The Intercollegiate Socialist, organ of the I. S. S., was founded in 1913 and displaced the *Bulletin* issued up to then. It was an imposing 24-page magazine published every two months, carrying articles and reviews by a wide variety of writers, thinkers, leaders: Victor Berger, congressman; Florence Kelley, social worker; Arturo Giovannitti, poet; W. J. Ghent, writer and theoretician; Anita Block, women's editor of the New York *Call;* and scores of others. An early article was by Jean Longuet, a son-in-law of Karl Marx, on "The Socialist Movement Among the Students of French Universities." One number bore a Ryan Walker anti-capitalist cartoon on the front cover.

The year 1913 was notable also as the publication year of Jessie Wallace Hughan's *The Facts of Socialism,* a book advertised by John Lane Company as "Especially adapted to college study groups." The I. S. S. "Study Course on Socialism," circulated in 1916, reminds students that Dr. Hughan's book "was written especially for I. S. S. chapters." The book gives a rather good exposition of Marxism. Dr. Hughan had written *American Socialism at the Present Day* two years earlier, and for both works had had the benefit of Louis Boudin's *Theoretical System of Karl Marx,* published in 1909. It was in 1909, too, that Joseph E. Cohen brought out the first edition of his useful manual, *Socialism for Students,* published by the Charles H. Kerr Company. This was a period when Marxist study was widespread.

An editorial reference in the December-January, 1914-1915, issue indicates in a small way the significance of the I.S.S. "John Reed reports," it says, "that when he attempted, a few months ago to obtain from Dr. Karl Liebknecht an interview for publication in a well-known American periodical, the famous German Socialist informed him that the only periodical in this country of whose existence he was aware was that 'little magazine, *The Intercollegiate Socialist.*' "

By 1916 there were Intercollegiate Socialist Society undergraduate chapters in about 70 colleges and universities, and, in addition, alumni chapters in seventeen cities. Field representatives of the Society, such as John Spargo, Rose Pastor Stokes, and Harry W. Laidler, spoke that year at more than 120 colleges, addressing 30,000 students. They talked

3. *The Intercollegiate Socialist,* April 9, 1910.

before some 80 economics and other social science classes, and to more than a score of entire student bodies.

The Socialist movement produced two outstanding educational institutions for the teaching of Marxism and allied subjects: the People's College of Fort Scott, Kansas, and the Rand School of New York.

The story of the People's College might be described as a 13-year effort to realize a great educational dream, which then had an actual but hard-up existence of perhaps five years. It could also be described as the story of a great educator, Walter Thomas Mills, whose place in American working class history surely cannot be denied though few know it. It might also be considered the progenitor of such modern cooperative schools as Commonwealth College, Mena, Arkansas, and Highlander Folk School, Monteagle, Tennessee—both with a strong heritage of populism and utopianism.

It will be simplest to follow the career of Walter Thomas Mills himself, for wherever he went, the People's College idea went too. Mills published his first important book, *Evolutionary Politics,* in 1898, under the imprint of Charles H. Keer & Company. This was a book of essays about "The Unemployed," "The Children of the Unemployed," "The Problem of the Poor," "Collective and Private Ownership," and so forth—a book with a distinct utopian flavor. In a brief opening chapter, Mills states his central credo: "I am a believer in the greatness of the future."

An important fact emerges casually in the first pages, as though it were a minor trifle: The title page says the copyright is held "by the People's University." And a sort of introduction is given, signed by "George McA. Miller, Chancellor of the People's University," an institution which had been chartered at Hopkins, Illinois, to carry out the "plans proposed by Walter Thomas Mills." That was in 1898, a year when Mills spoke in Hopkins, we are told, for forty-five consecutive Sundays. "Mr. Mills simply advertised to speak, and having spoken once kept speaking. The people having heard him once kept coming."

Two years later, according to *The Comrade,* Vol. I, No. 10, Walter Thomas Mills was in San Francisco, where he had set up the International School for Social Economy, with Frank P. O'Hare as one of the teachers. (O'Hare was later to be the husband of Kate Richards O'Hare and an editor of *The National Rip-Saw.*)

Correspondence courses were given. The Board of Examiners included such leading Socialists as Max D. Hayes, George D. Herron, Charles H. Vail, J. Stitt Wilson, A. M. Simons, and John Spargo.

A year after this, according to an advertisement in an early New York socialist paper, *The Worker,* April 28, 1901, the school had been transferred to Chicago, where the office was at 3962 Langley Avenue (and

shortly afterward moved to 6416 Ellis Avenue). "If you wish to understand Socialism or to be able to work for it, you should take this course
of lessons by correspondence," the announcement said, under the heading: "A School for Socialism."

The Chicago school kept going for some years, where Mills lectured
more or less regularly, and from where he accepted speaking dates
throughout the western and midwestern states.

We hear of Walter Thomas Mills again, however—according to Frederic
Cornell, in an unpublished doctoral dissertation—in Kansas City, Missouri,
as heading the International School of Social Economy there in 1902,
which assertedly already had 1,794 correspondence students.[4]

The next stage came in 1911, in Fort Scott, Kansas, with the establishment of the People's College, a really notable institution. Here, apparently, Mills came only to lecture. The venture was backed by local townsmen
and by leading Socialists throughout the country. The story is told by the
town's local newspaper, the Fort Scott *Tribune Monitor,* in issues dated
August 20, 1911, June 20th, 1914.

The College began in 1911, with a "Socialist Week's Camp" held at
Gun Park, featuring speeches and social events every day and evening.
The speakers included the local Socialist attorney, Hon. J. I. Sheppard,
and the Socialist organizers and journalists, George D. Brewer, Miss May
Wood (later Mrs. May Wood Simons), A. M. Simons, H. G. Creel, and the
Appeal to Reason editor, Fred D. Warren. "People's College Big Thing
for Fort Scott," exulted the editor of the *Tribune Monitor.*

After many delays and many months, the People's College was definitely chartered under Kansas state law. In an article in the paper, lawyer
Sheppard wrote that Fort Scott would "become, in a few years, the chief
center of education in the world." He added: "The school will be owned
and directed by the working class of the world."

At long last, the school obtained a suitable site: the $40,000 former
home of a deceased local judge at 1002 National Avenue, in Fort Scott;
and on July 1, 1914, headquarters were set up there for classes and for
correspondence courses. The first lecture scheduled in the new location
was by Eugene V. Debs, the second by Helen Keller. Debs was announced
as Chancellor of the People's College.

By December, 1915, the school had its own organ: *The People's
College News,* edited by Arthur Le Sueur (father of the writer, Meridel Le
Sueur). On its inside front cover were listed Debs as Chancellor, and a
Board of Administration which included such other outstanding Socialists
as Arthur Le Sueur, Caroline A. Lowe, Fred D. Warren, Charles Edward

---

4. Frederic Cornell, presently at Columbia University.

Russell, George Allan England, John M. Work (national secretary of the Socialist Party), Charles P. Steinmetz (electrical inventor), Kate Richards O'Hare of the *National Rip-Saw,* and George R. Kirkpatrick (soon-to-be Socialist candidate for vice president). The School's two basic aims were given as follows:

1) "To bring education within the reach of every man, woman & child.
2) "To teach from the viewpoint of the working class."

The College maintained a farm dairy, an orchard, mechanical and electrical plants and shops, where students could receive both instruction and practical training. The courses included English, arithmetic, book-keeping, penmanship, typing, algebra, American history, parliamentary procedure, and law. A *People's College News* editorial stated that 4,000 students were enrolled, and noted that of the correspondence students, "six are in penitentiaries." Occasional references were made to the *Appeal to Reason,* the *National Rip-Saw,* the *International Socialist Review,* the Chicago *Socialist,* the Minneapolis *Socialist.*

By February, 1916, the People's College sent an official congratula-tory message to Socialist congressman Meyer London, Washington, D. C., praising his fight against American involvement in what came to be known as World War I.

It is clear that the People's College had an uphill financial struggle throughout its existence. No millionaire came forward to back its work. It was unable to reach any concord with orthodox established educa-tional institutions. But it left behind a tradition of workers' cultural aspiration that, one hopes, will not completely fade.

The Rand School became a legal entity in 1905, when Carrie Rand (Mrs. E. D. Rand) of Burlington, Iowa, died, leaving a will which provided a fund to establish "a School of Socialism in this country." The money was a trust fund amounting to $200,000, naming her daughter, Carrie Rand Herron, her son-in-law George D. Herron, and the Socialist lawyer Morris Hillquit as trustees. The full number of trustees was set at nine, who were required to be members of the American Socialist Society (and the members of the American Socialist Society had, in turn, to be members of the Socialist Party of America.) The remaining six trustees were Algernon Lee, who became Director of the School; Job Harriman and Benjamin Hanford, who had both been candidates for vice president; William Mailly, national secretary of the Party; Leonard D. Abbott, an editor of *The Comrade,* socialist magazine of the arts and literature; and Henry Slobodin, first national secretary of the anti-De Leon faction which left the Socialist Labor Party in 1899 to merge with others to form the Socialist Party.

The Rand School became a fact on October 1, 1906, when it opened its doors to students at 140 East 19th Street, New York City, as announced in *The Worker* of that period. Later it moved to its better-known location at 7 East 15th Street. The trustees named an advisory committee of three: Charles A. Beard of Columbia, Dr. P. A. Levine of the Rockefeller Institute, and Herman Schlueter, editor of the *New-Yorker Volkzeitung,* a German language social-democratic paper which in past years had supported the Socialist Labor Party.

From then on the Socialist and progressive world had a congenial center at the Rand School. In 1912, the New York *Call* announced an addition to the staff: Dr. Helen L. Sumner, a member of the Socialist Party of Washington, D. C., and a former co-worker of Professor John R. Commons.[5] The regular teachers included the Director, Algernon Lee, who taught Socialism; Dr. Alexander Goldenweiser, who taught anthropology; David Berenberg, a former public school teacher; and August Claessens, teacher of public speaking. Concerning the latter, Irving Potash, one of his old students and at present a Communist leader, remembers that Claessens took his pupils straight from the classroom to the soapbox to try out theory in real practice. Among frequent lecturers there were Scott Nearing, Isaac Hourwich, and Morris Hillquit, as well as guest speakers from several college and university faculties.

Trade unions regularly gave selected members scholarships to the Rand School, to make them better organizers. Among other activities, the Rand School Ball became an annual social event.

In 1913, the Rand School Library began to be significant. Collections of books were contributed by Robert Hunter, Dr. Maxim Romm, William Dean Howells, Herman Schlueter, Jessie Ashley, W. J. Ghent. Among those who willed books to the Library were Ben Hanford (a fine collection of pamphlets); Joseph Weiss; and William Mailly. Noted authors contributed copies of their own works, including Jack London, Maxim Gorki, Edward Carpenter, Brand Whitlock, Charles Rann Kennedy, Percy Mackaye, David Graham Phillips, John Galsworthy and Arnold Bennett. Later, valuable collections by Eugene V. Debs, Meyer London, and C.H. Matchett (first Socialist candidate for vice president) were bequeathed to the Library.

In 1915, Alexander Trachtenberg came from Yale to establish and take charge of the Research Department, to organize the Library on a systematic basis, and to edit and publish the *American Labor Year Books,* which from then on became an annual Rand School undertaking. Trachtenberg also taught certain courses. In January, 1917, the late Jack Stachel, while still attending Cooper Union, signed up for a course in Labor Problems

5. New York *Call*, December 19, 1912, p. 5.

under Trachtenberg. (Stachel afterward became a Communist Party leader).

Then came World War I, the Red Scare, searches and seizures. The Rand School eventually closed its doors, but the Rand School Library still lives—known as the Tamiment Library, in the old premises at 7 East 15th Street, under the auspices of its present owner, New York University.

Local and *ad hoc* Marxist discussion groups were a prominent feature of the war and pre-war years, 1913-1917. Forums and debates became popular, in and outside of the Rand School. Morris Hillquit debated the merits of Socialism on the platform with Jacob Gould Schurman in New Rochelle, New York, and H. M. Tichenor, socialist editor of the *Melting Pot,* debated John Basil Barnhill in the columns of the St. Louis *National Rip-Saw.* On street corners, all across the country, in every sizable city, soapboxers like Joseph D. Cannon of the miners' union, taught mass classes in socialism night after night, on a specified topic, regularly announced.

We may take as typical examples of ephemeral but influential Marxist schools, one in Brooklyn, New York, the other in Detroit, Michigan.

In Brooklyn, the Brownsville Labor Lyceum grew up under the backing of local labor unions organized by two Socialists, A. Shiplacoff and Frank Smith. They put in active charge of the Lyceum a man named S. Hurok, who eventually made a world reputation as an impresario. Among the subjects taught in 1915-1916 was American History: the text was James Oneal's *The Workers in American History,* and the teacher was the youthful Will Weinstone (now a Communist teacher and writer) who himself was attending the separately organized lectures on Marxism under Harry Waton. (Waton was independent of the Lyceum; he held his meetings in a separate building in the same neighborhood.) The latter, who seemingly was a man born to teach, instructed a class of 150 young men and women in Karl Marx's *Capital* and Herbert Spencer's *Principles.* Weinstone describes Waton's classes as inspiring and markedly influential. "After he taught us *Capital,*" he told the present writer, "I went on and read it myself." Hundreds of young people attended these Waton and Brownsville Lyceum assemblies, took an active part in the discussions, and bought and read the recommended books.

In Detroit there were classes and lectures given by John Keracher, a shoe merchant, and Al Renner, a clerk and accountant, on Marxist themes and classics. Keracher specialized on expositions of *Capital,* especially of value and surplus value, and of historical materialism. He wrote pamphlets on these topics, such as *The Head-Fixers,* an exposé of press-and-church control over ideas. Keracher's friend, Renner, well-read and an able student of public affairs, centered on lecture-demonstrations—backed up by statistics—on the way in which workers were exploited, describing everyday facts of unemployment and of evictions of the poor from their homes, and in general the brutal concrete truths of the class struggle. Margaret Nowak, wife of Stanley Nowak (who became a member of the Michigan legislature), recalls from her youth the irrefutable convincingness of Renner's lectures, delivered with devastating objectivity.

The Keracher-Renner educational work developed soon (1917-1918) into the short-lived though important Proletarian University—but that leads to the outer limits of this study.

War and political reaction halted this many-sided nation-wide intellectual upsurge. Monopoly control of press and radio, buttressed by repressive legislation, changed the pattern of public life, and almost obliterated the memory of this brief hour from people's minds.

The Russian Revolution also—in a sense—interrupted this educational history; or, more accurately, lifted it to a new level of political struggle.

IX

Marxism
and American Prose

"Behold the literature of my Party!" said Jack London on a certain occasion.[1] He was referring to the founding of *The Comrade* in 1901, and the "party" was the Socialist Party, which he had lately joined. Perhaps we should say that by "party" he meant the entire movement initiated by Karl Marx: after all, he had become a member of the earlier Socialist Labor Party in 1895.

In speaking of literature Jack London had in mind also other publications, such as *The International Socialist Review* (1900) and *Wilshire's Magazine* (1900).[2] If we stretch his vision to include prophetically the next dozen years—before 1917—we can include *The Masses,* founded in 1912, *The Bulletin* of the Intercollegiate Socialist Society (1905), and an outstanding anthology, *The Cry for Justice,* edited by Upton Sinclair (with Jack London's Foreword) in 1915.

William Dean Howells, already the dean of American literature, hailed the birth of *The Comrade,* even though he wanted a different title for it. He said he didn't "like the name or anything that suggests soldiership." The editors replied that their comradeship was the fraternalism of peace, which they wanted so badly they were "even willing to fight for it." Howells was a socialist sympathizer who contributed financially to socialist political campaigns for office. His greeting to *The Comrade* appeared in the first issue.[3]

1. *The Comrade,* November, 1901, quoted in *Jack London, American Rebel,* edited by Philip S. Foner, p. 55, footnote.
2. H. Gaylord Wilshire, founder and editor.
3. Howell's greeting to *The Comrade* appeared in the issue of October, 1901. See also article, "The Nature of Liberty," by William Dean Howells, in *The Worker,* June 21, p. 4.

From England George Bernard Shaw saluted *The Comrade* in his own Shavian way. He concluded his "good wishes" with the joshing words, "After all, it [a socialist magazine devoted to literature] must succeed *sometime; and why not this?*"[4]

And not only were there periodicals devoted to literature—*socialist* periodicals, demanding a changed world, as they created a new art—but new authors and new novels gave evidence of "the literature of my party."

Even the political propaganda newspapers of the Socialist Party, such as *The New York Call, The Appeal to Reason, The National Rip-Saw,* and *The Worker,* gave space to poetry and short stories and critical comment. Every week in Anita Block's editorial domain in *The Call* there were verse and book reviews, and established writers did not hesitate to appear there.

But most important was the new generation of outstanding novelists, some of them members of and spokesmen for the Socialist Party.

There were of course Upton Sinclair's *The Jungle* (1906), and Jack London's *The Iron Heel* (1907), as well as his *The People of the Abyss* (1902). Also, there was Ernest Poole, whose *The Harbor* (1915) was notable. Edward Bellamy's *Looking Backward* (1887) belonged to literature as well as to politics. Floyd Dell was experimenting with social ideas as he sought to theorise on "The Literature of the Machine Age."

Upton Sinclair's *The Jungle* won deserved fame for two qualities: the uncompromising realism of its description of conditions in the Chicago stockyards, and the congressional investigation which it inspired, leading to the pure food laws of our time. It is interesting, that Ella Reeve Bloor, a Socialist Party organizer, did a good deal of on-the-spot research for Sinclair in gathering material among the stockyard workers.

Jack London's *The Iron Heel* is notable for its astonishing foresight in portraying a fascist government many years ahead of time. The supposed date of publication was set at 32 BOM or Brotherhood of Man, that is, in the new socialist era four hundred years hence. London deduced the rise of a fascist oligarchy from reading W. J. Ghent's *Our Benevolent Feudalism* (except that London regarded it as an utterly brutal—not benevolent—feudalism), and by pondering on the pitiless tsarist crushing of the 1905 revolution in Russia.[5] The heroes of the story are Ernest Everhard and his wife Avis. The central lesson of the book is Marxist.

Ernest Poole's *The Harbor* (1915) was praised and admired as a novel

4. *The Comrade,* October, 1901.
5. Jack London, *American Rebel,* opus cited, pp. 87-88.

about workers in New York. The story is told in the first person by a boy who, at the start, is listening to a sermon by the Reverend Henry Ward Beecher. There are references to Boss Tweed, the Haymarket Victims, strike leaders, suffragettes, and even "mass action." Eventually the terms "comrades" and "socialists" grow out of the narrative. In Socialist Party records at Tamiment Library, Ernest Poole is listed as a candidate for senator from the 17th District in 1914—the year before the book's publication.

William Dean Howells, hovering between Marxism and utopianism, wrote *A Traveler from Altruria* (1894), a utopian piece of fiction and its sequel, *The Eye of the Needle* (1907). These were preceded by *Annie Kilburn* (1891), a novel which indicated the "socialistic" trend of his thinking in those years. Howells may be said to have gone through fictional realism to social idealism. "Howells wished his books to rely on fidelity alone, and through this fidelity to serve as socializing instruments."[6] All three of these are impressive works tusseling with themes that cannot escape class struggle truths, while not quite establishing them.

Edward Bellamy was not a member of any Socialist organization, and his *Looking Backward* came more than a dozen years before the birth of the Socialist Party. Yet it set going a movement called "Nationalism" which had something of a socialist ideology and which merged actively with the Socialist political movement of the time. Many socialists regarded *Looking Backward* as a dependable picture of the society they wanted to establish.

Horace Traubel was a critic and social commentator rather than a novelist. In an article in *The Worker,* April 7, 1906, he wrote: "It is bound to come. The new world of men as against the old world of money." In another piece, October 13, 1906, in *The Worker,* Traubel said: "I know just how you feel about it, Dear Comrade," and urged socialists to keep on going, despite repression. In *The Call,* April 13, 1913, he declared: "I don't know what I am. But I do know what I want. What do I want? I want the earth."

In addition to London, Sinclair, Poole, Bellamy, Howells, and Traubel, the acknowledged leaders among socialist novelists and writers, there are others who deserve attention:

Leroy Scott produced a notable novel of trade-union organization titled *The Walking Delegate* (1905). Buck Foley is the walking delegate, Tom Keating is the foreman, a man named Baxter is head of the

6. *A College Book of American Literature*, Vol. II, p. 455, by Milton Ellis, Louise Pound, George Weida Spohn, 1940.

tyrannical Iron Employers Association, and one Nels Peterson is the scab. The narrative involves a big construction job, and the hero turns out to be Tom Keating.

Eugene Wood's most popular novel was *Back Home* (1905), a book that emphasized humor and plain realism, followed by *Folks Back Home* (1908), and *Our Town* (1913). Eugene Wood was a delegate to the New York State Socialist Constitutional Convention in 1914, as shown by records in the Tamiment Library.[7] In these same records we find a letter from Wood to the organizer, Julius Gerber, dated June 17, 1911, in which Wood offers to speak for the Party. "You can send me wherever you like to fill cavities or appointments where the speaker finds he cannot appear."

I. K. Friedman's novel, *By Bread Alone* (1901), involves a strike in a steel mill owned by Henry Marvin, for which the company mobilizes its pinkertons. There are a thousand pickets. Among the characters are a socialistic student named Blair Carrhart and Henry Marvin's daughter.

Albert Bullard, under the pseudonym of Albert Edwards, was the author of *Comrade Yetta,* a popular novel. Yetta is a socialist leader and delegate to the International Socialist Congress. In *The New Review,* May, 1913, Andre Tridon reviews *Comrade Yetta,* referring to it as "that rare thing, a radical novel which is also a work of art."

George Allan England, a Socialist Party leader, undertook a grandiose novel on *The Air Trust* (1915), with illustrations by socialist artist John Sloan. The book was dedicated to Eugene V. Debs. "This book," says a Foreword by the author, "is the result of an attempt to carry the monopolistic principle to its logical conclusion." If a monopoly can control coal, beef, steel, etc., why not air? The yarn begins with old Isaac Flint, a Wall Street billionaire, who says his power, though great, is not enough. He wants more! There are exciting developments, plots, air tanks, projectiles, airplanes, explosives, and "The Storming of the Works."

Bouck White, the radical preacher who founded The Church of the Social Revolution, also wrote a kind of utopian allegorical novel titled *The Mixing* (1913), designed to demonstrate what cooperation could do. He was a Socialist Party candidate for congress in 1914 from the 13th congressional district of New York.

James Oppenheim wrote *Pay Envelopes* (1911), a volume of short stories that had appeared in *Everybody's, Pearson's, The Metropolitan,*

7. In *The Call,* April 4, 1915, an article tells of Peggy Wood, actress daughter of socialist author Eugene Wood. Peggy Wood played a leading role in "Hello, Broadway."

about the unemployed, factory women, steel workers, shop-girls. His novel, *The Nine-Tenths* (1911), also dealt with factory workers, with strikes, with the unemployed. Oppenheim was not afraid of "problems" in literature, nor of socialism. He was clearly much interested in the organized working-class movement.

Perhaps the most dramatic instance of a socialist novelist is that of Joseph Medill Patterson, son of the publisher of the *Chicago Tribune,* a reactionary Republican paper. This son of wealth was elected to the Illinois legislation as a Republican at the age of twenty-four, then appointed Commissioner of Public Works in Chicago. Then, in 1906, he resigned with the announcement that he was joining the Socialist Party. He wrote *Confessions of a Drone* for *The Independent,* a liberal magazine, the next year. Then, in 1908, he wrote a satiric novel, *A Little Brother of the Rich,* in which he ridicules the wealthy bourgeoisie to which class he belonged. Walter B. Rideout, author of *The Radical Novel in the United States,*[8] says that Patterson "expands his attack on the empty and vicious lives of a leisure class made possible only through the wealth-creating activities of the workers." Rideout goes on to say that in a chapter "describing a yachting cruise, the dissolute pleasures of the rich passengers are contrasted in an ironic counter-point with the labors of the crew."

Oddly enough, Patterson was given the job of editing the 1908 Socialist Campaign Handbook, and it was a good job of editing! But Patterson did not last very long in the Socialist Party. He defected back to the class he came from, even before the Russian Revolution.

Socialist records put the outstanding novelist Sinclair Lewis in Branch One on January 16, 1911. His address is given as Care of Stokes Publishing Company, 443 Fourth Avenue, New York. It is the present writer's opinion that Sinclair Lewis' long-intended "labor novel"—which never got written—had its inspiration decades ago in his brief stay in the Socialist Party.

The evidence given here, incomplete as it admittedly is, should be conclusive on this one point: that Marxist social theories strongly affected American literature in pre-1917 times.

8. Walter B. Rideout, *The Radical Novel in the United States,* 1956, p. 67.

X

Marxism and American Poetry

The inspiration that U. S. poets discovered in Marx and in the socialist movement was profound, years before the 1917 revolution in Russia. Combing through the Socialist publications of those years, I have found copious and unmistakable examples.

There is, for example a poem by W. L. Benessi, a frequent contributor to *The Comrade*. It is notable as one of the earliest to embody the Marxist slogan: "You have nothing to lose but your chains: you have a world to gain." Thus in part:

The Battle Cry

(The Comrade, November, 1903.)

Close the ranks! Ho, fellow toilers,
    See! the foe is drawing near—
The fell army of despoilers
    Seeking courage in their fear.
               Arm'd with falsehood and confusion,
                   See them bungle, hear them howl!
               Blind with rage and vain delusion,
                   But with purpose drear and foul.
See! 'Tis trac'd in glowing letters—
    Liberty's divine refrain:
"Ye can only lose your fetters,
    But ye have a world to gain."
               Close the ranks, O fellow toilers,
                   Let each one be brave and true,
               Let us outvote our despoilers;
                   We are many—They are few.

Sarah N. Cleghorn's *Comrade Jesus,* circa 1912, quoted by William Rose Benet and Norman Cousins in *The Poetry of Freedom,* evokes the rank and file atmosphere of a typical oldtime Socialist Party local. It is clear, too, that Miss Cleghorn was not a bit bothered about *politicizing* her verse. There is—one senses—an obvious pride in her own *red card.*

Comrade Jesus

Thanks to Saint Matthew, who had been
At massmeetings in Palestine,
We know whose side was spoken for
When Comrade Jesus had the floor.
    "Where sore they toil and hard they lie,
    Among the great unwashed, dwell I.—
    The tramp, the convict, I am he;
    Cold-shoulder him, cold-shoulder me."
By Dives' door, with thoughtful eye,
He did tomorrow prophesy:—
"The Kingdom's gate is low and small;
The rich can scarce wedge through at all."
    "A dangerous man," said Caiaphas,
    "An ignorant demagogue, alas!
    Friend of low women, it is he
    Slanders the upright Pharisee."
For law and order, it was plain,
For Holy Church, he must be slain.
The troops were there to awe the crowd:
Mob violence was not allowed.
    Ah, let no Local him refuse!
    Comrade Jesus hath paid his dues.
    Whatever other be debarred,
    Comrade Jesus hath his red card.

Professor Jessie Wallace Hughan of Barnard College had a poem entitled "The Vanguard" in the *Bulletin* of the Intercollegiate Socialist Society for October-November, 1912, which also breathes a militant spirit. I cite the first stanza of a four-stanza poem.

The Vanguard

'Tis ours to haste through the desert waste where the hearts of strong men fail;
'Tis ours to blaze through hidden ways, when night has swallowed the trail;
To charge the height in the first wild fight, when lances meet in the fray;
And count the cost by the leaders lost at the end of a losing day.

This theme of the vanguard role of their contemporaries is a favorite one with socialists of the first years of the Twentieth Century.

*   *   *

"The Eagle That Is Forgotten" by Vachel Lindsay, circa 1902, reprinted in *The Poetry of Freedom,* is a tribute to Governor John P. Altgeld of Illinois, and at the same time, by implication, it is a memorial to the Haymarket Martyrs whom Altgeld defended. This is the final stanza:

> Sleep softly . . . eagle forgotten . . . under the stone.
> Time has its way with you there and the clay has its own.
> Sleep on, O brave-hearted, O wise man, that kindled the flame—
> To live in mankind is far more than to live in a name.
> To live in mankind, far, far more . . . than to live in a name.

In 1912, also, Vachel Lindsay wrote a three-stanza bit of verse on the prosaic theme, "Why I Voted the Socialist Ticket." The opening lines state:

> I am unjust, but I can strive for justice.
>   My life's unkind, but I can vote for kindness.
> I, the unloving, say life should be lovely,
>   I, that am blind, cry out against my blindness.

"The Man With the Hoe" by Edwin Markham, written about 1900 after seeing Millet's painting, might be described as a Marxist response to the picture. Its last stanza reads:

> O masters, lords and rulers in all lands,
> How will the Future reckon with this man?
> How answer his brute question in that hour
> When whirlwinds of rebellion shake all shores?
> How will it be with kingdoms and with kings—
> With those who shaped him to the thing he is—
> When this dumb terror shall rise to judge the world,
> After the silence of the centuries?

Another poem by Edwin Markham, in *The Comrade,* is "The Love of Comrades," of which the concluding stanza reads:

> O world, rejoice with me,
> For the joy that is to be,
> When far as the bright arch of heaven extends
> The world of men shall be a world of friends.

The slogan of "Workers of the World Unite," emphasized by Benessi, was a theme for many other poems. The song, "Solidarity Forever," written in 1912 to the tune of "John Brown's Body," by Ralph Chaplin, is an example:

> When the Union inspiration through the workers' blood shall run
> There can be no power greater anywhere beneath the sun,
> Yet what force on earth is weaker
> Than the feeble strength of one?
> But the Union makes us strong!

Art Shields tells the story of the writing of "Solidarity Forever" in *The Worker,* September 4, 1966. The occasion was a miners' strike in Cabin Creek, West Virginia, in 1912. Another stanza was added in Chicago during another strike some years later, when unity was again the inspiration.

*   *   *

In the *New York Call,* June 15, 1913, there was a poem by Louis Untermeyer, "Caliban in the Coal Mines." One of the stanzas reads as follows:

> God, if you had but the moon
> Stuck in your cap for a lamp,
> Even you'd tire of it soon
> Down in the dark and the damp.

Significant is "The Angel of Discontent," by Sam Walter Foss, in *The New York Call,* December 28, 1913. The opening lines were these: When the world was formed and the morning stars/Upon their paths were sent/The loftiest-browed of the angels was named/The Angel of Discontent./

"Why I am a Revolutionist," by Covington Hall, is in *Songs of Rebellion,* published by the author in 1915, New Orleans. Covington Hall was an IWW poet and organizer, several of whose volumes of verse are in the Labadie Collection, University of Michigan, Ann Arbor. I quote the last three stanzas:

> In these wild and frightful moments, I have felt my reason reel,
> Felt an impulse like the tiger's over all my being steal;
> Felt it would not be a murder if my hand the blow could deal,
> That would brand upon your temple the death angel's mark and
>   seal.
> Then I heard a voice crying, "Workers of the world, Unite!"
> And the vanguard of the Marxians broke upon my hopeless sight,
> Serried ranks of Rebels marching 'neath the crimson flag of right,

To call our class to action, to arouse it to its might.
Thoughts of murder vanished from me and demon ceased to reign,
For the scheme of life unraveled and the universe seemed sane;
And I took my place beside them, here upon Truth's battle plain,
And I stand beside them fighting till the world we lose or gain.

In the *International Socialist Review,* September, 1915, there is a poem by Carl Sandburg about "Billy Sunday". The opening lines are: You come along—tearing your shirt—yelling about Jesus./I want to know what the hell *you* know about Jesus?

In late 1912 Left-wing Socialists launched a fresh Marxist organ named *The New Review.* In its first issue, January 4, 1913, one of its devoted supporters, Bertha W. Howe, contributed a brief poem in a virtual consecration of the newly-born magazine:

The New Review

Soul of the working class
     Which is the life of me—
Strength of the toiling mass,
     Which speeds the heart of me—
Stamp thy evolving will,
     Which is the law of me,
Firm on these pages till
     Earth breathes, 'Equality!'

Charlotte Perkins Gilman, founder and editor of *The Forerunner,* had a poem on "Child Labor" in her December, 1909, issue. Here are two of its nine stanzas:

No fledgling feeds the father-bird!
     No chicken feeds the hen!
No kitten mouses for the cat—
     This glory is for men.
We are the Wisest, Strongest Race—
     Loud may our praise be sung—
The only animal alive
     That feeds upon its young![1]

The socialist writer, Rose Pastor Stokes, has a beautiful five-stanza poem named "The Slave Driver" in the *International Socialist Review,* August, 1912; the opening:

The brazen loud alarmclock whips my brain.
Its lash stings the raw thought. I curse, and rise,

---

1. See another poem by Charlotte Perkins Gilman, "The Socialist and the Suffragette," in VI, "The Battle for Woman Suffrage," herein.

> And drag my bleeding thought thru bogs of pain
> To where the gray mills grin as darkness flies.

While in his cell in Essex County Jail, Lawrence, Massachusetts, the IWW poet Arturo Giovanitti wrote his oft-quoted elegy, "The Walker," which appeared in the *International Socialist Review*, September, 1912. Here are some lines from the final stanza:

> My brother, do not walk any more.
> . . .
> I implore you, my brother, for I am weary of the long vigil, weary
> of counting your steps and heavy with sleep.
> Stop, rest, sleep, my brother, for the dawn is well nigh and it is not
> the key alone that can throw open the door.

"The Drum," by Mary Carolyn Davies—a four-stanza anti-war lyric in the *New York Call*, January 10, 1915—says in its second verse:

> And he doesn't know the reason for it all—
> But not to go is treason when they call,
> The wild and wicked drum, with its 'Come, come, come!'
> And the sun upon the bayonets, and all.

Well-known is "The Preacher and the Slave," Joe Hill's parody of a Christian hymn which was such a favorite of migratory workers in the I.W.W. It opens with the line, "Long-haired preachers come out every night"; I quote the final stanza:

> Workingmen of all countries, unite,
> Side by side we for freedom will fight.
> When the world and its wealth we shall gain
> To the grafters we'll sing this refrain:
> > You will eat, bye and bye,
> > When you've learned how to cook and to fry;
> > Chop some wood, 'twill do you good,
> > And you'll eat in the sweet bye and bye.

Clement Wood, whose textbooks on versification have been popular in recent years, wrote a sonnet which was widely circulated at the time of the Colorado coal strike in 1913-1914. No names are mentioned, but the allusions are clearly to the Rockefeller family. The title is "To a Certain Rich Young Ruler"; the first stanza reads:

> White-fingered lord of murderous events,
> Well are you guarding what your father gained:
> With torch and rifle you have well maintained
> The lot to which a heavenly providence
> Has called you. Laborers, risen in defense
> Of liberty and life, lie charred and brained

About your mines whose gutted hills are stained
With slaughter of these newer innocents.

Daisy Sanial Gill, contributed many poems to Woman's Sphere, of the *New York Call,* edited by Anita Block, and one was inspired by the same events that spurred Clement Wood to address a sonnet to that "Certain Rich Young Ruler." Her poem was titled, "Down With the Guards," and appeared in the *Call* of May 10, 1914, hailing the 80-odd deserters from Company B of the Colorado National Guard. Here is the opening stanza:

Hail and hope, you-men
Who straight became new-men
When ye hissed that mad, black Guard
That had gunned babes and women,
The workers' poor women
With their babes—that dastard Guard!
Think of Calumet—Homestead!
Ever the fight for bread
Ever new-gunned by these Guards;
Now machine-gunned and roasted,
Babes—women! gunned—roasted!
Are we *human?* Down with the Guards!

John G. Neihart's "Cry of the People," included in *The Poetry of Freedom,* surely emphasizes the Class Struggle! For example:

We are the workers and makers!
We are no longer dumb!
Tremble, O Shirkers and Takers!
Sweeping the earth—we come!
Ranked in the world-wide dawn,
Marching into the day!
The night is gone and the sword is drawn
And the scabbard is thrown away!

In July, 1900, Ella Wheeler Wilcox wrote a memorial poem in the Debs Scrapbook (Labor Scrapbook No. 5):

Oh, men bowed down with labor!
Oh, women young, yet old!
Oh, hearts oppressed in the toilers' breast
And crushed by the power of gold!
Keep on with your weary battle
Against triumphant might.
No question is ever settled
Until it is settled right.

As World War I was threatening, Eugene Gladstone O'Neill—known later as Eugene O'Neill, the dramatist—contributed a 19-stanza anti-war poem titled "Fratricide" to *The Call*, May 17, 1914:

> What cause could be more asinine
> 　　Than yours, ye slaves of bloody toil?
> Is not your bravery sublime
> 　　Beneath a tropic sun to broil
> And bleed and groan—for Guggenheim!
> 　　And give your lives for—Standard Oil!
> Comrades, awaken to new birth!
> 　　New values on the tables write!
> What is your vaunted courage worth
> 　　Unless you rise up in your might
> And cry: "All workers on the earth
> 　　Are brothers and we WILL NOT FIGHT!"

"The Female of the Species Speaks" was one of the earlier angry retorts by women, appearing in *The National Rip-Saw*, January, 1912. In it Kate Baker Heltzel replies to Kipling's well-known rhyme on "The Female of the Species." She summarizes as follows:

> Seems to me, that man would profit
> 　　If he took the thing to heart,
> Let him rule himself by all means,
> 　　And the woman rule her part.
> And we would not, if we knew it,
> 　　Dip our pen in blood or gall,
> But we ask for "abstract justice,"
> 　　For our sisters, that is all.
> 　　Half-truths seem to lull some people,
> 　　　　More than beasts we are to be,
> 　　When our brothers wiser growing
> 　　　　Grant to us equality.

Upton Sinclair's lyric, "The Red Flag," which he dedicated to Fred D. Warren, who had been given six months in prison for his protest against the kidnapping of Bill Haywood, appeared in *The Appeal to Reason*, July 17, 1909:

> Tremble, oh masters—tremble all who live by others' toil—
> We come your dungeon walls to raze, your palaces to spoil!
> Yours is the power of club and jail, yours is the axe and fire—
> But ours is the hope of human hearts and the strength of the soul's
> 　　desire!
> Ours is the blazing banner, sweeping the sky along!
> Ours the host, the marching host—hark to our battle song!

Chanting of brotherhood, chanting of freedom, dreaming the world
 to be—
We come in the right of our new-born might to set the people free!

Among other collections of labor and socialist songs, that by Harvey
D. Moyer, *Songs of Socialism,* Chicago, 1911, is outstanding.

American labor history has been unusually rich in its production of
labor songs, as Foner shows in his *History of the Labor Movement in the
United States.* Most of those extant belong to the period of the Workingmen's Party of the United States and the Socialist Labor Party. One of
those cited by Foner is the "Eight-Hour Song,"[2] which goes as follows:

> We mean to make things over;
> We're tired of toil for naught
> But bare enough to live on: never
> an hour for thought.
> We want to feel the sunshine; we
> want to smell the flowers;
> We're sure that God has willed it,
> and we mean to have eight hours.
> We're summoning our forces from
> shipyard, shop and mill:
> Eight hours for work, eight hours
> for rest, eight hours for what we will!

Foner culled this song first from *John Swinton's Paper,* May 16, 1886,
where it appeared at the height of the fight for the Eight-hour Day, a
fight which Marx personally endorsed. In a letter Professor Foner tells me
that the song's author was I. G. Blanchard, and that its first publication
was in the *Workingmen's Advocate,* August 18, 1866.[3]

* * *

"The Rip-Saw Mother Goose," No. 14, copyrighted 1912, was an
effective assault on tradition by a class-conscious rhymester. They were
written by Henry M. Tichenor, and published in a 32-page pamphlet with
line-drawings as illustrations in the usual Mother Goose way. Here are
some examples:

> Old Mother Hubbard went to the cupboard
> To get her a weeny wurst;

---

2. Philip S. Foner, opus cited, Vol. II, p. 103.
3. Professor Foner's letter, dated October 20, 1971, adds: "It was set to music by
the Rev. Jesse H. Jones and was published in the *Labor Standard* of July 21, 1876,
with the music."

The cupboard was bare—no weeny was there—
Morgan had got there first.

. . .

Hey-diddle-diddle the cat and the fiddle,
    Your daddy has got 'em again;
He's votin' to have the wealth he makes
    Belong to other men.

. . .

Big Biz is in the parlor, counting out his boodle;
His wife is in the drawing-room playin' with her poodle;
You are workin' like a mule, contented as a clam,
And everything is lovely and you don't give-a-dam.

. . .

Pluck me and skin me
And lay me down softly,
I'm only a workingman made to be skun;
I'll vote for you, work for you,
Fight for you, die for you,
You beautiful capitalist son-of-a-gun.

Besides revising Mother Goose, the infatiguable Henry M. Tichenor, himself a debater and editor, also experimented with journalistic verse forms of the type used by "Mr. Dooley" and other humorists. In one such effort he took on the "Men and Religion Forward Movement" which was boosted by J. Pierpont Morgan and other millionaires. This one appeared in the January, 1912, *National Rip-Saw:*

> Ho, all ye worn and weary ones in all this blessed land, sing Glory Hallelujah, for Salvation is at hand. Your miseries shall fade away, your troubles all shall hike—Saint Pierpont and his pious bunch are marchin' down the pike. They're comin' with their chloroform and theologic dope and handin' out large packages of holy hot air hope; they'll fill you full of slobberin' hymns and Billy Sunday rot, and teach you how religion means 'contentment with your lot.'

The instances given are only instances, not by any means a complete survey of the Marxist spirit in American verse. They show the creative urge a-borning in the people, and indicate a growing socialist-minded audience in the United States prior to the Bolshevik Revolution.

XI

Art: Marxist Political Cartoons in the United States

There is general agreement, I think, that American political cartooning has been outstanding over the years. The satirical treatment of bossism in the cities and of trusts as an influence in government is a fact of journalistic history.

Notable in all this has been cartooning on the left. The socialist artists of the late 19th and early 20th centuries were particularly good. Ryan Walker, Art Young, Maurice Becker, Rockwell Kent, John Sloan and Robert Minor, to name a few, were powerful in their converging social impact. Donald Drew Egbert, in *Socialism and American Life,* concedes that "Marxism has affected American art to a much greater degree than has utopian socialism."[1]

There was, to be sure, influence from abroad. The British artists, Walter Crane and William Balfour Ker, did a good deal of work for *The Comrade* and other American publications, including the liberal and muckraking journals. But Crane tended to be over-decorative and symbolic, as in his May Day designs; Ker was more vigorous and even violent in his technique, but at the same time his work was over-polished and slick. This is not to deny that Ker was in a way similar to Robert Minor in the vigor of his conception, as shown in his powerful drawing, "From the Depths" (1906).

But American socialist artists contemporary with them were more original and inventive, and more devoted than they to the working class. Compare Ryan Walker and Art Young with Ker, for example. Both Walker and Young dealt almost exclusively with the working class, and with class struggle themes. Ryan Walker originated the series featuring

1. Donald Drew Egbert, *Socialism and American Life,* page 636.

Capitalism: Boo-hoo! These Socialists are going to take all my property away from me!

Art Young in *The Red Portfolio* (1912)

What Would His Chances be in a Court of Today

Ryan Walker in *The Red Portfolio* (1912)

A Suggestion for the Average Man's Epitaph

Art Young in *The Red Portfolio* (1912)

THE COMRADE.

No. 9.   Vol. II.

THE COMRADE

UNCLE SAM: "I've had a good many doses of that stuff already, but it don't cure."

Ryan Walker in *The Comrade* (May, 1903)

The Farmer: "Well, I'll just turn things over with this spade."

Ryan Walker in *The Red Portfolio* (1912)

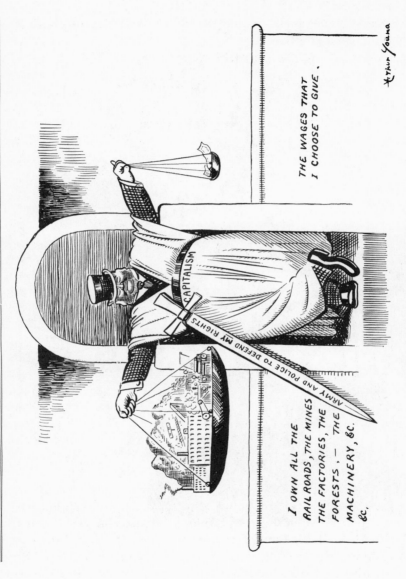

The Capitalist's Idea of Perfect Justice

Art Young in *The Red Portfolio* (1912)

"Henry Dubb," the worker who is always foolishly taken in by capitalist propaganda. Art Young was the sardonic creator of "The Poor Fish," another worker who tragically and comically goes through life without seeing how asinine he is in refusing socialism. Additionally, both Ryan Walker and Art Young were magnificent caricaturists.

Ryan Walker was born in Springfield, Kentucky, in 1870, and aside from contributions to *Life* and *Judge,* is known chiefly for his drawings in the *Appeal to Reason* and the *New York Call,* both being socialist newspapers. He is called by B. O. Flower, in the *Arena,* April, 1905, "A Cartoonist of Social Protest." Memorable, furthermore, are the many caricatures of well-known socialist men and women which he drew for the *Call,* notably entire pages in the issues of July 7, 1912, and December 7, 1913.[2]

Maurice Becker, who chummed with Ryan Walker in New York in the days of World War I, was born in 1889 in Novgorod, Russia—also the birthplace of Maxim Gorki—and grew up in the United States. As a conscientious objector, he served a term in Leavenworth Prison. Becker contributed drawings to the socialist press, beginning as early as 1911 in *The Coming Nation.* In a letter to the present writer dated January 24, 1961, Becker describes Ryan Walker thus: "A slight sprightly man, graying abundant hair, once sandy perhaps. Blue twinkling eyes behind glasses. As others of the fraternity, he wore a Windsor tie. A quality of gaiety hovered over him."

Walker and Becker were among the early contributors and founders of the *Masses* (1912), along with Art Young, Rockwell Kent, and John Sloan. The first International Show of Modern Art, known as the Armory Show, was held in New York in 1913, and socialist artists were prominent and influential in it. These Marxist artists worked also for the commercial press. Becker was on the staff of the *New York Tribune* (Karl Marx's old paper), and, later, the *New York World,* as well as the socialist *New York Call.*

John Sloan was basically a painter rather than a cartoonist, but as a conscientious Socialist Party member from 1908 onward, he did cartoons for socialist papers whenever requested to do so. In *John Sloan: A Painter's Life,* Van Wyck Brooks records that "On the Socialist ticket he ran for the Assembly in 1908 and six years later for a judgeship." Sloan, the story continues, "introduced speakers at socialist street meetings—on one occasion in Wall Street at the corner of Broad." He not only drew cartoons for the *Call,* but illustrations for socialist writer Ernest Poole whose stories appeared in the *Saturday Evening Post.* Sloan was abetted,

2. *N. Y. Call,* July 7, p. 7, and December 7, 1913, p. 9.

says Brooks, "by his wife, the tiny, devoted, bellicose, emotional Dolly." She—whose real name was Anna M. Sloan—sold literature at socialist mass meetings, and was generally active in all Jimmie Higgins duties.

Sloan's notable painting, "Backyards: Greenwich Village," executed in 1914, was acquired by the Whitney Museum of American Art in 1936. It was perhaps this work that led some cranky critic to say that Sloan belonged to the "ashcan school."

The Socialist Party election records at the Tamiment Library show that on August 24, 1912, the Socialist Party Committee of the 25th Assembly District "was called to order by John Sloan, the Chairman." When nominations were called for member of Assembly, "to be voted for by the enrolled Socialist Party voters at the official Primary to be held on the 17th of September, 1912 . . . John Sloan, residing at 155 East 22nd Street, City of New York, was nominated."

On the "Committee to fill vacancies," the name of "Arthur Young, residing at 9 East 17th Street," was included—the artist known to history as *Art Young.* He was candidate for Assemblyman from the 27th District of New York County in 1913. It is interesting that Art Young became a socialist—as he says in his autobiography, *Art Young: His Life and Times*—when he was "past forty years of age."[3] Like Ryan Walker, he made much of his living by contributing to *Life* and *Judge.*

I never knew Ryan Walker or John Sloan personally, but I did meet Art Young—at least once. It was on the 14th Street corner of Broadway and Union Square, and Young was waving to me from the northeast corner, and actually skipping kitty-corner across toward me, as I stood a few yards from the northwest corner. He introduced himself as Art Young, and said he had a sketch which he had done of Charles E. Ruthenberg at the latter's trial. Somehow or other he knew who I was and knew I was doing a Ruthenberg biography. He was then 86 years old.

Art Young's drawings have in the main been saved. He sketched the Haymarket martyrs in jail in 1886, and never missed a proletarian protest or a working class battle against bosses from that year to 1955, the day I met him.

It took forty years for Art Young to become a conscious Marxist, but the socialism of Rockwell Kent came to him in his early youth. I heard him speak on June 16, 1961, at a tribute in his honor at the Belmont Plaza Hotel, when he declared, "I was a socialist in my teens, and I'm a socialist now." A letter from him to this writer, written from Au Sable, New York, January 21, 1961, says: "I bought a copy of *Das Kapital*

3. *Art Young: His Life and Times,* page 269. Art Young's autobiography was edited by John Nicholas Beffel, 1939.

around 1902, shortly after its publication by Kerr. As with Darwin's *The Origin of Species,* I read but a little way in *Das Kapital* to recognize that here was the truth." He adds that he joined the Socialist Party when he was twenty, and among his friends were Horace Traubel, the associate of Walt Whitman; William English Walling, a prominent Socialist Party leader; and Rufus W. Weeks, a millionaire who called himself a Christian Socialist and who gave financial help to Piet Vlag, the founder of the *Masses.*

"I voted consistently for Debs," Kent declared, in this letter, "from my first vote to Debs' final retirement—which followed, I believe, his candidacy while in prison."[4]

Robert Minor, implacable satirist of two eras, was born in Texas in 1884, and had his share of cartoons in the socialist press of the pre-Bolshevik years, especially in the *Masses.* Although Minor began as an anarchist rather than a socialist, his caustic pencil assailed the Socialist Party's capitalist enemies, and its products found ready space in Left publications. His skill at character portraiture was shown in the commercial press too, as in the *St. Louis Post-Dispatch* of January 7, 1912, when he caricatured the beef packers on trial.[5]

Thanks to Minor, we also have a splendid drawing of Boardman Robinson, one of the *Masses'* outstanding aritsts.[6]

At this point there should be noted an art event of historic importance, namely, the publication of the *RED PORTFOLIO,* an anthology of socialist cartoons by socialist artists, selected from *The Appeal to Reason* and *The Coming Nation,* and brought out in Girard, Kansas. The book is undated, but Lee Baxandall's *Marxism and Aesthetics* (Humanities Press, New York, 1968, p. 179), gives the year as 1912, the year Socialist movement reached its highest point, before 1917, measured by the recorded vote of nearly a million for Eugene V. Debs for president.

This collection, as stated in the catalog of the Tamiment Library, includes works by "Ryan Walker, Art Young, Walter Crane, Balfour Ker, and other cartoonists." The Introduction is by Eugene V. Debs, accompanied by a short note by A. M. Simons. This is believed to be the first published compilation of Marxist cartoons in this country. Since 1917 there have, to be sure, been several, notably by *The Toiler* and *The Daily Worker,* but the *Red Portfolio* was the earliest.

Wilshire's Magazine, a privately owned socialist publication, featured the cartoons of F. Opper, which excoriated the trusts in the issue of July, 1902, p. 84. The originals had appeared in the *New York Journal.* In

4. See also, *It's Me, O Lord,* 1960, Rockwell Kent's autobiography.
5. See *Robert Minor: Artist and Crusader,* by Joseph North, 1956, p. 54.
6. Ibid., p. 65.

October, 1902, *Wilshire's* praised Opper as "A cartoonist of the people," and quoted a signed letter from that artist as saying, "I get your magazine regularly, and value it highly, and like to see my cartoons copied in it." In the same issue an Opper cartoon from the *New York American* satirized the Trusts, accompanied by a rhymed caption headed, "The Charge of the Trust Brigade."

Opper illustrated books by Bill Nye, Mark Twain, and Finley P. Dunne, and created such comic characters as Happy Hooligan. One of his Center Shot Leaflets showed "Socialism" as arrows hitting the bull's eye of the target labeled "Capitalism." Another of his anti-Trust drawings has the following caption:

"When will the little fellow quit pulling the capitalist load and begin pushing the Co-operative Commonwealth for himself? It is either pull or push. Take your choice and get busy. . . . Socialism is worth pushing."

Like Opper, Gordon Nye was also a liberal artist influenced by the socialist philosophy. In *The Call* for Sunday, February 21, 1915, Magazine Section, Gordon Nye has a cartoon showing *The Call* as The Statue of Liberty holding her torch to enlighten the world. The caption says: "Stop giving your support to the press of the enemy. Give your pennies to *your* press. Put your oil in your own lamp to light your own way."

In the Midwest, a lone socialist artist established his own publishing company and art school in Kalamazoo, Michigan. One of his first Center Shot Leaflets bore the slogan, "Workingmen of All Countries, Unite, You have nothing to lose but your chains.—Marx." There is a drawing of a worker and a farmer shaking hands, with a disappointed capitalist scowling in the background. The signature on the drawing is *G. H. Lockwood, 1901.* The accompanying discussion concludes with these words: "The political interests of all workingmen are identical and are represented by the Socialist Party." One of the many issues of Lockwood's magazine carries a letter beginning, "My dear Lockwood" and ending "E. V. Debs." The date is January 18, 1913.[7] Some of the titles of this homespun socialist magazine were as follows: "The Priest and the Billy Goat"; "Pa and Young America"; "The Prophet and the Ass," all illustrated by himself. Lockwood says that he joined the socialist movement in 1897.

To deal briefly with half a dozen socialist cartoonists—including some on the rim of the movement—and not mention the scores of others is perhaps a disservice both to those omitted and to art history. But mere mention is as far as I can go, for my purpose is only to show Marxist influence, not to offer a cyclopaedia of Marx-influenced artists.

---

7. The Lockwood pamphlets are in the Tamiment Library, New York City, formerly the Rand School Library.

I must, however, add to the previous reference to Boardman Robinson the name of Henry Glintenkamp, a prominent contributor to the *Masses;* and also, finally, the name of Hugo Gellert, who was younger than most of the others, but nonetheless managed to be represented in the *Masses* as early as June, 1916.[8]

The accompanying illustrations show one thing clearly: The power of Marxism, in a situation of social conflict, to bring to fruition an artist's genius.

8. *Masses*, June, 1916, p. 13.

XII

Marxism in American Academic and Scientific Thought

The scholar and philosopher, Karl Marx, was a product of European academic culture. Lenin has shown this in pointing out that Marxism grew out of Germany's idealist philosophy (Hegel and his followers), France's Restoration historiography (Thierry, Guizot, and others), and Britain's capitalist economics (Adam Smith, Ricardo, and others). It was early capitalist university study that formed the soil and produced the seed which—through the alchemy of this man's genius—grew into scientific socialist theory.

We should therefore expect that American university culture and American science would likewise produce something in the way of social thought to accompany or confirm Marxism, and exactly that has resulted, though in a limited fashion, in the pre-1917 period that we are examining.

I) First was the notable anthropologist, Lewis Henry Morgan (1818-1881), author of *Ancient Society,* first published in 1877. People may forget that Morgan was president of the American Association for the Advancement of Science, and that he founded its Anthropology subsection. (See Eleanor Burke Leacock's new edition of *Ancient Society,* with her annotations, 1963, Meridian Books.) Objectively, Morgan was a co-worker of Marx rather than a scientist *influenced by* Marx. Morgan's work became a genuine part of Marxism through Engels' brilliant interpretation of it in *The Origin of the Family, Private Property and the State.* This fact gives United States science a real share in Marxist theory, and our pride in it is pardonable.

II) Among Marx-influenced scholars in this country, let us start with C.

Osborne Ward (1831-1902), author of *The Ancient Lowly,* a two-volume work privately printed by the author in 1888 and re-published by C. H. Kerr & Company in Chicago in 1907. Osborne Ward, like Lewis Henry Morgan, was not a university professor, but carried on his studies unofficially, in the seclusion of his own home. Professionally, he was a newspaper correspondent and editor (Morgan was a lawyer). It must also be remembered that Ward was an American member of the First International, and that he took part in the December 17th, 1871, New York demonstration in honor of the Paris Commune.[1] His work was an immense collection of records and artifacts of ancient times, designed to reveal the basis for the Marxian interpretation of history and the upward progress of mankind. Incidentally, he was an older brother of the well-known sociologist, Lester F. Ward. (See discussion below.)

III) Among scientists, most notable in this connection was Charles Proteus Steinmetz (1865-1923), the "Electrical Wizard" of Rochester, New York, a lifetime socialist and a glory to all other American revolutionists. The *New York Call* of July 26, 1914, carried an illustrated feature piece on Steinmetz. He ran for municipal office as a socialist, was elected, and served. Most significant is the fact that some five years later Steinmetz corresponded with Lenin and offered advice on the latter's project for the electrification of Russia.

IV) Lester F. Ward (1841-1913), younger brother of C. Osborne Ward, was a prominent university sociologist at the turn of the century, and his social criticism often paralleled that of the socialists. "There is no doubt of the 'left wing' quality of the sociologists," wrote Charles Hunt Page, in his *Class and American Sociology: From Ward to Ross* (1940), "if by that is meant their recognition of the significance of class divisions and conflicts in community life." Arthur Morrow Lewis, a prominent speaker on the Socialist Lyceum Bureau, gave entire lectures on Ward's writings with the questionable claim—since Ward was *not* a Marxist—that they demonstrated the truth of socialism. Ward boldly used socialistic phraseology, as for example the sub-title of his famous *Applied Sociology: a Treatise on the Conscious Improvement of Society by Society,* published in 1908. It recalls the earlier and more famous phrase of Engels about humanity's "leap from the realm of necessity into the realm of freedom."[2]

1. See *The First International in America,* by Samuel Bernstein, Augustus M. Kelley, New York, 1962.
2. See Frederick Engels' *Anti-Duhring,* International Publishers edition, pp. 311-312. The whole passage (after the "seizure of the means of production by society") is

V) Henry Demarest Lloyd (1847-1903), publicist and economist, was author of an outstanding and indeed historic work, *Wealth Against Commonwealth* (1894). In it he pilloried great wealth, and exposed its crimes, with documentation. His own research led him toward Marxism, and only his untimely death kept him from carrying out his intention of joining the Socialist Party, as shown by his son-in-law, Harvey O'Connor, in a memorial essay, "Henry Demarest Lloyd: The Prophetic Tradition," an essay in Harvey Goldberg's *American Radicals* (1957). A manuscript found on Lloyd's desk, dated June 4, 1903, was entitled "Why I Join the Socialists."

VI) Gustavus Myers (1872-1964), a socialist himself, was the author of the mammoth *History of Great American Fortunes* (1910), and thereby he supplied the factual ammunition of polemical war to other socialist writers. His work has since been imitated and doubtless improved, and certainly brought up to date, by other researchers, notably Ferdinand Lundberg in his *America's Sixty Families* (1946), and Matthew Josephson in *The Robber Barons* (1934).

VII) Another socialist writer, A. M. Simons (1870-1950), who was for years editor of *The International Socialist Review,* produced *Class Struggles in America,* published by C. H. Kerr & Company, Chicago, in 1903. He revised and enlarged it and brought it out again in 1914 under the new title of *Social Forces in American History,* published this time by Mac-Millan, New York. Simons attempted with some success (and a number of shortcomings) to interpret United States history in Marxist terms.

VIII) Richard T. Ely (1854-1943), a Christian Socialist was fairly knowledgeable about Marx, considering the period in which he wrote. In *Recent American Socialism,* published in the John Hopkins University Studies in 1885, he refers to two parties: the "Socialist Labor Party" and the "International Working People's Association," the latter described as anarchists. [This "International" was an American grouping, not to be confused with the original Marx-led International Workingmen's Association.] Commenting, Ely says: "It may be stated that in general the teachings of Carl (sic) Marx are accepted by both parties [not accurate, of

___

as follows: "The objective, external forces which have hitherto dominated history, will then pass under the control of men themselves. It is only from this point that men, with full consciousness, will fashion their own history: it is only from this point that the social causes set in motion by men will have, predominantly and in constantly increasing measure, the effects willed by men. It is humanity's leap from the realm of necessity into the realm of freedom."

course] and his work on capital (*Das Kapital*) is still the bible of the Socialists. This work has not yet been translated into English, although a translation is announced for the near future; but extracts from it have been turned into our tongue and published, and brochures, pamphlets, newspaper and verbal expositions have extended his doctrines, while H. M. Hyndman (1842-1921, British socialist leader) has expounded the views of the great teacher in his *Historical Bases of Socialism* in England."

Herbert Aptheker in his "Marx and American Scholarship", first published in 1954, has provided material relevant to this chapter.* I shall therefore take the liberty of merging the results of my research with his, quoting from him at times, thereby enriching this discussion.

Dr. Aptheker's essay covers six outstanding figures in the social sciences and their individual attitudes toward Marx and Marxism, as follows: Charles A. Beard (1874-1948); John R. Commons (1862-1945); James Harvey Robinson (1863-1936); E. R. A. Seligman (1861-1939); Albion W. Small (1854-1926); and Thorstein Veblen (1857-1929).

Aptheker comments briefly on the distinguished character of these six scholars: Beard was a foremost historian, Veblen a foremost economist; Small was founder of the *American Journal of Sociology,* and for a long time its editor; Robinson, a professor of history at Columbia University, was a president of the American Historical Association; Commons was a professor of economics at the University of Wisconsin for nearly thirty years; Seligman, a professor of economics at Columbia University for forty-five years, editor of the *Political Science Quarterly,* and a president of the American Economic Association.

"All these great scholars," says Aptheker, "repeatedly referred in their lectures and writings to the ideas of Karl Marx, and—as befitted their stature—did not fail to mention explicitly the name of the man whose ideas they were considering or using. They were not themselves Marxists, but always they dealt with Marx respectfully and with a sense of responsibility. They did not use Marxism as an epithet; rather they treated it as one of the great seminal systems of world thought."

IX) Professor John R. Commons, editor of the many-volumed *Documentary History of American Industrial Society,* took part in a discussion of "Social Evolution" in the *International Socialist Review,* April, 1901.[3] While he was critical of the socialist philosophy, he conceded the following: "We may faithfully accept the theory that monopoly is inevitable and perpetual and therefore that freedom will be secured only through

*Reprinted in *The Era of McCarthyism* (New York, 1960, Humanities Press)
   3. *The International Socialist Review,* April, 1901, p. 608.

state ownership and operation." He adds that "the goal will not be reached except by participation of working people in their proportionate share of control over the legislative, administrative and judicial branches of government."

In his *Documentary History* Professor Commons surveyed utopian socialism and labor conditions in 19th century United States with an observant and critical eye, and left very useful records of the social currents he found. On his staff, incidentally, was Helen L. Sumner, an out-and-out Socialist Party member, belonging to a local in Washington, D. C.[4]

Aptheker found that Professor Commons, many years later, climaxed his career by a critique of "Marx Today" in the *Atlantic Monthly*, November, 1925. What he said was this: "Karl Marx, the founder of materialistic socialism, is recognized by economists as one of the three or four greatest minds who have contributed to the progress of economic science."

X) E. R. A. Seligman of Columbia University wrote *The Economic Interpretation of History,* first published in 1902. This was his understanding of what Marx called the "Materialist Conception of History." Seligman was following the Socialist Party's use of the phrase, "Economic Determinism," which was a softened form of the original term. Regardless of our estimate of Seligman's exposition, we must note that his estimate of Marx was very high. He asserts that the future historian "will be compelled to assign to Karl Marx a far more prominent place than has hitherto been customary outside of the narrow ranks of the socialists themselves." Continuing, he adds: "Marx will long be remembered as one of those great pioneers who, even if they are not able themselves to reach the goal, nevertheless blaze out a new and promising path in the wilderness of human thought and human progress."[5]

Aptheker notes that later in the same volume, speaking of Marx's philosophy of history, Seligman states: "Whether or not we are prepared to accept it as an adequate explanation of human progress in general, we must all recognize the beneficent influence that it has exerted in stimulating the thoughts of scholars and in broadening the concepts and the ideals of history and economics alike. If for no other reason, it will

4. Helen L. Sumner (Helen L. Sumner Woodbury): Her first book, *The White Slave* (1896), was brought out by the socialist publishing house, C. H. Kerr & Company, Chicago.

5. E. R. A. Seligman, *The Economic Interpretation of History*, 1902, pp. 162-163.

deserve well of future investigators and will occupy an honored place in the record of mental development and scientific progress."

XI) Charles A. Beard, proceeding in the footsteps of Professor Seligman, wrote *An Economic Interpretation of the Constitution of the United States,* published in 1913. He refers to President James Madison's well-known comment about the two classes in society—those with and those *without* property—and the likelihood that a conflict between them would come about in the future.

Said Madison: "The most common and durable source of factions has been the various and unequal distribution of property. Those who hold and those who are without property have ever formed distinct classes in society. Those who are creditors, and those who are debtors, fall under a like discrimination. A landed interest, a manufacturing interest, a mercantile interest, a moneyed interest, with many lesser interests, grow up of necessity in civilized nations and divide them into different classes, actuated by different sentiments and views."

Professor Beard declared this a "masterly statement of the theory of economic determinism"—which, as indicated above, was the softened phrase socialists used at that time as a substitute for Marx's *dialectic materialism.*

Stopping for a moment, we find on page 6 of Beard's book, in a surprising footnote, that "There are three works by socialist writers that deserve study: [A. M.] Simons, *Social Forces in America,* Gustavus Myers' *History of Great American Fortunes* and [his] *History of the Supreme Court."* This afterthought, in the form of a footnote, further attests, as the reader will observe, to socialist influence in Beard's thinking.

Incidentally, the first scholar to call attention to President Madison's axiom about class interests was Daniel De Leon, who eventually became the leader of the Socialist Labor Party. His essay, "The Voice of Madison," appeared in *The Nationalist,* August, 1889, a magazine which supported the views of Edward Bellamy, author of *Looking Backward* (1887). "Madison . . ."wrote De Leon, "was an honest, as well as earnest and profound thinker, peering deep into the future in order to foresee his country's trials and, if possible, smooth her path. Let us then enrich the discussion with the learning of this distinguished Revolutionary Father and give ear to the voice of Madison."

De Leon noted Madison's justified fear that "the class of the propertiless in the United States would increase from generation to generation" and would swell into a great majority. It was thus "a steady progress toward poverty" that Madison foresaw. And he foresaw therewith the danger of revolt and the need to make government changes to forestall that danger.

Aptheker, in the cited work, pointed out that Beard, after expressing points of disagreement with Marx, added: "Yet I freely pay tribute to the amazing range of Marx's scholarship and the penetrating character of his thought." Beard summed up in our own time as follows: "However much one may dislike Marx's personal views, one cannot deny to him wide and deep knowledge—and a fearless and sacrificial life. He not only interpreted history, as everyone does who writes any history, but he helped to make history. Possibly he may have known something. At least the contemporary student, trying to look coldly and impartially on thought and thinkers in the field of historiography, may learn a little bit at least, from Karl Marx." (*American Historical Review,* October, 1935.)

XII) Professor Albion W. Small was a very earnest student of Marx and of Marxist socialism, gathering intensity as he went on from a modest beginning. In *An Introduction to the Study of Society* by himself and George E. Vincent, published in 1894, this elementary statement is made: "Socialism is nevertheless a challenge which society cannot ignore. If the evils alleged by Socialism do not exist, the charges must be refuted. If they do exist, their cause must be discovered. If actual social evils are due to conditions which society can control, social programmes must be adopted accordingly." While Professor Small headed the department of sociology in the University of Chicago, he published his *General Sociology,* 1905, and *Between Eras: From Capitalism to Democracy,* 1913, progressing gradually to socialistic ideas.

"At Chicago," says Page in the work cited above, "Small conducted seminars on Marxism and class conflict." He also, Page adds, gave a course on "The Conflict of Classes." Small is quoted by both Page and Aptheker as having stated the following: "Marx was one of the few really great thinkers in the history of social science. His repute thus far has been that of every challenger of tradition. All the conventional, the world over, from the multitude of intellectual nonentities to thinkers whose failure to acknowledge in him more than a peer has seriously impeached their candor, have implicitly conspired to smother his influence by all the means known to obscurantism. From outlawry to averted glances, every device of repression and misrepresentation has been employed against him. . . .

"He is worthy of the most respectful treatment which thinkers can pay to another thinker whose argument has never been successfully answered. . . .

"I confidently predict that in the ultimate judgment of history, Marx will have a place in social science analogous with that of Galileo in physical science. . . ."

The above is an excerpt from Small's forthright essay, "Socialism in the Light of Social Science," in the *American Journal of Sociology,* May, 1912. The theme of the essay was this sentence: "Socialism has been the most wholesome ferment in modern society."

XIII) Thorstein Veblen, author of *The Theory of the Leisure Class,* which was first published in 1899 and re-published in 1912, never publicly aligned himself with Marxists, but A. K. Davis, in his essay, "Thorstein Veblen and the Culture of Capitalism," in Goldberg's *American Radicals* cited above, argues, "The core of Veblen's social theory is largely Marxian," and "Veblen's foundation consists of his insistence on change as the prime reality of social life. . . ." Davis also comments: "His terminology is entirely un-Marxian. But the biographical evidence is overwhelming that Veblen became permanently and intensely interested in Marxism early in his career." Finally Davis asks if it is not time "to acknowledge Veblen as a notable and original contributor to Marxian tradition?"

Paul M. Sweezy, in an essay, "The Influence of Marxism on Thorstein Veblen," in *Socialism and American Life* (1952), edited by Donald Drew Egbert and Stow Persons, agrees. Sweezy states that "the weight of evidence indicates that Marxism was one of the decisive factors shaping his thought." Veblen was, Sweezy adds, "a good deal more sympathetic to socialism than he was to the order of society under which he lived."

I quote the following on Veblen from Aptheker's cited essay, "Marx and American Scholarship":

> Thorstein Veblen, in a series of articles entitled "The Socialist Economics of Karl Marx and His Followers," felt it necessary to tell the academicians reading the *Quarterly Journal of Economics,* that Marx was to be studied with great care and attention, that he was "neither ignorant, imbecile or disingenuous" and that: "There is no system of economic theory more logical than that of Marx" (issues of August 1906 and February 1907). Joseph Dorfman, in his definitive biography of Veblen (Viking Press, 1935), cites Veblen's remark that Marx was "coming to be more widely appreciated as he becomes better understood." To his students, Veblen would often say, Professor Dorfman records, "Read Marx. Uncover the roots of the problem."

XIV) James Harvey Robinson gave what might be called a panegyric on

Marx in his *History,* Columbia University Press, 1908. The following passage from that work is cited by Aptheker:

> "It was a philosopher, economist and reformer, not a professional student of history, who suggested a wholly new and wonderful series of questions which the historian might properly ask about the past, and moreover furnished him with a scientific explanation of many matters hitherto ill-understood. I mean Karl Marx."

XV) Dr. W. E. B. Du Bois (1868-1963), American scholar, historian and innovator in social studies, has been discussed in this book in another connection, but his stature in all fields requires that he be at least listed in this chapter also. As already noted, he joined the Socialist Party in 1911, and was a critical contributor to Marxist discussion ever since. In his remarkable *Autobiography* (1968), he complains of the absence of reference to Marx in Harvard classrooms, and looking back, he says: "I began to read Karl Marx. I was astounded and wondered what other areas of learning had been roped off from my mind in the days of my 'broad' education." It was a matter of pride to him that, in London, the sculptor Lawrence Bradshaw, who had done "the great head of Karl Marx, did my head." In 1961 he joined the Communist Party.

XVI) Roy Wood Sellars (1880-   ) of the University of Michigan had an article in the socialist *New York Call,* May 25, 1913, on the topic, "Incentive to Labor." Professor Sellars—who joined the Department of Philosophy at Ann Arbor in 1905, becoming an assistant professor in 1913—refers to slavery and serfdom, where the incentive was "obvious," then to capitalism. Under capitalism, he points out, the incentive was low wages and high wages, which also was not particularly idealistic. Sellars argues that there may be higher motives, for "man is what he is made by his social and economic conditions." This was the rather diffident beginning of a genuinely honest academician interested in socialism.

Three years later, Sellars published *The Next Step in Democracy* (1916), in which he begins by saying: "I presume that every young man of today who has the capacity to be attracted by the thought of a juster and humaner world than that visible around us has been drawn in some manner toward socialism." In his discussion, Sellars does not ignore Marxism. On the contrary, he puts utopian socialism in the first stage, historically, and Marxism in the second. "Marxian socialism, on the other hand," he writes, "represents just the beginning of reflective analysis." Thus, while he does not *advocate* Marxism, he gives it a place of honor.

Professor Sellars, in effect, endorses Marx's call to workers to unite for victory, "on the true principle that the people must help to emancipate themselves." Hence, he argues, "In this realistic and democratic attitude rather than in its economic theories lies the permanent contributions which Marxianism [has] made." Sellars endorses socialism's central aim: "Finally," he writes, "socialism hopes to bring in its wake a society healthier physically and morally, and one ever more capable of developing sane and progressive institutions."

In later years, Sellars taught a course labeled "A Critical Examination of Socialism." He called himself personally a Guild Socialist, which took him from socialist politics to a mild form of syndicalism. It is interesting to note that Corliss Lamont, formerly of Columbia, in *The Philosophy of Humanism* (1949), credits Sellars with drawing up the first draft of the Humanist Manifesto of 1933. The Marxist theories he studied in pre-1917 years surely helped to shape his humanist beliefs and ideals.

Sellars' latest book—an autobiography—is entitled *Still Alive* (1968), a title which fits socialism as well as his term of existence.

XVII) Scott Nearing (1883-   ), who taught economics at the University of Pennsylvania until he was fired for anti-war teaching and radicalism, was a notable University advocate for socialism. He lectured at the Rand School, wrote pamphlets which the Socialist Party press published, and produced a most important study of monopoly, *Anthracite,* in 1915. He is the best-known academic figure of pre-1917 years who directly and openly supported the Marxist philosophy as taught by the Socialist Party. He has had an enormous influence. His autobiography, *The Making of a Radical* (1972), tells the story of a consistent activist and near-Marxist.

XVIII) Alexander Meiklejohn (1872-1964), a notable educator and scholar-liberal, looking back over a long life, summed up his impression of Marxism in response to an inquiry from the present writer. "I had an early affiliation with the Intercollegiate Socialist Society," he wrote, in a letter dated November 1, 1961, "but was not, as I recall, a member; I read a good deal of the fundamental literature and kept touch with current discussion. Yes, I am sure that the Marxist ideas influenced me, as they did my associates, so that, in attitude, I have regarded myself as a Socialist."[6]

Reflection will show, I think, that the stream of Marxist theory was a seminal and an abiding stimulus to American intellectuals through the last quarter of the 19th century and the first seventeen years of the 20th.

---

6. Written from the Hotel Adams, New York, where Professor Meiklejohn was staying for a few days, while attending a conference on socialism.

APPENDIX A

Platform of the Socialistic Labor Party

(adopted at National Convention, held in Allegheny, Pa.,
December 26, 1879 through January 1, 1880; published in
Detroit, Michigan, April, 1880)

Labor being the creator of all wealth, through and by it alone is
organized society and civilization possible. It rightfully follows that those
who labor and create all wealth are the most important part of society,
and hence should enjoy the full results of their toil; and we declare

That a just and equitable distribution of the fruits of labor is utterly
impossible under the present system of society. This fact is abundantly
illustrated by the deplorable condition of the working classes, who are in
a state of destitution and degrading dependence in the midst of their own
productions. While the hardest and most disagreable work brings to the
worker only the bare necessaries of life, others, who labor not at all, riot
in labor's production and everything that wealth can purchase; and we
declare

That the present industrial system of competition causes and intensi-
fies this inequality, concentrating into the hands of a few all means of
production, distribution and the results of labor, thus creating gigantic
monopolies dangerous to the people's liberties; and we further declare

That these monster monopolies and these extremes of rich and poor
are the natural outgrowths of the industrial system, supported by class
legislation, and are subversive of all democracy, injurious to the national
interests and destructive of all truth and morality. This state of affairs,
continued and upheld by the now ruling political parties, is against the
welfare of the people, and as the emancipation of the working classes
must be achieved by the working classes themselves, it now becomes their
duty to unite as a powerful labor party to free themselves from all forms
of tyranny and an unjust system.

For these reasons the Socialistic Labor Party has been founded, and in order to ameliorate the condition of the working people under the present system, we present the following platform and demands:

The material condition of the working people in all civilized countries is identical and results from the same causes, consequently the struggle for the emancipation of labor is international and naturally cooperative and mutual.

The wages system has become destructive of the highest interests of mankind, and to abolish this system, with a view to establish cooperative production and to secure equitable distribution, we demand that the resources of life, the means of production, public transportation and exchange, become as fast as practicable, the public property of the people under administration of the government.

Demands

First. Entire revision of the United States Constitution so as to institute direct popular legislation, and enable the people to propose or reject any law at their will, and thus secure self-government.

Second. The right of suffrage shall in no wise be abridged.

Third. Political equality before the law, of all citizens, without regard to creed, race or sex.

Fourth. The establishment of a national ministry of labor.

Fifth. All conspiracy laws operating against the rights of workingmen must be repealed.

Sixth. Congress shall provide for the immediate creation of a national bureau of labor statistics.

Seventh. The rigid enforcement of the eight hour law in all national public works. We also demand an amendment to the Constitution of the United States declaring eight hours a legal work day in all industrial employments.

Eighth. All uncultivated lands shall be taxed equally with cultivated lands in the same locality.

Ninth. The government alone shall issue all money, and such right should not be delegated to any banking or private corporation.

The Socialistic Labor Party struggles to carry out the following measures in those States where they are not now the law:

First. State bureaux of labor statistics.

Second. Eight hours as a legal working day, and strict punishment of all violators.

Third. Abolition of the system of hiring out by contract the labor of convicts in prisons and reformatory institutions.

Fourth. Strict laws making employers liable for all accidents resulting from their negligence to the injury of their employes.

Fifth. Entire legal restriction of the labor of children under fourteen years of age.

Sixth. Universal compulsory education; all schooling material to be furnished at public expense.

Seventh. Factory, mine and workshop inspection, and sanitary supervision of all food and dwellings.

Eighth. All wages shall be paid in the legal tender of the land, and violations of this law must be punished.

Ninth. All ballots to be printed by town and city governments. Ballots containing the names of all candidates for public office to be sent to all voters two days before each election, and all election days to be legal holidays.

Tenth. All property, whether used for religious or secular purposes, to bear its just proportion of taxation.

Resolutions

1st—Resolved, We favor the organization of national and international trade and labor unions for the protection of workingmen, and advise our members to assist and join them, and that in resisting aggressive capital we give to labor, exploited under whatever form, our full sympathy, and, according to our means, our material support.

2nd—Resolved, All so-called tramp laws punishing unemployed workingmen as tramps are unconstitutional and inhuman, as poverty is thereby made a crime, therefore we demand their repeal.

WHEREAS, Twenty-two different railroad corporations have failed to comply with the conditions under which they have received land grants aggregating over 125,000,000 acres, comprising an area of territory larger than nearly a dozen States, and

WHEREAS, Millions of the citizens of the United States are struggling for a bare existence, unable to procure homes and a competence, and

WHEREAS, Said railroad land grants would furnish farms of fifty acres to over five millions of our citizens, therefore be it

RESOLVED, We call upon the Representatives of the people in the Congress of the United States to revoke the charters of these railroad corporations and reclaim the land granted under them for the exclusive use, benefit and occupancy of the people.

WHEREAS, The so-called Democrats (landlords) of the South have joined hands with the so-called Republicans, (capitalists) of the North; and

Whereas, This combination of the wealthy men, both North and South, is made for the sole purpose of destroying the liberties of the common people of both sections of our country; therefore, be it

Resolved, That we urge the working people of the South, regardless of color, to unite with their brothers of the North against the attempts of the ruling class to further impoverish and enslave them by depriving them of the possession and enjoyment of the fruits of their labor.

APPENDIX B

Platform of the Socialist Party: 1901

(Adopted at a convention held in Indianapolis,
July 29-31, 1901)

The Socialist Party, in National convention assembled, reaffirms its adherence to the principles of International Socialism, and declares its aim to be the organization of the working class, and those in sympathy with it, into a political party, with the object of conquering the powers of government and using them for the purpose of transforming the present system of private ownership of the means of production and distribution into collective ownership by the entire people.

Formerly the tools of production were simple and owned by the individual worker. To-day the machine, which is an improved and more developed tool of production, is owned by the capitalists and not by the workers. This ownership enables the capitalists to control the product and keep the workers dependent upon them.

Private ownership of the means of production and distribution is responsible for the ever increasing uncertainty of livelihood and poverty and misery of the working class, and it divides society in two hostile classes—the capitalists and wage-workers. The once powerful middle class is rapidly disappearing in the mill of competition. The struggle is now between the capitalist class and the working class. The possession of the means of livelihood gives to the capitalists the control of the government, the press, the pulpit and schools, and enables them to reduce the workingmen to a state of intellectual, physical and social inferiority, political subservience and virtual slavery.

The economic interests of the capitalist class dominate our entire social system; the lives of the working class are recklessly sacrificed for profit, wars are fomented between nations, indiscriminate slaughter is encouraged and the destruction of whole races is sanctioned in order that the capitalists may extend their commercial dominion abroad and enhance their supremacy at home.

But the same economic causes which developed capitalism are leading to Socialism, which will abolish both the capitalist class and the class of wage-workers. And the active force in bringing about this new and higher order of society is the working class. All other classes, despite their apparent or actual conflicts, are alike interested in the upholding of the system of private ownership of the instruments of wealth production. The Democratic, Republican, the bourgeois Public Ownership parties, and all other parties which do not stand for the complete overthrow of the capitalist system of production, are alike political representatives of the capitalist class.

The workers can most effectively act as a class in their struggle against the collective powers of capitalism, by constituting themselves into a political party, distinct from and opposed to all parties formed by the propertied classes.

While we declare that the development of economic conditions tends to the overthrow of the capitalist system, we recognize that the time and manner of the transition to Socialism also depend upon the stage of development reached by the proletariat. We, therefore, consider it the utmost importance for the Socialist Party to support all active efforts of the working class to better its condition and to elect Socialists to political offices, in order to facilitate the attainment of this end.

As such means we advocate:

1. The public ownership of all means of transportation and communication and all other public utilities as well as of all industries controlled by monopolies, trusts, and combines. No part of the revenue of such industries to be applied to the reduction of taxes on property of the capitalist class, but to be applied wholly to the increase of wages and shortening of the hours of labor of the employes, to the improvement of the service and diminishing the rates to the consumers.

2. The progressive reduction of the hours of labor and the increase of wages in order to decrease the share of the capitalist and increase the share of the worker in the product of labor.

3. State or national insurance of working people in case of accidents, lack of employment, sickness and want in old age; the funds for this purpose to be furnished by the government and to be administered under the control of the working class.

4. The inauguration of a system of public industries, public credit to be used for that purpose in order that the workers be secured the full product of their labor.

5. The education of all children up to the age of eighteen years, and State and municipal aid for books, clothing and food.

6. Equal civil and political rights for men and women.

7. The initiative and referendum, proportional representation and the right of recall of representatives by their constituents.

But in advocating these measures as steps in the overthrow of capitalism and the establishment of the Co-operative Commonwealth, we warn the working class against the socalled public ownership movements as an attempt of the capitalist class to secure governmental control of public utilities for the purpose of obtaining greater security in the exploitation of other industries and not for the amelioration of the conditions of the working class.

Resolution on Socialism and Trade Unionism.

The Socialist Party, in convention assembled, declares:

The trade-union movement and independent political action are the chief emancipating factors of the wage-working class. The trade-union movement is the natural result of capitalist production, and represents the economic side of the working class movement. We consider it the duty of Socialists to join the unions of their respective trades and assist in building up and unifying the trades and labor organizations. We recognize that trades unions are by historical necessity organized on neutral grounds, as far as political affiliation is concerned.

We call the attention of trades-unionists to the fact that the class struggle so nobly waged by the trades-union forces to-day, while it may result in lessening the exploitation of labor, can never abolish that exploitation. The exploitation of labor will only come to an end when society takes possession of all the means of production for the benefit of all the people. It is the duty of every trades-unionist to realize the necessity of independent political action on Socialist lines, to join the Social Democratic Party and assist in building up a strong political movement of the wage-working class, whose ultimate aim and object must be the abolition of wage-slavery and the establishment of a co-operative state of society, based on the collective ownership of all the means of production and distribution.

Injunction Resolution.

"Whereas, The injunction has become, in the hands of the judiciary, an instrument by which the capitalist class seeks to destroy the civil and political rights of the workingmen.

"Resolved, That we, the Socialist Party, in convention assembled, call the attention of the working class to the fact that our judiciary is but a servile tool in the hands of the capitalist class and hostile to the interests of labor, and we call upon the working class to use the ballot in defense of their own interests by voting the Socialist ticket."

APPENDIX C

Panorama of Early Socialist Pioneers
(From interviews, correspondence, research)

A time-machine that would exhibit the activities of Marxist workers from coast to coast from 1900 through 1916 would provide revelations for historians.

In lieu of such magic, perhaps a literary spotlight focused now here, now there, jumping more or less chronologically from one central spot to another, will provide some illumination.

1900-1905: This was the new beginning, the period of rapid *clarification* of Marxist ideas.

KANSAS: J. A. Wayland, like Debs, a Bellamy-Populist before he knew of Marx, already had his *Appeal to Reason* in Girard, Kansas, before the turn of the century. . . . With him soon after was Fred D. Warren, the fearless editor. . . . And helping him from the first was Irish-born Mother Jones, who says in her *Autobiography* that she sold subscriptions for the *Appeal* to "almost every lad" at the Federal Barracks in Omaha, and even at the City Hall—"and the paper was launched." Later, in 1906, she and the *Appeal* and Debs defended Moyer, Haywood and Pettibone, heroes in an unforgettable labor war. . . . And with the Appeal, very soon, were the roving reporter, George H. Shoaf, and the father of American labor cartoonists, Ryan Walker, creator of "Henry Dubb."

NEW YORK: Grand old Lucien Sanial, survivor of the Paris Commune, and veteran of the Socialist Labor Party: indeed, author of its best platform, "basing its arguments on the Declaration of Independence" (Hillquit), and now sitting in conventions of the Socialist Party up to as late as 1912. . . . Also, Irish-born Tom Flynn, father of Elizabeth Gurley Flynn, engineer and dreamer, voting for Debs in 1900, reading "everything by Marx and Engels he could lay his hands on," attending meetings with his wife and daughters, and following *The Worker* of that day, the newly established paper of Hillquit, Ben Hanford and Algernon Lee. . . . Unknown to Tom Flynn, the engineer, was the artist, Rockwell Kent, who bought a copy of *Capital* around 1902. . . . Also jeweler and businessman, A. A. Heller, who had joined the Socialist Labor Party in 1893, became a voter for Debs in 1900 and a member of the Socialist Party in 1901. He put his money behind the Rand School and the publishing of Socialist literature. . . . Herman Cahn, who joined the Socialist Party in 1901, was the father of Anita Block, Barnard College graduate, who herself joined the Party in 1907. Later, Herman Cahn wrote *Capital Today* (1915) and daughter Anita Block became editor of the New York *Call's* "Woman's Sphere," featured every Sunday. One of the contributors to her page was Margaret Sanger, who also joined the Party. Anita Block's husband, S. John Block, was a Socialist lawyer. . . . Rose Pastor Stokes, former factory girl, joined the Socialist Party in 1905, and entered upon a scintillating career. Ahead of her in the Party was the former Knights of Labor organizer and suffragist, Leonora O'Reilly. Rose's millionaire husband, J. G. Phelps Stokes, also became a member of the Party.

OHIO: Walter M. Nelson, Detroit lawyer, living as a boy at the turn of the century in Columbus, Ohio, writes: "I remember going with my father on Sundays on the street car and then walking a distance to this man's house (an old German friend) where he read *Das Kapital,* translating from German into English." Old man Nelson came out of the Populist tradition, and was working toward socialism. . . .

To Cleveland, Ohio, in 1902, came Russian-born Simon Weissberg fleeing a Siberian prison sentence, and carrying in his pocket his Russian Social Democratic Labor Party membership card. Right away he joined the Socialist Party of America. Became Cleveland representative for Abe Cahan's Jewish *Daily Forward.* Was a presidential elector for Allan L. Benson in 1916. . . . With Simon was Anna, his wife, who also joined the Socialist Party, attending the same branch of which C. E. Ruthenberg and Tom Clifford were members. (She refused to go into a foreign language branch: "In the United States we speak English," she insisted.) She led the Socialist contingent of the Cleveland Woman Suffrage Parade in 1912, and a year later organized the Women's Socialist Educational League to carry on work among housewives. . . . Simon and Anna were the parents of Carl Winter, who at the age of 5 attended Socialist Sunday School with C. E. Ruthenberg's son Daniel . . . And others there were in Ohio: Tom Clifford (named above), printing leaflets on his little hand press; the Altenbernd family, John Fromholz, dozens of others, who all distributed countless leaflets; and Irish Ammon Hennacy, who feared and fought American entry into World War I.

NEW JERSEY: Ella Reeve Bloor in 1900 was writing articles for the Socialist Labor Party *Weekly People* and in 1902 helping Debs in the Socialist Party, organizing meetings, organizing workers, climbing stairs and caring for her babies, all at the same time, as she tells in her autobiography, *We Are Many*. In the course of her life, for decades after, she did organization work for the Party in Delaware, Pennsylvania, Ohio—in a good many of the states of the Union. (One of her sons, agricultural expert Hal Ware, was praised years afterward by Lenin: "Not a single kind of help has been for us so timely and important as the help shown by you.")

PENNSYLVANIA: Captain John R. McKeown, born in Pennsylvania in 1877, was a member of the Amalgamated Association of Iron, Steel and Tin workers from 1894 till CIO days, a veteran of the Spanish-American War of 1898, and a voter for Debs in 1900. Was for a time organizer of the Socialist Party in his home state. . . . Horace Traubel, literary executor of Walt Whitman, friend of Debs, and himself an unaffiliated socialist sympathizer, editing a little paper called *The Conservator* from 1890 to World War I. Like Henry Demarest Lloyd, like William Dean Howells, he could accept just about everything in Marx— but hesitated at class struggle. . . . One summer night in 1900, at the corner of Broad and South Streets in Philadelphia, 19-year-old William Z. Foster stood listening to a Socialist Labor Party soap-boxer for above an hour, and walked off with some pamphlets in his pocket. A year later he joined the newly formed Socialist Party. . . . Steam-fitter James H. Maurer, who had joined the Knights of Labor in 1880 and the Socialist Labor Party in 1889, also joined the Socialist Party in 1902, and was elected to the state legislature on the Socialist ticket in 1911.

ILLINOIS: From Chicago in 1904 went Mrs. Corinne Brown, suffragette and Socialist, to Amsterdam as a delegate from the Socialist Party of America to the Congress of the Second International. There, in that Marx-inspired parliament, she listened, consulted, argued, and voted, along with other delegates from around the world. . . . Socialist historian A. M. Simons, at first editor of the *Coming Nation* and, later on, editor of the *International Socialist Review*, found himself in June, 1905, translating an article by Karl Kautsky that mentioned a man named Lenin. The article was about the two factions in the Russian Social Democratic Party. This is what Kautsky had written: "One of these [factions] is the *Iskra* (Spark) among whose contributors are many who are well-known to the German comrades, especially Axelrod, Deutsch, Plechanoff, and Vera Sassulitsch. The other is *Wperjod* (Forward) whose most prominent representative is Lenin." . . . A couple of years later, also in the *Inter-*

national Socialist Review (July, 1907) was an article by William English Walling on "Evolution of Socialism in Russia." Walling discusses (rather vaguely) the possible role of the peasantry in the hoped for Russian revolution, and indicates that Lenin, leader of the "majority faction" of the Social Democrats, favored a more positive role on the part of the peasants than did the "minority faction." Walling adds: "Lenin thinks that Germany would not allow Socialism in Russia and would try to intervene." . . . Here in Chicago was Charles H. Kerr, scholarly publisher of Marxist books, taking time off in 1901 to compile *Socialist Songs with Music,* and even translating "The International Party" from the French of Eugene Poitier. "We American Socialists are only beginning to sing," he wrote in a preface to the first edition. . . . And in Chicago, too, was Henry Demarest Lloyd, discussing by mail with William Dean Howells his feeling that he should join the Socialist Party; and Arthur Morrow Lewis and Lena Morrow Lewis, both popular lecturers on Marxism, and salesmen of Socialist classics.

WASHINGTON: Westward in 1898 traveled pioneer Methodist preacher Ely C. Johnson to the town of Puyallup, Washington, and there saw copies of J. A. Wayland's *Appeal to Reason.* Then he read *Wage-Labor and Capital* and other books by Marx and Engels, and threw away his bible. Instead of sermons, he gave lectures on socialism, and organized Socialist locals from 1900 on. . . . Johnson's daughter Mattie joined the Socialist Party in 1908; Mattie's son Elmer T. Allison became editor of the Ohio *Socialist* years later; Mattie's daughter Hortense Allison joined the Socialist Party in Seattle in 1905 at the age of 18, got into the Seattle free speech fight in 1907-08, and was a member of the Socialist National Woman's Committee in 1912. . . . Westward too traveled German-born Alfred Wagenknecht and became state organizer of the Socialist Party of Washington from 1900 to the Russian Revolution. Married Hortense Allison, and they moved to Ohio. The Wagenknechts were friends of the Ruthenbergs (Charles E. and Rose), and both families became friends of Bishop William Montgomery Brown of Galion, Ohio. Bishop Brown joined the Socialist Party and brought in 30 new members. . . . A daughter of the Wagenknechts became Helen Winter, Communist leader and wife of Carl Winter (now an editor of the *Daily World*). . . . But can we forget those others in Washington State: Dr. Herman F. Titus, editor of the Seattle *Socialist,* and teacher of Marxism? And his many students, including Sam and Kate Sadler, he an organizer, she a famed orator?

MISSOURI: Kate Richards O'Hare—in the Socialist Labor Party in 1889 and the Socialist Party in 1900—became associate editor of the *National Rip-Saw* ("Blind as a bat to everything but right"). Lectured widely in many states, including once in Brooklyn—wearing, as some still remember, a flaming red dress. Her husband was Frank P. O'Hare, teacher and editor.

COLORADO: Mrs. Ida Crouch-Hazlett, one-time member of the Knights of Labor, lecturer and organizer for the Socialist Party from 1901 on, was in 1902 candidate for Congress from Colorado, "first woman parliamentary candidate in the world" (*American Labor Who's Who,* 1925).

CALIFORNIA: Albert Strout, born in Yuba City, California, in 1876—the year that saw the birth of the first American Marxist party— joined the Socialist Labor Party in 1898, and in 1899 the Social Democratic Party which was to unite with the Hillquit group to form the Socialist Party. While the soon-to-merge groups were quarreling over a name for the new party, Strout wrote a piece for the *Workers' Call* urging the name "Socialist Party"—and the idea took hold. Strout is important for one further contribution: In 1901 the repercussions of the Boxer Rebellion and the Chinese Exclusion Act were at a high pitch, and he openly took the position that "a Chinese was a human being and if he did his share of the world's work, he was entitled to receive the welcome hand of brotherhood." . . . Gaylord Wilshire, a Fabian Socialist who moved close to Marxism, founded *Wilshire's Monthly* in 1900, and ran for Congress in 1902 on the Socialist ticket. In an editorial reprinted in 1906, he wrote: "One who cannot see the necessity of a class struggle preceding the institution of Socialism has a very poor idea of the Marxian position, and in fact, he must be going through the world of today with closed eyes and ears."

1906-1912: This was the period of most rapid spread of Marxist ideas:

SOUTH DAKOTA: "I remember that Tom Ayres, my father, had the three volumes of *Capital* in the book case," says a letter from Homer Ayres, contributor to Helen Alfred's *Towards a Socialist America.* Tom Ayres and his wife, who lived then in Pierre, South Dakota, talked about Bellamy's *Looking Backward,* his son Homer also recalls, and adds that the "rural radicals" round about all subscribed to the *Appeal to Reason* and the *National Rip-Saw.* . . . Farmer D. I. Todd got interested in socialism in 1909, he said in a letter to this writer. That winter, he states, his wife, three hired men, and himself "joined in a winter's study of Walter Thomas Mill's *The Struggle for Existence.* Then, says Todd, he went on to read "everything in English that Marx and Engels ever wrote." Joined the Socialist Party in 1911, sold subscriptions to the *Appeal to Reason,* the *Milwaukee Leader,* the *New York Call,* and North Dakota's own Socialist paper, the *Iconoclast.* Then helped get fellow farmer Carl

Erickson elected sheriff of Williams County on the Socialist ticket in 1912.

MICHIGAN: Before he got to Chicago, where he got his start as a Socialist journalist, Reuben Borough writes, he attended high school in Marshall, Michigan, and there he heard about Marx from two sources. One was Ben Blumberg, a cigar-maker (later secretary of the Socialist Party of Michigan), and the other was the rector of the local Episcopal Church. In Chicago, where Reuben Borough went next, he became a reporter (1907) on the Chicago *Daily Socialist*. . . . Delbert E. Earley, itinerant Socialist soap-boxer, was a familiar figure in most Michigan towns from 1912 on, a candidate for state office many times, a peddler of Socialist classics, and a teacher of Socialism.

MONTANA: "I joined the Socialist Party in 1907 in a little town in Montana, where I worked as a stone mason," writes Andrew Omholt. He tells how 3,000 people met in 1913 in Williston, Williams County, with Walter Thomas Mills as chairman and Eugene V. Debs as featured speaker. At other times Kate Richards O'Hare spoke there, and also Emil Seidel of Milwaukee, and Carl D. Thompson of the Party's national office.

CALIFORNIA: John J. Ballam, London-born cigar-maker and Socialist soap-boxer, made his mark in Oakland, California, in the years 1903-1911, wrote Steve Murdock of the *People's World*. Ballam spoke every night on street corners, studied at the University, was active in the Cigar Makers' Union, and wrote for the Oakland *World*, socialist newspaper. He got to know Jack London, California's favorite son, and Thorstein Veblen, an academic dissident. . . . In California, too, was another pioneer Socialist soap-boxer, Tom Lewis, whose name is still legend as speaker, debater, and organizer. . . . "My first reading of Socialist literature was Engels' *Socialism; Utopian and Scientific,*" writes newsman and author, James Dolsen, and adds that he joined the Socialist Party in California in 1907. (It was years later that Dolsen wrote *The Awakening of China,* one of the first books on socialism in that new-ancient land.)

NORTH CAROLINA: W. G. Binkley, Southern farmer, descendant of a Swiss settler who came to America in 1749, recalls reading his first copy of the *Appeal to Reason* when he was eleven, an issue reporting the trial and speech of Fred D. Warren. Binkley listened to Gene Debs speak in Winston-Salem in 1911, and joined the Socialist Party in 1912. Later he heard Emil Seidel, Ida Crouch-Hazlett, Kate Richards O'Hare and Ryan Walker in that same city. "In 1916," he writes, "we polled 28 Socialist votes out of a total of 200 in my own precinct." He adds that "all the Binkleys supported the North during the Civil War, and hated the rich slave-owning class." . . . Another North Carolina farmer, Virgil Wilson, according to Binkley, was Populist candidate for governor in 1898, and joined the Socialist Party a few years later. . . . Schoolmaster Charles J. Hendley, son of a railroad worker, was a Socialist in his native North Carolina as early as 1912. He came north to a long career of school teaching and union activities in New York.

NEW JERSEY: Bryn Mawr-trained Anna Rochester read Marx's *Capital* in 1908 and voted for Debs that same year. She joined the Socialist Party in New Jersey in 1910. For the next two years she worked with Florence Kelley of the National Consumers League in the campaign to reduce the hours of labor for women workers; then was research worker for the National Child Labor Committee; next, more research for the Federal Children's Bureau in Washington. And so on in a devoted life.

NEW HAMPSHIRE: Farmer Fred B. Chase and his wife Elba were friends and supporters of Eugene V. Debs in 1912. (They were the parents of Homer Chase.)

WASHINGTON: E. B. Ault grew up in an old Socialist "Equality Colony," near the town of Edison, Washington, a utopian settlement that his parents had joined before the turn of the century. Ault went from utopian to scientific socialism, becoming publicity man for Debs in the earlier campaigns. In 1912, Ault became editor of the Seattle *Union Record.*

ALASKA: Up there in Nome, Alaska, from 1907 to the Russian Revolution, the Nome *Industrial Worker* was the *only* newspaper published. It was the organ of the Mine, Mill and Smelter Workers, and its editor (says journalist Art Shields of *The Worker,* who lived there a while) was the erudite John McGibney, who read and interpreted Marx in a somewhat leftist fashion.

KANSAS: German-born Ludwig E. Katterfeld, living in Topeka, first sold one thousand subscriptions to the *Appeal to Reason,* and *then* joined the Socialist Party in 1905. He was a Kansas delegate to the 1908 national convention and rode that year with Debs on the "Red Special". A leaflet he wrote at that time was entitled "Plenty for All." . . . In nearby Wichita lived Populist-reared Earl Browder, who joined the Socialist Party in 1907—and left in 1912 to do trade union work.

NEW YORK: In 1908 Cyril Lambkin was a member of the Young People's Socialist League. "One of the proudest moments of my young life," he writes, "was my acting as an usher at the Hippodrome in New York to celebrate the first issue of the New York *Call,* with Gene Debs as the main speaker." A few years later, in Detroit, Michigan, he joined the Socialist Party. Here he became acquainted with suffragette Frances Allaire, a descendant of one of the original French settlers in the Detroit area. She too became a Socialist, and supplied bail to war-time victims of reaction. . . . Office worker Bertha C. Howe was handed a copy of the *Communist Manifesto* by Courtenay Lemmon, one of the old Socialist intelligentzia, around 1905, and gradually grew into Socialism from then on. Until her death at age 102, she kept the delegate's badge she wore at a New York state convention of the Socialist Party in 1912. . . . In this same year Negro soapboxer Hubert H. Harrison was also at the state convention, along with Lucien Sanial and Charles H. Matchett. . . . It was a year earlier that W. E. B. Du Bois joined the Socialist Party—and resigned in 1912, explaining his reasons for doing so. . . . According to Socialist Party records at Tamiment Library (the old Rand School Library) Benjamin Gitlow was a member of Local New York around 1909, along with artist John Sloan and other well-known people. Gitlow helped organize the Retail Clerks' Union. His mother was a devoted and class-conscious Socialist. (No one thought, then, that he would one day write a book entitled *I Confess.*)

OHIO: Jacob S. Coxey, who had led "Coxy's Army" of unemployed to Washington, D. C., in the panic of 1894, joined the Socialist Party in Massilon, Ohio, about 1912. In Ohio's Socialist circles he met Charles E. Ruthenberg, candidate for governor (Ruthenberg had himself joined in 1909), and Mrs. Marguerite Prevey, veteran Socialist woman leader.

MINNESOTA: Catholic-reared Clara Strong Broms, a school teacher and outstanding woman leftwinger of Minnesota, joined the Socialist Party about 1910. She remembers (in a letter to this writer) meeting Rose Pastor Stokes, William Bross Lloyd (son of Henry Demarest Lloyd), Alfred Wagenknecht, Elizabeth Gurley Flynn, and John Reed. . . . Minnesota-born J. Louis Engdahl, long-time editor of Socialist papers, headed the staff of the Chicago *Daily Socialist* about 1907, then was labor editor of the *Milwaukee Leader,* then editor of the *American Socialist* (1914). Many Socialist newsmen served their apprenticeship under Engdahl.

ILLINOIS: Italian-born Frank A. Pellegrini, member of the Sewer and Tunnel Workers Union, supported the newspaper strike of 1912, read the *Chicago Daily Socialist,* heard Debs speak at the Armory on Washington Boulevard, and joined the Socialist Party that same year.

1913-1916: This was the period of *testing* of American Marxists.

NEW YORK: Ryan Walker was no longer alone among cartoonists, for now along came John Sloan and Maurice Becker, (Becker was soon to join hundreds of anti-war militants at Fort Leavenworth prison.) Another of the newer artists was Art Young, creator of the Poor Fish, . . . Teen-aged Horace B. Davis at an Intercollegiate Socialist Society meeting listened to a speech by Professor Scott Nearing in 1916, . . . Farmer Fred Briehl joined the Socialist Party in 1913, and recalls that his father, Herman Briehl, also read Socialist literature. A few years later Fred found himself in prison—at Fort Douglas, Utah, along with thirty other openly self-announced Socialist objectors to war. . . . From Russia in 1915, came M. J. Olgin, already a distinguished scholar and a devoted Socialist over there, to start a new scholarly and Socialist life here in America. . . . A. Philip Randolph, Negro intellectual inspired by W. E. B. Du Bois, joined the Socialist movement and prepared to launch that remarkable magazine, *The Messenger,* in January, 1917. . . . Pacifist A. J. Muste tells in his autobiography, *Not So Long Ago,* how attracted he was to Woodrow Wilson's he-kept-us-out-of-war slogan in 1916, but adds: "By the time Election Day came, however, I voted for Eugene V. Debs." . . . Dorothy Day, who later became a Catholic pacifist, worked as a reporter on the New York *Call* in 1916, and supported the radical left.

CALIFORNIA: Trade unionist and Socialist Party member Thomas J. Mooney was also anti-war in San Francisco, and imperialist reaction struck murderously at him in 1916. . . . Agnes Smedley joined the Party in college circles about 1915, and says of the 1916 election, "At the time I had been a Socialist, at least on paper, and had been one of the many Socialists who deserted the Party and voted for Wilson purely because of his anti-war slogan." . . . And also in California was J. E. Snyder, editor of the *Oakland World* from 1915 on through the war. He was well-known before that for his Socialist barnstorming through Texas, Oklahoma, Kansas and Nebraska.

WASHINGTON: Teen-aged Harvey O'Connor joined the Young People's Socialist League and then the Socialist Party in Seattle around 1915, and wrote for the Socialist press there. He recalls Kate Sadler Greenhalgh of Seattle, "where she was kind of a Rosa Luxembourg of the Socialist movement, a fire-brand with a glowing personality and tremendous appeal to mass audiences." O'Conner adds: "It would be presumptuous for me to claim to be a Marxist, in view of my ignorance of his doctrine. However, in the course of reading I have found no other explanations of world affairs which seem to make as much sense as those based on Marxism." . . . Another teen-ager in Seattle, Joe Pass, joined the Young People's Socialist League there about the same time, and then the Socialist Party. He remembers vividly speeches by Gene Debs, Elizabeth Gurley Flynn, Arthur Morrow Lewis, Bill Haywood, Tom Lewis, Walter Thomas Mills. Joe's brother, Maurice Pass, became a socialist artist, joining Maurice Becker and others in the ranks of artists.

WEST VIRGINIA: Val Reuther, according to Carl Haessler of *Federated Press,* was an organizer for the American Federation of Labor Brewery Workers Union in the years before World War I, and became a militant Socialist Party member. His sons, Walter and Victor, were born in Wheeling, West Virginia, where Val founded and headed the city central labor body.

ILLINOIS: Holland Roberts was a high school boy of 17 or so when he first tried in 1912-13 to read *Capital* in Peoria, Illinois. "Of course I could not understand a great deal of what I read, but nevertheless enough of it sank in to impress me deeply," he writes. . . . Independent newsman Carl Haessler was a Rhodes Scholar in 1911-12 and joined the Fabians at Oxford, England. When he returned to the United States, he joined the Socialist Party in 1914, while at the University of Urbana, and worked with Scott Nearing, Rose Pastor Stokes, George R. Kirkpatrick and others "to stave off United States participation in World War I." Haessler knew personally many Socialist old-timers: Ralph Korngold, organizer; Victor Berger, congressman and editor; John M. Work, national secretary; Oscar Ameringer, lecturer and propagandist; and scores of others.

MICHIGAN: Attorney Maurice Sugar joined the Intercollegiate Socialist Society in 1912 at the University of Michigan law School and the Socialist Party the following year. Like other Socialist students at Ann Arbor, he made himself available as a speaker on Marxism for the nearby local Socialist clubs.

MASSACHUSETTS: Congregational minister Albert Rhys Williams in Massachusetts joined the Socialist Party in 1914-15, and, in his church in East Boston, set up a Socialist Forum for public discussion of solutions to social questions.

CONNECTICUT: Alabama-born Helen Keller lived much of her adult life in Westport, Connecticut. She surprised many by writing an article, "How I Became a Socialist," for the New York *Call*, November 3, 1912, an article which was reprinted in 1920 in her book, *Out of the Dark.* Referring to it she says, in the book's preface, "Briefly, it sums up my position at the present time." First, she says, she read H. G. Wells' *New Worlds for Old,* then went on to articles in the *International Socialist Review,* the *Appeal to Reason,* and Kautsky on the *Erfurt Programme.* She wrote a letter of support to Fred Warren when he was on trial, and declared that she had a red flag hanging in her study. She was ironic about capitalist editorial references to her blindness in connection with social beliefs. "Marx was probably stone deaf and William Morris was blind," she wrote, indignantly, and went on: "It is not fair fighting or good argument to remind me and others that I cannot see or hear. I can read. I can read all the Socialist books I have time for, in English, German, and French."

Only a relatively few people are mentioned here: the literary spotlight has slid over the majority. There were many others: truly, thousands.

BIBLIOGRAPHY

The following list includes works referred to in the text plus others which relate to the theme as a whole and which influenced the author.

Alfred Helen, ed. *Toward a Socialist America;* A Symposium of Essays by Fifteen Contemporary American Socialists. 1958.
——. *Public Ownership in the U. S. A.:* Goals and priorities. 1961.
Allen, James S. *Reconstruction:* the Battle for Democracy. 1937.
Ameringer, Oscar. *Life and Deeds of Uncle Sam.* 1909.
——. *If You Don't Weaken:* Autobiography. 1940.
Aptheker, Herbert. *Essays in the History of the American Negro.* 1945.
——. *To Be Free: Studies in American Negro History.* 1948.
——. *A Documentary History of the Negro People in the United States.* Preface by Dr. W. E. B. Du Bois. 1951.
——. *The Era of McCarthyism:* A revised edition of *History and Reality.* 1962.
—— *John Brown: American Martyr. 1859-1959.* 1960.
——. *American Negro Slave Revolts.* 1943.
——. *One Continual Cry:* David Walker's "Appeal to the Colored Citizens of the World," 1829-1830. 1965.
——. *The Urgency of Marxist-Christian Dialogue.* 1970.
Asbury, Herbert. *The French Quarter* (of New Orleans), 1936.
Anderson, Marian. *My Lord, What a Morning: An Autobiography.* 1956.
Baxandall, Lee. *Marxism and Aesthetics: An Annotated Bibliography.* 1968.
Beard, Charles A. *The Economic Interpretation of the Constitution of the United States.* 1913.
Beatty, Bessie. *The Red Heart of Russia.* 1918.

Bellamy, Edward. *Looking Backward, 2000-1887.* 1887.

————. *Bellamy Speaks Again!* Re-published articles, editorials, speeches. Foreword by R. Lester McBride. 1937.

————. *Talks on Nationalism.* Foreword by Wm. P. Harvey. 1938.

Benet, Wm. Rose, & Cousins, Norman. *The Poetry of Freedom.* (Modern Library.) 1948.

Bernal, J. D. *Prometheus Books,* 1958, 1959. (Note especially Chapter VI. "The Advancement of Science.").

————. *World Without War.* 1959.

Bernstein, Samuel. *International Workingmen's Association, Papers of the General Council.* (Feltrinelli, Milan). 1961.

————. *The First International in America.* (Published by Augustus M. Kelley.) 1962.

Bestor, Arthur Eugene, Jr., *Backwoods Utopias.* 1950.

Bimba, Anthony. *History of the American Working Class.* 1927; 1937.

Blake, William J. (Pseudonym.) *An American Looks at Karl Marx.* (Alternative title: *Elements of Marxian Economic Theory and Its Criticism.*) 1939.

Bloor, Ella Reeve. *We Are Many:* An Autobiography. 1940.

Blumberg, Dorothy Rose. *Florence Kelley: The Making of a Social Pioneer.* 1966.

Boudin, Louis B. *The Theoretical System of Karl Marx.* 1907.

Boyer, Richard O., and Morais, Herbert M. *Labor's Untold Story.* 1955.

Borough, Reuben W. (An unpublished autobiography, kindly lent author)

Brisbane, Albert. *Social Destiny of Man.* 1840.

Brooks, Van Wyck. *John Sloan: A Painter's Life.* 1955.

Brown, Bishop Wm. Montgomery. *Christianism and Communism.* 1922.

————. *My Belief: The Autobiography of an Idea.*

Brownson, Orestes. *The Laboring Classes.* 1840.

Bruce, Robert V. *1877: Year of Violence.* 1959.

Bullard, Albert (Pseudonym: Albert Edwards). *Comrade Yetta.* 1913.

Cahan, A. *Bletten fun Mein Leiben.* (Five Vols.) 1926-1931.

Calmer, Alan. *Labor Agitator: The Story of Albert R. Parsons.* 1937.

Commons, John R. and Associates. *Documentary History of American Industrial Society.* (Seven Vols.) 1909; 1911.

Conrad, Earl. *Harriet Tubman: A Biography.* 1943.

Conrad, Earl, and Patterson, Haywood. *Scottsboro Boy.* 1950.

David, Henry. *The History of the Haymarket Affair.* 1936; 1963.

Davis, Angela Y., and Bettina Aptheker, eds., *If They Come in the Morning.* Foreword by Julian Bond, 1971.

Davis, Benjamin J. *Communist Councilman from Harlem.* 1969.

De Leon, Daniel. *Reform or Revolution.* 1896.

———. *What Means This Strike?* 1898.

———. *Two Pages from Roman History.* 1903.

———. *Flashlights of the Amsterdam Congress.* 1906

De Leon, Solon. *The American Labor Who's Who.* 1925.

Dietzgen, Joseph. *Philosophical Essays.* 1906.

———. *Positive Outcome of Philosophy.* 1906.

Dolsen, James. *The Awakening of China.* 1925.

Donner, Frank J. *The Un-Americans.* 1961.

Douglass, Frederick. *Life and Times of Frederick Douglass:* An Autobiography. 1892: 1962.

Draper, J. W. *History of the Intellectual Development of Europe.* (2 vols.) 1864.

Draper, Theodore. *The Roots of American Communism.* 1957.

Du Bois, W. E. B. *Black Reconstruction.* 1935.

———. *The Souls of Black Folk.* 1953.

———. *John Brown.* 1909; 1962.

———. *Dusk of Dawn.* 1940.

———. *The Autobiography of W. E. B. Du Bois.* 1968.

Egbert, Donald Drew, and Persons, Stow. *Socialism and American Life.* 1952.

Ely, Richard T. *Recent American Socialism.* 1885.

Engels, Frederick. *Peasant War in Germany.* 1850.

———. *Condition of the Working Class in England in 1844.* 1845; 1885.

———. *Origin of the Family, Private Property, and the State.* 1884.

———. *Socialism, Utopian and Scientific.* 1892.

———. *Dialectics of Nature.* 1940, in English.

———. *Speech at the Graveside of Karl Marx.* 1883.

England, George Allan. *The Story of the Appeal.* (A history of the *Appeal to Reason,* newspaper founded by J. A. Wayland.) 1917.

———. *The Air Trust.* (A novel.) 1915.

Finkelstein, Sidney. *Art and Society.* 1947.

Fine, Nathan. *Labor and Farmer Parties in the United States, 1828-1928.* 1928.

Flexner, Eleanor. *Century of Struggle.* 1959.

Flynn, Elizabeth Gurley. *I Speak My Own Piece:* An Autobiography. 1955.

———. *The Alderson Story:* Her prison years. 1963.

Foner, Philip S. *History of the Labor Movement in the United States.* (Four vols.) Vol. I. 1947; II, 1955; III, 1964; IV, 1965.

———. *Jack London: American Rebel.* 1947.

———. *Helen Keller: Her Socialist Years.* 1967.

———. *The Bolshevik Revolution: Its Impact on American Radicals, Liberals, and Labor:* A Documentary Study. 1967.

———. *The Autobiographies of the Haymarket Martyrs.* 1969.

Ford, James W. *The Negro and the Democratic Front.* 1938.

Forsythe, Robert (Pseudonym). *Redder Than the Rose.* 1945.

———. *Reading from Left to Right.* 1938.

Foster, William Z. *From Bryan to Stalin.* (Autobiography). 1937.

———. *Pages from a Worker's Life.* 1939.

———. *History of the Communist Party of the United States.* 1952.

———. *The Negro People in American History.* 1954.

———. *The Three Internationals.* 1955.

———. *Outline History of the World Trade Union Movement.* 1956.

Friedman, I. K. *By Bread Alone.* (A novel.) 1901.

General Council of the First International, The. *Minutes, 1864-1866.* Foreign Languages Publishing House. Moscow.

Ghent, W. J. *Our Benevolent Feudalism.* 1902.

———. *Mass and Class.* 1904.

Gilman, Charlotte Perkins. *Women and Economics.* 1898.

Ginger, Ray. *The Bending Cross:* a Biography of Eugene Victor Debs. 1949.

Glazer, Sidney. *Labor and Agrarian Movements in Michigan, 1876-1896.* A doctoral dissertation, University of Michigan, 1932.

Godwin, Park. *Democracy, Constructive and Pacific.* 1844.

Gold, Michael. *The Hollow Men.* 1941.

———. *Life of John Brown.* 1960.

Goldberg, Harvey. *American Radicals: Some Problems and Personalities.* 1957.

Gompers, Samuel. *Seventy Years of Life and Labor.* 1925.

Gronlund, Laurence. *The Cooperative Commonwealth.* 1884.

Hanford, Benjamin. *Fight for Your Life.* (Pamphlet). 1909.

Hardy, Jack, pseudonym. *The First American Revolution.* 1937.

Harris, Rev. W. S. *Capital and Labor.* 1907.

Hart, Henry, editor. *American Writers' Congress.* Foreword by Waldo Frank. 1935.

———. *The Writer in a Changing World.* 1937.

Haywood, Wm. D. *Bill Haywood's Book.* 1929.

Heath, Frederic. *Socialism in America.* 1900.

Hicks, Granville. *The Great Tradition.* 1933.

———. *Proletarian Literature in the United States.* An Anthology. Edited by Gramille Hicks. 1935.

Hillquit, Morris. *History of Socialism in the United States.* 1903.

————. *Loose Leaves from a Busy Life:* an autobiography. 1934.

Howe, Irving, and Coser, Lewis, with the assistance of Julius Jacobson. *The American Communist Party, A Critical History.* 1957.

Howells, Wm. Dean. *A Traveller from Altruria.* 1894.

————. *The Eye of the Needle.* 1907.

————. *Annie Kilburn.* 1891.

Hughan, Jessie Wallace. *American Socialism of the Present Day.* 1910.

————. *The Facts of Socialism.* 1914.

————. *The Socialism of Today.* 1916.

Johnson, James Weldon. *The Autobiography of an Ex-Colored Man.* Introduction by Charles S. Johnson. 1912; 1927.

Johnson, Oakley, C. *The Day is Coming: Life and Work of Charles E. Ruthenberg.* 1957.

————. *An American Century: Recollections of Bertha W. Howe.* Edited and with an Introduction by OCJ. 1966.

————. *Robert Owen in the United States.* 1970.

Jones, Mary H. See Mother Jones.

Kautsky, Karl. *The Class Struggle* (English edition), 1910.

————. *Bolshevism at a Deadlock.* 1931.

Keller, Helen. *The Story of My Life.* 1902.

Kelley, Florence. *The Working Child* (Pamphlet). 1896.

————. *What Women Might Do With the Ballot:* The abolition of Child Labor. (Pamphlet). 1912.

Kennell, Ruth Epperson. *Theodore Dreiser and the Soviet Union.* 1969.

Kent, Rockwell. *It's Me, O Lord.* An Autobiography. 1960.

Keracher, John. *The Headfixing Industry,* Pamphlet. 1935. (This material was delivered by Keracher—"The Head-fixers"—as a lecture for nearly twenty years before publication.)

Kipnis, Ira. *The American Socialist Movement, 1897-1912.* 1952.

Kirkpatrick, George R. *War—What for?* 1910.

Klein, Nicholas. *The Socialist Primer:* First Lessons in Socialism for Children. 1908.

Lafargue, Paul. *Karl Marx: His Life and Work; Reminiscenses.* (English Edition.) 1943.

————. *The Religion of Capital* (Pamphlet). 1902.

Lamont, Corliss, ed. *The Trial of Elizabeth Gurley Flynn by the American Civil Liberties Union.* 1968.

————. *The Philosophy of Humanism.* 1949; 1957.

Lawson, Elizabeth. *Thaddeus Stevens* (a pamphlet). 1942.

————. *Lincoln's Third Party.* (a pamphlet.) 1948.

Lenin, V. I. *"Left Wing" Communism: An Infamtile Disorder.* 1920.

————. *State and Revolution.* 1917.

————. *Imperialism.* 1917; 1920.

————. *A Letter to American Workers.* 1919.

Lofgreen, P. A. (Pseudonym for Laurence Gronlund) *The Coming Revolution: Its Principles.* 1878.

London, Jack. *People of the Abyss.* 1902.

————. *The Iron Heel,* a novel. 1907.

————. *Revolution,* a lecture. 1908.

Lloyd, Henry Damarest. *Wealth Against Commonwealth.* 1894.

Lunacharsky, A. *On Literature and Art.* Progress Publishers, Moscow. English Edition. 1965.

Lusk Committee, New York State Legislature. *Report: Revolutionary Radicalism.* (Four vols.) 1920.

Madison, Charles A. *Critics and Crusaders:* A Century of American Protest. 1947.

Malkiel, Theresa Serber. *Woman and Freedom.* 1911.

Mandel, Bernard. *Labor: Free and Slave.* 1955.

Mark Twain (Samuel L. Clemens). *A Connecticut Yankee in King Arthur's Court.* 1889, & later.

Marx, Karl. *Class Struggles in France.*

————. *Civil War in France.*

————. *Eighteenth Brumaire of Louis Bonaparte.* 1852; 1869.

————. *Capital:* Vols. I, 1887; II, 1893; III, 1894. (English.)

————. *Value, Price & Profit.* 1865; 1898 (7).

————. *Wage-Labour & Capital.* 1849.

————. *Critique of the Gotha Programme.* 1876; 1891.

————. *Poverty of Philosophy.*

————. *Inaugural Address.*

Marx and Engels. *Communist Manifesto,* 1848.

————. *Letters to Americans.* 1953.

Marcy, Mary E. *Shop Talks on Economics.* 1911.

Melish, John Howard. *Franklin Spencer Spalding: Man and Bishop.* 1917.

Merriam, Eve. *Emma Lazarus: Woman With a Torch.* 1956.

Morell, Parker. *Lillian Russell: the Era of Plush.* 1940.

Mayer, Gustav. *Friedrich Engels: A Biography.* 1936.

Minton, Bruce, and Stuart, John. *Men Who Lead Labor.* 1937.

Mills, Ethelwyn. *Legislative Program of the Socialist Party.* 1914.

Mills, Walter Thomas. *Evolutionary Politics.* 1898.

Morais, Herbert M., and Cahn, William. *Gene Debs: The Story of a Fighting American.* 1948.

Morgan, Lewis H. *Ancient Society,* or Researches in the Lines of Human Progress through Barbarism to Civilization. 1877.

Morlan, Robert L. *Political Prairie Fire.* 1955.

Mother Jones (Mary H. Jones). *Autobiography.* Edited by Fred Thompson. Foreword by Clarence Darrow. Published by C. H. Kerr & Co. 1925; 1972.

Muste, A. J. *Not So Long Ago:* An Autobiography. 1957.

Myers, Gustavus. *History of Great American Fortunes* (3 vols.) 1910; 1911.

——. *History of the Supreme Court.* 1912.

Nearing, Scott. *Anthracite: An Instance of Natural Resource Monopoly.* 1915.

——. *The Making of a Radical:* An Autobiography. 1972.

——. *The Great Madness: A Victory for the American Plutocracy.* (Pamphlet). 1917.

——. *Open Letters to Profiteers: An Arraignment of Big Business in Relation to the World War.* (Pamphlet). 1917.

Nordhoff, Charles. *The Communistic Societies of the United States.* 1875; 1960.

North, Joseph. *Robert Minor: Artist and Crusader.* 1956.

——. *New Masses: An Anthology of the Rebel Thirties.* 1969.

Novosti Press Agency. *The Year 2017.* One Hundred Years After the October Revolution. 1968. Moscow.

Oberman, Karl. *Joseph Weydemeyer, Pioneer of American Socialism.* 1947.

O'Connor, Harvey. *Revolution in Seattle.* 1964.

O'Hare, Kate Richards. *Sorrows of Cupid.* 1909.

——. *Law and the White Slaver.* (Pamphlet). 1911.

——. *The Church and the Social Problem.* (Pamphlet). 1911.

Oneal, James. *The Workers in American History.* 1910.

Oppenheim, James. *Pay Envelopes.* 1911.

——. *The Nine-Tenths.* 1911.

Page, Charles Hunt. *Class and American Sociology: From Ward to Ross.* 1940.

Parrington, Vernon L. *Main Currents in American Thought.* Vols. I & II. 1927.

Patterson, Joseph Medill. *Confessions of a Drone.* 1906.

——. *A Little Brother of the Rich.* 1908.

Patterson, Wm. L., *We Charge Genocide.* 1951; 1970, with Preface by Ossie Davis.

——. *The Man Who Cried Genocide,* an autobiography. 1971.

Pauling, Linus. *No More War.* 1958.

Petersen, Arnold. *Daniel De Leon: Social Architect.* 1941.

Pickens, Donald Kenneth. *The Program and Principles of Oklahoma Socialism.* (Doctoral Dissertation.) 1957.

Poole, Ernest. *The Habor.* 1915.

Pound, Louise, and others. *A College Book of American Literature,* Vols. I & II. 1939; 1940.

Porter, Kirk B. & Johnson, D. B. *National Party Platforms.* 1956.

Quarles, Benjamin, and Fishel, Leslie H., Jr. *The Negro American: A Documentary History.* 1967.

Red Fox, Chief. *The Memoirs of Chief Red Fox.* Introduction by Carl Asher. 1971.

Richmond, Al. *Native Daughter: The Story of Anita Whitney.* 1942.

Rideout, Walter D. *The Radical Novel in the United States.* 1956.

Rischin, Moses. *The Promised City.* 1962.

Robeson, Paul. *Here I Stand.* 1958; republished with preface by Lloyd L. Brown, 1971.

Rochester, Anna. *The Populist Movement in the United States.* 1943.

Rogers, J. A. *World's Great Men of Color:* 3000 B.C. to 1946 A.D. 1947.

Russell, Charles Edward. *Why I Am a Socialist.* 1910.

Sachs, Emanie. *The Terrible Siren* (About Victoria Woodhull). 1928.

Sanger, Margaret. *What Every Mother Should Know.*

———. *What Every Girl Should Know.*

———. *Margaret Sanger: An Autobiography.* 1938.

Schlueter, Herman. *The Brewery Industry and the Brewery Workers Movement in America.* 1910.

———. *Lincoln, Labor and Slavery.* 1913.

Scott, Leroy. *The Walking Delegate.* 1905.

Scudder, Vida D. *Social Ideals in English Letters.* 1898.

———. *Socialism and Character.* 1912.

Seldes, George. *You Can't Do That.* 1938.

Seligman, E. R. A. *The Economic Interpretation of History.* 1902.

Sellars, Roy Wood. *The Next Step in Democracy.* 1916.

Simons, A. M. *What the Socialists Would Do If They Won in This Election.* (Pamphlet.) 1901.

———. *Class Struggles in America.* 1903. (Expanded and re-titled *Social Forces in American History.* 1911.)

Sinclair, Upton. *The Jungle,* a novel. 1906.

———. *The Cry for Justice,* an anthology. 1915.

———. *The Brass Check:* A Study of American Journalism. 1919.

Small, Albion W. *General Sociology.* 1905.

———. *Between Eras: From Capitalism to Democracy.* 1913.

Small, Albion W. and Vincent, George E. *An Introduction to the Study of Society.* 1894.

Smith, Bernard. *Forces in American Criticism.* 1939.

Socialist Party. *Socialist Congressional Campaign Handbook.* 1914.

Socialist Labor Party. *Daniel De Leon, The Man & His Work: A Symposium.* 1919.

Stalin, Joseph. *Marxism and the National Question.* (English edition.) 1942.

Stanton, Elizabeth Cady, with Susan B. Anthony, and others. *History of Woman Suffrage.* (3 vols.) 1881-1886.

Steffens, Lincoln. *The Autobiography of Lincoln Steffens.* 1931.

Stern, Meta L., Translator. *Bebel's Woman.* 1910.

Suhl, Yuri. *Ernestine Rose and the Battle for Human Rights.* 1959.

Sumner, Helen L. (Helen L. Sumner Woodbury). *The White Slave.* 1896.

Symes, Lillian, and Clement, Travers. *Rebel America, the Story of Social Revolt in the United States.* 1934.

Titus, Dr. Herman F. *The Four-Hour Day.* Pamphlet. 1909.

Todes, Charlotte. *William H. Sylvis and the National Labor Union.* 1942.

Trachtenberg, Alexander, ed., *The American Labor Year Books.* 1916; 1917-18.

——. *The Heritage of Gene Debs.* Pamphlet. 1929.

——. *History of May Day.* Pamphlet. 1931.

Twain, Mark (Samuel L. Clemens). *A Connecticut Yankee at King Arthur's Court.* 1889; 1917; 1955.

——. *The Adventures of Tom Sawyer.* 1917; 1955.

——. (With Charles D. Warner) *The Gilded Age.* 1873; 1899.

Vail, Rev. Charles Henry. *Modern Socialism.* 1897.

——. *The Principles of Scientific Socialism.* 1899; 1908.

Veblen, Thorsten. *The Theory of the Leisure Class.* 1899.

Ward, C. Osborne. *Labor Catechism of Political Economy: A Study for the People.* 1878.

——. *The Ancient Lowly.* 1888; 1907.

Ward, Lester F. *Pure Sociology.* 1903.

——. *Applied Sociology.* 1906.

Weeks, Rufus E. *The Most Interesting Phenomenon of the Twentieth Century.* Pamphlet. 1905.

Wesley, Charles H. *Negro Labor in the United States.* 1927.

White, Bouck. *The Call of the Carpenter.* 1911; 1914.

——. *The Mixing.* 1913.

——. *The Carpenter and the Rich Man.* 1914.

Williams, Albert Rhys. *The Bolsheviks and the Soviets.* 1919.

——. *Through the Russian Revolution,* edited by Lucita Williams. 1970.

Williams, William Appleman. *The Contours of American History.* 1961.

——. *The Great Evasion.* 1964.

Wise, David, and Ross, Thomas B. *The Invisible Government.* 1964.

Wood, Eugene. *Back Home.* 1905.

―――. *Folks Back Home.* 1908.

―――. *Our Town.* 1913.

Woodbey, Rev. George W. *The Bible and Socialism: A Dialogue Between Two Preachers.* 1904.

Work, John M. *What's So and What Isn't.* 1905.

Yellen, Samuel. *American Labor Struggles.* 1936.

Young, Art. *Art Young: His Life and Times.* Edited by John Nicholas Beffel. 1939.

INDEX

Author's Commentary:
AN EPILOGUE

How did the Marx-influenced people described here react to the actual Revolution when it came in 1917?

The truth is that even *before* 1917 there was a division within the Socialist ranks: the Left Wing and the Right Wing. The dividing line was between those who wanted a "Workers' Government" which would run the nation's affairs in the interest of workers, and those who wanted a mixed collaboration of "business unionism" and businessmen.

The American Left welcomed Lenin and the Bolshevik Revolution and supported both in the years following; the Right rejected them and became leaders of the counter-revolution.

George Creel, once a reporter on the *Appeal to Reason,* became a war propagandist for President Woodrow Wilson. Albert Bullard, the highly praised author of *Comrade Yetta,* joined the U.S. diplomatic staff in Moscow and, as Albert Rhys Williams tells in his memoirs, failed to understand Lenin and the working class character of the Revolution. George Allan England, who fought so mightily against the *Air Monopoly,* became a defender of American imperialism; the theoretician, Morris Hillquit, finally led the Right Wing into a betrayal of the working class.

Nonetheless there were those who did indeed hail the Bolshevik Revolution and remained staunch supporters of the USSR. Albert Rhys Williams was one example; so were Bishop Wm. Montgomery Brown, and the Rev. Eliot White; so were the artists, Ryan Walker, Maurice Becker, Bob Minor, Hugo Gellert, Lydia Gibson; so the writers Mike Gold, John Reed, and others; so the mass leaders, Wm. Z. Foster, C. E. Ruthenberg, Mother Bloor, Elizabeth Gurley Flynn, Alfred Wagenknecht, and others.

I think that the rank and file of those who studied Marxism, despite moments of uncertainty, remained in the growing socialist legions.

I'LL CALL YOU IN KATHMANDU
THE ELIZABETH HAWLEY STORY

I'LL CALL YOU IN KATHMANDU

THE ELIZABETH HAWLEY STORY

BERNADETTE McDONALD
Foreword by Sir Edmund Hillary

THE MOUNTAINEERS BOOKS

THE MOUNTAINEERS BOOKS
is the nonprofit publishing arm of The Mountaineers Club, an organization founded in 1906 and dedicated to the exploration, preservation, and enjoyment of outdoor and wilderness areas.

1001 SW Klickitat Way, Suite 201, Seattle, WA 98134

First edition, 2005

Manufactured in the United States of America

Developmental Editor: Helen Whybrow
Acquiring Editors: Helen Cherullo and Christine Hosler
Project Editor: Mary Metz
Copy Editor: Brenda Pittsley
Cover, Book Design, and Layout: Mayumi Thompson
Cartographer: Brian Metz/Green Rhino Graphics

Cover photograph: upper right: *Portrait of Elizabeth Hawley by Gopal Chitraker* (Courtesy of the Elizabeth Hawley collection) lower: *Durbar Square, Patan, Nepal* © Earl and Nazima Kowall/Corbis
Frontispiece: *Portrait of Elizabeth as a young woman* (Courtesy of the Michael and Meg Leonard collection)

Text excerpt on page 152 © Kurt Diemberger from *Spirits of the Air.*
Text excerpt on page 159 © Ed Webster from *Snow in The Kingdom.*

Library of Congress Cataloging-in-Publication Data
McDonald, Bernadette, 1951-
 I'll call you in Kathmandu : the Elizabeth Hawley story / by
Bernadette McDonald.-- 1st ed.
    p. cm.
 Includes bibliographical references and index.
 ISBN 0-89886-800-9
 1. Hawley, Elizabeth, 1923- 2. Mountaineers--United
States--Biography. 3. Women mountaineers--United States--Biography. 4.
Mountaineering--Nepal. I. Title.
 GV199.92.H37M33 2005
 796.52'2'092--dc22
                              2005012738

CONTENTS

ACKNOWLEDGMENTS

I am grateful to the people who assisted me in this writing adventure. To Helen Cherullo of The Mountaineers Books, I offer thanks for inviting me to do this project, and for her ongoing support and encouragement. I would have been unable to accept the invitation if The Banff Centre had not granted me a six-month leave, during which time I researched and wrote parts of the manuscript—thank you to Banff Centre President Mary Hofstetter for allowing me that flexibility. Thanks also go to the Mountain Culture dream team for their unwavering interest and support of this project. Richard Salisbury provided me with important cooperation and insights, even in the midst of his own Elizabeth Hawley project. Paula Rondina helped me with valuable research. Woody MacPhail ensured that the audiotapes I recorded in Kathmandu were of the highest quality, and Yvonne Dixon kindly lent me her recording equipment. Fran Hunziker gave me the use of her backyard cabin in Cape Town, South Africa, as well as German shepherds Max and Murphy to protect me. Catherine Destivelle provided a writing space with the most inspiring view in Provence. At the beginning of the project, Charlie Houston wrote a letter to Elizabeth Hawley promising her that I wasn't an ogre, and Sir Edmund and Lady Hillary assured me (and Elizabeth) that this was a good idea. Broughton Coburn lent me books and was always interested and encouraging. Meg and Michael Leonard trusted me with a priceless box of letters and photographs that opened the door to Elizabeth's early life. Maria Coffey lent me her interview tape from a previous book project and was supportive, as was Lisa Choegyal, who sent many helpful emails and images. Thank you to Ang Rita for delivering faxes to Elizabeth when I couldn't get through to her directly. Special gratitude also goes to the people who generously read through early versions of the manuscript and advised me: Geoff Powter, John Porter, and Leslie Taylor, as well as to Anne Ryall for her meticulous fact checking.

Additionally, I want to thank all those who wracked their memories for Liz Hawley stories to share. Although not all are mentioned in this book, their interviews helped inform the effort. A sincere thanks to: Sir Edmund Hillary, Lady Hillary, Sir Chris Bonington, Reinhold Messner, George Band, Tomaž Humar, Ed Viesturs, Jean-Christophe Lafaille, Doug Scott, David Breashears, Audrey Salkeld, Tom Hornbein, Tashi Tenzing, Charles Houston, Robin Houston, Arlene Blum, Kurt Diemberger, Rebecca Stephens, Voytek Kurtyka, Greg Child, John Porter, Silvo Karo, Marija and Andrej Štremfelj, Junko Tabei, Conrad Anker, Frances Klatzel, Ken Wilson, Carlos Buhler, Christian Beckwith, Geoff Powter, Bernard Newman, John Roskelley, Richard Salisbury, Harish Kapadia, Reudi Eisland, Tamotsu Ohnishi, Erhard Loretan, Stephen Venables, Ed Webster, Catherine Destivelle, Dave Hahn, Eric Simonson, Lisa Choegyal, Leo Dickinson, David Schlim, Ed Douglas, Bill Crouse, Broughton Coburn, Mary Lowe, George Lowe, Russell Brice, Lindsay Griffin, Heather Macdonald, Sharon Wood, Michael Brown, Meg Leonard, Michael Leonard, Alex Lwow, Elaine King, Lee Kneerim, Will Kneerim, Eleanor Schwartz, Bernadette Vasseux, Kunda Dixit, Ang Rita, Lydia Bradey, Jean-Michel Asselin, Dr. Bekha Bahadur Thapa, Gopal Sharma, and Bahadur Garung.

Those who generously provided photographs include Heather Macdonald, Meg and Michael Leonard, Elizabeth Hawley, Lisa Choegyal, Colin Monteath, Alex Lwow, Ed Webster, and Jimmy Chin.

Elizabeth's life in Nepal is fundamentally tied to the mountaineering achievements of the past forty years, and so the efforts of countless climbers play a major role in her story. Many climbs and climbers of great significance are not included, however, because the selection of stories for this book was driven by a connection to Elizabeth, rather than their place in mountaineering history. I sincerely thank all the climbers whose stories have so enriched this book.

My deep appreciation goes to Christine Hosler of The Mountaineers Books for her patience as she gracefully walked me through the process; to my editor, Helen Whybrow, for the enlightening—and surprisingly enjoyable—experience of working on this manuscript; and to Brenda Pittsley for her meticulous copy editing. Thank you to Sir Edmund for writing the foreword with such enthusiasm, as well as to my husband,

Alan, for tolerating and encouraging me as I lived, ate, and breathed Elizabeth Hawley stories for eighteen months.

Finally, thank you to Elizabeth Hawley, for putting aside her skepticism about the project and for cooperating with me in such a wholehearted and enthusiastic manner. She opened her home and her files to me, gave me access to her personal papers, offered me glimpses of her wonderful sense of humor, and dug deep into her memory bank to provide me with more stories and images than I ever dreamed of. It was a rare privilege to work with her.

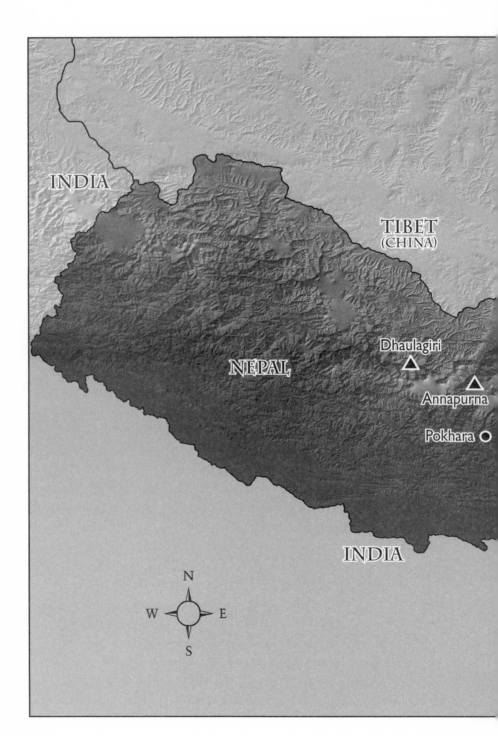

FOREWORD

I have known Elizabeth Hawley for forty-five years or more. When she settled in Kathmandu she quickly became a member of that unique group of people who added color and vitality to a city that had only recently moved into the new age—people like Inger and Boris Lissanevitch, Desmond Doig, Father Moran, Barbara Adams, Jimmy Roberts, and maybe to a lesser degree, myself.

In her early days, she was a researcher in New York, but she soon found that dull and uninteresting. She started traveling around the world and reveled in new experiences and adventures. She was a brave woman—never afraid to meet challenges or travel in areas of uncertainty and possible danger.

Finally, Nepal became her home; she enjoyed the people, the culture, and the intense political changes. She knew everyone she considered worth knowing, and when she became a Reuters correspondent she dispatched dramatic stories of the remarkable happenings that were so frequent in Kathmandu and on the Himalayan peaks. Her old-model Volkswagen was recognized by everyone, and if anything of consequence was going on, then Elizabeth and her VW would be there too.

Elizabeth was never a climber, but she interviewed every Himalayan expedition passing through Kathmandu and, on their return, reported on their adventures and their successes or failures. No one has a wider knowledge of Himalayan mountaineering. She is respected and admired by all the famous climbers.

She played an important role in the establishment of Col. Jimmy Roberts' Mountain Travel trekking agency. She is a formidable lady and does not suffer fools easily, but she is kind and generous to those she admires.

When I established the Himalayan Trust more than forty years ago and started building schools and hospitals for the people in the mountains, Elizabeth Hawley became a godsend to us. She is our executive officer and supervises our programs and finances with remarkable common sense and wisdom. Our Sherpa staff admire and respect her, as we do, and they work together as a most effective team.

So Elizabeth continues to work energetically on all her projects, be it reporting on Himalayan climbing, guiding the Himalayan Trust programs, or serving as Honorary Consul for New Zealand in Nepal. She is a woman of efficiency and courage who does everything well. She is widely respected around the world and has, in consequence, received many important decorations and awards.

I am particularly pleased that her unique and eventful life has finally been documented, as she has lived through interesting times, in fascinating places, with some remarkable people.

May she long remain her very special, formidable self.

—Ed Hillary

ENIGMA 1

I came to Nepal. I never planned to stay.
I just never left.
—ELIZABETH HAWLEY

I was well aware of Elizabeth Hawley's formidable reputation as the "grande dame" of the Himalaya and foremost authority on climbing in Nepal. She has been described as the single most reliable source of statistics on Himalayan climbing and "a one-woman Nepal Himalayan mountaineering institution." So when The Mountaineers Books asked me if I would be interested in writing her biography, I was intrigued, sensing there must be a remarkable personality behind that reputation. I had previously corresponded with Elizabeth on various mountain matters through my work with the Banff Mountain Festivals, but our contact had been cursory at best. What was her story? How—and why—did this woman from Middle America create such a unique role for herself as the doyenne of the world's highest mountains? Despite prolific mountaineering reports and published articles written by her over the course of forty years, almost nothing had been written about her. This surprised me, until I started talking to people who know her.

With discouraging unanimity, her acquaintances warned me that Elizabeth is an unequivocally private woman and, despite her having led a fascinating life in Nepal and elsewhere, they doubted she would reveal much of interest to me. All have asked her about her past, and her typical response is to hand over a one-page bio that reveals the basic facts: date of birth—1923; citizenship—American; occupations—journalist, honorary consul, Himalayan chronicler. New Zealand guide Russell

Brice has known her for thirty years, but could offer no insight into her personal life.

It was apparently hard work getting to know Elizabeth Hawley. American climber Carlos Buhler met her for the first time on an expedition in Nepal in 1979, when he was in his early twenties. He was focused on the climbing at hand and the logistics that had to be sorted out before leaving Kathmandu, so when she called him for an interview he was not enthused. "She was nosy and I didn't know her from Adam, and I thought, 'Wow! Goodness gracious, who is this gal?'" Looking back, he estimates it took at least five trips to Asia to begin to know her and appreciate what she was doing—"Sort of like your mother's antiques," he says. "I feel lucky that I went back and saw through that initial period of consternation and confusion about who she was." But even after dozens of meetings with Elizabeth, Buhler doesn't think he ever "cracked her." She is just as abrupt with him now as she was in 1979. Only his reaction has changed: "I'm not offended by it—I love her for all of those reasons. While at the beginning, I just didn't have enough life experience to know where to put this type of person."

Eleanor Schwartz, a good friend and colleague from Elizabeth's twenties, implored me to do more than list her accomplishments. "Try to capture her personality," she urged. Even though it might be difficult, "Elizabeth is worth the effort."

Heather Macdonald, Elizabeth's assistant in Nepal for a time, once approached her about writing a biography. Elizabeth responded that it would be a waste of paper. Heather knew there were great stories tucked away in this woman's memory, but she was not successful in drawing them out. When she asked Elizabeth why she stayed in Nepal, her answer was vague: "I came to Nepal. I never planned to stay. I just never left." Despite her reluctance to talk about herself, Elizabeth always leaves an impression—of mystery.

She has been a woman in a world of men—athletic, focused, devoted, egocentric, powerful men. Most of these men seem to be either in awe of her or terrified. At least one has thought of using her as a thinly veiled character in a novel. He describes this character as the ultimate schoolmarm type from the 1930s or '40s, with an aura of fear and terror radiating around her. Others are more prosaic: "She's just Liz. She's blustery and opinionated and outspoken and eccentric and, to many people, rude." Some have learned to "keep their mouths shut" and stay out of her line of fire.

Sir Edmund Hillary describes her as "a bit of a terror. If you get on the wrong side of Liz, it can be a bit difficult, but if you befriend her, you have a good friend, and one for life." He wonders if perhaps the only people who are not afraid of her are himself and his wife. One author muses, "It's always fun to speculate what Liz is doing when she's not terrorizing people." British author Ed Douglas agrees that people are afraid of her, but he thinks she is a "sexy old gal."

American climber Conrad Anker describes her as a diminutive, fragile, wickedly witty person exuding confidence and a no-nonsense authority. She is known far and wide as Miss Hawley. He has seen her on a regular basis for fourteen years, but on his last visit in 2002, he said, "She was definitely getting older and frailer. She's still beautiful and athletic, although a bit stooped." And he smiles as he observes, "She likes climbers, especially guys!" He admits he has always been curious about her private life—particularly the rumors of affairs with famous climbers.

In fact, many people are prone to speculating about the kind of fabulous private life Elizabeth might have had—mysterious men, maybe a broken heart in New York, royal family connections, and so on. Himalayan climber and writer Greg Child is one of these. After post-expedition interviews with her, he and other climbers have discussed her in private, imagining and speculating. "What's she doing? Who has she been with? What's she hiding from?" There have been a lot of theories, especially about potential lovers, among them Col. Jimmy Roberts, Eric Shipton, and Sir Edmund Hillary.

American climber and doctor Charles Houston is convinced that Elizabeth is not the marrying type. She is too independent. There are many stories about how and why she came to Kathmandu, including one in which a boyfriend leaves her, another where she stays in Kathmandu when she runs out of money while traveling. Italian alpinist Reinhold Messner agrees that she is a completely independent woman, free and modern—and has been since the 1960s. He believes she knew exactly what she wanted—and she went out and got it. But if this is true, she is also a woman of contradictions. He has seen her prudishness firsthand and cites an incident when she was talking with a climber who told her about having children with his girlfriend, whom he hoped to marry at some point in the future. She let him know that it should be the other way around: marry first and then have children.

British filmmaker Leo Dickinson interviewed Elizabeth in 1990 when he was in Nepal to fly over Everest in a balloon, as well as to work on a film about British climber Don Whillans. Dickinson remembers her as "inscrutable" and "buxom," and found her difficult to interview. Others who knew her during the same period described her as short and stocky, a busy woman who didn't bother much with her appearance. Others said she was tall, slender, well groomed, and elegant. One climber remembers her as standing 6 feet 7 inches tall and weighing 90 pounds—at least that's the impression she made. Could they all be talking about the same person?

According to Dickinson, Elizabeth always sticks to facts and figures like an encyclopedia. He felt a barrier descend when he attempted a more personal line of questioning, comparing the experience to a medieval moat: "you can go in one way, but you can't get out the other way." He is convinced she thinks that what others are doing is much more interesting than anything about her. He thought—but didn't dare ask—that she agreed to do the interview about Don Whillans because she and Whillans had had a romantic fling.

British climber Doug Scott agrees there may be something in the Whillans romance theory. He remembers an interview with Elizabeth, Whillans, Hamish MacInnes, and himself in the early 1970s, in which she singled Whillans out and, Scott believes, was enamored with him. Whillans thought so too. After she left, he commented to the others, "I think she likes me . . . I think I'll follow this up. . . ." Scott doesn't know what happened, and he can't help but chuckle at the incongruous image of the two of them together—the "buxom" Miss Hawley, and Whillans, who was 5 feet 2 inches and somewhat round at belly height. Another story has Elizabeth arriving in Kathmandu in the early 1960s with a man who was a climber and a scientist.

Probably the most persistent rumor about love affairs with climbers is one that almost every Himalayan climber believes—that Elizabeth and Sir Edmund had a long-standing romantic relationship. Doug Scott sums it up: "Of course, Ed's the one!" Elizabeth has been an ardent Hillary defender throughout her years in Kathmandu, and there is a story that she physically stood up for him at the Tiger Tops lodge when something disparaging was said about him. Observers claim she took a swing at the heckler with her fists. Elizabeth vehemently denies the incident.

Romantic theories aside, Scott is sure that most mountaineers and countless others are interested in Elizabeth's knowledge and opinions on the inside dealings of mountaineering in Nepal. Ed Viesturs agrees. Every climber he knows who has met and worked with her wants to know the story—and opinions—of Elizabeth Hawley. After all, she has interviewed climbers and reported on expeditions to Nepal for more than forty years. She has seen and heard some amazing stories, yet her seasonal mountaineering reports have always been straightforward journalism without overt opinion. What did she really think?

After interviewing dozens of climbers and friends, and reading thousands of her letters given to me by Elizabeth's nephew, it was time to go to Kathmandu and meet her in person. I was warned "there's a side of her that's very robotic." Several people advised me to have a drink with her first to "take the edge off." Anything from whiskey to gin and tonic to wine would do.

I was further advised to do my homework. "You need to know the big events . . . the epochal events" because "if you don't know your stuff, she will arch her eyebrows." I was told that when I asked a question, a typical response would be for her to turn the question around and make me feel ignorant for asking such a thing. I was repeatedly instructed to "never, ever, call her anything but Miss Hawley." Friends cautioned me to be emotionally prepared for a belligerent, antagonistic, rude woman. I was urged to be patient, to work with her, to not go on the offensive. Repeatedly I was told to bring whiskey.

But there was positive reinforcement as well. Lady Hillary advised, "just be yourself." Elizabeth had called the Hillarys about this project, and, despite being reticent in the beginning, was now said to be somewhat

"chuffed" about the idea. Elizabeth was flattered, but still couldn't understand why I'd want to do it, and wondered aloud who on earth would want
to read it. Sir Edmund encouraged me by saying that it was high time her
story was told, and he was confident she would cooperate.

Climbers regaled me with stories about how, upon their arrival in
Kathmandu, they would no sooner be checking into their hotels, or
unpacking their bags, or jumping into the shower, when they would
receive a call from Elizabeth Hawley asking to set up a meeting as
soon as possible. I found this to be encouraging—maybe she'd be eager
to meet me too. But the difference was that they had something she
wanted—information about a climb—and I didn't. Yet she had something
I wanted—her life story.

I left my home in the Canadian Rockies, and started the long journey: Calgary, London, Frankfurt, Bangkok, and, finally, Kathmandu.
A couple of days of bad meals, long lines, important bits of paper,
cramped seats, and ever-rising temperatures. The Kathmandu airport
was crowded and steaming. I crammed myself into a taxi and rumbled
off to my hotel, located conveniently near Elizabeth Hawley's residence.
I was in the hotel just long enough to unpack my suitcase and brush my
teeth when the phone rang—it was her! I took it as a good omen.

She gave me directions to her house and wanted to meet immediately, so I packed my briefcase with whiskey and headed out. I didn't
follow her directions too well, though, and ended up walking an extra
hour in the late-afternoon monsoon heat. Her street was packed with
postage stamp–sized shops selling everything from bathroom fixtures
to silk fabric to aspirin, while vendors crowded the sidewalks hawking
fresh vegetables and roasting corn. The pungent smells were overwhelming—a sensation intensified by unrelenting traffic and billowing clouds
of black diesel smoke. Two narrow driving lanes were choked with rat-
tling buses and sleek SUVs, as well as what seemed like thousands of
clanging motor scooters, all pouring into town with horns blaring. The
sidewalks were an obstacle course of unexpected drop-offs and ankle-
bending steps, piles of rotting garbage, and giant open sewage holes.
Attractive, traditional, three-story brick buildings were juxtaposed with
four- and five-story cement monstrosities. Beautifully carved, ancient

wooden doorframes leaned into the street, providing stark contrast to those made of aluminum and cast iron. It was a cityscape in transition, from the traditional to the modern, from medieval times to the twenty-first century. It bordered on mayhem.

At last, I came to a gated black iron fence on the north side of the street. The gate was open and to its right a formal brass plaque read "Elizabeth Hawley, Honorary Consul, New Zealand." The sign suggested order in a world of chaos. I walked through the gate, greeted the guard, wandered down a slight incline, and found myself in a courtyard surrounded by flowering trees and shrubs and a small plot of green grass. It was suddenly, unbelievably, quiet.

Within the courtyard were several houses. Elizabeth Hawley's home for more than forty years occupies the central position. A ground floor entrance leads to the headquarters office of the Himalayan Trust, an organization founded by Sir Edmund Hillary to provide educational and health support to the Sherpas of the Khumbu region of Nepal. I walked around to the left and up a short set of stairs leading to an unlocked screen door adorned with a string of bells, presumably to announce visitors.

On the other side of the screen door, a steep set of stairs ascended to a small landing, from where it was possible to see directly into a neat, orderly office. And there she was, at her desk playing solitaire on the computer.

Peering over her reading glasses, she turned her head to greet me: "Did you get lost? Don't worry, everyone does." She rose from her desk and walked purposefully over to shake my hand, still peering over her glasses. She was smaller than I expected, thin, and well groomed. Her eighty-year-old eyes were clear and dark, never wavering as she looked me over. We moved to the sitting area, where she offered a cool drink. Within the first half hour of meeting Miss Hawley, she asked me to call her Elizabeth. And so we began.

The puzzle remains unsolved, and her tenacity won't allow her to let it go.

The next day, I watched as Elizabeth, Sherpa Pemba Dorje, and two companions engaged in the kind of investigative cross-examination that perpetuates Elizabeth's reputation as being honest, relentless, and not easily fooled. Pemba, a wiry, sun-blasted, super-confident athlete, perched on her couch like a coiled spring, there only as long as it would take to convince her of his latest climbing feat, which was being contested by other climbers.

For the twenty-seven-year-old speed climber, this was a matter of pride, and his place in history. He had made big news in the climbing world, appearing in the "Breaking News" section of *Rock & Ice* magazine, as well as *Gripped*. But was this new exploit true? Did Elizabeth believe him? Pemba claimed to have climbed 3500 vertical meters from base camp on the Khumbu Glacier to the summit of Mount Everest in 8 hours and 10 minutes during the night of May 20/21, 2004. He climbed alone, using artificial oxygen above the last camp at around 7900 meters. The announcement of this astonishing climb was met with skepticism from other climbing Sherpas, however, and was immediately challenged by his rival Lhakpa Gelu Sherpa, who had beaten Pemba's time the previous year.

It did seem amazing that Pemba could lop four and a half hours off his time from just one year ago, and it was this that Elizabeth was probing. But he had a plausible explanation for her; on May 16, just a few days before his historic climb, he had climbed the mountain completely without bottled oxygen. That ascent had prepared him mentally and physically for the May 20 speed ascent—with bottled oxygen. Others on the team said he had used oxygen intermittently on the earlier climb, however, and any discrepancy in his story aroused Elizabeth's curiosity.

One of the problems with his claim was that he reached the summit in the middle of the night, on a night when nobody else was on the upper part of the mountain. Since his camera malfunctioned, there was no summit photograph. She asked him what he could tell her that would prove he was there. He answered that, when he was on the summit, he saw headlamps coming up from the north side. She double-checked his statement to ensure she had heard it correctly, making a note to cross-reference her other sources and records.

After an hour of questions, answers, repeat questions, more elaborate answers, and copious note taking, Elizabeth concluded with, "Congratulations, you have made an admirable effort." Pemba and his team stood up with an audible sigh of relief and bade this formidable, investigative force of a woman good-bye. For Elizabeth Hawley, this was but the first of many interviews concerning this ascent. It would occupy much of her attention and sleuthing abilities during the weeks to come.

———————

Before we settled into a serious interview session of our own, Elizabeth showed me around her home, pointing out items of interest. Her office is filled with mementos, photos, mountaineering books, and a few Tibetan paintings. Most of the furniture is made of wood and simply built. A small sofa and two chairs upholstered in interesting fabrics are a little worn. Fully one-third of the room is taken up with a large desk, a smaller table, upright wooden chairs, and the usual office equipment. This room, functioning as both her office and living room, is all hard surfaces—there is nothing soft about it, and it feels a little severe.

Old-fashioned wooden file cabinets stuffed with mountaineering files stand against the office walls. Every climb Elizabeth has covered is documented in a file organized by year, mountain, and route. Each file has an arrival form, bio forms for each expedition member, a return form, letters, photos, and route drawings. On an interesting or unusual climb, she makes notes regarding exact locations of camps, landmarks, distances, times between camps, oxygen information, and so on. If any letters or photos are supplied to her, she attaches them to the file. In some cases, she has the leader give her a detailed, blow-by-blow, day-by-day account of the climb. There are thousands of folders. The history of Himalayan climbing in Nepal is contained within these files. Upon closer examination, I see that all of the bookcases and file cabinets are firmly attached to the wall, and the computer and fax machine are chained to the desk. "Earthquakes," she explains. "They're not uncommon here. We're due to have a major one any minute now," she adds with a grin.

Adjoining the office is a dining room, lovely in its simplicity. A wooden table with ample seating space for six presides in the center of the room. On it lies a small notepad. A china cabinet holds dishes—and that's it, very simple. Tall French doors open onto a spacious balcony. I imagine Elizabeth holding court at the head of the table as famous mountaineers and adventurers regale her with their stories. This is the kind of dining room meant for interesting people, languid lunches, stimulating conversation, and laughter.

A hallway leads to a curious little bathroom—nooks and crannies peek out from the walls, each with a specific purpose. A large nook housed a water heater in days gone by; another is an alcove for towels; on a small shelf rests another notepad. The toilet has an old-fashioned elevated water tank dangling a long, slender chain for flushing. The tub looks barely big enough for a leisurely soak. It's a good thing she's not any taller.

In her bedroom, nothing is king-sized, queen-sized, or even double-sized. The wardrobes are conservative, the dresser is small, and the proportions of her canopy bed are elegant but diminutive. Draped with mosquito netting, the narrow mattress looks functional but hardly comfy. Another notepad is handy on a small bedside table.

Passing from room to room, I notice that all the walls are similar shades of ivory, though Elizabeth points out slight differences in hue, each individually selected by her. It's a sensory shock, then, to walk into a screamingly bright mustard yellow kitchen. Did she choose this color too? "Oh Lord no," she scoffs, "my cook chose this color. He's the one who spends all his time in the kitchen. I certainly never do." It's a tiny kitchen, but looks well organized and efficient—and very yellow.

Two massive truck batteries are lashed to her balcony, standing by ready to power lamps and other items such as her computer when the power goes off—which it frequently does. In addition, she has rechargeable, battery-operated flashlights close at hand to navigate the rooms not connected to the truck batteries. The wiring in her apartment is an eclectic mix of two-pronged plug-ins, narrow three-pronged plug-ins, fat three-pronged plug-ins, and plug-ins for both narrow and fat prongs. It's a living history of the evolution of electricity in Kathmandu.

Finally, I ask about the notepads. A distinct twinkle in her eye makes me think she's been waiting for the question. She explains she never knows when she might think of something, and she detests the thought of losing an idea, or a detail, or a to-do item. "I'm full of systems," she offers. "I'm very systematic. When you went into the bathroom, everything was neat and tidy, and that wasn't just for your benefit, you know." We then go back to the bathroom, so that she can explain her bath towel system: "When I get out of the bathtub, I take my towel and divide it into quadrants. Each quadrant is carefully used for a portion of the body, ensuring that, at no point, will I be drying myself with a wet towel." As a postscript, she proudly points to the notepad within easy reach of the bathtub.

Although her mind is robust and agile, and she is clearly having fun at my expense, Elizabeth appears fragile and thin. She wears a light cotton, short-sleeved, pastel, patterned frock. Her hair is neatly done and those reading glasses still rest on her nose. Her legs are slender, bare, and tan. At about five feet two inches, she isn't as tall as I expected, but she may have been taller at one time. Her eyes are dark brown, large and clear, and I'm sure she's wearing eyeliner, as well as a bright shade of lipstick.

The tour ends and, back in her office, the phone rings frequently. Her response varies—sometimes she's smooth as silk, other times she's impatient to the point of rudeness. Her voice can be quite sharp, a marked contrast to the conversational tone I've enjoyed so far. Occasionally, someone from the Himalayan Trust or one of her staff comes in; she speaks sharply to each one. The only exception is her driver, a nice-looking young man named Suben, who confers with her about a metal part somewhere in the depths of her car's motor. It is not working, and he is attempting to get it fixed. He seems to know what he's doing, so she agrees that he should keep doing it and gives him money to pay for whatever he needs. Maybe it's due to her lack of expertise in auto mechanics, but he's the only one who escapes reproach this afternoon.

A painting she cherishes has fallen off the wall and leans against a file cabinet. She explains that it was hung probably 30 years ago on a string that finally rotted. Two of her staff arrive to make it right, and she barks out orders, which are followed by considerable banging and scraping. Soon the painting is hanging again, but at a sharp tilt. She fumes that the only way to get anything done right is to do it herself.

She describes a typical Hawley day: It begins with an early breakfast and a thorough read of the two local daily papers. Meetings begin at 8:00 A.M., when Ang Rita from the Himalayan Trust usually comes upstairs to discuss funds he needs for a school or hospital project he's working on. Elizabeth doles out money from the Trust account and confirms what needs to be done.

Next, she calls climbing expedition leaders and makes appointments for interviews. She normally goes to their hotels because they can't easily find her (I'm relieved to learn I'm not the only one who ever got lost). She does two or three interviews in the morning, with her driver delivering her from hotel to hotel. The locations vary from elegant, expensive hotels to mean hostels, depending on the expedition.

Back home, she eats an early lunch in the dining room, noting "It takes me two minutes to get from my desk to my lunch." She has an excellent cook who prepares a light meal, such as a soufflé, shrimp, or rice. Then it's time to take the information she gleaned from the expedition interviews and type it up in the afternoon—and into the evening if necessary. During the afternoon, she calls trekking agencies and hotels: Is the expedition coming tomorrow? Have they checked in yet? Have they changed their plans? She knows when the daily Thai Airways flight arrives, so shortly after touchdown she's on the phone calling expedition leaders at their hotels to arrange meetings for the following day.

Dinner is at six. Evenings are a good time to phone people she wasn't able to catch during the day, as well as for more writing. Although her work is computerized, she prefers to do some things manually. She keeps several lists—lists of trekking agents, hotels, and expeditions. This third list is organized by mountain, leader's name, hotel name, and the expected arrival and departure dates. To best organize her time, she also makes a fourth list that is a chronological order of the expeditions' arrival dates. Several times a week, she revises the five-page chronological list, which is essentially her work schedule, because plans change constantly. But she resists doing it electronically "because it would take a lot longer." She describes the task as "a great evening's entertainment."

When Elizabeth stops working, at around 9:00 or 10:00 P.M., she reads the *International Herald Tribune*, a daily ritual begun in her early days of travel, and an Indian daily paper. To relax, she does the *Tribune*'s crossword puzzle. Then it's time to shut down the computer and place her backup files in a locked tin trunk beside her bed—in case of an earthquake she can escape with it out the back stairwell. Finally, it's time to choose her clothes for the next day and then retire. Sixteen-hour days are normal.

Each week also provides a few diversions; for example, Thursday morning is her weekly hairdresser's appointment. In addition to getting her hair done, she catches up on local gossip, and since she uses the same hairdresser as the queen of Nepal, there's always something interesting going on. "It's pretty good entertainment for a Thursday morning," she says. On Saturdays, the telephone doesn't ring as much and there are fewer interruptions. Weekends are her time for writing end-of-month reports for the adventure travel company Tiger Tops, working on a seasonal mountaineering report, and tidying up any leftover accounting for the Himalayan Trust.

The Tiger Tops report is a kind of "state of Nepal" analysis that includes political, economic, and tourism news that she writes for the company's executive director. In preparation, she faithfully clips anything of interest from the daily papers and saves it for the weekend writing exercise. She says she actually hates writing, but she loves the research.

She tells me there is virtually no day that she doesn't work, even at age eighty. On reflection, she concedes that every once in a great while there comes a day—usually a Saturday, maybe near the end of July—when she doesn't have anything pressing to do. On that glorious day, she luxuriates in an all-day read of a murder mystery. She hasn't indulged herself for a few years now, she says, but remembers a day a few years ago, and it was wonderful. She prefers murder mysteries because they are full of problems and puzzles, and she loves problem solving.

Elizabeth's excursions out of the apartment are all business. She never shops for food. "Me? Shop?" Her recurring theme is "the staff does what they can do, and what they cannot do, I do." Shopping for food is something they can do. She doesn't even tell the cook what she wants to eat; he knows what she wants and he finds it.

The greatest chunk of her time is devoted to mountaineering interviews. They form the core of the mountaineering reports she provides for a number of journals and mountaineering magazines around the world: the *American Alpine Journal* in the United States, *Desnivel* in Spain, and *Klettern* in Germany, among others. She doesn't ask for a lot of detail from climbers who climb the most frequented routes, but she does expect detailed feedback from those doing anything out of the ordinary. She asks them exactly where their camps were—in a crevasse, beside a rock outcropping, or on a ledge? From those details, she builds her information base.

Her forms have evolved little over the years. "What is your email address," was introduced after a request from Christian Beckwith when he was editor of the *American Alpine Journal*. She used to ask for "nationality," but changed it to "citizen of" because of the complex nationality issues that emerged as large countries broke into smaller nations. Anatoli Boukreev was a prime example. On the form, he said he was Russian. She pointed out that he was traveling on a Kazakhstani passport. "But I am Russian!" he insisted. In fact, his father and mother were ethnic Russians, but he lived in Kazakhstan. Just as a Sherpa would sign on as Sherpa rather than Nepali, Boukreev's nationality under the Soviet system was Russian because of his parents. She also got "Jewish" as a nationality because the old Soviet system identity papers identified people as Jewish, not Soviet. Someone else wrote "gypsy" under the nationality question.

Many have questioned her need for all this detail on the biographical forms, and some have been irritated by her insistence that everything be filled out. What does she need this for? She explains that one of her reporter jobs is writing obituaries for the climbers who don't come back.

American climber Dave Hahn, who has done eleven 8000-meter-peak expeditions, visits Elizabeth before and after every trip. He laughs at her unwillingness to change her form to accommodate changing times. She still has a box to check for "living with girlfriend," but none has emerged for "living with boyfriend." She doesn't see the need to change that, although she agrees that the combinations are endless—she once received a form filled out by a woman climber with a check beside "living with girlfriend." Assuming it was an error, Elizabeth corrected it while the climbers were on the mountain, but when they came back, the woman laughingly pointed out that "living with girlfriend" was the correct answer.

Elizabeth covers all of the expeditions that climb inside Nepal or on the other side of the border mountains. As she explains, "You can't do just half of Everest." Although the Nepalese Ministry of Tourism issues an expedition permit list, it's not that useful to her, as it arrives too late each season and is incomplete. Some of the teams listed don't show up and others not on the list do. Instead, she calls the trekking agencies to determine what teams are coming through which agency, when they are arriving, which hotels they are using, and the names of the expedition leaders. The interviewing work takes about three and a half months each year, with three main climbing seasons: spring, fall, and winter. The fall season is the busiest, as many teams prefer the calm period between the end of the monsoons and the beginning of the winter winds. Even though the spring brings warmer weather, especially up high, there is a constant fear of the onset of the monsoons. During the climbing seasons, Elizabeth spends "half my waking hours" doing interviews and recording the results.

American climber Ed Viesturs loves it when the phone rings in his hotel, often just as he's checking in. "We expect it—it's fun." Elizabeth fills him in on the latest gossip, and he does likewise. He finds that she's easygoing with him most of the time, but occasionally she's in a grumpy mood and really grills him about something. He remembers being cross-examined after one expedition about the location of his Camp II. He couldn't remember, but she insisted on an exact location for her seasonal mountaineering report, so he made something up. Unfortunately, he chose the wrong location and was chastised for the mistake. In retrospect, he says, it was funny. Viesturs says she always shows up punctually and nicely dressed, and her hair is always "fixed up." In fact, he makes sure he's properly dressed and combed when he meets her, too. "It's only common courtesy and respect," he says. He feels he must be careful about what he says and how he says it.

But not everyone is as cooperative as Viesturs. Robin Houston, a climber, physician, and son of Dr. Charles Houston, has had many occasions to see her in action. He has observed mountaineers paying her limited attention, or possibly not respecting her because of their difficult experiences with her. But more experienced mountaineers, those with a bit more savvy and consideration, do cooperate, he says. They respect her accuracy and diligence. They appreciate the fact that she makes it easy for them to get their story told. They don't have to chase her down; she does that for them. All they have to do is tell her their intentions, give her accurate information, tell her what actually happened, and she does the rest—carefully and precisely.

Tashi Tenzing, grandson of Tenzing Norgay, doesn't understand why some climbers won't cooperate. "They think that she's taking their valuable time, but in fact it's she who is making time for them—making time and effort to record accurately what it is that's so important to them."

But some find her cold and dismissive. American climber and filmmaker David Breashears once overheard her scold someone for not reading a particular book in preparation for the interview. He has seen her be dismissive to the point of arrogance—almost belligerence—and thinks it comes from having had deferential and accommodating Nepali staff for years. Some find this side of her irritating. In his opinion, it is her only negative side.

Australian climber Greg Child recounts a story about her coming to interview him after his attempt to climb Menlungtse. She asked if he had summited; when he said no, she replied, "Well that was easy," and left. He had ordered a pot of tea for them, but she left before it arrived. He believes there was someone else in the hotel she wanted to interview but she came to see him first. His summation: "Kind of a thorny old dame."

By contrast, Houston has often observed her work hard to get to the bottom of a complex or controversial story. She does multiple interviews on the same expedition, getting different points of view and triangulating her data to ferret out the truth, particularly if she suspects that new ground has been broken or there was friction within the team. He remembers her sitting at the Summit Hotel asking tough questions of youthful mountaineers and "holding court."

That's what I observe over the next few days too. Following Pemba Dorje's interview, Elizabeth goes into detective mode, checking her files to discover whether anyone was climbing high on the north side of Everest at that time. Not a soul reached the summit that day, although three Bulgarians had gone to 8300 meters. Checking her notes, she sees Pemba's claim that he saw headlamps above the last camp. She goes back to the Bulgarian file to learn that just one climber went out that night to search for a missing climber. So, if there were three headlamps, where did they come from? Puzzled, she puts the matter aside for the moment.

Late that night she remembers a Sherpa friend who has summited Everest from the north. She will ask him about the probability of seeing headlamps in that situation. Two days later, Chuldim sits on her couch poring over photographs. He is firm: "You can't see down that side of the mountain from the summit." He explains it would be impossible to see headlamps coming up on the north side because a small ridge blocks the view.

The puzzle remains unsolved, and her tenacity won't allow her to let it go. Next step: she needs to verify Pemba's timetable, which he says he radioed throughout the night to the Sagarmatha Pollution Control Committee man, Nuru Jangbu, at base camp. This is Elizabeth Hawley, Himalayan detective and mountain chronicler, in action—ruthless with her questions, dogged with her fact checking, and tireless in her efforts to know the truth.

Over the ten days I spend with Elizabeth Hawley, I learn about her insatiable interest in politics and history, her belief in a good education, her extensive world travels, her eclectic friends, her strong work ethic, her quirky sense of humor, and, of course, her deep knowledge of Himalayan climbing. Austrian climber and filmmaker Kurt Diemberger once told me, "I'm sure if she would open her mouth she would tell a whole book of stories about mountaineers . . . I hope she will do that for you." That she did—and as she told her stories, I learned an entirely new perspective on the history of climbing in Nepal.

*She knew one thing she didn't want to be—
somebody's secretary.*

Where Elizabeth came from has been the subject of much speculation in the climbing community. A number of American climbers were convinced she was British. Some speculated she was American but adopted a British accent as part of her image. Others were positive she came from Boston. Her nephew indicated she came from *Mayflower* stock—the source of her abruptness and stiff upper lip.

Sitting opposite her penetrating stare, I asked for details of her personal family history with a trepidation that soon evaporated. She was extremely forthcoming: family trees, lineage charts, photographs, letters, and stories that she obviously enjoyed retelling. Her memory was impressive. After hearing only the slightest reference to something I had read in one of her thousands of letters written decades earlier, she would launch into another anecdote. One story led to another, and the hours slipped by.

Elizabeth's maternal grandfather, Edward Everett Gore, was born in the coal-mining community of Carlinville, Illinois. He attended Blackburn College, a business school in Jacksonville, Illinois, and "read law" for four years in a Carlinville law office.

In 1895 Edward and his wife, Amanda, and their first child, Florelle, moved to Chicago, where he had been offered a job as an accountant. The first day he reported for work, his employer announced that there was no job after all. In shock, he dug into the entrepreneurial depths of his character and opened his own office. In recounting the history, it became clear that self-sufficiency, making do, and getting on are traits and values Elizabeth shared with her grandfather.

Edward became a leader in Chicago's business and civic circles, taking an active interest in educational and public affairs. His role as president of the Chicago Crime Commission led to several threats against his life by the Capone syndicate. He retaliated by organizing the "Secret Six," an undercover group that collected evidence to help indict Chicago mobsters during the height of the gang wars.

Elizabeth's grandmother Amanda was college educated, as was her mother, a rare achievement for women of that era. If Elizabeth's favorite memory of her grandmother is that she was college educated, her favorite memory of her grandfather is the ample size of his comfortable lap—possibly due to his fondness for chocolate. Every Friday afternoon, he allegedly bought ten pounds of chocolate and by Monday morning, it was gone.

Their eldest daughter, Florelle, was Elizabeth's mother. Born in 1894, her unusual first name was a combination of two beloved aunts, Flora and Cinderella. Florelle hated the name and tired of people asking about it. She graduated summa cum laude from Northwestern University in English literature and went on to work in labor relations for the League of Women Voters for most of her career. She was also treasurer for the organization in the state of New York.

On the other side of the family, the Hawleys landed in Connecticut in the seventeenth century, initially settling in Hawleyville. Born to them in 1893 was Elizabeth's father, Frank. Frank and Florelle met, fell in love, and married while at Northwestern University. He served in the Navy during World War I, then came home to qualify as an accountant and join his father's Chicago accounting firm. The couple settled in La Grange, a Chicago suburb.

Elizabeth Anne Hawley was born in Chicago on November 9, 1923. The infant Elizabeth had severe digestive problems, and as a young girl, she came close to dying before her condition was finally diagnosed as gluten intolerance. From then on, starch was banned from her diet. This was bad news for a little girl who loved birthday parties. Not only could she not eat the cake, she couldn't even eat the ice cream. Instead, she got Jell-O and bananas. However, a pediatrician suggested that when her digestive system was finally ready for starch, she would ask for it again. And so she did. One fine day when she was eleven years old, she asked for mashed potatoes. She had outgrown the intolerance. In a letter to her grandfather in 1937 at age fourteen, she wrote, "Dear Grandpa, I went to a party last night. . . . We had a lot of fun and then ate ice cream and cake." In an unfortunate postscript, her gluten intolerance returned at the age of seventy-five. Once again, it was Jell-O and bananas for dessert.

Shortly after Elizabeth's birth, the family moved to Yonkers, New York. There were four of them: Frank and Florelle, Elizabeth, and her brother John, nine years her senior. Soon thereafter, however, Florelle and the two children returned to Huntington, Indiana, to settle some issues surrounding Florelle's deceased father's estate. He had been president of a bank and his affairs were complicated and confused. It took four long years to sort out, and during this time, they lived apart from her father. Perhaps because of this, Elizabeth never really felt close to him. Though devoted to her father, she did not feel the profound connection with him that she felt with her mother.

Although the Hawleys were neither strict nor religious, they were a family of some social prominence and therefore Elizabeth was expected to attend Sunday school. It was here that a seed of skepticism was planted that would flourish over the years. One day at Sunday school, when she was four, the children were asked to sing, "Dropping, dropping, dropping/hear the pennies fall/every one for Jesus/he will get them all." Her practical little brain thought about it and concluded, "No way, he won't get my pennies."

Elizabeth was not active in sports as a girl, but her practical side showed in her love of sawing, hammering, and chopping wood. She liked to do useful things and was always a bit of a loner. Her brother was more socially inclined; he mixed easily with people and loved to tease her.

Elizabeth remembers summer vacations at her great-grandfather's place on Lake Minnetonka, Minnesota, as "hot as hell." There were huge family get-togethers at the lake—a beautiful spot that had yet to be "discovered." Few cars traveled the unpaved roads during the Depression, and farmers still used horse carts. The kids ran freely in the woods from dawn to dusk, untethered by parents or responsibilities.

Once the family estate business was cleared up, Elizabeth's father joined them and they moved to Birmingham, Michigan, where she attended grammar school. But when reports of infantile paralysis (polio) closed down the school, Florelle took the children to their grandmother's for safety. On the way there, Elizabeth became restless and fevered. Soon she couldn't raise her right arm. Polio. The standard treatment was to immobilize the limb, but, luckily for Elizabeth, her doctor knew of more modern treatments, which may have saved her arm from deformity. She was given a brace to immobilize the limb in an upward position for twenty-three hours a day. But for one hour each evening, the brace was removed while her mother massaged her arm and tried to move it for Elizabeth as best she could. This continued for three and a half months, and feeling and mobility eventually returned. According to family lore, there were three cases of polio in Birmingham that year: one died, one was paralyzed for life, and the third was Elizabeth.

The family next moved to New York for her father to find work because, then in the depths of the Depression, the business climate in Michigan could no longer support them. Before moving, her parents researched where the best schools were located, finally deciding on Scarsdale. The school was excellent—they even managed to "fix" Elizabeth's Midwest accent, which her mother wanted her to lose.

After that, they moved several times to increasingly comfortable houses. The last one was large and filled with antiques and masses of books, but generally they lived quite frugally. They made good use of the local library, but if their friends wanted to give a gift to the Hawleys, it was easy—give them a book.

Elizabeth inherited this love of reading and was an insatiable reader the rest of her life. While staying with family friends in Woodstock when she was eighteen, she listed the books she had read thus far that summer in her weekly letter to her mother: *You Can't Do Business with Hitler, I Saw It Happen in Norway,* and *The White Cliffs,* with

Europe in the Spring next on her list. Her brother John was already at Princeton, where he proved to be an excellent student, although not a bookworm. He was active socially and athletically and was on the Princeton rowing team.

Three years later, she was ensconced at camp in Sackets Harbor, New York, where she was to spend the summer. Weekly letters to her mother—a tradition that would be lifelong—reveal a mixed response to the highly scheduled days of swimming, riding, games, and excursions, as well as a penchant for detail. Her mother wanted to know what she had been eating at camp. Elizabeth's response left nothing to the imagination and indicates an early fondness for lists:

Breakfast—1 glass tomato juice
    2 rolls with butter
    1 glass milk
    1 banana
Lunch—potato salad
    glass of water
    bread and butter
    raspberries and blackberries
Supper—baked beans (I didn't like them)
    glass of water
    bread and butter
    chocolate candy bar with peanuts

She summarized her camp experience as, "It's quite strange here—but I like it."

While she was in high school the family bought an old-fashioned summer home in the Green Mountains at Dorset, Vermont. Called "Hollow's End" because it was at the end of Hollow Road, the house was her parents' joy. They enjoyed big family gatherings there and worked endlessly on the house. Elizabeth spent hours watching the carpenters, loving the fact that something useful was being created. As a family, they spent their time swimming in the brook, gathering stones, fishing, and wandering in the woods and getting lost. Elizabeth often hiked with her father, clarifying years later that it was hiking—not climbing—that they did. Her highest point was Mount Mansfield at just over 4000 feet (1219 meters). Elizabeth loved the hills around Dorset and later found reminiscent hills around Kathmandu.

Although Elizabeth was closer to her mother than her father, it would be unfair to ignore him as an influence in her life. Some describe him as a typical accountant, immersed in his work and distant from his family, but correspondence between Elizabeth and her father reveals a respectful relationship. He took an active and specific interest in her doings, her education, and her friends and often gave her names and introductions to people he thought she would be interested in meeting or who could help her. His financial training was probably a blessing, as the family struggled somewhat, especially during the war, to keep up their comfortable, middle-class lifestyle. This included the summer home in Dorset as well as supporting two children through college. Her father agonized over the smallest details of their finances. A letter to his wife in 1942 reveals his concerns: "Have spent hours more on our budget and, after chiseling away here and whittling away there, I think I have at last produced something for us to follow."

Even as a young girl, Elizabeth felt fortunate to be born into a family that was reasonably well-to-do. But looking back, she thinks that at the time she did not fully fathom the hardships her parents endured to ensure her comfort and a good education.

While in high school, she took particular pleasure in grammar bees—"I was a hot shot." Always the competitor, she quickly learned that when the teacher distributed the bits of paper with the questions, it was best to avoid the long pieces of paper because those questions were harder! One of her high school teachers asked the class what they wanted to do when they finished school. Elizabeth sassily replied that she didn't know, but she knew one thing she didn't want to be—somebody's secretary. And she purposely did not take shorthand or typing, firmly rejecting that stereotypical female role. Years later, a newsletter was prepared for her sixtieth high school reunion (which she did not attend) to update everyone on various classmates' activities. One of her schoolmates wrote "Elizabeth has some sort of job where she interviews all the climbers who attempt to scale Mount Everest and other tall mountains in Nepal." She had delivered on her promise to refrain from being somebody's secretary.

In 1941 Elizabeth enrolled in the University of Michigan. More than sixty years later, as she tells about those formative years, the personalities, classes, and incidents float to the surface with clarity and focus, as though it happened yesterday.

It didn't take her long to become completely immersed in classes, starting with political science, English, zoology, and history. She was particular about choosing her professors, and the biggest coup of all was landing Professor Slosson for history. He was a well-known—almost revered—professor, and it was her own determination that got her into his much-coveted class.

Orientation week included a number of tests. Elizabeth did well, scoring in the ninety-sixth percentile in English and the ninety-third percentile in aptitude. The other big event early in her first semester was sorority rushing. She received open-house invitations to fourteen sororities and was pleased when several asked her back after the initial meetings. She decided that the most interesting was Alpha Xi Delta. Phones rang off the hooks as the girls in the dorm scrambled to get the best possible sorority membership. But there was to be no sorority for Elizabeth—nobody picked her up. In the end, she was relieved. She couldn't imagine living in a house full of "chummy" girls, expected to do all kinds of social things together. Although her mother didn't care whether she joined a sorority, her grandmother was disappointed and let her feelings be known.

By October, there were a number of extracurricular lecture and concert series to attend, and Elizabeth showed an eclectic curiosity in her choices: from British labor law to the war in Europe to symphony concerts. But she was disappointed in her fellow classmates and didn't mince words in a letter to her mother, where she observed that most of the students seemed to be leading an "awfully artificial life here. They don't read the papers; they don't know what's going on in the world and they aren't the least bit interested. It's like moving to a different planet where there is no war." She remembers several students in her dormitory asking about the location of Pearl Harbor when it was bombed later that year.

College wasn't all books and exams, though. Elizabeth's wicked sense of humor was apparent as she described her social plans to her mother. "Well hand out the flag and ring all the bells: I'm going to a dance next Saturday.... The gentleman in question is a sophomore, would-be constitutional lawyer, from Rochester, Indiana. He isn't too wonderful, but he might have a roommate." And lest she be perceived as too bookish, she was as concerned as many other young university students about things like her waist size (which apparently changed by three-quarters of an inch from before to after dinner) and her need for a yellow pullover sweater, black spectator pumps with toes, and a full plaid skirt, as well as the recently published *Secret History of the American Revolution* by Carl Van Doren. Her mother bought all her clothes for her in New York, so Elizabeth kept her updated on her precise measurements. As always, Elizabeth was exact: "waist—27½", hips—35½", bust—33"."

Her first midsemester exams yielded Bs in zoology, political science, and history. She was madly in love with her history course, less so with political science, and detested zoology. By the semester's end, she had maintained these grades and was relieved to have moved her history grade up to an A. Her father even received a congratulatory letter from the University of Michigan registrar lauding her efforts and expressing the hope that she would continue to be as successful.

With barely a moment to catch her breath, she was now looking forward to arranging her courses for the next semester. As in any big university with thousands of students and few popular professors, it was difficult to get the courses she wanted: "Tomorrow I go forth to do battle with the most cold-blooded members of the darned institution I've ever known—the University of Michigan—in other words I am going to register." In a revealing self-analysis, she adds, "It will be interesting to see what happens when an indestructible force meets an immovable object!"

Curious about unknown places, Elizabeth decided to attend a lecture and film night about India. She was disappointed, commenting to her mother that it was "superficial, silly and misleading, if not altogether insulting." Even more disappointing was the reaction of her friends, who thought the evening interesting. Elizabeth was brutal in her evaluation: "Interesting, hell! That was supposed to be an educational lecture, not an ignorant travelogue." Famous in later life for her impatience and sharp tongue, those habits were developing even now, as her standards were very high.

In fact, her standards were rarely met, but when they were, as with her favorite professor Dr. Slosson, she exuded enthusiasm. He was charmed by her as well. He and his wife included her in social functions where they had intense discussions about the war, education, the economy, government, or whatever they chose.

She describes his lectures as masterpieces in form and content, perfect combinations of history and metaphysics, of the particular and the general. It was easy to learn from him. He made it interesting. He made it come alive. She admits to having had a crush on him and cherished the informal evenings in his home, where he proved that he was not only incredibly smart, but also good, kind, and even funny. She was friendly with Mrs. Slosson for a time, but they eventually drifted apart. She didn't respect Mrs. Slosson's intellect, and thought she took up "air space with idle chatter." The trait that rankled Elizabeth the most was that Mrs. Slosson was a domineering woman, and Elizabeth didn't like (other) domineering women. "That poor man!" she exclaimed in a letter to her mother.

Many of the informal discussions and formal debates at the university were about the ongoing war, and Slosson surely influenced her thinking on this topic. He was not an either-or kind of person, but took the historian's perspective of relativity. No matter who won the war, he felt sure that civilization would not be lost. He was equally sure that a pure state of democracy would not be the result—it was a matter of degrees. Others disagreed with him, and Elizabeth relished the debates as stimulation for her ever more curious mind.

Elizabeth's interests moved beyond the borders of America. Partly because of the people (primarily professors) she surrounded herself with, partly because of the lectures and debates she attended, and partly because of the war, she found herself more interested in international affairs than national. She sympathized with Britain's stand against Germany, and didn't agree with the isolationist views of many Americans who wanted no part of a "foreign" war.

She became fascinated with social philosophy, the meaning of free-dom, and the materialistic conceptions of history, democracy, fascism, and socialism. It began to dawn on her that she was leaning toward an honors history program, but for this she needed to be recommended by one of her professors. As much as history interested her, she wondered what she would do with this knowledge. "Is teaching the only answer?" Sensibly, she decided, at age nineteen, that she could be patient; her future might yet reveal itself. It's doubtful she could have imagined what that would look like.

Although there were few students with whom she shared her increasingly awakened consciousness, she and her mother communicated constantly about ideas, giving Elizabeth an outlet for her thoughts. It was a healthy outlet since, as she pointed out to Florelle, the university experience, stimulating though it was, centered on input from her professors: "I don't have the time I would like for thoughts of my own, but it is fascinating gathering those of others." In letters to her mother, she began to develop—and test—her own theories of a moral order within the reality of a world at war. And although she missed her family, New York, and the Green Mountains at Dorset, she admitted, "I really wouldn't trade places for anything."

Discussions with her father were more wrangling in nature, as he tried to channel her academic program into a more practical vein, namely math and calculus. She humored him for a while, but eventually made her own choices, and they didn't include calculus. Her father was not pleased, calling her "selfish and unpatriotic" while pointing out that calculus and other practical courses would prepare her for factory work where she could make a real contribution to the war effort. But she held her own in an argument stretching over a period of months, responding that devoting herself to current history would better prepare her to "win the peace." Her parting shot was, "If this be treason, make the most of it."

Her social life continued, but the men she met did not impress her greatly. "A graduate student who was half bald, a Frenchman who got me smoking a cigarette, and a very nice architect who walked me home," was how she described them. Eventually she began to see a young man named Fred. They attended movies and dances and went for long walks together. She appreciated his company and his intelligence, but didn't find him especially exciting or attractive, and he was conservative in his political views too. She recalls that when they were feeling particularly "dangerous" they might sip some wine. Fred eventually pressed her to marry him, but she was not in the mood for marriage, particularly not to Fred. They continued to see each other, however. Unlike her brother, she wasn't interested in sports, although she did attend the odd football game. After a particularly conclusive win against her mother's alma mater she wrote, "But one might ask, so what?"

She began to involve herself with the Post-War Council, a student organization that coordinated a series of extracurricular lectures and events. A wide-ranging program included philosopher Bertrand Russell and the Beethoven scholar and pianist Arthur Schnabel. She was also instrumental in pulling together a regular series of student-faculty discussions that resulted in good debates on topics such as hate, particularly in relation to the war. One point of view was that there must be more organized hate in order to win the war. Elizabeth strongly disagreed with this, but she didn't see Churchill as a solution either. "Churchill just doesn't seem to be able to see beyond his nose in regard to planning for the future." She concluded that "the British simply muddle their way through things, and tend to shy away from people with too many brains."

The Post-War Council provided her with an opportunity to learn about organizations and how they worked, and how she could influence how they worked. An opening came up on the executive committee, so she offered her services on a temporary basis. Thinking strategically, she realized the role would put her in close proximity to professors, campus advisors, and other decision makers at the university, a place she enjoyed being. By spring, she had been elected Council chairman and not long after she was asked to be president of her dormitory—the largest one on campus. As she moaned to her mother, "I'm sure only Mrs. Roosevelt is as busy a woman as I am."

But Elizabeth's tendency to speak her mind got her in trouble with the Post-War Council—a messy situation ensued that resulted in her being "relieved" of her job as chairman, although she ended up with the position of executive secretary-treasurer. She was strongly criticized because she had been part of a decision that no member of the Council could appear on stage with guest speakers—and then she broke that rule. She was subsequently viewed as a self-promoter and asked to step down. Seriously disappointed, she confided to her mother that the process "left your little daughter a much sadder and wiser person." She was demoted once again shortly thereafter, this time to program chair. Nevertheless, she continued to pour energy into the organization because she believed its work had value.

Elizabeth relied on her mother, not only for intellectual sparring, but also for practical needs. In addition to continuing to buy her clothes for her in New York, her mother was also in charge of mending them, which in January 1943 happened to be a sock. Elizabeth's quirky sense of humor was in evidence as she sent a single green sock home and begged her mother to mend it because it was "vital" to her wardrobe. Her mother teased her about this attachment to a sock, but Elizabeth defended herself, explaining that her mother obviously didn't know her socks: "I have them so well trained that when I whistle one tune the green ones come out, and when I whistle a different tune another color comes out." And she constantly pleaded with her mother to send her care packages of food: "It would be grand if some day a box of lemon cookies or some fudge or something came for no apparent reason except that you acted like a normal parent with her child away in school and sent her something extra to eat!" She wasn't afraid to ask for what she wanted.

Elizabeth was elated in February 1943 when the academic committee approved her plan to do honors work in history. They took her grades into consideration as well as her considerable efforts in producing a term paper on the causes of war. Elizabeth herself was pleased with the paper, as it proved to her that she could work independently, do her own research, and come to her own coherent conclusions. In this case, it was a complicated subject for a nineteen-year-old to tackle, but she did it well, digging beyond the superficial to argue that the psychological state of people's minds made them willing to fight, thereby facilitating war. She concluded that, in order to prevent war, it wasn't the incidents that needed to be prevented, but rather the state-of-mind factors that should be eliminated.

Her mother challenged her, maintaining that if man could learn to live under law and order and regard war as taboo, peace would be achieved. But Elizabeth insisted that this was a restrictive point of view, that more could be achieved by concentrating on the "spirit of brotherhood" where men worked toward the same goal—peace. She agreed that law and order was necessary, but achieving real peace required something more creative and dynamic than simply obeying rules.

It was during this time that she began to formulate her thoughts about the role of an historian, an interesting foreshadowing of her future work. It started with an article in the *New York Times* on whether American history should be required study at universities. Elizabeth saw immediately that its required inclusion was irrelevant if it wasn't taught correctly, citing her high school American history courses, where she had learned facts, but not their relative importance or proper perspective. She had learned about the trees, but not the forest. She was beginning to understand that facts were important, but something was needed on which to hang them. She equated the learning of facts to the work of an antiquarian, while the understanding of context was the sign of a true historian. Little did she know that fifty years later many in the mountaineering community would debate these same issues around her life's work documenting the history of Himalayan climbing.

A new man entered her life in the form of Harold Sokwitne, secretary of the Post-War Council. They had many opportunities to work together, and they now began seeing each other socially. A tall redhead from Hillsdale, Michigan, he came from a religious background and had intended to follow that line of work himself but rebelled. Now twenty and a freshman, his liveliness and conversational abilities attracted Elizabeth. She also continued to see Fred. They were two strikingly different personalities and she saw good points in each of them. Fred was pleasant to be with, but was too complimentary: "He likes my eyes, he thinks I'm brilliant, he thinks I have great ability." It was all too much for Elizabeth. Harold (nicknamed Sok), on the other hand, didn't have Fred's polished manners, and he didn't compliment her at all—he was perfectly aware of her faults. But in August 1943 Sok was called for induction into the Naval Air Corps. They had one last wonderful evening together in Detroit, and he was off.

By November Elizabeth was beginning to pay her own way with an assistant position in the history department. Taking attendance and correcting papers brought her a grand total of $250 per semester. She was proud of herself, partly because of the money, but mostly because of the recognition. In addition to her work for the history department, she was beginning to get speaking opportunities, often arranged by Slosson (whom she now called by his first name, Preston). The local Business and Professional Women's Club, Rotary Clubs, and high schools all had the benefit of her keen interest in, and growing knowledge of, international affairs.

Her personal relationship with the Slossons deepened as their working relationship matured. She now spent most Sunday afternoons and evenings with them, frequently staying overnight. In the summer of 1944, against her mother's advice, she moved in with them.

By September of that year, she had wrapped up her classwork and was excited about her family's arrival for graduation. Her brother John couldn't attend because of a serious illness. After majoring in philosophy at Princeton, John had gone on to medical school at the Physicians and Medical School at Columbia University—where he was a brilliant student. He then joined the Navy, during which time he contracted tuberculosis and was sent to a sanitarium in Trudeau, Vermont. Because of his illness, he was subsequently discharged from the Navy.

Shortly before graduating, Elizabeth made a decision to carry on with her studies and immediately begin work on an advanced degree. As a graduate student, her classes were different from before—much smaller or in an individual study format. She thrived in this environment.

The tides of war seemed to have changed and she felt a sense of relief. She was beginning to think seriously about her future now, as various ideas presented themselves. One was to enter the service as an officer in training, providing a chance to go overseas and be attached to the Allied military government. Another option was to go into State Department work, but when she inquired with the State Department she was told that, although they were impressed with her qualifications, returning veterans would fill any openings.

One offer she considered was a teaching position at the Oklahoma College for Women. The president of the college told her that their goal was the "development of capable young women with beauty of character, personal charm, gracious manners, and social insight, willing and able to perform successfully the duties of life in their generation." She wasn't excited by the thought, in part because of concerns about the overall intellectual atmosphere of the college. But, being practical, she knew it would provide her with the experience needed to compete successfully against the returning servicemen for good jobs in good universities in the future. Another benefit of taking the job was that it was permanent, with possibilities for promotion. To her mind, the drawbacks were serious: it was a small college in the middle of nowhere, and her mother was dead set against it, skeptical about the quality of life that Oklahoma could provide her daughter. Florelle's opinion prevailed—after college Elizabeth went, not to Oklahoma, but to New York.

As often happens when a long period of intensity nears its end, she had had enough of Ann Arbor and the University of Michigan and was ready to leave, vowing that if she did continue with doctoral studies, it would definitely not be in Ann Arbor. Above all, she was tired and needed a break. A time of rest and relaxation at the country home in Dorset was just what she needed. The only problem was the lack of a job; Elizabeth was a doer and she liked to have a plan of action. Not having one was a worry.

The Sherlock Holmes of the mountaineering world . . .

Before I met Elizabeth, many people told me about her attention to detail and dogged insistence on getting things right. It's her signature style. Heather Macdonald, Elizabeth's assistant for a couple of years in the 1990s, asserts that Elizabeth insists on knowing the source for every bit of information, grilling climbers to ascertain whether it was 7550 meters or 7555 meters. The climbers could be exhausted and their "brains half-melted" after being at altitude for weeks, Heather remembers, but Elizabeth wouldn't let up. In time, she came to be affectionately known as the Sherlock Holmes of the mountaineering world. Where did this diligence and attention to detail come from, I wondered. Who taught her these techniques and how did she gain the confidence to cross-examine world-class climbers in such an authoritative manner?

Independence is another of her strong traits. Living alone most of her adult life, Elizabeth carved out a place for herself in a new and strange environment. Lady Hillary describes her as "one of the original feminists," adding that she doubts Elizabeth will thank her for saying it. Heather Macdonald is convinced that her early self-confidence grew from her insatiable curiosity. If so, it allowed her to evolve into a woman who is comfortable with high-profile climbers, royalty, government officials, and writers. She has an innate sense of protocol. I was curious how this young American woman became so worldly. As she recounted the next decade, parts of the mystery were revealed.

Back in New York in 1946, she went job hunting, honors degrees in hand, at a number of organizations and foundations, finally arriving at *Fortune* magazine, part of the publishing family that included *TIME*, *Life*, and *Sports Illustrated*. It was her lucky day. She started immediately as an editorial researcher earning $39.40 a week. Researchers were initially assigned six months of training in "the morgue," where thousands of files on people and issues were kept. Each file had original material—tear sheets, letters, photographs—supporting and informing that particular topic. It was her job to learn what was in those files, to update them constantly from newspaper clippings and other materials, and to access that information whenever the magazine needed it. It's easy to see the similarity between the morgue system and Elizabeth's future mountaineering archive.

Unfortunately, there was a not-so-subtle hierarchy at *Fortune* at that time. Without exception, researchers were women and writers were men. She saw no way to break that mold. In retrospect, she's not sure she had the makings of a writer, and others agree with her. Former colleagues described her as "brilliant and literal," but not terribly imaginative. Even as a lowly researcher, however, she found opportunities. Sometimes she traveled with a writer and took notes, and sometimes she traveled alone, throughout the States as well as to Canada and Brazil. After the writer finished the piece, it would come back to her to be checked—every word required a dot above it to indicate it had been checked, re-checked, and cross-checked. It was an arduous system that took considerable time and effort, but it appealed to her sense of order.

She lived in an apartment at 226 Madison Avenue and her first office was in the Empire State Building, later moving to the Time-Life Building near Rockefeller Center. She started her day at about 10:00 or 11:00 A.M., worked until 2:00 A.M., and then walked home. The first thing she did each morning was read the *New York Times*.

From her recent university studies in world politics, she had developed a curiosity about far-off places. That led to an interest in travel and, now that she was working and had a salary, she began to use her annual vacation to do just that. Although her salary was small, she lived frugally, eating a tomato sandwich with mayonnaise for lunch most days. This gave her the freedom to travel widely and in good style—usually alone.

Elizabeth's first trip abroad was to England in 1948 when, in October, she boarded the RMS *Queen Mary* for Southampton. Her first stop was London and all that it had to offer. She loved it: Big Ben, the Houses of Parliament, London cabs, the architecture, and the fog. Then it was north to Scotland and into the countryside of Wales and rural England. After all that she had studied and read and observed in movies, it astonished her how different and rich the experience was when seeing it for herself. "Britain is a fascinating place and I'm having the time of my life," she wrote her mother.

After cramming in as much of Britain as possible, Elizabeth moved on to immerse herself in the great cities of Europe, including Paris, Rome, and Florence. She walked endlessly, mentally cataloging the sounds and smells of the streets, inspecting museums, historical monuments, palaces, gardens, and churches.

But it had to end, and she reluctantly sailed home. It had been an unforgettable experience, one she hoped to have again. Her appetite for travel had been whetted in a serious way—back in New York, where it was work and more work, she immediately began scrimping and saving for the next big trip.

A family tragedy awaited her. Shortly after she returned from Europe, her brother John died suddenly. Having recovered from tuberculosis and completed his medical degree, John had begun practicing as a physician and married Anne, whom he met while doing medical research. They had a child and named him Michael. But John's health took another downturn when he was diagnosed with Hodgkin's disease. The disease appeared suddenly, developed swiftly, and was fatal. Elizabeth's brilliant brother and only sibling died in 1949 at age thirty-five.

Family members and friends recall that Elizabeth appeared to be cool and stoical about this loss. They described her as a model of the stiff upper lip—even though she was inwardly devastated by the premature death of her brother. John's wife remarried and had more children, but young Michael didn't adjust easily to this new arrangement and his adolescence was troubled. Elizabeth kept tabs on him through her correspondence with her mother and worried constantly about his future.

Years later, Michael was touched and surprised to learn she had been an advocate for him in his adolescence, that she understood what he was going through, even from a distance. She had never told her nephew about her early and ongoing concerns about his troubled childhood and youth. Nor did she tell him how pleased she was when he later appeared to be settling down to a good education. Her pride, like her earlier concerns, went unspoken.

Back at *Fortune*, Elizabeth's routine continued with research for the magazine's writers. She worked hard, but made time for a few friends, too. Eleanor Schwartz, who sat next to her at work, was one of them. She remembers Elizabeth as somewhat shy and "terribly smart," not very feminine, and lacking a "sizzling social life." Years later, Eleanor moved into Elizabeth's apartment when she left for Kathmandu. Elizabeth also admired and befriended her boss, Mary Johnston, who was an avid traveler like herself. Fred still came around to pursue her—with no results.

In 1951, her cousin, Lee Kneerim, an aspiring actress, moved in with her. Elizabeth knew that Lee had a wish to meet the great actress Judith Anderson, so she decided to do something about it. First, she bought a copy of Robinson Jeffer's translation of *Medea*, a play Judith Anderson was starring in. Then, she tracked down the elusive Anderson, asked her to sign the play, and gave it to Lee for her birthday, along with a ticket to the performance in a good seat. This act of kindness meant a great deal to Lee, and the signed play remains one of her most prized possessions years later. She describes Elizabeth as a "typical Vermonter"—somewhat taciturn—but remembers that when Elizabeth gave her that thoughtful gift, "her face revealed warmth and love."

Another relative, a rather famous distant cousin and a friend of her grandmother, came to visit. Irma Rombauer, author of *Joy of Cooking*, was affectionately called "Cousin Irma" by the family. Elizabeth had never shown any interest in cooking, so was unaware of Cousin Irma's connection to the well-known cookbook. Elizabeth could boil an egg and make toast, but there wasn't much else in her repertoire. While Irma was in New York, however, she called Elizabeth, resulting in an invitation to dinner. Her mother was aghast—"Elizabeth is going to cook for Irma!" During dinner, Elizabeth asked Irma what brought her to New York, and found out, to her discomfort, that she was in town to do book signings for the famous cookbook. It was the first time Elizabeth realized who she was.

Her mother called the next day to ask, "What did you serve?" Elizabeth first chastised her mother for not having warned her, but then replied, "Oh, just a regular dinner." Her mother pressed, "Yes, but what was it?" "I had lamb chops, mashed potatoes, and canned peas, and for dessert I served Jell-O." Her mother was horrified, but Cousin Irma later sent Elizabeth a signed *Joy of Cooking*, inscribed with a note thanking her for the simple meal. Of course, she didn't know it was the only meal Elizabeth knew how to cook.

Over the next eight years, Elizabeth traveled extensively, keeping a tight budget at home in order to go ever farther afield as her interests widened and her confidence grew. She almost always traveled alone. Traveling through Germany and Austria in the summer of 1949, she began to understand just what the ravages of war look like. Her curiosity led her to visit the Eagle's Nest, Hitler's retreat on top of a mountain in Obersalzberg, and the crematory at Dachau.

She gambled in Monte Carlo and lost 1000 francs—representing a sum of three dollars at the time. Next, she caught the *Simplon-Orient Express* to Trieste, Italy, before venturing into more adventuresome terrain—Yugoslavia—with letters of introduction from Time Inc. to a State Department official in hand. She was delighted to discover that her train compartment companion was a *TIME* researcher who was on assignment in Yugoslavia. Her name was Judy Friedberg.

The meeting with Judy was fortuitous, as they continued to be traveling companions throughout Yugoslavia and beyond. The Ministry of Information had arranged a number of interviews for Elizabeth; between interviews, she and her new friend met various interesting foreign correspondents stationed in Belgrade. Gathering information for a *Fortune* story was more difficult than Elizabeth imagined. Things moved slowly in Belgrade. It was common to have appointments canceled or postponed with little or no notice, and it was hard to find the right person to answer a particular question. She did interview the deputy minister on law, a member of the Central Committee of Trade Unions, and an executive of the Women's Anti-Fascist Front.

Traveling through Macedonia, Bosnia, Herzegovina, and the Dalmatian coast, she witnessed, for the first time, isolated and primitive villages.

She saw scenery that was wild, barren, and dramatic. She experienced her first exposure to the Islamic religion, and she obtained interviews with people who had never been interviewed by a foreigner. Upon her return to Belgrade, she was thrilled to be invited to a gala reception celebrating Yugoslavia's national holiday, where she was introduced to Marshal Tito. She delighted in writing her mother that he was "courtly" and had chatted with her on a number of topics. She knew that *Fortune* would be pleased with the results. She was proud that she had learned to move effortlessly between the high society of government officialdom and the rough conditions of the countryside.

In 1951 Elizabeth traveled to Berlin, where she had arranged letters of introduction to various interesting and influential residents. She was entertained at cocktail parties and shown around the city in fine style. But there wasn't much to see. Berlin was so badly destroyed in the war that she concluded the most interesting places were where important buildings had once stood.

She went on to Helsinki, Finland, where she connected with the foreign ministry's press section and arranged for tours of factories and interviews with individuals involved in Finland's reparations payment program. She discovered a dramatic story of a country that was surmounting its postwar problems and beginning a revival. At the moment, consumer goods were still scarce and expensive, but when war reparations payments to Russia ended the following year, it was generally thought that Finland would move into the world market with confidence. Perhaps her best interview yet was with the woman commonly known to be the prime minister's mistress, who was also a part-time correspondent for the Associated Press. Elizabeth noted: "She must have good inside sources."

She went to Rovaniemi, the principal town of Finnish Lapland, near the Arctic Circle, where it was minus twenty-four degrees Celsius at night and dark by 3:00 P.M. every afternoon. She was there to see the Lapps and reindeer and, more importantly, to see the reconstruction efforts after the Germans torched Lapland in 1944. When she expressed an interest to see some of the country north of Rovaniemi, the local police chief accommodated by sending her to the Swedish border in a police car accompanied by two Finnish policemen—officially, they were on a smuggling patrol.

She enjoyed three entertaining days traveling through rolling country covered in pine, birch, and snow. The colors were magnificent—mauve and purple with a sky of blue and pink—which was due, she thought, to the low angle of the sun. They didn't find any smugglers, but she doubts they were seriously looking.

She also experienced her first sauna, and wasn't overly impressed with this Saturday night tradition. But she was amused to learn that when the Finns began rebuilding their towns after the war, the saunas went up first. In answer to her mother's persistent questions about Finland, Elizabeth's observations to her mother were peculiar: "The Lapps are some kind of mysterious people with an unknown ancestry, but they don't have much resemblance to an Eskimo, and I believe their cultural level is supposed to be a bit higher—at least they all belong to the Lutheran Church."

In 1953 Elizabeth headed to Tunisia, Algeria, and Morocco, her first time on African soil. As usual, she contacted the local public-affairs officer at the U.S. consulate, who went out of his way to ensure that she saw everything of interest. In addition to touring the city of Tunis and nearby Carthage, she traveled for a couple of days with some visiting Americans to Kairouan, a Muslim holy city 150 kilometers from Tunis. After spending so much time in Europe, where the land had been inhabited and worked for centuries, she found it fascinating to travel through a landscape that was majestic in its emptiness. Wandering through the labyrinthine Casbah in Constantine, Algeria, she found it dark, dirty, and mysterious—alluring, but also a primitive and difficult place to live.

In the middle of one all-night journey, she was obliged to change trains at a remote station in Algeria. As there were few people around, she struck up a conversation with a man who then pummeled her with questions in French about the famous Rosenberg spy case—a laborious discussion to have at 1:00 A.M. On another train journey, from Marrakesh to Casablanca, a French expatriate sat down next to her and proposed marriage. She declined, but he persisted. "Why not? Do you not find me handsome?"

Throughout Morocco, she was struck by the number of men who seemed to have nothing to do, and by the notable absence of women in public places. The exception was when there was heavy work to be done; here she saw heavily veiled women carrying heavy loads. Extreme poverty was evident everywhere. It was hard for her to accept, and disturbing to behold, that people here lived in conditions only slightly better than their animals.

She continued her annual travels for the next three years, spending more and more time in the Middle East. On one of these trips, she fell in love with a Sudanese man named Mamoun El Amin in Khartoum. He was a tall, very dark, Muslim Arab. They met on a Nile steamer traveling upriver from Aswan to a town named Wadi Halfa, now at the bottom of Lake Nasser. They spent many hours together on the steamer deck, watching the palm trees glide by, talking, discovering each other.

At the time, Sudan was officially the Anglo-Egyptian Sudan, ruled jointly by Britain and Egypt. It had a British-trained, British-style civil service, and Mamoun was a senior administrator in Khartoum. He fascinated her. He was a study in contrasts—exotic, mysterious, and educated, with a proper English accent. They spent hours in the cool of the evening sipping whiskey on the veranda of her hotel and talking about his work and her travels. It was a short, intense romance. After she left Khartoum for Kenya (British East Africa, as it was then known), she never saw Mamoun again. Decades later, they exchanged letters, trying to reconnect their lives. His began with "My dear Eliza." Handling the faded letters, she admits he was one of the few men she ever considered marrying.

After working for eleven years at *Fortune*, Elizabeth, at age thirty-four, was a little bored. By 1956 it was clear she wouldn't advance any higher than a researcher, even though her work was appreciated and admired. Unsure what to do next with her life, and with no strong emotional ties, she decided the best thing was to get out of New York and really see the world. She took her profit-sharing funds from Time Inc., *Fortune*'s publisher, and set off for as long as the money would hold out. It was the beginning of a new life for Elizabeth Hawley, but one for which she was well prepared.

⸻ ◦ ⸻

And so in 1957 she embarked on an around-the-world journey, master of her own schedule, seeing what she wanted, going where she wished and when it suited her—no more assignments and deadlines as she had known them in New York. In order to be assured of meeting interesting people along the way, she collected numerous letters of introduction before departing. For the next two years, she explored Eastern Europe and the Soviet Union in 1957; the Middle East, Turkey, Israel, Iran, and a number of Arabian countries in 1958; and South and Southeast Asia, including Nepal and Japan, and finally back to the United States in 1959.

She traveled with panache. In each new city, she would stroll into the office of the Time Inc. correspondent as though she were of a different stature—a higher one. She assumed a certain "presence" to pull it off time and time again. As a clever, curious woman traveling alone, she stood out, and she met interesting people wherever she went.

She launched her journey on the SS *Satendam*, leaving New York on April 16. Using Paris as her initial base of operations, she caught a train for Warsaw, a lengthy journey that revealed a countryside and architecture in transition as she moved from the Western styles of France and Germany into Czechoslovakia and Poland. Throughout her travels, trains were her preferred mode of transport in order to see and absorb the country at a civilized pace. Arriving in Warsaw, she was delighted to run into Judy Friedberg, her former traveling companion from Yugoslavia. Working on articles for American magazines, Judy already knew the lay of the land, so she introduced Elizabeth to several American, British, and German journalists.

Elizabeth's first impression of Warsaw was one of shock—so much destruction, so many gaping empty spaces in the center of the city where buildings once stood. But rebuilding had begun, and she walked the city thoroughly, exploring the churches, the Palace of Culture, and the old section that had been rebuilt in its original baroque style. The locals joked with her about the Palace of Culture—a gift from Stalin to Warsaw, and truly ugly. They told her that the best view in town was from the palace's thirtieth-floor observation deck—because it was the only place in the city where it couldn't be seen.

Together with her new journalist friends, she attended the May Day parade, where there was enthusiastic response to the new party secretary, Gomulka. That was nothing compared to the frenzied response to the cardinal of Poland when he led a parade of half a million Poles in the town of Częstochowa for the annual dedication of Poland to the Virgin Mary. Recently released from three years' imprisonment, Cardinal Wyszynski would soon appear on the cover of *TIME*, courtesy of Judy Friedberg.

In Lódź Elizabeth interviewed the chairman of a Jewish civic group in Poland, whose family was in the process of immigrating to Israel, along with most of Poland's seventy thousand other remaining Jews. He explained to her that anti-Semitism persisted in Poland and there was no future for them there. The family story was astonishing. The parents and one of the daughters had spent the last nine months of World War II hidden behind bookstacks in a convent library in Vilna (now known as Vilnius), which was in Poland before the war but now was the capital of Lithuania. Behind the bookstacks was a small room where they lived with nine others. There were three beds, and that was all. They could never raise their voices above a whisper and could only use an upstairs bathroom quietly and secretively at night. While they were in hiding, the Germans systematically destroyed the Vilna ghetto. The Vilna Jewish population went from eighty thousand to five hundred, leaving only eight families intact, including the Lódź family. It was a chance for Elizabeth to hear of a war experience that she could not have imagined while living those war years in Ann Arbor, Michigan.

Traveling around Poland was an extraordinary learning experience. It was a study in contrasts—a devoutly Roman Catholic nation struggling to build a socialist state. Contrasts also existed in the economic well-being of the people. It was an obviously poor country, yet there were well-dressed people in the streets of Warsaw who ate as much caviar as they could manage. Finally, after three weeks in Poland, she felt an "accumulation of drabness in her soul," brought on by the grayness and dustiness and absence of anything well designed or in good working order. So it was with relief and a light heart that she moved on to Sweden and Finland, where "they know a bit about color and design," she wrote her mother.

While in Helsinki, Elizabeth was at the train station, press pass in hand, when Bulganin and Khrushchev arrived from Russia. It was a strange sensation to see, stepping down from the train, a man whose picture she had seen a million times before—the president of the U.S.S.R. Later in the week, she spent an hour seated just below the two men at a union rally in the Olympic Stadium and, at a government reception, Bulganin actually smiled at her. She sensed a coldness in this man with his blank, pale blue eyes, but she found Khrushchev to be amiable, with shrewd and piercing deep-set eyes.

From Helsinki, she took the train to Leningrad for a long-awaited, monthlong trip to the U.S.S.R. She visited Moscow, Stalingrad (now Volgograd), and the provinces, always accompanied by a guide/interpreter who seemed to think Elizabeth was some kind of working journalist in disguise. Therefore, he made sure she saw only the "best" sights. As always, she arranged to connect with people living in the area.

She floated down the Volga and the romantic Don River to Rostov, and eventually ventured on to Georgia. On her flight to Tbilisi, Georgia, she was impressed by the snowcapped Caucasus Mountains and the deep, sun-baked valleys. Everything about this part of the world intrigued her, particularly the dark, fierce-looking Georgians. She tromped through monasteries and fortresses from the second and fifth centuries and visited Gori, where Stalin was born, and where the crude house in which he spent the first four years of his life still stood, carefully preserved.

Then it was on to Kiev and finally the long train journey back to Moscow. She was joined in her double compartment by a Muscovite, who became amorous during the night and attempted to molest her. She managed to fend him off, but found the event unnerving. She did encounter this kind of harassment occasionally, she says, but it was rare. In general, she met a lot of men, and most of them were interesting. In fact, she preferred men. She didn't meet many women in her travels, and admits she found few among them to interest her. It was unusual at the time for a woman to travel alone, especially to such remote places, but Elizabeth was undaunted.

Back in Moscow she met up with some friends from the *New York Times* who were gathering the pieces of a story about recent political machinations in the Central Committee. She tagged along with them to the telegraph office, fascinated to see how they filed their stories, submitted them to the censors, waited for telephone lines to London to send them, and finally retired to a reporter's apartment for a late evening of conversation, scrambled eggs, and whiskey. She had her first taste of a reporter's life, and she loved it.

By July 12 Elizabeth was relieved to arrive in Vienna, a city that she knew, a language that was at least a bit familiar, newspapers that carried stories that made sense to her, a comfortable room with a splendid bath featuring hot and cold running water, and a bed with a reading lamp! Life in Vienna was luxuriously lazy. She slept each day until 10:00 A.M., enjoyed hot chocolate and rolls in her room, read the *New York Times* and the *Herald Tribune* in a nearby park, and then ate lunch. She worked a little on her report on Finnish socialism for *Life*, but more often than not became distracted by a book.

She was also planning the next leg of her trip, this time to Romania and Czechoslovakia. Disappointingly, the Romanians informed her they weren't accepting individual tourists that year. She had more luck with the Czechs and was in Prague by the end of July. Fortunate to have escaped a lot of destruction during the war, the city was mostly intact, with fabulous castles, towers, old bridges, palaces, and churches.

The next few months found Elizabeth traveling throughout Czechoslovakia, West Germany, Greece, Italy, and Yugoslavia. Back in Belgrade she met up with *New York Times* reporter Elie Abel, so she was able to get in on the latest happenings and social functions. The city had transformed itself since her visit six years earlier: her hotel now had soap and stationery for its guests, street lights were working, new buildings had gone up, and the shops were full of goods, many of them imported from Germany, Italy, and France.

She continued hounding the Romanian embassy for a visa to visit that country, only to be frustrated with endless delay tactics, along with a need to do everything multiple times. She described her Belgrade visit to her mother: "Just a mad social whirl by night—and the interior of the Romanian embassy by day."

She remained in Belgrade until mid-December, watching winter descend on the city with a blanket of snow. Walking in the streets was a joy. Each morning she strolled to a newsstand selling the international edition of the *New York Times*, which she would devour cover to cover. It was her way of keeping in touch with the rest of the world, and a daily routine that she treasured. It was a habit she would never break.

There's no reason I know of to hurry away.
—ELIZABETH HAWLEY

B y the end of 1957, tired of waiting for a decision from the Romanians, Elizabeth decided to move on to the next stage of her
travels—the Middle East. Her mother's interest in the life of British
explorer and political power broker Gertrude Bell sparked her initial at-
traction to the region. Elizabeth had read Bell's published letters recounting
tales of desert adventures and nation building in the Middle East, and now
she wanted to see this part of the world for herself. Beyond Gertrude Bell,
however, a whole parade of wandering women inspired Elizabeth: Isak
Dinesen, who had moved to Kenya and struggled to build a farm in Africa;
Alexandra David-Néel, who had disguised herself as a pilgrim to wander
throughout the wildest parts of Asia; and others. Years later she met Freya
Stark in Kathmandu, listened to her stories of adventure, and rode horses
with her up in the hills. Elizabeth devoured all of their stories, admired their
bravery and curiosity, and proceeded to create some stories of her own.

She took the *Balkan Express* from Vienna to Yugoslavia and Greece
and finally, to Istanbul. It was a long journey made entertaining by the
people she met. The Greeks were friendly to her, giving her advice and
introducing her to Greek red wine. But they were critical of her plans to
go to Turkey, and warned her that Turkey was dirty, the Turks themselves
were dirty, and the city smelled. She didn't take them too seriously though,
because none of them had actually been to Turkey. In fact, most of those
traveling through Greece to Turkey were Yugoslavian emigrants looking
for a better life.

In Istanbul Elizabeth marveled at the skyline of minarets and rounded domes. The view up close was less romantic, since it was impossible to ignore the dirty alleys, the buildings in disrepair, and a general state of grime. But it was lovely from a distance. Upon seeing the harem section of the old sultan's palace, she confided to her mother that it must have been "fantastically lovely in its heyday, but an awful bore for the ladies." And she was amused one afternoon to observe Premier Nuri al-Said of Iraq enjoying a parfait in the Hilton coffee shop. She wondered what he thought of it.

From Istanbul she took a berth on the *Taurus Express* to Aleppo, Syria, home of desert explorer Gertrude Bell's much-loved servant, and the beginning of some of Bell's desert wanderings. In Aleppo Elizabeth befriended a young Armenian boy who took her around the city to mosques and palaces, the souk, and a thirteenth-century citadel.

From there she took a seven hour *dolmush* (car) ride to Beirut, where she settled in. Before a week had passed, she was reacquainted with old friends and had acquired a few new ones, including a curious young man named Kim Philby, who later became famous as a double agent for British Intelligence and the Soviet KGB. She also met his father, the famous Arabist John Philby, who had been the first European to visit the southern provinces of the Nejd. John had known Gertrude Bell, and commented to Elizabeth that he thought Gertrude's much-lauded Arabic language skills were questionable. Elizabeth thought he was being a chauvinist.

But the world's politics were urging her to move on. February 21, 1958, was the date set for a plebiscite in Syria and Egypt to confirm the new union of the two countries; although the results were more or less a foregone conclusion, she was sure the event would be memorable and she wanted to be in Damascus to see it. Just then, the United Nations Relief and Works Agency (UNRWA) offered her a six-month job writing articles about the hundreds of thousands of Palestinian refugees, and the work being done for them by UNRWA. The job would entail traveling to places where the refugees lived, such as Lebanon, Syria, Jordan, and Egypt. To support the refugees, UNRWA needed to raise money; therefore, they needed to raise their profile, particularly in the English-speaking world. How could she resist? She was pleased, not only because of the financial implications, but also because she wanted to see what she could do as a writer.

Before the job began, she had just enough time to go to Damascus for the plebiscite. She was disappointed with the city, which had been described to her as the loveliest Arab city. But the plebiscite produced the effect she was expecting. The city came alive when Egyptian president Nasser flew in from Cairo, with tens of thousands pouring in from all over Syria. Huge groups marched, shouting slogans in favor of Nasser, the Union, and Arabism in general, and against Israel, Hussein of Jordan, Eisenhower, and other symbols of imperialism. It was out of control, and eight small children were trampled to death in this spontaneous outpouring of support for Nasser. She found him to be tall, dark, and handsome, a striking person with a commanding presence.

But the atmosphere was tense. She believed she was being watched constantly, as in the Soviet Union. A military policeman even asked her to turn over the film in her camera. When she refused, she ended up arguing her case at military police headquarters—successfully, as it turned out. During the mob scene, a kind man had taken her under his wing to ensure she wasn't swept away by the masses, but she later learned he too was a secret-police officer. Even her hotel concierge constantly asked where she was going and with whom.

Back in Beirut Elizabeth luxuriated in the lack of surveillance, enjoying relaxing conversations in her hotel lobby and on the outdoor veranda, talking about current events to anyone of interest who came through. Subjects ranged from Nasser's future to charges of Saudi plots, rumors of the assassination of Jordan's King Hussein, the strengths and weaknesses of Iraq's Premier Nuri, and the general state of Arabia. She was also looking forward to her new job, but then came an unpleasant surprise. While she was in Damascus, the job had vanished into thin air. Disappointed, she went back to her original plan and headed to Egypt on an Italian boat.

She arrived in Cairo on March 17 and settled into the Semiramis Hotel, where she had a private veranda with a commanding view of the broad and placid Nile. She was immediately greeted by an Egyptian doctor she had met on her 1955 trip. Her rarely seen romantic side surfaced, and she plotted the next three weeks with an eye to ensuring she would be in Cairo when the full moon cast its magical light on the pyramids. She had worried that Cairo would be "another slightly quaint, slightly annoyingly Eastern city," but that was not the case. It had many attributes: the Nile, palm trees, the sandy desert, the pyramids, and the vivid colors of sand, sky, and palm.

Donning blue jeans, she climbed to the top of the highest pyramid, amazed by the views. Unused to physical exertion, her muscles protested with each step the following day. She attended political rallies, visited new friends at their homes, attended the Bolshoi Ballet, and was entertained by her Egyptian doctor friend. The time passed agreeably, and she decided to stay longer than originally planned. "There's no reason that I know of to hurry away," she wrote her mother. It was a cosmopolitan city filled with people of many nationalities, bringing with them many different ways of thinking. To Elizabeth, it felt like a meeting place experiencing a three-way awakening: Arab, Asian, and African, all at the same time.

One of her most memorable experiences was a trip to St. Catherine's Monastery on the Sinai Peninsula. The Sinai wilderness was the bleakest, driest, hottest, sandiest, most inhospitable place she had ever seen, a mass of steep, jagged, barren mountains rising out of the sand. While at the monastery, she exerted herself more than usual, ascending two mountains in the vicinity, mostly by camel, but on foot for the top difficult bits. One of them was Moses Mountain, where the Prophet was said to have received the Ten Commandments. The second was St. Catherine's Mountain, about 8000 feet (2438 meters) in height. She enjoyed the magnificent views, with wonderful hues of yellow, brown, and red and small patches of the Red Sea in the distance. Once again, her muscles needed a few days to recover.

Her mother, traveling at the same time in Western Europe, expressed concerns over Elizabeth's safety, having heard there was an element of fanaticism in the country. Elizabeth assured her that she was conducting herself properly and prudently, and there was absolutely nothing to worry about. But she couldn't be completely honest with her mother because the Arabs censored all letters leaving Egypt. It was only later, during a ten-day boat trip to Beirut, Cyprus, Rhodes, Istanbul, and Izmir, that she was able to write freely about her plans to travel on to Israel. It was impossible to mention this in a letter read by Arab censors because she would not have been allowed back in again. To facilitate her freedom of movement, she carried some curious documents with her, such as her Methodist Sunday school certificate. This humble scrap of paper was sufficient proof that she wasn't Jewish. When she traveled between Arab countries and Jerusalem, the authorities were obliging and stamped her visa on a separate piece of paper so it wouldn't appear in her passport.

In southern Turkey, she traveled to Izmir and Antalya, which became her jumping-off point to explore the ruins in the surrounding mountains. Together with a Danish architect, she decided to visit a ruin called Side. They took a taxi for a certain distance, and then got out and walked about three miles from the highway to its seaside location. After exploring the ruin, they took a swim and enjoyed a good lunch at a seaside café. They began their return at about 5:00 P.M., walking back to the highway to wait for a bus or a taxi. At 6:45 P.M., a tractor came by, pulling a farm wagon loaded with several men and boys. They climbed in and went as far as he was going—about half an hour to his village. He explained to them in sign language that they were still a long way from Antalya, and as there were no more buses, why not spend the night at his place. They declined, as Elizabeth had a plane to catch the next morning. So they began to walk. Soon a private Jeep came by filled with two men, one woman, and four children, along with two large suitcases, various bundles, gasoline cans, and tool kits.

Despite the congestion, everyone adjusted to make room for the two strangers—Elizabeth perched on the lap of the Dane. Then the engine died. While one of the two men attempted to fix it, a taxi came by, but it too was overloaded. However, the taxi driver said—again by sign language—he was dropping off a couple of passengers shortly and he promised to come back for them. As a guarantee, he left one of his other passengers to assist with the Jeep repairs. He returned, but in the process of turning around, his car also died. Finally, an ancient Vauxhall came by. Elizabeth and the Dane climbed in and proceeded to the next town, where they decided to revive themselves with a meal. In a café, the local schoolmaster treated them to dinner and several rakis (a local liquor) because he wanted to chat with them in English. The newly

repaired taxi showed up, and at last they made their way back to Antalya, arriving at about 10:30 P.M. Such was travel off the beaten track in
Turkey, mid-twentieth century style. She did make the flight.

What most impressed her about that day—and many others in
Turkey—were the unexpected acts of kindness from fierce-looking
characters. She had observed this characteristic in a bus driver who
swerved to miss a pigeon, and in another bus driver who, at the sight of
a legless beggar, stopped his vehicle so that all the male passengers, who
were poor themselves, could disembark and give the man some money.
She wondered if this would be the case in militant Israel.

She arrived in Haifa on June 18 to find a city that felt more European
than Middle Eastern, with many modern buildings and a splendid location on the slopes of Mount Carmel. As always, Elizabeth had prepared
herself by reading related literature well in advance of her visit. In this
case, she was enlightened by Sholem Asch's controversial novel, *The
Nazarene*, in which he sought to reconcile Judaism and Christianity.

In Jerusalem, as the sun set and the Sabbath was proclaimed one
Friday evening, men and boys began to emerge from their small homes
and walk slowly and with dignity to nearby synagogues. They were
dressed in the medieval garb they had worn in the ghettos of Eastern
Europe, and their quiet procession of devotion impressed her.

When people learned of her recent trip to Lebanon, they immediately engaged her in intense conversations about the situation there.
They wanted to know if it was true that the Lebanese might like to
make peace with Israel. She sensed they had real hope that peace might
have a chance. She couldn't respond positively, though, because she was
convinced it was unlikely, especially since it would be impossible for
any one Arab country to make peace with Israel for fear of retribution
from its Arab neighbors. She was interested to hear the other side of
the Arab-Israeli conflict in order to better understand it. And she was
impressed with the speed at which the Israelis were building a country
for their citizens, although largely financed, she knew, by outside sources.
She found the social, religious, and political conflict complex, intriguing,
and disturbing, but she didn't imagine it would still wrack the region
forty years later.

By September Elizabeth was off to Amman, Jordan—a village that seemed to have grown up overnight to become the capital of a struggling nation. No ancient walls confined its growth, and its modern buildings were rapidly creeping up the seven hills on which it was built. With introductions to friends of Mahmoud Reish, the city opened its doors to her. "Here in Jordan I am beginning to find the charm of the Arab as described by the romantic orientalists of earlier times," she tantalized her mother.

She learned about the complexity of the various brands of Arab nationalism still alive and competing with each other: the Hashemite family, which led the Arab revolt of World War I; the religiously fanatical Wahabbis of Saudi Arabia; the followers of the ex-Mufti of Jerusalem, whose family quarreled with the Hashemites in Palestine and who led the Arab terrorist activities in Palestine under the mandate; and the pan-Arabists, who idolized Nasser. These family feuds were complicated by power politics and a general high state of emotional tension made worse by the existence of Israel on the western border. In Jordan, she found that these were not just theoretical discussions, but life-and-death struggles for power, wealth, and glory.

Through her connections, she arranged a trip through the southern part of Jordan as the guest of an Arab Legion colonel whose military district it was. Now she would see T. E. Lawrence country: Al Kerak, Petra, Aqaba, and the great southern desert. It began in an unorthodox manner, driving with the colonel to a camp outside of Kerak where she was fed. That night she slept on a hospital cot. They continued on to Ma'an, a scraggly, mud-brick town in an oasis, inhabited by conservative Muslims who forbade movies or liquor in their town and who locked the women in their houses when the men went out. She explored the ancient city of Petra on horseback and foot with another army major, and went to Aqaba, Jordan's single tenuous contact with the sea. She drove across a wide expanse of the Wadi Rum desert, where she paused beside a fresh spring a few hundred meters up a slope from a group of black Bedouin and ate freshly killed pigeons roasted over a fire. The trip back to Amman turned into a marathon of driving the rough desert route for fourteen hours to arrive at 4:00 A.M. After a bath and a few hours' sleep, she reconnected with Mahmoud and returned to Jerusalem.

After a good rest, Elizabeth continued on her Middle East journey, arriving in Baghdad by the end of October. Armed with introductions to friends and contacts at the American embassy, she set about seeing the country she'd read about in Gertrude Bell's travels—and the Bible: The Tower of Babel, Nineveh, Ur, the supposed location of the Garden of Eden. She saw many evocative ruins in a state of recent excavation; some of the contents were in the archeological museum in Baghdad, a place she visited frequently and thoroughly.

Slightly farther afield, she managed to get permits from the security department to visit the important Islamic center of Karbala, sixty-five miles southwest of Baghdad, as well as the well-preserved ruins of Al-Ukhaidir and Basra. She was almost the only tourist in Baghdad, according to the locals, but she didn't mind because she found that "most of the Americans one meets traveling in these parts are better kept at home." From Basra, she flew to the sheikhdom of Kuwait.

Kuwait was fascinating because of the contrasts between the old, traditional, and poor Eastern way of life and the new, brash, and rich Western style that had burst upon the land with the discovery of huge oil deposits. She saw barefoot men in desert garb driving gigantic Cadillacs, traffic jams of huge American cars in narrow, winding alleys, and men dressed in western suits alongside women completely veiled and clothed in black. She met Egyptians working in Kuwait who earned ten times what they could make in Cairo. She was amused to see the first two and a half pages in the telephone book devoted to "sheikhs."

An unusual invitation arrived from the secretary of the deputy ruler, Sheikh Abdullah Mubarak es Sabbah, to visit him at his seaside palace (one of several). She didn't know why she was invited, but she had a pleasant time at his sumptuous palace, particularly enjoying the ceiling of one remarkable room painted with portraits of lovely European ladies—an unusual sight in a country that hides their women. As she traveled through the area, she read Lawrence's *Seven Pillars of Wisdom*, constantly connecting his famous stories with her own observations.

By mid-December she was in Tehran, Iran, just in time for winter. Nighttime temperatures plummeted and snow draped the mountains in white, providing a spectacular backdrop to the city. Her friend Judy Friedberg arrived in mid-January, and they made plans to depart for India. Their first stop was Karachi, which Elizabeth described as an "overgrown, ugly town" with nothing to hold the interest of a casual tourist. There only because of Judy's freelance assignment, they continued on to Bombay as soon as they were able. She and Judy found themselves sharing a taxi with a man who looked remarkably like Arthur Koestler, author of *Darkness at Noon*. In fact, he *was* Arthur Koestler. Traveling alone, he was keen to share their company and provided many hours of good conversation. Particularly interesting were his views on the totalitarian tactics of the Soviet Union, provoking lively discussions on the relationship between the state and the individual. From there, it was on to Delhi and finally—Kathmandu.

> *. . . a place where you can see what the world*
> *is becoming.*
> —ELIZABETH HAWLEY

Elizabeth arrived in Kathmandu on February 8, 1959, near the end of her two-year, round-the-world trip. It was to be a short visit—only a couple of weeks—but Nepal had been in her mind since 1955 when she read a *New York Times* article about the first tourists to the kingdom. Thinking it would be an interesting place to visit, she had tucked the information away for future reference.

Her excitement grew as her plane from Benares (now known as Varanasi), India, approached the southern border of Nepal. She was struck by the dark forests of the Terai, imagining the wildlife prowling in what appeared to be an impassable barrier. As she continued north, the landscape changed as brown hillsides emerged from the jungle depths. A jigsaw maze of terraced fields was dotted with small thatched cottages, and the hills were laced with pathways connecting remote villages. Suddenly, a broad valley opened up and the city of Kathmandu appeared. Surrounded by hills and the shining Himalayan peaks in the distance, it appeared, she said in a letter, as "a kind of fairy tale mirage, an oasis of fertility in a sea of verticality." It had a sense of intimacy, as though cut off from the rest of the planet by the towering peaks. Her first impression was one of remoteness—remote in the sense that the twentieth century was less apparent here than in most of the other countries she had visited. "Here one really feels oneself to be in Asia—timeless Asia," she wrote her mother.

Kathmandu had a medieval feel. Ancient, three-story houses leaned over the narrow streets, their intricately carved wooden window frames a testament to the skills of local craftsmen. The gods of Nepal were carved above every lintel, offering many opportunities for ordinary Nepalis to stop momentarily and offer *pujas* (Hindu prayers). Tiny shops with brightly colored fruits and vegetables and startling slabs of meat provided a visual feast as she made her way through the city. The proportions of the city were balanced, giving a sense of harmony and prosperity. The relative prosperity was real; the valley's strategic location between Tibet and India had made its Newari citizens wealthy from trade between the two countries for centuries.

Elizabeth visited the government offices, housed in the hundred-year-old Singha Durbar palace. The great structure presented an impressive gateway at its entrance, but the gardens were neglected. Lavish banquet rooms with gleaming marble floors and sparkling chandeliers were used for special occasions, but the only rooms accessible to the public were the administrative offices—a rabbit warren of small, badly lit rooms that had been used by the palace concubines in days gone by. As the residence of the prime minister, it had been a marvel of opulence. Four stories high, reflected in the still waters of a lake, it appeared to float in space.

She discovered Durbar Square and the *maidan*, a huge grass parade ground with tall, stately bamboo at one end. Alive with activity, the *maidan* was an ideal place to get a sense of the pulse of Kathmandu. Young boys came by the dozen, marching and exercising under the watchful eyes of Gurkha soldiers. Cows grazed contentedly, and squealing children competed in sporting events and gymnastics.

The other lifeline in Kathmandu was the sacred Bagmati River. It was here, rather than on the streets, that she saw the women of Kathmandu, washing their hair, their bodies, and their clothing. The Kathmandu bazaar was a place of mass confusion and activity. Bicycle shops, beggars, cows, the odd camel, and the occasional Rolls-Royce all shared street space. Mounds of spices and rice, piles of peppers and bananas, bolts of brilliant silk and cotton, cheap plastic jewelry, and the all-important moneychangers caught her eyes. The smells and sounds were overwhelming: bells rang ceaselessly from more than five thousand temples in the valley, drums drummed, and horns honked. Even though there were few cars, each seemed to have a functioning horn and a highly motivated operator. The evenings were strangely silent.

But Elizabeth Hawley's arrival in Nepal was of a professional as well as personal nature. Before she left India, she had learned that Nepal was about to hold its first general election in history, so she dropped in at the Time Inc. bureau in Delhi and asked the correspondent if he would like her to do some work for him there. He said yes, so she immediately met up with two journalists, her friend Elie Able from the *New York Times*, a man she described as wonderfully bright, and a correspondent for the *London Observer*, Cyril Dunn, who struck her as gentle and witty. The three of them traveled as a pack, doing interviews with leading Nepalese politicians and others. Watching the two experienced journalists work, Elizabeth found herself exactly where she wanted to be—on the inside track of an interesting period in the political history of Nepal, when King Mahendra would institute the nation's first constitution.

The chronology leading to the first parliamentary elections was one of intrigue and a massive shift in power that was centuries old. The Ranas had ruled Nepal since the mid-nineteenth century, and the Rana prime minister normally held his position until death. To accomplish their stranglehold on power, they had devised a crafty refinement of the caste system that split the powerful Rana clan into A, B, and C classifications. Only the A's could rise to the upper levels of power, and of course it was an A-class Rana who devised the system. They were known for their keen interest in women, whiskey, and hunting. They didn't tolerate freedom of speech in religion or politics, and the prison was full of political prisoners to prove it.

Under the Ranas, the members of the royal family were powerless and lived as virtual prisoners in their own palace. Needless to say, there was some tension between these two most powerful forces in Nepal. The king at this time was named Tribhuvan, meaning "dweller of three worlds": material, spiritual, and human. Not as magnificent as the prime minister's palace, the king's palace was nevertheless impressive, Elizabeth wrote, with grounds resembling a "fairyland version of an English country garden." His title was hollow, but the throne was maintained because, to the Nepalis, he was a deity. The Ranas arranged his marriage and by the time he was fourteen he had fathered two children by two wives who were sisters. To foreigners, he was a symbol of self-indulgence, rumored to be interested only in opium and women. In fact, this was not the case, and history would prove that he had intelligence, self-discipline, and the courage to mobilize his people to a new way of governance and life that would emerge at just about the time Elizabeth arrived in Kathmandu. The nation had begun its rebellion against the Ranas and its long road to democracy.

By 1950 King Tribhuvan and his family had escaped bondage in their palace, finding refuge in the Indian embassy at Kathmandu and then in India itself. There, they were welcomed by Pandit Nehru. While the king was in India, armed Nepali Congress supporters invaded southern Nepal and captured the Rana government, setting up a provisional government. In the west, peasant guerrillas leapt into action. Nehru's opinion was made clear in his statement: "We are anxious that there should be peace and stability in Nepal. At the same time, we felt that the introduction of substantial political reforms was essential for this purpose." With the fall of the Ranas, the king returned as constitutional head of the country. He announced that an interim cabinet would be set up with seven Ranas and seven representatives of the popular party. All political prisoners would be freed and there would be a constituent assembly chosen by adult suffrage the next year.

It was a strange kind of revolution—in part inspired by the population, in part by the monarchy. But despite his best intentions, Tribhuvan seemed unable to replace the oppressive Rana rule with anything other than unworkable, short-lived, compromise governing councils. To make things more complicated, his son, Crown Prince Mahendra, insisted on marrying a Rana woman named Indra. Defying his parents on an issue as important as marriage was unheard of, but Mahendra did it, marrying first Indra and then her sister Ratna after his first wife died. After several years of recurring illness (and probably exhaustion from his recent efforts at reform), King Tribhuvan died in a Swiss hospital.

In 1952 Prince Mahendra was crowned king and his second wife became Queen Ratna. A precedent had been set—it was possible for a crown prince to choose his own queen. The significance of this became clear fifty years later when Queen Ratna was the septuagenarian queen mother in residence at the palace when yet another crown prince rebelled against his parents' marriage plans. Only this time, it would end in a bloodbath such as the country could hardly comprehend, the slaughter of almost the entire royal family. But now, after a century of Rana rule, King Mahendra was keen to move his country into the twentieth century, and so he held the first general election in Nepal's history. It was this election that Elizabeth had come to observe.

After several days of voting, victory was declared by the Nepali Congress Party (NCP), which won 70 percent of the votes. Elie Able of the *New York Times* had to leave, but first he asked Elizabeth to file a couple of stories for him on the results of the election. He also told his foreign news editor in New York about Elizabeth. She was flattered, and also pleased from a practical point of view because she was running out of money. After reporting the results, Elizabeth left for Benares and a gradual journey east, meandering through Calcutta, Rangoon, Penang, Singapore, Bangkok, Hong Kong, Yokohama, and, finally, San Francisco, arriving in time for spring.

Elizabeth recalls a mélange of sensory pleasures upon returning to America after two years abroad—a rush of familiarity, but also the dawning awareness that America had less to offer her than before. After sailing under the Golden Gate Bridge into San Francisco—an event she remembers vividly—she went directly to Bloom's candy shop in Union Square and ordered a chocolate sundae smothered in chocolate sauce and walnuts. With that treat in hand, she proceeded to wander around the square, feasting her eyes on scenes of "typical" America that she hadn't seen for two years. It was a pivotal moment. During that wander, she had a little discussion with herself: "This is a great place, but it's not the real world. I would like to live a few years in the real world—a world that's like what most people in the world live like." Her travels had made an impact. Her life would never be the same.

But she was also practical. She wanted to live comfortably, and it dawned on her that Kathmandu was the place. It had a pleasant climate, a low cost of living, beautiful hills that reminded her of Vermont, and she would be able to hire staff to look after her everyday needs. (No need to cook!) At no point did climbing and exploration enter the equation in her decision-making process. She was blissfully unaware of the Herculean efforts taking place on the Himalayan peaks. The names Herzog, Buhl, and Hillary meant nothing to her. But in order to mobilize this new plan, she first needed to return to New York and find a job.

She moved back into her apartment on Madison Avenue, settling in with the treasures she had accumulated in the far-flung corners of the world, and worked at a series of temporary jobs until she had enough money to depart for good. One of these was for *Life* magazine's new book publishing arm. As always, she did research. Then she did a stint for Nelson Rockefeller's brief presidential campaign, where she proved to be a useful member of the staff because of her access to the morgue and all those files.

In the meantime, she applied for a job at the U.S. Information Agency (USIA) within the State Department. This was the domestic name for what was known abroad as the USIS (United States Information Service). Its role was to understand, inform, and influence foreign policies in promotion of the U.S. national interest. Information activities in overseas operations included reading rooms and libraries, and personnel in missions, embassies, and field posts around the world. President Eisenhower set up an Operations Coordinating Board to run the USIA, which consisted of several high-level people: the Undersecretary of State, the Undersecretary of Defense, the head of the Foreign Aid Agency, the head of the CIA, and the head of USIA. This tight group met for lunch once a week, speaking freely about what was going on in the world, which at the time included atomic energy tests, secret information relating to the Soviet Union, shifts in political regimes, and citizens movements.

Although she had good credentials to work for the USIA, it didn't look promising, as revealed in a letter from Deputy Director Washburn: "She made a very good impression here, but jobs for women in the Foreign Service are extremely limited." This was tough to accept for a woman as independent, experienced, knowledgeable, and capable as Elizabeth.

She was also waiting on a decision from the Ford Foundation Foreign Area Training Fellowship, for which she had applied. She proposed a study of Nepal's post-war history—its political and economic development since World War II, with particular emphasis on its penetration by influences from outside its borders, specifically India and Tibet. Albert Furth, assistant to *TIME* magazine founder and editor Henry R. Luce, wrote an effusive reference letter for her:

"Elizabeth Hawley was among the top few researchers on *Fortune's* staff . . . she was always in demand by our ablest writers. . . . The writer knew he would not only have the benefit of thorough, penetrating reportage; he also knew he would have the benefit of a mature and uncommonly intelligent mind in debating the implications of the material gathered."

In early December Elizabeth was asked to come to Washington to appear before a panel of three USIA men: one from personnel, one from the press section, and one from the cultural-affairs section. They grilled her for an hour and a half about her past experience, her views on American foreign policy, what she would do if she were running the USIA, and whether she understood what her duties would be. She obviously made an impression because ten days later she received a letter asking her to proceed to the next steps: a security check, medical examination, and psychological-psychiatric examination. She was being seriously considered for a Foreign Service appointment.

By April 1960 she had received a "no" from the Ford Foundation because she didn't have enough academic background in South Asia. The USIA eventually did offer her something in a foreign country but she didn't get to choose the country, so she turned it down. Her mother also discouraged her from working for the USIA, as she was sure it would be too bureaucratic for Elizabeth's free spirit.

By this time, Elizabeth had become fixated on Nepal. Fascinated by Nepal's politics and the idea of an isolated state emerging into the twentieth century, she decided to live there for a few years. She wanted to watch the country change and develop. She described it as "a place where you can see what the world is becoming." During the summer, she hammered out an arrangement with Time Inc. in which she returned to Kathmandu in September of 1960 accredited as their part-time correspondent. Two years later it would be the Reuters News Agency. She had also been offered fairly lucrative work with an organization calling itself the Knickerbocker Foundation. She accepted the offer—an arrangement that would cause some raised eyebrows back in New York, since many of her colleagues and friends assumed she was really doing intelligence work for the U.S. government under the cloak of a foundation. So with her contacts made and her contracts signed, she was off.

The mountains hereabouts are infested with men mad enough to want to slog to the tops.
—Elizabeth Hawley

N ow that she was to make it her new home, Elizabeth began to explore Kathmandu and its environs with even keener interest. She discovered the adjoining ancient city of Patan. Bazaars filled with tiny shops selling exquisite silk, silver, and gems were the reward for navigating its maze of narrow lanes and alleys. Along each brick-paved street, spacious houses were decorated with dragons, gods, and goddesses carved into wooden frames.

She drove to Bhadgaon, where hundreds of gilded roofs glared in the harsh sunlight. While Patan is a Buddhist center, Hindu temples dominate Bhadgaon, and the two styles often intertwine in evocative imagery. Religious festivals are common, and to Elizabeth the entire valley seemed to embrace ancient religions of all kinds.

And of course she went to Bodhinath, the holiest Tibetan sanctuary outside Tibet. The cone-shaped Buddhist shrine, known as a *stupa*, was dazzling in its whiteness, topped with gold and emblazoned with the unblinking blue eyes of Lord Buddha at its base. Surrounded by prayer wheels, it resonated with the sound of their turning, and the smell of lamps floating in clarified butter permeated the air. Elizabeth took in the great number of Buddhist pilgrims milling around the stupa. What a sight: monks in crimson robes, pig-tailed hermits, scholars, and peasants crowding to the sacred site, accompanied by the sounds of bells, gongs, and horns—and the ever-present smell of butter. It wasn't just pilgrims that she saw; Tibetan refugees had flooded into the area after the Chinese takeover of Tibet, and the streets swarmed with fierce-looking warrior figures.

Her new home seemed uncomplicated, peaceful and contented, centuries removed from the hustle and bustle, strife and warfare, and rapid rate of change in the rest of the world. Of course, that was not the case, as Elizabeth would discover. But for now, she reveled in the novelty of making a home in such a foreign place.

While staying at the Royal Hotel, she began searching for an apartment. Within a week she found what she was looking for—a two-bedroom apartment in a central part of town. It had spacious rooms and plenty of windows, three of which had balconies. She was pleased to find electricity in every room although the power was a bit feeble. The kitchen was somewhat bare, with a sink and cold running water. The bathroom had a small hot-water tank, as well as a flush toilet—all for ninety-five dollars a month. She rearranged the basic furniture, removed the heavy draperies off windows and doors, and purchased some brass vases to fill with colorful flowers from her garden. The overall effect pleased her.

To make it feel like home, she had brought a few "essentials" with her from the United States, such as record albums like *My Fair Lady*, *Oklahoma*, and *The King and I*. She had her autographed copy of *Joy of Cooking*, and a recording of Handel's *Messiah*, as well as a Bible, but joked to her mother, "God knows what reason." On the practical front, she brought a plastic dinner set, some sheets and towels, an atlas, the Webster's *Collegiate Dictionary*, a thesaurus, a condensed paperback encyclopedia, a book on English usage, and a Finnish hot plate.

By mid-October she reported to her mother that she had not only settled in, but had acquired a cook as well. Kumar had worked previously for some Americans, spoke a little English, and was already trained in "our ways of cooking and cleanliness." She was pleased that he could bake bread and sugar cookies, make soup and mayonnaise, keep the household accounts, and "do all sorts of things I couldn't possibly do." She also hired a gardener and a man to come in twice a week to do her laundry. Her staff was complete.

Kumar wasn't the cook for long, as she replaced him with Ran Krishna, but he remained to take on other responsibilities. Kumar and

Elizabeth had what can only be described as a "difficult" relationship. Looking back, she admits she treated him badly: "He simply exasperated the hell out of me." According to Elizabeth, he was completely disorganized. This was a recipe for disaster as Elizabeth is extremely organized. She mocked him routinely, but now acknowledges her behavior was inexcusable. He annoyed her, and in return, she was mean to him, but they continued to work together for forty long years. Many of Elizabeth's friends describe her as "very much memsahib," or someone who thinks of Nepalis as people you hire to get work done. Her cousin's son, Will Kneerim, views her relationship with her Nepali staff as classic nineteenth-century master-servant style. When Kumar retired in 2003, he thoughtfully hired his replacement six months in advance in order to fully train him. She appreciated that parting gesture and realized she had underestimated Kumar all along.

Kathmandu had only a couple of shopping streets and few "useful" stores. One, run by the American embassy, was called The Blue Bucket. It was somewhat like a country general store, with tinned and packaged foods. Most foodstuffs came from the markets and street vendors. The choices of vegetables were limited: cauliflower, carrots, radishes, potatoes, onions, and garlic. There was a bakery (it still exists) named Krishna Loaf that was the first to bake bread in the valley. Western-style clothing was unavailable, as there was no place to buy it; everything was individually tailored or brought in from abroad. There were no streetlights and few paved roads. Most people walked or rode bikes. There was no international mail service, although there was a post office for domestic mail. Elizabeth sent and received her mail through the American embassy and sent telegraphs at the Indian embassy.

It was unusual to see a single Western woman in the streets in 1960. Once, when she encountered some Tibetan refugees on the street near her house, her knee-length skirt and nylon stockings caused them to flee, giggling uncontrollably as they went. She knows she stood out because years later she was chatting with a young office clerk who admitted, "I remember you from when I was a little boy twenty years ago." Elizabeth initially rode about town on a bicycle, but everything changed when she borrowed a bluish-green, 1952 Fiat 500 convertible. She was thrilled to get out of the rain, and it was the perfect size for her. Finally, in 1965, she bought a used, robin's egg blue Volkswagen Beetle from Prince Basundhara. It was two years old and she paid him fifteen hundred dollars for it. That car became her trademark in Kathmandu, and it was still parked proudly in her garage in the spring of 2004. She drove it herself until 1996, after which she employed a driver.

As a young, single, American woman, Elizabeth was immediately embraced by the Kathmandu social scene. Social occasions usually took place in private homes rather than restaurants or hotels. One hotel she did frequent, however, was the Royal Hotel, run by the infamous Boris Lissanevitch. This luxurious watering hole occupied one wing of a former Rana palace named Bahadur Bhawan. Actually, it wasn't the hotel or restaurant that she frequented, but Boris' fabulous apartment above, the scene of many parties. Of all the fascinating characters she would know in Kathmandu, Boris was one of the more colorful. He was dark and good-looking in a mysterious kind of way, with hair parted straight down the middle. His past was almost unbelievable: he grew up in Russia, escaped during the Russian Revolution, became a celebrated dancer with Diaghilev's Ballets Russes, traveled the world as a performer, opened the exclusive 300 Club in Calcutta, and befriended royalty and adventurers alike. While running the 300 Club, he became a close friend and confidant of Nepal's former King Tribhuvan, as well as a number of the people who assisted Tribhuvan in overturning the Rana rule. It was this friendship that brought him to Nepal. Now he was in partnership with Tribhuvan's son, Prince Basundhara, running the Royal Hotel, sometimes described as "Kathmandu baroque."

Despite his royal connections and friendships with the most powerful people in the country, Boris had already done a stint in prison for bad debt. Debt was something he was familiar with, having an impractical business sense. Shortly after being released from prison, he was asked to produce a series of lavish banquets for the coronation of King Mahendra. Entertaining on a scale never before seen in Nepal, Boris quickly became the center of the social elite.

His scene also included climbers, as virtually all the expeditions coming through the valley stayed with Boris. He boasted a unique rock collection in connection with his mountaineering friends: a bit of the summit of Everest from Barry Bishop, a piece of the top of Dhaulagiri from Norman Dyhrenfurth, a rock from the top of Makalu from Jean Franco, and more. In return for high-altitude rocks, he gave the alpinists fruitcake; his famous Genoa fruitcake was standard fare on the early expeditions to all the highest peaks. It was in Boris's apartment that Elizabeth first glimpsed the exciting things that were happening up in the mountains. And it was there that she began to meet climbers.

Elizabeth supported her lifestyle with two sources of income. The first was as a stringer for her former employer Time Inc., the publishers of *Fortune*, *TIME*, *Life*, and other magazines. Her job was to research political news and other stories and send that research to New York or the New Delhi bureau for one of their writers to do a story.

The rest of her income came from the Knickerbocker Foundation, which hired her to send them regular reports on the political scene in Nepal. Elizabeth was uncharacteristically uncurious about the work she did for Knickerbocker. During the early sixties, in many parts of the world and particularly in strategically located Nepal, there was an enormous amount of intelligence gathering going on—by Britain, the United States, Russia, and others. This mountain region was considered an essential buffer, and had long been a place of intrigue. Every foreigner living in Kathmandu was aware of this. According to the 1967 Facts on File yearbook, the Knickerbocker Foundation was suspected of being a cover organization for the CIA. But Elizabeth remains adamant that, if her monthly reports to the Knickerbocker Foundation were used for government purposes and analysis, it didn't bother her. "Why not? What's wrong with that?" she asks. She never thought of her work as "espionage." She believes it is natural for governments to gather intelligence in other countries in whatever way they can.

Elizabeth's daily routine included listening to the newscasts on BBC Radio and reading the *Herald Tribune*. She began calling on some of the top political figures she had met the previous year, and it paid off; she was invited to embassy cocktail receptions and her network continued to expand. Then the United Nations Association of Nepal held a series of meetings in celebration of the UN's birthday, and as a representative for *TIME* and *Life*, she was invited to attend. One of her appointments was with a leading politician who would soon become the country's next prime minister—B. P. Koirala.

In her free time, she explored the nearby countryside with Jeeps and motor scooters. In mid-November, she embarked on her first trek: ten days of hiking north of Kathmandu as far as the village of Melamchi. It was definitely roughing it, with long days of walking, steep trails, and cold nights. Although she enjoyed herself, she recalls that it felt considerably longer than just ten days. But the compensations were numerous: the scenery, which she described to her mother as magnificent, and the people she met, particularly the Sherpas, who were unaware of the political changes in Kathmandu and whose isolated existence included considerable hardship. She was pleasantly surprised at how quickly she became physically fit.

Fresh from her mountain experience, Elizabeth learned that B. P. Koirala (B. P., as she later called him), now the new prime minister, was planning a trek of his own in December. He was an informal, intelligent, and friendly man, and one who knew how to flatter, telling Elizabeth she was pretty. She suggested to his office, and to the prime minister himself, that she accompany him on the trek and do a story for *Life* about how the head of government must overcome all kinds of obstacles to make democracy work. He was enthusiastic, and she was hopeful.

All of her well-laid plans vanished into thin air the day before they were to leave, however, for the singular reason that Koirala was no longer prime minister. At noon on December 15, 1960, all cabinet members who could be found (some were in hiding, some were out of the country) were taken into custody on orders from King Mahendra, who had lost patience with what he considered gross inefficiency and erroneous policy making. It was just one year since Koirala had been elected. Elizabeth believed the confrontation was the result of a power struggle between the king and the prime minister. Koirala soon learned that the king had no intention of stepping back to become a symbolic leader because that would negate everything his father, Tribhuvan, had believed in.

The king retained sweeping powers in emergency situations; as he was the one who determined what was an emergency situation, this was one. He promised to substantially carry out the policies of his predecessor, but to do so scientifically and efficiently, without corruption and without the pressures of political parties. This meant that all parties were now banned for an indefinite period. There was still a constitution and parliament, but they were there to rubber-stamp decisions that came down from the palace. It was the king who nominated the cabinet ministers as well as the prime minister.

Mahendra devised a system of government, also used in India, called *panchayat*, essentially a council of five advisors. He released a few politicians from jail and recycled them into the council. Koirala was not appointed and, after a stint in confined quarters, subsequently fled the country, remaining abroad for several years. Elizabeth now had some news worth reporting for Time Inc., but she worried about what they would do with the information—would their interpretation of her material make it difficult for her to work in Nepal in the future? It was a tricky situation because on one hand the king was moving his country forward, opening it up to foreign aid and development programs. But he was doing so with an iron glove; the royal palace had become the real center of power. The juxtaposition of his open-minded goals for Nepal and his inward-looking style of rule fascinated Elizabeth.

Despite the delicate nature of the situation, Elizabeth was excited by the fact that this wasn't small-time politics in an isolated corner of the world. Because of its strategic position between China and India, Nepal became skilled at playing the big powers against one another other. The king's main goal was to retain Nepal's independence—a feat he managed in part by playing China against India and the Soviet Union against the United States, all while ruling with his own brand of autocracy. As a wire service reporter, Elizabeth had to stick to the facts, being careful not to voice an opinion regardless of what she thought of the goings-on.

Professionally, Elizabeth managed a small coup in January 1962 when Time Inc.'s chairman of the board and the Delhi bureau chief arrived, expecting Elizabeth to entertain them and introduce them to all the important people. Thanks to her infiltration of the upper echelons of Nepal society, she was able to secure interviews and lunches for them with important ministers and, more impressively, a half-hour interview with the king—his first press interviews since taking over the government. She was fascinated to hear him articulate his thoughts in his soft-spoken manner.

In early February she met an Englishman named Micky Weatherall on a plane heading south to Simra near the Indian border. He lived in an enormous palace belonging to one of the most prominent members of the Rana family. A civil engineer, Weatherall was in business with his Rana host to build bridges under contract to the Nepalese government. He had grown up in Darjeeling and spoke Nepali, Hindi, and half a dozen other languages. They decided to drive back overland from Simra together. It turned into an adventure of several days, as they were hauling enormous steel girders behind a couple of tractors, one of which was driven by Weatherall. Elizabeth pulled up the rear in a Land Rover. They traveled through steep, rough country with some challenging driving, becoming good friends in the process. Weatherall invited Elizabeth to his palace, Baber Mahal, for a party he was throwing for one of the Rana family members. It was an introduction into a part of Nepalese society that Elizabeth otherwise would have had difficulty penetrating. In particular, it opened the door to a friendship with General Mrigendra Shumsher Jung Bahadur Rana, his wife, and their children.

Elizabeth and Weatherall became close, spending a lot of time together in Kathmandu, as well as heading into the nether regions of the country where he had construction projects. They were also friends with American journalist Barbara Adams and Prince Basundhara, brother of the king. Barbara was something of a curiosity in Kathmandu, as she had arrived in 1961 from Long Island with her husband, an Italian photographer. After their brief vacation in the country, he was ready to leave and she wasn't—so she stayed. Shortly thereafter, she became romantically involved with the prince. Barbara Adams did some reporting work in Nepal, but spent most of her time socializing. She was flamboyant and talented in linguistics, speaking at least four languages.

The two couples often traveled around the country together, which usually meant an adventure. Barbara and her prince wanted to marry, but it was not to be. The prince, who was already married, had to ask permission from the king to remarry under the recently created remarriage laws. The king said yes, but only if Basundhara's wife agreed to the divorce. She refused—apparently she didn't want to give up being a princess. So the prince and Barbara remained lovers for years.

When Barbara and her prince finally split up, both Weatherall and Elizabeth tried to mediate, but it was irreconcilable. Elizabeth thought Barbara was egocentric and their friendship eventually waned, but not before they'd had a few more adventures. Many years later, the friction between them finally exploded at a garden party. Barbara had been writing regular columns for a local newspaper about political and environmental issues and was openly critical of the current prime minister and the cabinet. At the garden party, she complained bitterly about problems she was having trying to renew her visa for Nepal. Elizabeth remarked, "Well what do you expect when you write that kind of stuff?" Insulted, Barbara allegedly threw her out. But as difficult as their friendship sometimes was, they continued to see each other occasionally and were polite.

Kathmandu had a small social community in those days; everyone in the expatriate circles knew each other. One of the more unusual characters was an American named Father Moran. A Jesuit, he was affectionately called the American Lama. He had set up a secondary school for boys in the valley and was recognized by everyone as a scholar, a diplomat, and a man about town—racing around the city, sometimes in a Jeep, sometimes on his motorcycle, but always racing.

Another local character was the Swiss geologist Toni Hagen. Here was a man who not only knew his way around Kathmandu, but around the entire country, as Elizabeth would learn. For twelve years, he had roamed Nepal, exploring hundreds of valleys, covering thousands of miles of trail, identifying dozens of different dialects, and infiltrating places no foreigner had ever been. Many speculated on ulterior motives for his extensive wanderings, especially near the Tibetan border, but he was a true explorer and had the stories to prove it.

A much quieter man, though no less intriguing to Elizabeth, was the Austrian Peter Aufschnaiter. Famous for the seven years he had spent in Tibet with fellow Austrian Heinrich Harrer, Aufschnaiter wasn't a willing storyteller. But occasionally Elizabeth coaxed him into sharing stories of his years in close proximity to the young Dalai Lama. After escaping from a prison camp in India into forbidden Tibet, he and Harrer had worked with the citizens of Lhasa long before the country was open to foreigners, building infrastructure and growing close to the Dalai Lama's family before they were eventually forced to flee the country.

At the beginning of March 1961, Britain's Queen Elizabeth arrived with a contingent of foreign press in her wake, some of whom stayed with Elizabeth. There were a lot of press events and, in the course of covering one of them, she found herself engaged in a brief chat with "the other Elizabeth," as some of her friends called the queen. Her job was to supply information for both *TIME* and *Life* so that writers based in New York could produce their stories. One of these was to be a "human interest" story. A Sherpa family from the Khumbu valley wanted to come to Kathmandu to see the queen. The only problem was that the mother was extremely pregnant and expecting to deliver any day. They came anyway, walking several days down from the hills. En route to Kathmandu, the appointed time arrived. They stopped for a couple of hours, she had her baby, and they continued. In honor of that royal visit, they named their newborn baby Philip, after Queen Elizabeth's husband.

The royal visit provided Boris Lissanevitch of the Royal Hotel with an ideal opportunity to display his talents. He did it all: banquets, picnics, tent camps, a model of Mount Everest, and more. And for the coup de grâce, he organized a royal tiger shoot, a tradition for any foreign dignitary coming to Nepal. But there was a problem. The Duke of Edinburgh was closely linked with several international conservation bodies and he simply could not be seen shooting a tiger or—even worse—photographed standing over a slain one. At the same time, he couldn't insult his royal hosts. A diplomatic solution was found. On the morning of the shoot, the duke emerged from his tent with an apparently injured trigger finger firmly encased in plaster. Elizabeth was amused that an international "incident" had been averted.

There are many Boris stories, but the one that put him on the international map was his elephant salute. As the queen, Prince Phillip, and their entourage left their tiger shoot camp, Boris arranged no fewer than 376 elephants, decorated and painted with gold and silver, into one immense, breathing wall. When the queen drove away from her jungle adventure, each elephant lifted its trunk one after the other in a solemn and majestic royal salute. As Elizabeth (Hawley) recalls the event, "nobody thought on the same scale as Boris."

On her first New Year's Eve in Nepal, Elizabeth attended a gala party at the Royal Hotel where she met New Zealand climber Sir Edmund Hillary. He had just come out of the mountains with what was alleged to be the skin of an abominable snowman. Hillary's yeti expedition was one of the largest and most international ever to enter the Himalaya to that point. More than twenty expedition members had come from New Zealand, England, India, the United States, and Australia. The team included five journalists and photographers, eleven scientists, one radioman, one builder, and seven veterans of one or more Himalayan expeditions. The primary objectives were scientific research in high-altitude physiology, meteorology, and glaciology. The much-publicized "yeti fur" brought back by Hillary ultimately proved to be the skin of a Tibetan blue bear.

The most important of the expedition's scientific objectives was to research and document the effects of high altitude on the human body. They erected a hut at 5791 meters and equipped it with a physiological laboratory manned by a team of eight physicians and physiologists for five months. They also did the first winter ascent in the Himalaya on Ama Dablam, angering the Nepalese government by doing so without a permit. The disgruntled government ordered them to leave the country, but Ed Hillary flew back to Kathmandu and successfully negotiated permission to stay, as well as a permit for the 8481-meter Makalu, fifth highest mountain in the world and situated 20 kilometers east of Everest. Their attempt on Makalu was without bottled oxygen and although they did not reach the summit, they did accomplish a successful bivouac at 8230 meters as well as a rescue operation when Hillary became ill. The climbing party included three strong New Zealand climbers: Hillary, Peter Mulgrew, and George Lowe.

Later that spring, Elizabeth was asked to do a story on Hillary's health, as he had experienced a mild stroke while at high altitude. She was convinced that the famous climber's climbing days were over, and she wondered whether he would go back to New Zealand and run for parliament. Or maybe "he'll just go back to his bees," she wrote to her mother, referencing his previous means of livelihood.

These early days of mountaineering in Nepal were exciting, as there were major peaks still to be climbed. For example, nobody had tried to climb 7861-meter Nuptse. Although photographic evidence by Sir John Hunt had suggested a possible summit route by the South Ridge, British climber Chris Bonington and expedition leader Joseph Walmsley found a better route on the Central Ridge that led more directly to the summit. Within a six-week period in 1961, two summit teams reached the top, enjoying some difficult technical climbing as well as a view of nearby Everest.

Although Elizabeth was increasingly drawn into the world of mountaineering, with its daring stories of courage to report, the politics of Nepal continued to occupy her time. In October she was assigned a *TIME* story to ascertain the contents of a boundary treaty signed by the king of Nepal on a state visit to China, in which he and the chairman of the People's Republic of China had "disposed of the question of who owns Everest." Nobody in Kathmandu knew the answer, so it took some behind-the-scenes digging to discover that the treaty outlined the southern slope, as well as a few hundred meters down the northern side, to be Nepalese territory. Her network of highly placed contacts served her well in getting an answer, and getting it in time for their deadline.

At this time, Elizabeth began a frustrating exercise: she tried to learn Nepali. Confessing to not having a good ear for languages, she also bridled against the inflexibility of scheduled lesson times. It was a half-hearted attempt from the beginning; secretly she was convinced that anyone she really needed to speak with would speak English better than she could ever speak Nepali. All of which added up to her decision, after only a few lessons, to give up the struggle for good. Years later, when her assistant Heather Macdonald informed her that she was learning Nepali, Elizabeth asked why. Heather responded that she wanted to understand the culture better, but Elizabeth patiently explained that, "everyone here speaks English." Heather describes her attitude as a combination of New York cosmopolitan and British raj. Elizabeth never did learn to speak Nepali.

In May 1962 her professional life changed once again, although not too dramatically. At the time, Reuters had a part-time correspondent stationed in Kathmandu, an Indian man who also worked for the *Times of India*. When King Mahendra put a sudden end to the constitution, slapped all the members of the government that he could find in jail, and declared political parties illegal, the Reuters reporter naturally reported on it. The authorities were not pleased with what appeared in print, and so they demanded that he leave. One day shortly thereafter, Elizabeth was sitting in her office when two Reuters executives and the Reuters bureau chief in Delhi appeared at the top of her stairs. They were looking for a replacement and asked Elizabeth if she would do it. She knew the job would not pay well, but it would allow her even more access to the inner circles of current affairs in Nepal, and so she said yes.

Initially it meant little more than having a young Nepali journalist arrive at her door each morning to tell her what was in the local newspapers and the government's publicity department bulletin, as well as the National News Agency report. Her job was to check for accuracy, which she did on her newly acquired telephone. But with the upcoming weeklong celebration of King Mahendra's birthday starting June 11, she knew her Reuters work would increase.

Her first news exclusive was not about politics, however, but about a small climbing expedition headed by Woodrow Wilson Sayre (the president's grandson). Sayre was thought to be lost in bad weather on a remote mountain. The climbers eventually showed up, but upon interviewing Sayre, Elizabeth declared him to be a strange and irresponsible sort of person. Privately to her mother, she suggested that the expedition had been asking for trouble, as they were not especially experienced, had never been to the Himalaya before, and had left their Sherpas at base camp to go alone into dangerous terrain. She was not impressed, particularly when she later learned from her mother that he was planning to write a book—which he eventually did, entitled *Four Against Everest*. She suggested that it wouldn't be worth buying, ending her tirade with "God preserve us from more climbers like Sayre."

And while her work was changing, so was her domestic scene, for she had acquired a dog, a male Lhasa apso, black except for white paws and a bit of white on his breast. She described him as a shaggy-dog type, "much hair falling down over his eyes and a bushy tail that curls up over his rear end when he's walking, and isn't noticeable until he wags it." His name was Sindhu—Sherpa for "little lion." To Elizabeth, he looked more like a bear.

Elizabeth left her new housemate to spend Christmas in the United States with her family. She returned to Nepal to find that her relationship with Micky Weatherall was winding down, much to her disappointment, as he was choosing to spend more of his time with other people. Over the past two years, they had developed an easy pattern of spending a lot of time together, sharing thoughts, problems, feelings, and good times. They continued to see each other because they were in the same social circle, but now they often attended parties separately.

To complicate things more, Elizabeth had the awkward task of declining an offer of marriage from a pleasant American highways engineer, for whom she had no strong personal feelings. A short time later, she was surprised to be the object of considerable affection from the foreign secretary, Major General Padma Bahadur Khatri, whom she described as "sweet, quite bright, and amazingly well read." She went on to tell her mother, "He's a terribly nice person, who has the one major drawback of possessing a wife." Despite the wife, they did see a lot of each other. He had a good command of English and they delighted in banter: puns, double entendres, and generally joking around at the endless banquets and cocktail parties. He had a silly saying that she can still recite forty years later:

> *"What a man can do, a cat can't do,*
> *What a cat can do, a man can't do,*
> *But here is a man from Kathmandu."*

Her lively personal life was not unnoticed in Kathmandu, where rumors circulated swiftly. One was that she was going to marry Weatherall as a cover-up for an affair she was having with his closest friend, General Mrigendra. It wasn't true. But it made for good conversation at the parties.

An important expedition was now taking her time as a reporter: the 1963 American Mount Everest Expedition led by Norman Dyhrenfurth, including climbers Jim Whittaker, Barry Bishop, Lute Jerstad, Willi Unsoeld, Col. Jimmy Roberts, and Tom Hornbein. Before they went to the mountain, Elizabeth met Bishop and Unsoeld and learned of their ambitious plans for a complete traverse of the mountain.

During the expedition, daily press briefings were based on regular reports coming in from base camp. But Elizabeth was privy to additional information as she gained access to ham radio communications from Everest base camp through a friend of hers, Bill Gresham, who was the military attaché at the U.S. embassy. Through these radio transmissions, she obtained interesting bits of information to file at the telegraph office. Reuters used these bits and, at a press briefing the next day, the other reporters attacked her "special treatment." She then had to admit that she had listened to the ham operator, pointing out that "the airwaves are free." But, in fact, they weren't. The other reporters didn't have the access that she did, and she took considerable criticism for that and was discouraged from going into the embassy entirely.

Luckily, her friend loaned her an extra sideband, which she promptly set up in her bedroom, continuing to listen. Things on the mountain progressed smoothly, as far as her work was concerned, until the first summit was achieved. Then all hell broke loose. She learned that the American team had not only climbed the summit but also made the first ascent of the West Ridge and the first traverse of the peak. This was now a really significant and newsworthy climb. She knew that the other reporters would call the Americans for current information, but she wanted the scoop. So she had her assistant call the American office and tie up the phone line so nobody else could get through. At the same time, she called the telegraph office on her other phone line and got the story out. It gave her just a few minutes' advantage, but it worked. Elizabeth's Reuters dispatch got the message out first to the world, and it was her story that Pierre Salinger showed to President Kennedy to break the news. As a result, she was in good standing with Reuters but unpopular with her colleagues in Kathmandu. Shortly thereafter, *TIME* and *Life* offered her work covering the story in depth.

Elizabeth considers this the most important climb of the 1960s. It was also one of the first expeditions for which she kept massive and detailed notes. It was not only the first American ascent of Everest, but also the first attempt to traverse the mountain. They first tackled the mountain from the normal route to make sure that someone reached the top, and then two members, Tom Hornbein and Willi Unsoeld, split off to make an attempt on the West Ridge. Nobody had seriously looked at it before, so this was a true pioneering effort. It wasn't without its serious moments—they were running out of time and supplies and they were nearly blown off the ridge—but they made the complete traverse, descending the normal route without fixed lines. Their original plan for the two teams climbing different routes to meet at the summit didn't work out because the West Ridge team was slower. The normal-route team consisting of Lute Jerstad and Barry Bishop reached the summit first, waited a bit before beginning their descent, and were soon overtaken by darkness. This unplanned bivouac gave them a chance to flash their flashlights and shout to the others coming over from the West Ridge. Finally, the two teams joined for an uncomfortable bivouac in which Willi Unsoeld suffered severe frostbite to his feet.

Willi was living in Kathmandu at the time, working as deputy director of the newly established Peace Corps in Nepal. Elizabeth knew him quite well and was friendly with his family. She recalls visiting their house after the Everest climb: "I remember he was lying on his bed. He would play with his toe—one of his little toes—as though it were a loose tooth, just like a child would play with a loose tooth, until finally it came off." The unexpected bivouac high on Everest eventually cost him nine toes to frostbite.

Shortly after the expedition's success, Elizabeth threw a cocktail party with Unsoeld, enthroned on a bed, as the guest of honor. Other important guests included Prince Basundhara, ex-minister Rishikesh Shaha, and General Mrigendra. Unsoeld was interesting, well educated, articulate, and passionate about mountaineering and his work in the Peace Corps. He could well express the mystique of climbing. In a letter to her mother, Elizabeth contrasted his style with Ed Hillary's, whom she affectionately described as "the ex-beekeeper who doesn't appear to be the least introspective and has quite a hard time with anything more complicated than straight narrative."

Willi Unsoeld would eventually die in the mountains while guiding a group on Mount Rainier in the United Sates. His daughter, Nanda Devi, also died climbing, on an expedition to the mountain after which she was named. Elizabeth was fond of him, and describes him as a "very memorable person in my life."

After the expedition members had all gone home and the press conferences had ended, Elizabeth reflected on the excitement of her Reuters scoop and on the personalities she had encountered, writing to her mother on June 21, "The mountains hereabouts are infested with men mad enough to want to slog to the tops. I sometimes wish they'd all stay home with their wives and kiddies."

For her fortieth birthday, in November 1963, Elizabeth threw a cocktail party. As with all the evening parties in Kathmandu at the time, dress was formal and she appeared in a long gown. Her guest list was impressive: Ranas, royalty, diplomats, political figures, painters, climbers, and all the "characters" of Kathmandu. Among them was Micky Weatherall—and his new wife. In three short years, Elizabeth had emerged as an integral part of Kathmandu: she had interesting work, she met fascinating people, and she had enough money to live comfortably. She had no intention of leaving.

LEARNING THE ROPES 8

He would rant, and she would go on with her work. It seemed to work for both of them.

In the early spring of 1964, Elizabeth's routine was interrupted by a two-week adventure when she covered King Mahendra's tour of western Nepal for *TIME* and *Life*. They flew to the town of Nepalganj and then headed into the hills on horseback, spending the nights at semipermanent camps in wild, rugged country. Perched high on an elephant, Elizabeth watched while the king indulged himself by killing three tigers and two deer. The hunting system was unusual. They would erect a white cloth fence around a large area where tigers were known to frequent, and then beaters would enter the ring and make enough noise to scare the tiger out into the open. The white cloth created a psychological barrier to the tiger so it was essentially trapped—and easy prey for the hunters. Although this method was usually effective, Elizabeth also observed what could happen when the tiger was shot but only wounded. The tiger became half crazy from the wound, crashing through the white barrier followed by dozens of army personnel "gallumping" off on their elephants to finish it off.

In the evenings, the king sat for hours while long lines of humble petitioners presented themselves to tell him their needs. A program of song and dance performed by local people followed. Although Elizabeth realized that traveling in the wilds of Nepal with the king was a unique experience, she was glad to return to the comforts of her apartment and wash off the fatigue and dust. It wasn't only Elizabeth who found the journey rugged; the king's frenetic schedule was wearing on him too.

But ignoring his doctor's warnings (his father had died of a heart attack at a young age and Mahendra seemed to have inherited his frailty), he insisted on pursuing his favorite sport.

An expedition of the true adventuring kind came to Elizabeth's attention when a British group led by Dennis Gray came to town. After weeks of trekking, hacking trails through wild country, fixing ropes, and discovering ever more valleys hidden between them and their peak, the team, which included Don Whillans, finally reached the slopes of the 6257-meter Gaurishankar. But horrific ice conditions and avalanches defeated their goal of a first ascent. It was Elizabeth's first meeting with Don Whillans, someone who would come through Kathmandu again in the ensuing years. He was already famous for his combination of gruffness, great skill, and cruel wit. She was amused by him, and would sit with him as he smoked cigars and told humorous tales. She told him she thought he was too fat to be a climber and she was amazed that he added to his calorie intake by drinking enormous quantities of beer in Kathmandu. He explained to her that he'd lose the extra pounds on the expedition—and he did. Questioned about a persistent rumor that she and Whillans were romantically involved, she howls, "I can't believe that!" She goes on to say that if he was smitten with her, it was not mutual. And so fell the first of the Elizabeth Hawley "lover of famous climbers" myths.

Because of the delicate relations between Nepal and Chinese-occupied Tibet, climbing was banned in Nepal from 1965 to 1969. China regarded all climbers along the border region as spies—and some of them were. Elizabeth thought that Sayre's foray into Tibet in 1952 factored in to Nepal declaring a halt to all mountaineering. In 1955 a Welsh expedition led by Sydney Wignall went into the far northwestern corner of Nepal and was arrested in Tibet. Forty years later Wignall wrote a book, *Spy on the Roof of the World*, about his daring deeds for Indian intelligence. And in 1963 a Japanese expedition went into the same area and also got caught. Then in the mid-sixties a Scottish missionary ventured across the border to film the brave rebellion of Tibetans in the Kham region against the repressive Chinese, and returned to the west with his images. During the Cultural

Revolution, the Chinese grew even more paranoid about the border; because of Nepal's close proximity to China and sensitivity to China's wishes, Nepal closed its border with Tibet.

———※———

It was during this time that a new kind of tourism began to emerge in Kathmandu. As early as 1963, British defense attaché Col. Jimmy Roberts began to hatch a plan to create a means of employment in Nepal that would enable him to remain there after he retired from the army. He had fond memories of the old days in Kashmir, when agents organized hunting trips with camping gear, porters, guides, and equipment, and so he decided to try it on a commercial basis. He gathered the necessary gear, placed an ad in *Holiday* magazine, and the world of trekking was born. Mountain Travel was Nepal's first trekking company and likely the first trekking company in the world.

In his first Mountain Travel newsletter, produced in 1965, Roberts described himself to prospective clients: "With nearly thirty years' experience of Himalayan exploration and travel, ten years' residence in or on the border of Nepal, and a more or less intimate knowledge of large tracts of the mountains, I can claim to be fairly well qualified to undertake this task." In a supplement to the newsletter, dated March 1965, he included his price list for the Everest Trek: five hundred dollars per person for a thirty-day trek. After many requests, he organized and accompanied a small trekking party comprising three American women to visit the Everest region.

Roberts had an interesting history that prepared him well for this new venture. He was born in India of a doctor in the Indian army. Asia was his home. He too became an army man, spending his first career with the British Gurkhas and finishing as a military attaché. He told Elizabeth ghastly stories of his time in the jungles of Burma with the Gurkhas. It was clear the experience had been harrowing. He went on countless expeditions into the mountains, sending back a certain amount of military intelligence: information about the sentiments of the local people, the border situation, what Nepalis thought about their government, and the general feel of things. When that career wound up, he found himself at loose ends, drinking too much whiskey and growing depressed. Then he came up with the idea of a trekking industry, and virtually saved his own life. It was during this time that he and Elizabeth became friends.

His passion was the mountains—climbing and exploration. His knowledge of climbing history in Nepal was prodigious and he was generous in sharing that knowledge with Elizabeth. He helped familiarize her with the mountaineering world. He was also shy and sensitive, and Elizabeth observed that he was easily hurt. Many people misjudged this shyness, thinking he was a bit dazed or vague. In 1953 John Hunt invited him to join the famous Everest expedition, but only after the expedition had arrived in Nepal. In fact, it wasn't until Roberts arrived at base camp with some late-arriving oxygen that he was invited to take part. He declined. Considering his already stellar climbing record in the Nepal Himalaya, he was insulted by the belated invitation, and many in Kathmandu thought he was justified.

Roberts was a confirmed bachelor and did not have lady friends. Another rumor made the rounds of Kathmandu that he and Elizabeth were romantically involved, but she sets that one straight, too. She doesn't believe he ever made passes at women and thinks there was probably credibility to the theory that he didn't care for women at all. She saw him at parties, often drinking heavily, but never with a woman. One of his closest friends was Pertemba Sherpa, and they adored each other, according to Elizabeth. Pertemba worked with him in the trekking business but eventually left for another company. Roberts was hurt by this apparent betrayal. But he was a brilliant organizer and his idea was not only original but also right for the times, and so the business began to grow.

As it grew, he needed someone in Kathmandu to handle correspondence because he preferred to go with clients on the treks. He asked Elizabeth for help, and she said yes. Her first assignment for the company was to help organize a trek into the region between Dhaulagiri and Annapurna for a physiologist from the University of California's oceanography lab. She met him at the plane, took him shopping for a bath towel, soap, and other personal things for the trip, answered endless questions, and saw him off on the plane. "The helpless scientific type," she concluded. Other clients began trickling in, attracted by the description of exotic locales, as well as the chance to meet famous explorers such as Eric Shipton (another rumored lover of Elizabeth's—also firmly denied), who worked briefly as a Mountain Travel guide.

In the early days of climbing in Nepal, there was no legal requirement for an expedition to be represented by a trekking agent, but even then Mountain Travel coordinated a lot of expedition logistics. Now an employee of Mountain Travel, Elizabeth handled their mail while they were on the mountain. In return, she asked them to send her regular correspondence from the climb, letting her know how they were doing. They did this exchange via a simple cloth mailbag lined with plastic. Using planes, trucks, and runners, she stayed on top of each expedition's progress.

At the same time that Mountain Travel was growing in Kathmandu, a private American investment company named Tiger Tops was bringing travelers to the southern Terai region of Nepal. It was the creation of two Texas oil investors, Herb Klein and Toddy Wynne Jr. They hired John Coapman, the son of missionary schoolteachers in India, to go to the Terai and build a lodge in what was then a game preserve but which later became a park (after the royal family had systematically killed much of the wildlife). This lodge became the first jungle lodge in Nepal.

Tiger Tops quickly became famous as an adventure destination. Between Christmas of 1964 and New Year's, Elizabeth was a guest at the lodge, where she viewed big game, including tigers, from the back of an elephant. The lodge itself was attractive, with a main building on stilts and a huge circular fireplace in the middle of the dining and lounge area.

By February 1966 business was picking up for Tiger Tops; it was then that John Coapman asked Elizabeth to help out with lodge bookings from her home office in Kathmandu. The lodge only had eight rooms at the time, so she used a school copybook in which she ruled out lines for eight spaces for each day of the week. Although she was already working as a stringer for *TIME*, *Life*, and Reuters, as well as her Knickerbocker Foundation work and her new job at Mountain Travel, she was happy to have the extra income. Her responsibilities consisted of answering telegrams, handling Coapman's correspondence, and answering questions from local hotels and travel agencies about Tiger Tops reservations. Within a year, this job began to take an inordinate amount of her time. But though the business was growing, the profits, strangely, were not.

By 1971 the Texas backers of Tiger Tops were tiring of the logistical and administrative problems and questionable profits, although they remained convinced that it was a good idea. They were used to making money, not losing it. Tiger Tops was not even able to pay their staff during this time and Coapman had the unpleasant experience of a general strike. So he fled, not just from Tiger Tops, but from Kathmandu altogether. This didn't affect Elizabeth as much as it could have because Coapman had fired her shortly before the company went bust. He had a terrific temper, and Elizabeth's strong and stubborn character had been too much for him.

In the meantime, another Kathmandu resident and keen hunter, Jim Edwards, joined up with Chuck McDougal to start a hunting company in Nepal. Jim had had his eye on Tiger Tops, so when Coapman fled, Jim met with the Texans and was appointed manager of the company in 1972. He knew Elizabeth and wooed her back to the company, after which they set about trying to straighten out the mess that John had left behind: unpaid salaries, dead elephants, a staff on strike, no credit in Kathmandu, and so on. Soon, they dramatically increased their business.

With their newfound success, they even managed to coax Royal Nepal Airlines into offering daily flights to their lodge—not an easy task. Jim had worked for Pan Am in New York before he came to Nepal, and he was a successful salesperson, not only selling the lodge to tourists, but also bringing in more investors. He was generally a charming man, but not always. Elizabeth didn't find him to be the easiest person to work for. She recalls that when he became angry with her he would rant and rave on the office intercom, but she knew how to turn it off and he didn't. So he would rant, and she would go on with her work. It seemed to work for both of them.

At the same time, Jim wanted to open a trekking agency. Elizabeth happened to know that Jimmy Roberts was getting bored with the management of Mountain Travel, so she introduced them to each other with a merger in mind. It worked. Jim continued to bring in new investors for the expanded company. Mountain Travel maintained its own name, as did Tiger Tops, and Jim then went on to open Himalayan River Exploration and two more jungle lodges. It was an exciting time for the travel industry: Mountain Travel was the first adventure travel company in Nepal and the world; Tiger Tops was the first jungle lodge in Nepal. Together they were not only successful, but they changed the way people thought of travel. The company eventually became known as Tiger Tops Mountain Travel International.

In 1975 a young British woman, Lisa Choegyal, joined Tiger Tops and began to invite a number of high-profile customers to the company, building its reputation internationally and having some interesting times in the process. It was a parade of stars: Robert Redford, Henry Kissinger, Goldie Hawn, and Jimmy Carter. Lisa remembers that for the most part they tried to steer the guests clear of Elizabeth, as she had a brusque manner that the guests did not find endearing. But perhaps Elizabeth was just selective—somehow she managed to sufficiently charm Jimmy Carter into lobbying on her behalf to the king when she had some problems with her journalist accreditation. It didn't work, but she appreciated his efforts. Carter found himself in a curious situation when his round-the-clock bodyguards, who accompanied him to Everest base camp, almost dropped dead from the combined effects of altitude and sheer exhaustion. Kissinger had his own problems down at the Tiger Tops lodge when he attempted to get on an elephant. He couldn't bring himself to do it—it turned out he suffered from vertigo. He ended up taking a Jeep tour instead, regaling Lisa Choegyal with stories of high-level intrigue and diplomacy.

Years later, in 1995, one of the Tiger Tops celebrities was Hillary Clinton. Lisa came up with the idea of introducing Hillary to the other Hillary—the knighted one—who happened to be in town. Elizabeth and Lisa choreographed the event, which ended up taking place on the hot tarmac of the airport. Hillary Clinton was particularly enthusiastic, gushing about how excited she was, announcing that her mother had named her after Sir Edmund. Former President Bill Clinton's best-selling biography of 2004, *My Life*, repeats the story of his wife being named after the man who first climbed Everest. There is only one problem with this anecdote: Sir Edmund Hillary did not reach the summit of Everest until May 29, 1953, when Hillary Clinton was already five years old. At the time of her birth, he was an obscure New Zealand beekeeper. Both Lisa and Elizabeth doubted her story at the time, but basked in the ink the event produced with headlines like "Hillary meets Hillary."

As the company matured, Jim created an executive committee, employing Elizabeth in that capacity. Then she became an executive advisor and finally more of a consultant, providing a monthly report that outlined the political, economic, and major tourism news in the country.

Elizabeth finally had her own opportunity to see a part of Nepal she had frequently written about—the Khumbu, land of the Sherpas and jumping-off point for many important expeditions. It was a place she was eager to experience firsthand. In 1965 she and her friend Barbara Adams joined a small group of Americans living in Kathmandu to fly to Lukla and trek for a couple of weeks. Among the group members were Willi Unsoeld and his wife. In a letter informing her mother of her plans, Elizabeth reassured her in a postscript: "I won't be doing any attempts at climbing, you understand—only trekking or hiking." Back in Kathmandu, having trekked to Namche Bazaar, Thyangboche, and Khumjung, she was tired, describing the experience to her mother: "This slogging up steep mountainsides and back down again for hours on end when one is not in training is bound to be tiring." But she thought it was worth the struggle—for the scenery, and to see where and how the Sherpas lived.

March 9, 1967, was an exciting day for those living in Kathmandu, and the beginning of even greater exposure and business for Tiger Tops. A Boeing 707 landed at the Kathmandu airport, the first time an intercontinental jet had ever landed there. Experts had said it was impossible to land a jet on the short, 6900-foot runway in a small valley surrounded by tall mountains, but the Lufthansa jet did it in just 3500 feet. Only a test flight, it was expected to pave the way for more in the future, which is exactly what happened a few months later when the Nepal government opened the airport to Thai International flights direct from Bangkok twice a week. As the Thai flights became established, they became an important supplier of clients for Tiger Tops. But Royal Nepal Airlines wasn't pleased with the competition and demanded that Thai Airlines pay a substantial fee to keep operating in Nepal. Elizabeth became involved, and arranged a meeting between the crown prince's secretary and some of the senior Thai officials, resulting in a smoothing of relations—and a free ticket for Elizabeth on Thai Airlines to an Asian city of her choice. By the beginning of June, yet another important transportation link had opened up—a paved road from Kathmandu to the Tibetan border. And in March, a casino opened in Kathmandu's newest hotel. The owners were a mixed group: Bhutanese, Albanian, and Anglo-Indian, and the manager was a former acting prime minister of Bhutan—a real "man about town," according to Elizabeth. The secret of Nepal was getting out.

But even as the city became more accessible and cosmopolitan with each passing month, the political situation took a major setback in March 1968 when King Mahendra had a heart attack while hunting tigers in western Nepal. He took two months off to convalesce and made his first public speech in May, sounding perfectly normal. Perhaps it was his brush with mortality that prompted the next momentous political event.

To give the event some context, it is necessary to reflect back to 1960 when the prime minister of Nepal, B. P. Koirala, was arrested and his authority replaced by that of the king. Koirala had been in custody without a trial or in exile ever since. One morning near the end of January, Elizabeth received a call from Koirala's former home minister, who had lived quietly in Kathmandu since his own release from prison seven years earlier. He invited her to come and have tea with Mrs. Koirala that evening at her home. Elizabeth knew something was up when she arrived to find several other journalists there as well. At about 8:00 P.M., a Russian Jeep belonging to the Nepalese army pulled up with two familiar faces: Koirala and his transport and communications minister, both of whom had been in jail or in exile all these years.

Koirala looked thinner but healthy, despite his prison ordeal. Now some interesting times would unfold, she thought, as these two men, the king and the former prime minister, would once again have to figure out how they were going to join forces—or not—in running the country. She was disappointed when, instead of Koirala, a deputy prime minister who had been suddenly dropped from the cabinet the preceding year was appointed as prime minister. Although Kirtinidhi Bista was a pleasant man, she doubted he had the experience and vision of Koirala.

The political intrigue continued when a close political friend of Elizabeth's, Rishikesh Shaha, who had been arrested three months before under a vague Security Act, was suddenly released on technical grounds. On his way home from court, he was re-arrested, this time with all the technicalities worked out. She concluded that the present government considered him to be a very real political threat and wanted him well and truly out of the way. Personally, it was a discouraging development, as he had always been a reliable source of inside information for her.

———— • ————

With her beloved dog Sindhu showing signs of age, Elizabeth decided to get a nine-month-old Lhasa apso, a male bundle of brown, black, and white fur, with a face remarkably like an owl's. He was sweet and affectionate and she named him Tigger. Sindhu wasn't overjoyed by this new addition and was rather cool to Tigger. But Tigger didn't notice and initiated endless play with Sindhu and Elizabeth or, if all else failed, with his ball, which he would chase around the apartment, leaping on it, letting it roll away, skidding to a stop to catch it, and sliding beyond it. He was excellent entertainment for Elizabeth, who described him as "so cute it almost hurts." Sindhu eventually allowed himself the indignity of playing with Tigger, although he appeared to tire easily of the silliness. During an important Hindu festival that fall, poor neurotic Sindhu had to endure fireworks, loud bangs, and strange light flashes scaring him half to death. Tigger slept through it all. Sindhu was beginning to show his age. Several of his front teeth had shifted position by 45 degrees and now pointed outward, giving him a bucktoothed effect. At least he could still chew.

In the spring of 1969 a young *Fortune* researcher from New York, Elaine King, showed up on Elizabeth's doorstep, stayed a while, and eventually worked for her. For the first few days, Elaine explored the sights of Kathmandu. The evening before she left, Elizabeth invited her for a drink at the Annapurna Hotel and asked, "Well, what do you think?" Elaine responded, "I think it's wonderful." Then Elizabeth announced she had a job opening at Tiger Tops and offered it to Elaine.

It was a foreign-correspondence position in charge of reservations for the company. Initially Elaine said no—she had a definite itinerary in mind for her travels, and it didn't include settling in Nepal. But the offer dangled in front of her and by the time she reached Iran she was seriously questioning her refusal of Elizabeth's offer. "How many times in your life do you get the chance to run away from home?" she wondered. She had a strong desire to break from the mold and so, at the age of twenty-four, she went back to Kathmandu.

However, she neglected to contact Elizabeth in advance. So when they met in Kathmandu, Elizabeth regretfully informed her that the job opening was gone. In the two weeks that had transpired, the job had been farmed out to a travel agent. Elaine was devastated. But she "suspended her emotions" and decided she would cope. She obtained a few names from Elizabeth and started looking for a job.

She eventually found one that combined teaching English and helping out with an English-language newsletter. Returning to Elizabeth to let her know, she learned that her friend had spoken to the travel agency and suggested that if they hadn't found anyone to do the job, she might have just the person for them. Now Elaine had two job offers. She weighed the difference between a job teaching English and a job that would give her an opportunity to ride an elephant on occasion—she chose the elephants.

So she went to work for Tiger Tops in the same office as Elizabeth. It was exciting, with clients coming in from all over the world. Sir Edmund Hillary came to the offices frequently to see Elizabeth—Elaine remembers that she called him Eddie.

Elaine's impression was that Elizabeth always adhered to her standards. She had two staff working for her, a cook and a bearer. "Elizabeth stayed Elizabeth—she didn't become Nepali." Although Elizabeth maintained a tough exterior, Elaine believes she was one of the few people allowed to see her softer side. They shared a similar sense of humor and enjoyed hilarious times together. Through Elizabeth, Elaine met a cross section of Kathmandu society, including politicians, royalty, climbers, and writers.

But when Tiger Tops went through its darkest hour and Coapman fled, there was no money left to pay staff, so Elaine was let go. She hated to leave and it was a sad day for both of them when Elaine left Kathmandu. Over the years they've remained in touch, partially through the "newsy" Christmas letters that Elizabeth claims to send. Elaine laughingly describes them as more "cryptic" than "newsy."

In addition to the work Elizabeth was doing in the travel industry, she was still a reporter. One of her dispatches was on an important American delegation in Kathmandu, led by U.S. Vice President Spiro Agnew. She actually dreaded the event because, in her opinion, "the man involved doesn't deserve all this attention." But she had to be intimately involved with the advance arrangements, as well as the visit itself. There were rumors of impending student demonstrations and hippie protests, but they didn't come to pass. The visit actually came off quite well. "He put his foot in his mouth only once," she reported to her mother, and then it wasn't that important. He referred to Nepal as India, a common occurrence for visiting dignitaries. His speechwriters had prepared him well, and the visit was mercifully short.

Elizabeth was beginning to realize that mountaineering news was an important part of reporting for an international wire service in Nepal. In those pioneering days of first ascents and mountain exploration, there was a lot of media interest in expeditions, much more so than now. So she began meeting all the expeditions coming into Kathmandu, and keeping files on them. This work, and the personalities involved, became a bigger part of her life each year, consuming a huge amount of time. Her life became devoted to mountaineering and it was increasingly difficult to separate Elizabeth Hawley from mountaineering in Nepal.

Her education in history and her experience as a researcher in New York prepared her for precise data collection, and statistics appealed to her. Her Reuters stories were objective, but her real opinions often came through when writing to her mother about the various expeditions and personalities. In the spring of 1969 she told her mother about an American expedition tackling Dhaulagiri I, on the western side of the Kali Gandaki Valley in the Central Himalaya, led by Boyd Everett, a security analyst when he wasn't climbing. She described him as "the coldest person in a body that's still alive whom I've ever met." She thought he would have been more at home among his stocks and bonds than in the mountains of Nepal. News began to trickle out from the expedition that things had gone disastrously wrong; an ice cliff high on the mountain had collapsed on seven climbers, sending them all to their deaths. As climber Al Read recounted in his report for the *American Alpine Journal*, "Death is not uncommon in mountaineering. Its cold fingers follow you into the rotton [*sic*] couloir. You see it above as you traverse below the cornice. . . . Most certainly it stalks in the incessant animation of an active Himalayan glacier." But on Dhaulagiri he saw something on another scale. "This was annihilation."

Elizabeth was thoroughly involved in this tragedy. She arranged rescue flights, filed news reports, and made arrangements with the next of kin. She saw a great deal of the expedition members, both before and after, and, except for the leader, thought they were a pleasant bunch of men. She believed they hadn't fully comprehended the immensity of the mountain before they tackled it.

By this time Mountain Travel was handling all climbing expeditions' logistical needs in Kathmandu, and Jimmy Roberts sent much of the work in Elizabeth's direction. They worked together closely. She credits him as an important influence, helping her in the early days of mountaineering reporting and giving her important archival materials. He explained the significance of certain expeditions and gave her a solid grounding in the history of Himalayan climbing.

It was he who told her about how Nepal had opened its doors to climbing in 1950, and of the early expeditions with climbers and explorers like Maurice Herzog on Annapurna and Charles Houston and Bill Tilman, and later Raymond Lambert, on Everest. She didn't arrive in Nepal an expert on mountaineering: she became one, largely with the help of Jimmy Roberts.

While she was still learning the ropes from Roberts, it was Mike Cheney who did most of the actual reporting to the various alpine journals. Elizabeth gave him the basic information from her meetings with the climbers and he crafted it into a report. She found Cheney to be a peculiar gentleman. He was an ex-Gurkha like Roberts, but she didn't consider his climbing background to be impressive and thought he misrepresented himself as an expert in his reports.

In the *American Alpine Journal* in the 1970s and '80s, it was Cheney's byline at first, then both his and Elizabeth's, and finally only Elizabeth's byline after Cheney died in the late '80s. Upon his death, she contacted the journals and magazines to offer her services, although pointing out that she would follow a different style. The difference in style had to do with editorializing. Cheney often included his own commentary. Elizabeth thought personal opinion was inappropriate and said she would be happy to provide a list of all expeditions, a list of expedition leaders, basic information on each climb, and a list of deaths, as well as a narrative story of the season's climbs—but no editorial comment. Although she suspects her opinion may have surfaced between the lines at times, she avoided overt editorializing. She didn't feel qualified to provide subjective commentary because she wasn't a climber and she didn't have the "big picture" that some people thought she did. She didn't feel entitled. Over time, this approach became a point of discussion—and a bone of contention—for climbers who read her work.

However, Elizabeth was generous about sharing her knowledge, particularly with climbers, and especially if she sensed a pioneering effort in the making. American climber Carlos Buhler remembers an example when he was searching for specific information about an obscure face on Annapurna. He questioned Elizabeth, and was surprised to be entrusted with a file from her collection, handed to him with "Carlos, promise that you will bring this back in perfect condition. You may take it down and get it photocopied." He was astounded by the gesture, her complete folder on Annapurna, a piece of her life's work, entrusted to him. He vowed at that moment to never, ever withhold a piece of information from Elizabeth Hawley, because he finally understood that it wasn't just for her records and her reporting; it was for the climbers of the future—those who would come and tell her about their dreams and be helped by her in turn.

But if she was going to share information, she insisted on intelligent, well-researched questions. She was impatient with people who would demand, "Liz, tell us all about Dhaulagiri." She interacted best with people who were prepared and specific in their needs.

"Memshab, we have accident."
"What happened, Kumar?"
"We have bad accident—plane crash."

One of the most outstanding friends from Elizabeth's years in Nepal is Sir Edmund Hillary. He was already a celebrity in Kathmandu when she first arrived, because of his 1953 ascent of Everest, and it was inevitable that the two would meet.

She grasped the significance of his climb in several ways. First, of course, was the fact that Hillary and Tenzing Norgay reached the summit and came back alive. Second, she understood the difficulty of the pitch high on the mountain, named the Hillary Step, and that by solving this particular riddle Hillary had found the key to the summit. "He forged a route using his knuckles, and God knows what all, to go up a crack and find himself at the top of it and pull himself over," she wrote to her mother.

Elizabeth also understood that Hillary's background had prepared him for this achievement: his climbing experiences, his fitness level, and his ambition. But she also instinctively recognized the difficulty he faced being thrust so quickly onto the world stage. "So here he was, going from a humble, modest beekeeper to a world hero." As she grew to know him, her respect grew. "This man has been a remarkable person in many ways, but one facet of his being remarkable is that he has never lost his modesty, he has never lost his unassuming ways and it didn't go to his head."

In Elizabeth's early days in Kathmandu, Hillary came back to Nepal to climb Baruntse, Kangchungtse, and others. But it wasn't just for climbing that he returned to Nepal. He began bringing New Zealanders with him who were capable of building things. Using local materials and local help, they began building schools at the urging of Nepalis. This developed into the Himalayan Trust, which became another link in the deep and complex friendship between Hillary and Elizabeth, and another important source of work for her. Her responsibilities grew over the years to include the logistics of shipping, travel arrangements, scheduling, hiring, finances, and much more.

The Himalayan Trust started modestly, as befits a modest man. Hillary had developed a great affection for the Sherpa people. He wanted to give something back to them in return for their help and friendship, so he enlisted the financial backing of the World Book Encyclopedia company to build a school in the village of Khumjung in 1961. It was the first of many schools that he built, as well as bridges, pipelines for fresh water, hospitals, and airfields. The funding for these projects was always a challenge and it occupied a lot of Hillary's time and effort. By 1972 Elizabeth's official role was to manage the finances and negotiate the necessary permissions from the government for all the Trust projects. She frequently accompanied Hillary to the mountain villages when they were opening a new school or hospital.

Another of Elizabeth's close friends, Boris Lissanevitch, met with trouble in early 1970 when he was arrested for collecting Nepalese and Tibetan works of art. He and his wife were avid collectors of statues, woodcarvings, and thankas, and recently there had been a concerted hunt for people dealing in items stolen from temples. Elizabeth thought it was strange that the authorities went after him. She knew his mother-in-law dealt in antiques, but this was hardly unusual in Kathmandu. She was convinced that it was an excuse to get Boris out of the way. Prior to this, he had done all of the catering for royal functions. Then the king and his brother opened the Soaltee Hotel, and it occurred to the wife of one of his brothers that perhaps the Soaltee, rather than Boris, should do the catering. So they effectively moved him aside. While he was in jail, they closed the Royal Hotel completely.

It took some time and negotiating, but by April he was free. What did he do? He created the Yak and Yeti Hotel. But Boris was not a business-man. All his businesses were financial failures. Prince Basundhara had bankrolled the Royal Hotel, and it was the prince who found an Indian investor, as well as the World Bank, for the Yak and Yeti. Boris hired architects and designers to realize his vision, and for a while it looked promising. But he eventually fell out with his major investor and was not even there when the hotel opened.

Boris then opened a series of failing restaurants. Many said they were unsuccessful because his middle son had his hand in the till to feed his drug habit. Boris once said to Elizabeth, "Look at my three sons. One's a kleptomaniac, one's a nymphomaniac, and one is a drunkard." Elizabeth was inclined to agree, but blamed their upbringing. They grew up living upstairs in the Royal Hotel and were raised by a woman she described as an "ignorant, superstitious, illiterate, fat Newari nurse" who had no control over the boys.

Boris himself was tremendous company and a great entertainer. In his upstairs apartment he had a huge living room, often full of fabulous guests: Agatha Christie, Freya Stark, movie stars, politicians, climbers, and royalty. Sir Edmund was impressed and amused by Elizabeth's eclectic friends. "No question, she really liked people who were interesting, who had done things, who were not stuffy . . . she liked the unusual." She thoroughly enjoyed the friendships she made with these quirky characters, as well as her acquaintances with the more established and important members of the community. Although she was friendly with several royals, Sir Edmund recalls that those closest to her were not the "most respected members of the royal family." They were a little on the out-side of the circle of power, and he doubts she had much to do with the king and queen themselves. Hillary never understood her friendship with Barbara Adams, though. He saw Barbara as a "real character, al-though . . . not one that fit into Liz Hawley's sort of ideas." Many saw Adams as Elizabeth's polar opposite; she was flamboyant, outgoing, and outrageous. Nevertheless, the two were close friends for a long time. They even went on an adventurous train trip across Russia, something that was regarded as quite a challenge in those days and something that Hillary suspects they endured rather than enjoyed.

Two decades after Hillary's ascent of Everest, climbers were already contriving various stunts, hoping to be remembered in the history of the highest mountain. The mountaineering world was amused in 1970 when the Japanese skier Yuichiro Miura attempted to ski down Everest. A film titled *The Man Who Skied Down Everest* was made, but according to Elizabeth he did nothing of the sort. "He didn't ski down Everest. He didn't start at the top, and he damned near killed himself skidding to a lucky halt just before a gaping crevasse at the start of the icefall."

At the same time, a climb of real significance was taking place on the great South Face of Annapurna. Chris Bonington put together a strong team: British climbers Don Whillans, Martin Boysen, Mick Burke, Dougal Haston, and Nick Estcourt, and the American Tom Frost. They struggled and pushed their way through a difficult technical route (and some difficult interpersonal wrangling), finally placing a potential summit pair—Haston and Whillans—in place. High on the mountain they endured screaming winds and extreme cold, but they kept going. With a superhuman effort, they reached the top at 2:30 P.M. on May 27, 1970. It was a great mountaineering story, marred by the death of Ian Clough, who was killed by falling ice as the team was leaving the mountain. Reports of the expedition reverberated in the mountaineering world and throughout Britain. Elizabeth, a relatively neophyte reporter on mountaineering matters at that time, understood the significance of this climb—a fundamental shift from the Himalayan ridges onto the more difficult and dangerous faces—and reported it accordingly.

One year later, in 1971, the disastrous International Himalayan Expedition came to Everest. Elizabeth was connected with the expedition through her responsibilities concerning their communications with the outside world. In return for this work, she was given their exclusive reports, which she sent directly to Reuters.

The expedition was something of an experiment in understanding and cooperation among nations. There were representatives from thirteen countries, plus a BBC film crew of nine and an Australian journalist, bringing the total to thirty. It was co-led by Norman Dyhrenfurth and Col. Jimmy Roberts. Their approach was two-pronged—one team would attempt the Southwest Face and the other would ascend the West Ridge along its entire length. But relationships came unraveled, with expedition members refusing to carry loads, leaving the mountain, or trying to change objectives to the South Col route while Dyhrenfurth remained adamant that it was the Southwest Face route they needed to climb. An Indian member of the expedition was killed early on the Southwest Face, and that added momentum to the resistance. Two Swiss, one Italian, and one French climber quit early—referred to by Dyhrenfurth as "the revolt of the Latins." The Frenchman, Pierre Mazeaud, said to Elizabeth, "I will not be a Sherpa for the Anglo-Saxons" (the Anglo-Saxons being the Americans and Japanese). Elizabeth's wry comment was, "That's the first time I ever heard of a Japanese described as an Anglo-Saxon." He continued, "It's not just me, Pierre Mazeaud, who is insulted. It is France who is insulted!" Eventually, Elizabeth's private opinion of the group turned to scorn, not just for the leader Norman Dyhrenfurth, but for members of the team as well. "It was a shame that Norman didn't choose his team much more carefully, and get them still in their primes and without such enormous egos," she commented.

Dyhrenfurth defended the team and his leadership and, although he did a certain amount of finger-pointing (particularly at the Latins), tried to take the high road and examine why individual priorities and objectives changed during the course of the difficult climb. There are some who say that what they interpreted as harsh criticism from Elizabeth was somewhat opportunistic, and that her words would have been completely the opposite had the expedition succeeded. But she defends herself, saying that she never printed anything other than the facts. "And if the facts tell the story, then so be it!"

Elizabeth herself was getting an international reputation. The *Bangkok World* wrote a flattering piece about her in August 1970 titled "She Wears Two Hats." And the *Kuala Lumpur Straits Times* headlined an article about her with "A Hippie Though She Does Not Look Like It." During a visit with her parents in California in 1973, Elizabeth did an interview in their home with the *San Jose Mercury News*. The questions for this "Socially Yours" column indicate a reporter with no real knowledge of Nepal but a great deal of curiosity for Elizabeth. She was asked the usual questions about why she went to Nepal, why she stayed, and how she made a living. Showing her journalistic savvy of what readers of such a column might like to know, Elizabeth answered with some quaint anecdotes and exotic images. In describing her various "hats," one of which was Tiger Tops, she explained, "It's the only airport in the world where the passengers are met by elephants." On her work with mountaineering expeditions: "They rely upon me if they need something such as a rescue aircraft. . . . " And on Hillary's Himalayan Trust, the reporter wrote, "We sensed her enthusiasm for its founder, Sir Edmund Hillary, conqueror of Mount Everest. . . . " Elizabeth made sure they understood his contribution. "He is one man who has taken something out of a country and is giving something back." She went on to describe him: "Sir Edmund is a casual, genial, friendly sort of person, but he is no puppy dog wagging his tail. He knows where he is going. He is the guiding light of the Himalayan Trust whose purpose is to help the people of Nepal." Asked about her social life, she explained that a lot of her friends were foreigners, but she was also close to several members of the Rana family, which had ruled Nepal for more than a hundred years. She described the social whirl of cocktail and dinner parties and tried to give readers some understanding of life without television. It was a feature article with a large photo of a smiling Elizabeth reclining on her mother's sofa.

But the reality of Elizabeth's life in Nepal was a little less romantic. By the end of 1971 most flights into and out of Nepal had ceased. The country was more or less cut off due to the conflict between India and Pakistan. Virtually everything came into Nepal through India, but India's preoccupation with the war meant that Nepal was a low priority. Banks in Nepal no longer accepted foreign checks, the mail and newspapers arrived only erratically, and gasoline shortages were common. The tourism industry temporarily ground to a halt.

Then Nepal was stunned in January 1972 when King Mahendra, at the age of fifty-one, had a heart attack and died less than twenty-four hours later. He died while on a hunting expedition, his greatest passion. Mahendra's sudden disappearance from public life affected everyone, as there was no political decision in Nepal that had not required his approval. He was cremated at Pashupatinath, Nepal's royal cremation site. Elizabeth stood with other members of the press on a knoll across the river from the site. They had a perfect view of the ceremony, which she describes as unforgettable. It was dark when Prince Birendra brought the king's body to the cremation site and placed it onto the cedar wood pyre, which he then solemnly lit. As the fire came to life, cedar and incense combined to produce a pungent fragrance that billowed across the river. Suddenly, the fire exploded into a huge flame and soared skyward as a great orange full moon gradually rose over the hills.

The new king, twenty-six-year-old Birendra, was expected to make some changes, and she wondered how difficult it would be for him. He seemed to be an impatient man who would probably not put up with the delays that Mahendra had tolerated, although she understood that many of those delays were caused by Mahendra's inability to delegate authority. But there were other major differences between the two. Birendra had been raised in a different era. He had only just been born when the Rana rule was drawing to a close. He had traveled widely and spent five years at Eton, one at Harvard, and part of a year at the University of Tokyo. Despite his exposure to the modern world, Birendra had an ominous connection with an ancient prophecy. Two centuries earlier a prophet had predicted that the direct descendants of the founding monarch, Prithvi Narayan Shah, would rule for ten generations—and no more. If this were true, Birendra would be the last.

Another expedition was in town, again for the Southwest Face of Everest. Elizabeth was much involved, dealing with their mail, film shipments, and entertainment. She knew a number of the climbers on this European team, including Don Whillans, whom she had met in 1964. The British team members included Whillans, Doug Scott, and Hamish MacInnes. But difficulties arose, particularly between the British members and their leader, Dr. Karl Herrligkoffer.

Elizabeth speculated privately whether these multi-nation attempts were doomed before they set out. It was easy to understand why Herrligkoffer had included the three Brits, as they were experienced on Everest and had gotten high on this face the previous year. But their climbing strategies were not compatible, and this led to misunderstandings. The Brits thought the Germans were squandering their energy and resources, and the Germans thought the Brits were lazy. "Whillans, for instance, likes a lie-in, a cup of tea, and a cigar or two before he starts work, and it is after 11:00 A.M. or even noon before he sets out for the day's climb at great altitudes," she wrote.

The expedition was also plagued by strikes by the Sherpas, and Herrligkoffer had to fly back to Munich twice during the climb to get more climbing equipment to satisfy these demands. He finally left the expedition early and it fell apart some time later.

By fall of 1972 the Brits were back again on the Southwest Face route. Led by Chris Bonington, the strong British team included Jimmy Roberts as co-leader, Doug Scott, Mick Burke, Dougal Haston, Hamish MacInnes, and Nick Estcourt. Elizabeth was in charge of their communications, receiving letters from them periodically, and reporting their progress. But by November they too gave up at 8230 meters because of terrible cold and wind. She felt bad for them and thought they had deserved the summit.

A death in the Khumbu Icefall strained her friendship with Chris Bonington. It was near the end of the expedition and, though Bonington did not have permission for Australian Tony Tighe to go any farther than base camp, he had allowed him to go into the icefall a couple of times. The last time in the icefall, a serac collapsed, burying Tighe under hundreds of tons of ice. Bonington received some terse reprimands from the authorities in Kathmandu for defying their regulations, and he felt that Elizabeth had made too big a story of the "nonpermission" part of the tragedy. The headline in the *London Daily Telegraph* on November 16, 1972, read "Bonington May Face Ban Over Everest Death," referring to a threat by Nepalese authorities to restrict Bonington's chances of returning to Nepal. He was saddened by Tighe's death but irritated with Elizabeth for her troublesome reporting. They had words. As Elizabeth remembers the incident, "He has a hot temper. I have felt the wrath of his temper once or twice. But I have forgiven him."

Her work was not limited to tourism and climbing, however, as she was still reporting political news for Reuters. A big event early in 1973 was Indian Prime Minister Indira Gandhi's visit to Kathmandu. Elizabeth was impressed with her, particularly at a press conference where she and other reporters were asking difficult questions, and Gandhi managed to evade their questions yet kept them all happy. "She may be short, but she packs plenty of poise and mental agility," she wrote her mother.

The expeditions continued to arrive. Next was a huge Italian expedition with sixty-four team members led by Guido Monzino. Two helicopters were enlisted to airlift food and equipment over the icefall from base camp to Camp II in the Western Cwm. Early in the expedition one of the helicopters crashed, so another was immediately sent for. They were supposed to use the helicopters strictly for rescue, but the climbers openly ignored the order, having fresh vegetables delivered on a regular basis to Camp II.

Elizabeth didn't think much of the size of the enterprise, and she was supported in her thinking by Hillary, who was in the country working on his hospital and school construction projects. Hillary was outspoken about it, providing excellent grist for the Reuters mill: "What Signor Monzino has shown is that if you have a couple of platoons of alpine troops, which is what he has, and a couple of helicopters, which is what he has, and unlimited equipment and funds, which he also has, then the climbing of Everest by the South Col route is a relatively straightforward procedure. We shouldn't regard this as a mountaineering expedition . . . it's more of a training program . . . it has nothing to do with mountaineering." The Italian embassy subsequently asked for an apology from Hillary. In 2003 at the celebration in Kathmandu of the fiftieth anniversary of the first ascent of Everest, a delegate from Italy stood up and denounced him. Hillary responded that he hadn't meant to hurt anyone, but his opinion remained unchanged.

At the other end of the mountaineering spectrum, Elizabeth was also reporting on a small American expedition to Dhaulagiri, one of whose members was the young John Roskelley from Spokane, Washington. After twenty days above 7132 meters, Roskelley, Lou Reichardt, and Nawang Samden summited, but the price was high for Roskelley. In base camp his frozen feet were thawed by the expedition doctors, and for the next three days he was carried by Sherpas down the glacier and across two passes to the village of Tukche, where a plane arrived carrying the finance minister of Nepal to an event in the district. The minister graciously offered to walk the seventy miles back to Pokhara so that Roskelley wouldn't have to. When Elizabeth saw him back in Kathmandu, his toes were badly frostbitten. But from what she observed of this outspoken American climber, she was sure that he would recover and return to Nepal.

A Hawley Reuters scoop occurred in 1973 when Elizabeth enlisted the help of a Himalayan Trust doctor. A Japanese team was on Everest trying to be the first to climb the Southwest Face and the first to climb the mountain in autumn. As a result, the Japanese media was giving it a lot of coverage. The team was providing media reports direct from base camp via a runner. As in 1963 with the American Everest expedition, Elizabeth was determined not to be outdone. So she organized the Kunde Hospital doctor to engage a local Sherpa runner to go up to the base camp to find out what was going on. He heard gossip about a Japanese climber getting to the top (not by the Southwest Face) by befriending the runner hired by the Japanese, who was on his way to get the word out to the Lukla airport. Elizabeth's runner got the details of the climb from the expedition's runner, and then sped down the trail to the hospital, leaving the other runner enjoying drinks in a bar. Her runner gave the news to the doctor, who wrote down what the Sherpa told him, and sent the news in a hospital mailbag by air to Kathmandu. Elizabeth received the bag and then had to decipher the somewhat confusing contents. The two climbers' names had been transmitted orally from a Japanese to a Sherpa to another Sherpa to a New Zealand doctor to an American correspondent—one Elizabeth Hawley. One name could have been Kartok, Kato, Kano, or Kondo. She decided on Kato, and filed the story. Thirty years later, Elizabeth describes the incident with glee. "Their expedition had a mail runner too, but my guy was faster—by a day. We got that story! [The other reporters] complained and the AFP guy was a particular moaner and groaner . . . I got chastised . . . I was naughty!"

In fact, the moaning *Agence France-Presse* guy did more than groan; he caused her serious trouble. Within a year the Ministry of Tourism banned her from reporting on mountaineering expeditions. By 1975 her "very friendly competitors," as she described them, had lodged a complaint with the minister of tourism and that cinched it. She was not even allowed on the ministry premises to learn of mountaineering news. She solved that through a friendly Kyoto correspondent with whom she had previously cooperated. He would go to the ministry and pick things up for her, but she still could not report on what she learned.

The first expedition attempting to climb one of the highest peaks in winter arrived in Nepal in December 1974. The Polish team led by the famous mountaineer Andrzej Zawada had 8511-meter Lhotse as its goal. They reached 8230 meters by Christmas Day, but continuous high winds and bitterly cold temperatures finally defeated them. A new variation on the Himalayan climbing theme was born—winter ascents.

By spring the Hawley household was facing serious problems, as both Tigger and Sindhu were sick with distemper. The vet attended to them both, but within two weeks her "dear, loveable, lively Tigger" died during the night. She missed him terribly. The indestructible Sindhu hung on, although his near blindness caused him to wander from one piece of furniture to the next, bouncing and colliding as he went. It didn't seem to bother him though—he would simply change directions and carry on. Now age seventeen, he had become an institution.

Upon returning from a short trip to Europe, Elizabeth became the proud owner of a new apso dog. The three-month-old puppy was "lively," causing considerable annoyance to poor old Sindhu but providing endless entertainment value for Elizabeth, chasing and chewing everything in sight. She couldn't think of anything better to name him, so finally settled on Tigger II.

She had also been tasked with finding the Hillarys a house in Kathmandu, and she found one by mid-January. When Sir Edmund, his wife, Louise, and their daughter Belinda arrived, Elizabeth threw them a fabulous welcoming party. One of her goals was to ensure that the country's powerful and elite were aware of the important work Hillary was doing in Nepal, and to that end she stacked the party with notables such as Prince Basundhara, the chairman of the newly formed Nepal Mountaineering Association, the American ambassador, and others. The big event of the season, though, was the king's coronation, which took place on February 24, 1975. The city dressed itself up for the who's who of the world's leaders arriving for the event: Prince Charles of England, the crown prince and crown princess of Japan, the husband of the queen of Denmark, the president of Sri Lanka, the crown prince of Laos, and many others. The city was aglow with decorative lights and colored lanterns. The round of official parties and receptions and black-tie dinners was endless, and Elizabeth was in the thick of it. She watched the colorful, elephant-back procession and the king's speech to the public, where he spoke about his country's needs and aspirations. It was very festive and she felt a little let down when it was over.

Shortly after, she received the sad news that her father had finally succumbed to the wear and tear of a number of illnesses. Although he had been ill for years, the end came quite quickly. Elizabeth was concerned about her mother and her ability to cope with the logistical and legal matters she was faced with. Elizabeth offered to come over to help, but her mother managed it on her own, efficiently and competently. She urged her mother to come to Nepal for an extended visit, and to this suggestion Florelle said yes, she would come later in the year.

No sooner had her father died than Elizabeth became a major player in yet another tragedy, this one closer to home. Hillary was in the Khumbu region building the Phaphlu hospital, and his wife and daughter were in Kathmandu, so he decided to charter a Royal Nepal Airlines flight to bring them and their dog to Phaphlu. The New Zealand pilot, Peter Shand, had met them the night before at the British embassy and was thrilled to have them as his passengers. But his fatal mistake the next morning was that in his haste to get going he failed to do a walk around the plane—wiggling the flaps, turning the propeller, jiggling the rudder, and checking everything as pilots of small planes do. They piled in and took off in a southerly direction. He immediately had trouble negotiating a turn to the east, so he attempted to return to the airfield. He managed the turn to the north but was unable to finish the turn to land the plane. At the north end of the runway was a steep drop-off to the river, and it was into that great hole that the plane crashed. He had failed to remove the wedge from one or both ailerons, and the plane's ability to fly was tragically compromised.

At 7:30 A.M., Elizabeth's helper, Kumar, was at the airport and Elizabeth was at home asleep. The phone rang.

"Memshab, we have accident."

"What happened, Kumar?"

"We have bad accident—plane crash."

Impatiently, she asked for someone else to come to the phone to verify—but it was true, the plane had crashed and everyone had been killed. She rushed to the airport and came upon an American helicopter pilot who was about to take his mother out sightseeing. Elizabeth knew him and implored him to take her to Phaphlu where Hillary was working. She returned home, changed her clothes, wrote and filed the story for Reuters, and flew to Phaphlu. She landed at the Phaphlu airfield, and Hillary later told her that when he saw the helicopter fly in and her get off, he immediately knew something terrible had happened. She told him the news and his first response was "oh shit, how will I tell the parents?"

His in-laws had been helping him with the building project, so he did tell them—immediately. A few days later, Louise and Belinda were cremated on the banks of the Bagmati River in the untouchables area because, of course, they were not caste people.

Hillary's other children, daughter Sarah and son Peter, were summoned to Nepal and they huddled together trying to grasp the significance of what had happened—to contemplate a future without two members of their family. Initially they went back to Hillary's rented house, but he couldn't bear it and retreated to Elizabeth's place. He couldn't sleep. Every night they ate at Elizabeth's place or another friend's house. Everyone wanted to feed them and look after them, but what they really needed was privacy—and a good friend. After some days in Kathmandu, they returned to Phaphlu as a family group, trying to find some peace in the mountains, in their work, and through each other.

Years later, Elizabeth sadly recalls watching her friend struggle with such a loss as the most difficult week of her life. She was swamped with arrangements regarding the tragedy. She arranged for last-minute flight changes for family members, tried to get reimbursements for flights not used, negotiated the termination of the rental contract for their house, and answered numerous letters of condolence on his behalf. She did her best to protect them from all the people who wanted to be around them, including the press.

Though Hillary busied himself with construction projects, they kept in close touch and he was deeply grateful for her help. In a letter written shortly after the accident, he said, "I can't claim that all is light and joy here but life goes steadily on and we have many happy moments amongst our family group. . . . We hear few Sherpa laughs, I fear, and I find the nights rather long but I have been assured that time cures all that sort of thing. Thanks for your terrific help—it's something I won't easily forget. I am very much in your debt."

After a couple of weeks, Hillary and his children were back in Kathmandu staying with Elizabeth before heading to the United States and New Zealand. She found him to be somewhat improved, although suffering from lack of sleep and depression. She was worried about him going back to his home in New Zealand. Her worries were justified, as he wrote to her shortly after: "Everything could almost be normal if the house didn't seem so empty without Louise and Belinda . . . and if I didn't have this unworthy ambition to be dead. No doubt I will become all jolly again in due course but it does seem to be taking a little time."

It was apparent to Elizabeth that some of the Hillary spirit had been broken; whether it was temporary or permanent she wasn't sure. He referred to it as a loss of the "Hillary dynamo," although he ruefully wondered if that had ever existed other than in the minds of the press. His health wasn't good and he found himself impatient with situations he would have coped with easily in the past.

One such incident involved his sister who, while helping him build the hospital at Phaphlu, was nearly killed by soldiers engaged in military exercises using live ammunition. A small bomb landed near her, nearly blowing her off a high trestle. Metal shrapnel flew overhead, barely missing a number of Sherpas and patients awaiting treatment. Hillary lost his patience and rushed to censure the soldiers, but immediately felt badly that he had lost his temper. He wrote to Elizabeth: "Tell me Liz—should one be calm when one's sister is nearly blown up? Clearly I would never have made it in the diplomatic world." He underestimated himself on that point, as time would tell.

By 1984 he had been invited by the New Zealand government to become high commissioner to India and Nepal. It was a great honor, but she wondered how he would handle both this and his Himalayan Trust responsibilities, speculating that more of them would fall her way. He accepted the post, and was duly installed in Delhi as high commissioner, a title that was the equivalent in rank to ambassador.

In May 1975 Elizabeth met Junko Tabei, the Japanese climber who had just become the first woman to climb Everest. It was an all-women ex- pedition except for the Sherpas. Because of these male Sherpas, there was speculation that Tabei was "pulled and pushed" by the men to get to the summit, but Elizabeth didn't buy it. She could see that Tabei was a strong climber and a determined lady. "She had her eye on Everest and she went out and climbed it."

Although Elizabeth was impressed with Tabei's determination to climb the mountain, she was somewhat cynical about the "first woman to climb Everest" ambition. To her mother, she confided that she didn't think it was the most exciting event that she could think of, but con- ceded that it did sell newspapers. Her Reuters report opened with "The first woman to conquer Mount Everest has come down from the clouds around the summit and talked of her love of adventure, science and music—and of her dislike of public life."

As Elizabeth grew to know Tabei better over the years, her respect grew, and some of that respect came from what Tabei did after Everest. She con- tinued climbing, including two more 8000-meter peaks—Shishapangma and Cho Oyu—and in other mountain ranges all over the world. Tabei stays in touch with Elizabeth by sending her an annual Christmas card filled with lists of the climbing she has done in the previous year. Elizabeth Hawley, master keeper of lists, views Tabei's annual climbing list with approval. She also approves of Tabei's efforts to help fight pollution in the Everest region with her donation of an incinerator at the Lukla airfield. Her assessment of this diminutive, record-breaking woman was surprisingly measured: "Quite modest ... not a great climber in terms of expedition climbing abilities, but a good climber and a determined one."

The great climbing accomplishment of the year, though, was the British Everest South West Face Expedition led by Chris Bonington.

The team was a handpicked group that functioned well throughout most of the expedition, consistently moving the lines up increasingly difficult pitches on or ahead of schedule. By September 24 Doug Scott and Dougal Haston were on the summit. They arrived at the top in the twilight, noting the strange metal structure that the Chinese had brought to the summit earlier that year. Now began their ordeal—the reality of a high-altitude bivouac. They reached the South Summit and dug a hole for some shelter, boiled up some tea, and spent most of the rest of the night rubbing each other's feet to avoid frostbite. They survived the night at an astonishing 8748 meters.

Two days later, still ahead of schedule, Bonington okayed the second summit attempt, by Martin Boysen, Mick Burke, Pete Boardman, and Pertemba Sherpa. Boardman and Pertemba made the summit and on the way down met Mick Burke resting a bit before continuing on. Boysen had already turned back. Within an hour, weather conditions had deteriorated dramatically and it was the last anyone saw of Mick Burke. What had seemed an uncontested success was now marred by tragedy.

Despite the death of Burke, Bonington took an enormous amount of pleasure—and pride—in this effort, proud of his team and of his own logistical and climbing performance on the mountain. He credited a lot of the success to the team of Sherpas, whom he had never seen carry such heavy loads and bring with them such an excitement and positive spirit.

Elizabeth gave a lot of credit to Bonington, who was, in her opinion, the most outstanding climber of the seventies. Even though he did not summit on either of his signature climbs, the South Face of Annapurna or the South West Face of Everest, she believes he was the force behind their success. "He showed the way to great face climbs on 8000-meter mountains, instead of just going up ridges in accordance with the history of mountaineering development." She laughs at her memory of Bonington after the Annapurna climb, when he said to her, "Never again a high mountain, never again a big expedition." Of course, he was back two years later. She learned never to believe a mountaineer when he says never! The seventies and eighties were not kind to these pioneers though. As

Elizabeth points out, "A whole generation of British climbing has been decimated . . . Bonington is alive, but most of his friends are gone."

Their relationship has had its ups and downs. Bonington remembers her being "a bit of a battle-ax" in the early seventies, but says she has definitely softened and has contributed a great service to the mountaineering community in sharing information and going the extra mile to help. He recalls their interviews as "very intense" because she really knew the terrain and was precise in her questioning. One of the star climbers on the expedition, according to Bonington, was Pertemba Sherpa. A frequent partner of Bonington's, Pertemba told Elizabeth some years later that he had since been forbidden to climb by his wife, who was afraid he would be killed. But, says Elizabeth, "He's snuck in an expedition or two since then!"

As excited as she was about the British Everest South West Face Expedition, Elizabeth wasn't allowed to report on it because she was still being punished for her earlier indiscretions. She was learning the fine art of patience—and diplomacy. It would take her a while. The reporting ban was not the last time that Elizabeth would run into trouble with the authorities. The next would be much more serious.

*"Two mountaineers from Austria and Italy
have conquered Mount Everest without oxygen
for the first time...."*
—ELIZABETH HAWLEY

T he political face of Nepal changed again when the king accepted his prime minister's resignation in September 1977.
Later in the year, B. P. Koirala, the former prime minister
who had been in power shortly after Elizabeth's arrival in Nepal and
who had been imprisoned or in exile for much of the time since then,
returned to Asia from the United States, where he had been receiving
medical attention. His arrival in India elicited a warm reception from
his old supporters, who were now in power there, irritating the Nepalese
authorities considerably. He subsequently arrived in Nepal, where he was
promptly arrested. He was later acquitted on five of the seven charges
brought against him, and the two remaining were postponed indefinitely
because the prosecution's evidence was incomplete.

Elizabeth was shocked at Koirala's physical state. He appeared thin
and weary. She hoped that Koirala and the king would get together and
find a way to solve what she saw as a process fraught with endemic
problems—the endeavor to combine democracy with a hierarchical system of family relationships. She recalled how the embassies would send
invitations to members of the royal family, and then be insulted when
they never received a reply. But the royals couldn't answer because they
never knew whether their father, uncle, or someone else would suddenly
demand that they be somewhere else. She realized it was unrealistic to
think that the road to democracy would be smooth.

In fact, there was greater unrest in Nepal now than at any time in the last fifty years. Even when the Rana family was being pushed out of power, Kathmandu was peaceful. The cause of the current unrest was hard to pinpoint, but seemed to be general discontent with inflation and corruption; unfulfilled—and rising—expectations; and the restlessness of youth. By the spring of 1979 student demonstrations had taken a violent turn. In the southern town of Hetauda, three people died when police opened fire on them. Following that violence, many leading politicians were arrested, and Koirala was again placed under house arrest.

The king moved swiftly to defuse the unrest by announcing a referendum to decide whether to keep the present panchayat system, under which political parties were forbidden, or to establish a multiparty system similar to what existed before his father ended it in 1960. This was considered an amazing announcement, since this very king had insisted since he ascended the throne in 1972 that the panchayat system would be permanent. Political maneuvering began immediately, with leaders campaigning for or against a new system. Political activity that had been dormant or clandestine for two decades, now burst into the open. Sporadic violence occurred. A group of men and women tried to assassinate Koirala by rolling boulders down a steep hillside toward his car. Uninjured in the incident, Koirala was nevertheless shaken by it, citing the dangers of the upcoming referendum. Some of those dangers, he believed, were coming from outside the country, as there was foreign interest in sabotaging the referendum and creating instability in a country that lay strategically between China and India. The king was undoubtedly aware of this too, and he made official visits to both India and China, emphasizing his country's good relations with both.

The referendum was held in 1980. Elizabeth was convinced that many voters would not understand what they were voting for or against, confusing the issues of multiparty vs. panchayat with problems of corruption, inflation, bureaucracy, and monarchy. Reporters flocked to Nepal to see what would happen. Despite the violence of the previous year, the referendum was peaceful. Long lines of voters had formed by 7:00 A.M., more than two hours before the polls opened. Seeing the huge voter turnout, Elizabeth was sure it signaled change to a multiparty system. But when all the results were in, the panchayat system had won—narrowly—with 55 percent of the votes. With such a narrow margin of victory, it was clear that some kind of constitutional change was needed, and the king announced that he would consult with various leaders on the nature and timing of reform.

In the process of consultation, many additional layers of administrative structure were created. The grander the administrative machine became, the greater number of resources were required to maintain it. In a country as poor as Nepal, Elizabeth thought it preposterous that this self-perpetuating bureaucratic organ could occupy so much money, time, ink, and effort when it appeared to be largely insensitive to what was going on in the rest of the country. With rapid and frequent changes in the top political positions, actually making a decision was one of the most dangerous things a senior politician could do. Commissions and councils resorted to delegating decision-making up, and up—ultimately to the king, where the sheer volume of decisions often resulted in stagnation. The paternal nature of this kind of rule flew in the face of genuine democratic reform, but it was a fact of life in Nepal—deeply rooted in the national character of patriarchal dependency.

The government's preoccupation with reform may have contributed to its reluctance to decide the fate of Elizabeth's journalist accreditation. Although the ban hadn't stopped her from doing the annual mountaineering reports, she was cut off from the excitement of a potential journalistic scoop. She heard rumblings from her Nepali journalist friends that the decision would be reversed, giving her the freedom to work again, but the decision was slow in coming and the waiting was frustrating. After more than a year, the prime minister and the king finally came to an agreement to renew her license, just in time for the 1976 spring climbing season.

Elizabeth's work with mountaineering expeditions was increasing and looked likely to continue to do so in the future, as the Nepalese government announced it would grant a total of twenty-six permits for the 1978 fall season. This would be by far the largest number of permits issued for one season. The most interesting of the spring expeditions was that of two men attempting to climb Everest without supplementary oxygen. The two were Reinhold Messner and Peter Habeler.

The climbers reached the summit without incident—or bottled oxygen—and with a small movie camera to record the historic event. Some people expressed doubts that they had not succumbed to dipping into the oxygen supplies at the South Col, but other team members later checked the supplies and found them to tally perfectly with the amount recorded prior to their ascent. Others expressed concern over the anticipated "brain damage" that the two would experience, but a physician who examined them after their descent found them to be tired but in excellent physical and mental condition, except for Messner's painful eye condition caused by removing his sunglasses while filming on the summit ridge.

Elizabeth's Reuters account announced: "Two mountaineers from Austria and Italy have conquered Mount Everest without oxygen for the first time...." She went on to add that this climb should settle once and for all the debate over whether humans could survive without oxygen at such rarified heights. But it didn't—as she soon found out.

After Messner and Habeler's ascent of Everest, a strange situation arose in Kathmandu. The Sherpas called a press conference to denounce Messner as a liar. They didn't believe his claim to have climbed without bottled oxygen, asserting that he had hidden tiny bottles of oxygen under his down jacket and had breathed it all the way to the top. It became clear to Elizabeth that the Sherpas believed that if they couldn't do it, nobody could. At the press conference she noticed that it was, "Messner this and Messner that." She challenged the Sherpas with "what about Peter Habeler?" No answer. She realized that they didn't like Messner—at all. He was perceived as condescending and demanding—"get my food, get my sleeping bag"—and they were intent on giving him a hard time in return.

The fall season brought an all-women's team to Annapurna led by American climber Arlene Blum. Elizabeth had met Arlene before and thought she was an intriguing personality. This time Arlene was taking on a much more onerous role as leader, and Elizabeth expressed to her mother that she was glad she wasn't going with them. After making the first American ascent of Annapurna I, the expedition came to a tragic end when two members of the second ascent team fell to their deaths on

October 17, 1978. There was speculation in various publications about whether their deaths could have been prevented if other (male, it was implied) climbers had been with them, but Elizabeth thought that the two who died were experienced, they knew what they were doing, and the nature of their fall would not have been prevented by having more people around. She responded to criticism of Arlene Blum not going high on the mountain with the logical observation that expedition leaders often do not go high on the mountain due to their logistical responsibilities down low. All of this was captured in a long piece about the expedition that Elizabeth submitted to *People* magazine.

This era in climbing, which began in the late seventies, saw an increasing number of experienced and often smaller expeditions attempting, and sometimes succeeding on, significantly difficult objectives—new routes on previously climbed peaks, as well as unclimbed peaks. This was a marked shift away from the large, siege-style expeditions that had produced notable successes on routes such as the Southwest Face of Everest. Now climbers began to bring a new, lightweight aesthetic to the Himalaya. They came from Britain, the United States, Yugoslavia, and Japan. Some of the most experienced climbers almost lived in Nepal now, going from one mountain to the next, seemingly having abandoned their lives back home in favor of the forbidding Himalayan faces. Many were familiar to her, and a few she counted as her friends.

In 1979 one of the most impressive of the spring's mountaineering objectives was a Yugoslav effort on a new route on the true West Ridge of Everest, which forms the border between Nepal and China. The team was led by Tone Škarja and included strong climbers like Andrej and Marko Štremfelj and Viktor Grošlej. They found the difficult climbing was sustained almost to the top, and the entire route was exposed to horrific winds. However, five climbers reached the summit on this impressive effort.

British climber Doug Scott was back with a small team that included Pete Boardman and Joe Tasker to attempt a new route on the 8598-meter Kangchenjunga from the glacier northwest of the peak. Not only were they trying a new route, they were doing it without oxygen or radios, and they limited their support to two Sherpas. The four team members had a total of more than twenty Himalayan expeditions under their belt, so they were well qualified for the task. After ten weeks, two serious summit attempts, frighteningly high bivouacs, and variable weather, they reached the summit in time for sunset on May 15.

The beautiful and remote twin-summited Gaurishankar, located on the frontier between Nepal and Tibet, had just been opened to climbing after a twenty-year ban—with the provision that any climb be a joint effort with Nepalese climbers. At 7144 meters, it was the last major unclimbed summit in the Nepal Himalaya. Its two revered summits represented two Hindu deities: Gauri—goddess of love, and Shankar—god of destruction. Not only was it remote, its approaches were largely unexplored since the Japanese attempt in 1959, and it was expected to be tremendously difficult. Al Read of Mountain Travel put together a formidable team including Nepal's most experienced Sherpa, Pertemba Dorje, and America's most experienced Himalayan climber, John Roskelley.

Once on the mountain, the climbers changed their route a couple of times, once because the border delineation with China changed, making the Northwest Ridge part of Tibet, and once because the West Face looked slightly more feasible than their other ridge alternative. Extremely difficult climbing at high altitude, rockfall, threatening ice bulges, aid climbing on shifting pitons, and uncomfortable camps were their partners, but on May 8 Roskelley and Dorje fought their way successfully to the summit. The last great Himalayan summit in Nepal had been climbed.

It was during this time that Elizabeth became better acquainted with Roskelley, a young, somewhat controversial climber from Spokane, Washington. Since his 1973 Dhaulagiri expedition, he had been racing up peaks in the Soviet Union, Bolivia, India, Pakistan, and Nepal. Roskelley was a professional climber, and so logically he should have been interested in having as much publicity for his climbs as possible. But he was a private person and didn't really appreciate the fact that Elizabeth's Reuters reports were being picked up by newspapers everywhere, particularly back home in Spokane, where he generally didn't inform people of his plans. It embarrassed him, as he described his motivation as "just to go with some friends and do a good climb." But Elizabeth did report on his climbs, and her reports undoubtedly helped his career. She understood what he was doing and the significance of his achievements, although she wouldn't tell him directly, saying to him only that he had done a "worthwhile ascent—not a great ascent." And that was fine with him. He accepted her taciturn style, partly because it reminded him of his father, who was also an old-school journalist.

A climbing event that made a big impression on Elizabeth was the death of Hannelore Schmatz in 1979. Her husband, Gerhard Schmatz, was the leader of the Everest expedition, and Hannelore was in charge of the logistics and trekking arrangements. She was not a terribly experienced climber, according to Elizabeth, but she did reach the summit with about nine other team members. It was on the descent that she died from exposure and exhaustion. Her body would be seen for years to come, lying beside the trail of the normal South Col–Southeast Ridge route, providing an unnerving sight because her head and upper torso were completely out of the snow. Climbers reported that her eyes appeared to follow them as they approached and passed her. Elizabeth remains caustic in her assessment of Gerhard Schmatz: "It didn't seem to unnerve her husband. He found consolation with somebody else, another woman." Elizabeth characterized Hannelore as a "hard-working woman," perhaps not with the charm of the beautiful French climber Chantal Mauduit, or the skill of Polish climber Wanda Rutkiewicz, but nevertheless a determined climber. "Her determination got her up the mountain, but not down."

Then, on October 25, 1979, Elizabeth was awakened by a telephone call from the airport saying that a radio message had come through from the New Zealand expedition on Ama Dablam requesting a rescue helicopter. Peter Hillary was on that team, and she agonized for several hours until she saw Peter emerge from the helicopter with a broken arm, cracked rib, broken finger, and sprained ankle. She shuddered to think of how Ed Hillary would have handled yet another death in the family. The team had been hit by falling ice; luckily, however, a team of Austrians was nearby and came to their rescue. One of that team was Reinhold Messner, who, much to Peter Hillary's chagrin, not only rescued him but left with Hillary's Canadian girlfriend! Elizabeth found this amusing.

From the other end of the world, another accident, again connected with the Hillary family, was reported. An Air New Zealand sightseeing flight in Antarctica crashed and initial reports said Ed Hillary was on it. They were mistaken. Although Hillary was safe, his good friend and climbing partner, Peter Mulgrew, was on the flight and was killed. Elizabeth had met Peter Mulgrew's wife, June, several times in Kathmandu and knew she would be devastated. Already on the board of directors for the Himalayan Trust, June began spending much more time in Nepal, working on the Trust projects, supporting Hillary in his work, and becoming close to him in the process. This was not easy for Elizabeth. Eventually, June Mulgrew became Hillary's second wife.

*"When I came with crazy ideas to Kathmandu,
she was listening—she never said it was
impossible."*
—Reinhold Messner

As the eighties began, climbing in Nepal saw some exciting new developments and notable achievements: winter climbs, difficult face climbs, a solo climb of Everest. In Elizabeth's mind, a few personalities leading these interesting developments stood out, and they helped make her work rewarding.

Polish climbers were the first to climb to a height of over 7000 meters in winter in 1973 on the 7492-meter Noshaq, and they did it again in 1974 when they reached 8250 meters on Lhotse. In both cases, Andrzej Zawada was there. Zawada was a great innovator, the first to convince the Nepalese government to open a winter climbing season; and for the 1979–80 season, he convinced the ministry to open Everest in winter. Elizabeth remembers him as tall, courtly, and charming.

Zawada's mission looked hopeless almost from the beginning as winds roared in from the north at up to 160 kilometers per hour, and temperatures averaged minus 25 degrees Celsius in the Western Cwm. The peaks grew dark as the winds stripped them of snow, and the days were even darker. Elizabeth heard horrific tales of hardship: throats inflamed from the cold, dry air; clear, hard ice; and camps destroyed by incessant hurricane-force winds. To make matters worse, the team received word from the government that they had to vacate the mountain by February 15. They negotiated a two-day extension, and with this new deadline and the thought of getting off the icy mountain spurring them on, Leszek Cichy and Krzysztof Wielicki reached the summit at 2:40 P.M. on February 17.

Two days later they were off the mountain and heading back to Kathmandu, where Elizabeth announced their landmark achievement to the world. She shuddered to think of what they had endured. Some of the Poles stayed on in Nepal, and by March, again under the leadership of Zawada, a team that was reinforced with several new members headed back to Everest for a successful ascent of a new route via the South Pillar. On May 19, Andrzej Czok and Jerzy Kukuczka reached the summit. The Poles were dominating. Some called it the Golden Age of Polish mountaineering in Nepal, and Elizabeth was inclined to agree.

Nearby on Makalu, an American team led by John Roskelley was attempting a route on the West Pillar. Roskelley described this expedition as one in which they were going to try and rise to the level of the mountain rather than pull the mountain down to theirs. That meant no bottled oxygen, a small team of four climbers, and no Sherpas above base camp. It was his tenth trip to Asia in seven years, and his third time as leader of an expedition, so he was clearly qualified to make the call.

Despite his having a team of highly experienced climbers who were as tenacious as he was, in the end it was up to Roskelley to actually tag the summit. In an impressive solo effort, with frighteningly technical and exposed climbing, he reached the summit in late afternoon on May 15. His descent was wracked with indecision about whether to bivouac or continue, interrupted frequently by lapses into a restless sleep. On his return to Kathmandu, he told Elizabeth an amusing story about how, as he emerged from one of these stupor-like states, he thought he heard voices. He called down to his teammate, Chris Kopczynski, who yelled back, "John, is that you?" Even in his hypoxic state, John couldn't help laughing as he thought, "Who the hell else could it be?"

Then, on August 20, 1980, Messner created another first—Mount Everest solo, partially by the Great Couloir on the Tibetan side, without supplemental oxygen. He did the climb in just three days after a six-week acclimatization period. He carried a 33-pound pack that included a small tent. For his final climb, he took only his camera and ice ax. Many would refer to this ascent as the ultimate alpine-style climb—elegant, pure, and bold.

In October, Messner was back, going from the 5395-meter base camp to 7399 meters in two mornings' climbing on his solo attempt of the South Face of Lhotse. On the third morning, he climbed to 7803 meters, where bad weather defeated him, forcing him back down to base camp.

In Elizabeth's opinion, Messner was the climber who really stood out in the eighties. She remembers their first meeting, when he made his ascent of Manaslu in 1972. He remembers it, too, having immediately sensed that she was serious about chronicling the history of mountaineering. She greatly admired Messner's philosophy of "fair means," which meant no supplemental oxygen, limited fixed rope if any, and few camps, Sherpas, or support team members. Messner and Peter Habeler shattered preconceived ideas of what was possible with their ascent of Everest in 1978 without bottled oxygen. But it was during the eighties that Messner proved you could climb two 8000ers in one season, and that you could traverse two 8000ers if they were close enough. Then he made his historic solo ascent of Everest—a truly solitary climb with no one else on the mountain. She regards him as a pioneer because he constantly showed the world new ways of doing things—ways that were thought to be impossible.

Elizabeth likes Messner. Many others say they don't, but she thinks they simply envy his skills and successes. They had long conversations about his expeditions, and about others as well. As he began to trust her with his plans and dreams, he found that she was an invaluable source of information that was always accurate. Perhaps more importantly, she encouraged him. "When I came with crazy ideas to Kathmandu, she was listening—she never said it was impossible."

As his career blossomed and peaked, Messner became more interested in what others were doing in the Himalaya—the next wave. They spent hours discussing the young, up-and-coming climbers. He says she had a good understanding of what was new and exciting in climbing, and that she had a good sense of who the outstanding new climbers would be. "We never disagreed on this point—never," he says.

They had many good evenings together, sharing ideas and stories. "I have to be thankful to her for her ideas," Messner says; "in some cases it helped me decide my projects." This is high praise coming from the man recognized as the greatest Himalayan climber of all time. In addition to ideas, he got information from her—information about who was planning to do what, where, and when—and this helped determine the order in which Messner launched his own plans. He describes their meetings as "giving and getting, giving and getting," and their conversations as between equals.

As Elizabeth recollects her relationship with Messner, she reveals pleasure in having inadvertently influenced his climbing plans. At one point, she read in the paper that Naomi Uemura was planning a solo attempt of Everest, and mentioned it to Messner, noting, "This is going to be a very interesting climb, isn't it." He didn't say anything at the time, but told her later that he had been thinking of doing just that. And with this bit of information, he decided to advance the timing of his solo attempt.

One of Elizabeth's favorite stories about Messner has nothing to do with climbing. She was sitting with him as he filled in the biography form that she used for each and every climber. On the form, she asked each member for basic data such as name, address, birth date, nationality, and marital status. Marital status had four possible categories: single, married, living with girlfriend, or divorced. On this expedition to Nepal, Messner ticked all four boxes! She asked him why, and he responded, "I was married in Italy and divorced in Germany, but Italy doesn't recognize divorce, so in one country I am married and in the other country I am divorced. I am also living with a girlfriend." Elizabeth acquiesced, saying, "Okay, I understand all that, fair enough. But single?" Messner responded, "I feel single."

A much less gregarious yet no less accomplished alpinist during this time was the Polish climber Jerzy Kukuczka. The second person to climb all fourteen of the 8000-meter peaks, Kukuczka did many of them in winter. She describes him as having been a tenacious climber, remembering the Manaslu expedition where he sat in base camp for over three weeks waiting for the weather to improve. And when it did, he got his summit. She knew that most climbers would have lost patience long before and gone home. She considered him a real mountaineer, and blamed his eventual death on the South Face of Lhotse to an inferior grade of rope used as a fixed line.

Elizabeth's close friendship with Messner and other famous climbers sparked discussion about the true nature of her "relationship" with the climbers on whom she reported. American filmmaker David Breashears suggests that, for the majority of climbers, her reporting style was somewhat critical. He thinks it would have been more difficult, but perhaps more useful, if she had developed a more constructive, or even congratulatory, style. And he also found that she could be somewhat "hung up" on high-profile climbers and big achievements like Messner's, losing sight of some of the smaller, subtler accomplishments. He believes she had good instincts for an exceptional achievement—as long as it was on a really big peak. But he is convinced that her reporting has been directly connected to her interest in the climber as an individual—that her reports were not just pure historical data, but a way of connecting to the personalities she felt closest to—personalities like Messner.

Dr. Charles Houston doesn't agree. He describes her reporting as unbiased and scrupulously accurate. He does, however, remember the sharp tongue and pointed criticism in her conversations. "She didn't hesitate to say that so and so was a fool, so and so ran a terrible expedition, and so and so made terrible mistakes."

Elizabeth admits that she was interested in meeting climbers and learning about the human dimension of why people climb mountains and how mountains affect them. Over the years, she says, she became close to a few climbers and watched them change. She singles out Messner with his "articulate passion and ecstasy for the mountains," as well as the great leadership qualities of Chris Bonington. But on the possibility of being influenced by the personalities themselves, she says, "I guess I'm human, but I try not to be influenced by the personalities. I would hope the answer is no. I try not to." She thinks her most detailed seasonal mountaineering reports reflected the most interesting climbs. She is amazed that the climbing community would even bother to have this discussion and is genuinely surprised by their interest. "I'm astonished that all these people would even think of this stuff. They must have something better to do than this."

Elizabeth seems unaware of just how enigmatic she has been. People enjoy speculating about those who keep so much beneath the surface. One person who found Elizabeth mysterious was American author Broughton Coburn, who was in Nepal working on the Namche micro-hydroelectric project. The Himalayan Trust was involved with their shipping logistics, so he coordinated them with Elizabeth. He found her to be difficult to work with and thought there might be a couple of reasons why. First, he doesn't think she relates well to men who are not climbers. He recalls seeing her with Reinhold Messner and a few other Austrian climbers at a Kathmandu restaurant, and was astonished to see her lively and smiling and almost flirtatious. He was a few tables away and couldn't take his eyes off her. He had never seen her like this! Although Coburn climbed, he wasn't in Nepal in that capacity and never presented himself to her in that context.

Second, he was working for UNESCO and as a consultant to Sagarmatha National Park, and he thinks Elizabeth had her loyalties firmly placed in the Himalayan Trust projects, regarding other agencies as somewhat suspect. Other people involved with aid agencies also observed that the Himalayan Trust group had subtly appointed themselves as the "colonists of Sagarmatha National Park"—expressing a kind of *noblesse oblige* toward that area. They sometimes gave the appearance of having staked their claim in the area of helping Sherpas, and everyone else was an intruder. These observers hastened to add that the work done by the Trust was admirable and valuable, making their claim to the area real and worthy. But a perception existed that the Trust was the self-appointed "royal envoy" to the area and Elizabeth Hawley, as the Trust's Kathmandu manager, was the self-appointed "queen of good work."

However, Elizabeth and Coburn's inability to really hit it off may have been due to a difference in style. As Coburn recalls, he was trying to coordinate flights into Lukla and Elizabeth was extremely particular about how it should be done. He describes his style as "winging it." It apparently drove her crazy that he didn't know the precise weights of things. After decades of working closely with her in Nepal, he admits that he never got to know her. She remained an enigma to him.

Canadian parks specialist Frances Klatzel brought her skills to Sagarmatha National Park in the eighties and developed a close working relationship with Elizabeth too. Frances first arrived in Nepal in 1980. While trekking in the Khumbu area, she jokingly volunteered her assistance to help the newly emerging park. They took her up on it, and thus began a long and fruitful relationship. For years she worked in the Khumbu and had her mail delivered to Elizabeth's mailbox in Kathmandu. Elizabeth had a mail runner who would do the trip from Kunde, back and forth to Kathmandu, with short rests in between. It was the only way to get mail up there at the time. Frances moved back to Canada from 1989 to 1995, but Elizabeth kept the little pigeonhole mailbox for her. "I guess she was expecting me back," Frances laughs.

And back she came. After some years, Frances began giving Elizabeth a bottle of red wine for Christmas, a gesture that seemed to surprise Elizabeth. But the annual gift created a connection in Elizabeth's mind between Frances and wine. Years later, they were at a party thrown by Ang Rita of the Himalayan Trust for Sir Edmund Hillary, and Ang Rita's wife, holding a glass of red wine, approached Elizabeth and Frances. Elizabeth acted surprised and wondered aloud where she had found red wine, commenting that only diplomats and foreigners could source red wine. She then looked at Frances, "Did you bring it?" Frances laughed and explained that red wine had been available in the supermarkets for several years now. Since Elizabeth never bought her own food, she had no idea that red wine was openly available in the supermarkets of Kathmandu. To Frances, it was a sign of Elizabeth's self-imposed isolation from real life in Kathmandu.

After twenty years of knowing each other, there are very few situations that Frances can describe as "personal" moments with Elizabeth Hawley: "She was cut-and-dried with me." But she does remember one incident that might just qualify as approval. After working with Sagarmatha National Park for a number of years, Frances became an expert on the Sherpas, learning the language and gaining a deep understanding of the culture. She was also leading treks to various parts of the country. After hearing that Frances was about to lead a trek to the Annapurna region—far away from the land of the Sherpas—Elizabeth ranted, "Why on earth are they sending you there? You're one of the world's leading experts on Sherpas. Why don't they just keep sending you to the Khumbu?" Frances isn't positive, but she thinks it might have been a compliment.

⁕

It had been a while since Elizabeth had been on an adventure of her own, and so in 1980, shortly after China opened its doors to tourism, she decided to go to Mongolia, which was still under Stalinist-style communist rule. Barbara Adams joined her. They traveled by train from London all the way to Hong Kong, stopping in East Berlin, Poland, and Russia. From Moscow, they took the Trans-Siberian Railway through Siberia, Mongolia, and China, ending up in Hong Kong. It was an adventure worthy of Paul Theroux or Eric Newby.

But all was not as it could be. By the time they arrived in Moscow, tensions had flared between the two friends and Barbara insisted on a single room. She hadn't paid for a single room, but, as Elizabeth remembers it, she was sufficiently persistent that the tour guide took pity on the situation and invited Elizabeth to share her room. The poor tour guide got into some trouble with her supervisors about that, but at least it kept the peace between Barbara and Elizabeth.

They continued east and, after plunging into the clear, icy waters of Lake Baikal, boarded a twice-weekly train to Ulan Bator. It was a slow but determined train, which chugged and steamed its way across the never-ending Mongolian hills and plains. The most vivid memory Elizabeth has of this trip is the vast sameness of the landscape. "I like birch trees, but this was something else!" she comments about the limitless stunted forests. She loved surface travel; the train was full of colorful characters, most carrying passenger-crushing loads of consumer goods from Russia, for which they must have traded Mongolian wool. From their faces and dress, they could have been Tibetan. The stations were alive with people coming in from the countryside, many with horse-drawn carts. Elizabeth and Barbara had the best the train could offer—a two-person compartment. This too became a source of irritation when "Princess Barbara," as Elizabeth was wont to call her, insisted on taking the preferred lower berth, but it wasn't just that. Elizabeth often felt she was babysitting Barbara, picking up after her, finding her lost this, her forgotten that. It was not

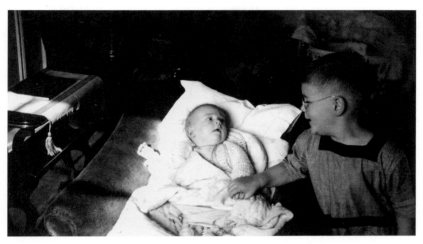

Elizabeth with her brother John (Courtesy of the Michael and Meg Leonard collection)

Young Elizabeth fishing in waders (Courtesy of the Michael and Meg Leonard collection)

Four-year-old Elizabeth on her favorite toy (Courtesy of the Michael and Meg Leonard collection)

Elizabeth on a trip into rural Nepal in 1964 with King Mahendra (Courtesy of the Elizabeth Hawley collection)

Elizabeth and her friend Barbara on the steps of "the most expensive hotel in Nice," the Negresco, on a photo postcard Elizabeth sent home. October 25, 1950 (Courtesy of the Michael and Meg Leonard collection)

Elizabeth's first car, parked in front of her Kathmandu apartment (Courtesy of the Michael and Meg Leonard collection)

*Elizabeth enjoying
a drink and the
scenery at the British
embassy bungalow,
Kakani, December
1975 (Courtesy of
the Michael and Meg
Leonard collection)*

*Elizabeth chatting, after a parade, with Lt. Gen. Surendra Bahadur Shaha,
Chief-of-Staff of the Royal Nepal Army. Kathmandu, October 24, 1963
(Courtesy of the Elizabeth Hawley collection)*

King Mahendra (left) and Minister Padma Bahadur Khatri (right) on November 4, 1963 (Courtesy of the Elizabeth Hawley collection)

Elizabeth with Chris Bonington (Courtesy of the Elizabeth Hawley collection)

Elizabeth with her parents in 1974 (Courtesy of the Elizabeth Hawley collection)

Elizabeth with United Press International correspondent Bhata Rana and Polish climber Andrzej Zawada (Courtesy of the Elizabeth Hawley collection)

Colonel Jimmy Roberts, Elizabeth, and Al Read of Mountain Travel on New Year's Eve in 1978 (Courtesy of the Elizabeth Hawley collection)

Elizabeth with Sir Edmund Hillary and Inger Lissanevitch (Boris's wife) in Phaphlu, January 1976 (Courtesy of the Michael and Meg Leonard collection)

Elizabeth with Italian mountaineer Reinhold Messner in Kathmandu in 2004 (Photo by Lisa Choegyal)

Elizabeth holding her favorite dog, Mallory (Photo by Colin Monteath)

Colonel Jimmy Roberts, Sir Edmund Hillary, and Elizabeth enjoying a visit together in the spring of 1995 (Courtesy of the Elizabeth Hawley collection)

In Kathmandu, Elizabeth interviews Paul Teare and Stephen Venables before their departure for Everest's Kangshung (East) Face, in 1988 (Courtesy of Ed Webster)

Elizabeth lighting the pyre at her mother's cremation in 1998 (Courtesy of the Elizabeth Hawley collection)

Elizabeth greeting U.S. First Lady Hillary Clinton at a U.S. Embassy reception on March 31, 1995 (Courtesy of the Elizabeth Hawley collection)

Elizabeth, August 1994 (Photo by Gopal Chitrakar, Courtesy of the Elizabeth Hawley collection)

Elizabeth meeting King Gyanendra (Courtesy of the Elizabeth Hawley collection)

Elizabeth's famous blue VW Beetle (Courtesy of Heather Macdonald)

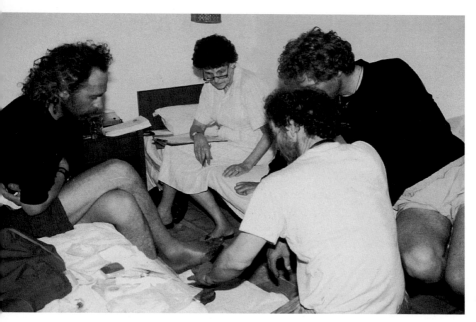

Elizabeth interviewing a climber with frostbitten toes (Courtesy of the Elizabeth Hawley collection)

American climber Ed Viesturs talking with Elizabeth in 2004 (Photo by Jimmy Chin)

Elizabeth working late at her desk (Courtesy of the Elizabeth Hawley collection)

Elizabeth with Russian climbers Valeri Babanov and Yuri Kochelenko in autumn 2003, around the time of their expedition to Nuptse (Courtesy of the Elizabeth Hawley collection)

Elizabeth with American filmmaker David Breashears and British historian Audrey Salkeld in 1996 (Photo by Lisa Choegyal)

Door to Elizabeth's apartment, including the sign identifying her as the New Zealand Consulate (Photo by Bernadette McDonald)

A street in Kathmandu, 2004 (Bernadette McDonald)

Caricature of Elizabeth at work, by Desmond Doig

something the fiercely independent Elizabeth enjoyed. She decided that she definitely preferred traveling alone.

The problem with the train was that it had no dining car and, worse yet, had neglected to stock any food or drink for the long and grinding trip. Finally, perhaps due to the protests of the passengers, or maybe because the train staff itself was hungry, the train ground to a halt at what looked like an oasis in the desert but turned out to be a *momo* tent set up in the middle of nowhere. That was almost the last human habitation the train passed until they reached Ulan Bator.

Barbara and Elizabeth appeared to be the only tourists in the typically Stalinist-style hotel in Ulan Bator and, except for the faces of the staff, they could have been anywhere in the world. This was a letdown for both of them, having read tales of horse races on the steppes, exotic yurts in the wild, fermented mare's milk, and colorful costumes. Instead, they were installed in a comfortable but plain square block of a cement room, with only one magazine to read.

Elizabeth noticed the richly adorned monasteries filled with golden brocade and statues scattered around the country, much as in Tibet. In Communist Mongolia, however, at least in Ulan Bator, the monasteries were treated as museums of past history and kept mostly locked except for the occasional tourist group. She remembers visiting the most important monastery in Ulan Bator. Their professional but unfriendly guide unlocked the monastery and they entered. Before he had time to lock the door, an old bent couple in traditional Mongolian dress followed them in.

As Barbara and Elizabeth listened to their guide's explanation of what they were seeing (similar to what one sees in the Buddhist monasteries of Kathmandu), the two old people did their religious rounds, touching their heads to the feet of the golden Buddhas and chanting prayers. The guide was noticeably irritated by the appearance and genuflections of these relics from an earlier feudal era, and he spoke to them harshly and asked them to leave. They looked up nervously from their devotions, gathered their belongings, and were pushed unceremoniously out the door. When Elizabeth and Barbara tried to intervene on their behalf, they were told to mind their own business. She remembers the expressions on the wrinkled, careworn faces—from fear to fervor and back to fear.

———— ✦ ————

Shortly after returning home, Elizabeth had a visit with Mother Theresa, who had started a mission in Nepal to care for the destitute. Speaking to an impromptu gathering at the Indian embassy, the honored guest asked everyone to "storm heaven" with prayers, that she might be given a house in which to do her work in Nepal. Elizabeth was impressed by her firm voice and fluent English.

Another international visitor was Britain's Prince Charles. While in Kathmandu, Prince Charles attended a press conference and noticed Elizabeth speaking with a couple of Nepalese reporters. He was surprised to see a white woman in this context, so he came over and introduced himself. She subsequently introduced him to the two reporters. He asked them if they enjoyed freedom of speech in Nepal, and they enthusiastically assured him they did. Elizabeth pounced on them: "Manindra, you know you were shut down twice last week!" Prince Charles was amused by this and insisted that she accompany him for the rest of the trip—which she did. She found him to be charming and approachable. He had an ability to connect with all kinds of people and appeared to be truly enjoying himself.

Jimmy Roberts of Mountain Travel organized a special trek for the prince, and Jimmy and his partner Pertemba Sherpa did the entire route ahead of time to ensure it had good locations for sketching, which was Prince Charles's passion. Charles did the trek, and proclaimed it ideal. They subsequently named it the "Royal Trek," and packaged it as such.

The fall 1981 mountaineering season brought forty-five expeditions to Nepal. Elizabeth could remember when seventeen was considered outrageous, and wondered how she would deal with so many people. But she continued to find the work interesting, the people fascinating, and the climbing "family" one that she felt comfortable with. One of the highlights of the year was a climb of Manaslu, which had always remained sheltered from the sight of climbers while other peaks attracted numerous expeditions. H.W. Tilman's comment, when he saw it in the fifties, was that it was "impossible without wings." Maybe so, but a four-person French team led by Pierre Béghin came to see what they could do with the West Face in the fall of 1981. One of the highest faces in the Himalaya, rising 3962 meters above the moraines to 7498 meters, it was complex and regularly scoured with avalanches. To make it even more challenging, escape from the entire face was blocked at the top by a serac barrier. Throughout the trip, the team experienced constant demoralizing and dangerous avalanches, but it was during the night of September 27 that all hell broke loose when a violent storm struck Nepal, flooding valleys, destroying villages and homes, and eventually killing 1500 people. They escaped the mountain and waited for conditions to calm down. As the weather cleared and cooled, they got their chance at the end of the month. On October 7, they succeeded.

Meanwhile, on the Tibetan side of Everest, a large American expedition was attempting an ambitious new route—the vast Kangshung Face. The team, led by Dick Blum of San Francisco, included Himalayan heavyweights like John Roskelley and Lou Reichardt, with David Breashears doing camera work. Even Hillary joined them as far as base camp. Fairly early in the trip, Roskelley declared the route too dangerous, and argued for a change of plans to the north side. Arguments ensued and tempers flared, with Hillary weighing in as well, imploring the team to not abandon their original objective. He obviously inspired them, because most opted to stay with the face. But Roskelley left, and others followed, after expending significant energy on the route. A weakened team continued to pick away at it, but they ultimately failed. After hearing all of the reports, Elizabeth thought that the expedition (like so many others) failed because they functioned as a group of prima donnas rather than as a cohesive team.

Hillary, meanwhile, was forced to return to New Zealand because of cerebral edema that he experienced while at base camp with the team. He wrote in a letter to Elizabeth that he would probably not be able to go higher than 3962 meters in the future. His altitude ceiling had decreased steadily ever since his first trouble in 1961 on Makalu. He was sadly correct; as time went on he even had to limit his time in the Solu Khumbu from two weeks to one. And then he wasn't able to go as high as Kunde, but only to Phaphlu, and finally not even to Phaphlu. Elizabeth worried that some day he might not be able to come to Kathmandu.

There were still first ascents to be done in Nepal, and in the spring of 1982 Roskelley and his team managed one. Cholatse was only 6492 meters high, but was the last unclimbed peak in the Mount Everest region and a prize worth going for. The team severely underestimated its difficulty, though. Hidden high in the Gokyo Valley, it didn't appear on the permitted list until Al Read of Mountain Travel finally convinced the government in late 1981 for the following year. Roskelley put together a five-person team and, despite some bizarre equipment failures and questionable weather, they made the summit. Roskelley explained that to save time he ended up leading all of the top fifteen pitches of steep ice, often with completely unprotected belays. They reached the top on April 22 in a howling blizzard with electricity crackling the air. Elizabeth arranged a grand party to celebrate their achievement, but while they were celebrating, she received a report from Rome that Reinhold Messner had been killed on Kangchenjunga. Much to her relief, he turned up in Kathmandu a couple of days later, thoroughly alive and triumphant over reaching the summit without the use of artificial oxygen. This was his seventh 8000er.

Soon after, an important figure in Elizabeth's life was to die. Elizabeth was on her way back from the United States after her annual trip to see her mother, when she ran into the brother of former prime minister B. P. Koirala at the Bangkok airport boarding gate. She greeted him, only to learn that he was taking Koirala to Kathmandu. She asked where he was and was informed that he was in an ambulance. The charismatic Koirala was near death; he had been in the hospital in Bangkok and had been told that his throat cancer was terminal. His brother was taking him home to die. Before the plane left, she spent almost an hour talking with his brother and with Koirala's son, who was a doctor. On the plane trip, she wrote her Reuters story and began filing it as soon as she reached home. Before she could finish, she received a phone call that he had died. It was her biggest scoop. Reuters had the news before any other news agency; as far as she knows, it was the only time a story of hers hit the front page of the *New York Times*.

Koirala's impact on Nepal had been huge. In 1947 he founded the

Nepali National Congress, which in 1950 became the Nepali Congress Party; he led the armed revolution of 1951, which overthrew 104 years of Rana rule; and he became Nepal's first prime minister in 1959. But Koirala was too powerful and too influential for the ruling monarchy, and his career became a series of confrontations, almost always leading to arrest and imprisonment. In addition to several stints in Nepalese prisons, he spent years living in exile. Yet each time he returned, his influence was felt. Tens of thousands of Nepalis revered him, forming a huge procession as they took his body through the streets of Kathmandu to Pashipatinath for cremation. Elizabeth admired him greatly and wondered who would have the leadership abilities and clear political vision to take his place.

When the People's Republic of China opened its autonomous regions, including Tibet, to non-Chinese mountaineers in 1979, new opportunities opened up on the north side of Mount Everest. Two important expeditions with different objectives found themselves in Tibet in the summer and fall of 1982. One was from the United States, led by Lou Whittaker, and the second was from England, under the leadership of Chris Bonington. Although the teams traveled through China, Elizabeth kept close track of their progress.

The American team consisted of a strong group of Mount Rainier guides from Washington, and Bonington's British team had only four climbers, a sign that he was moving away from the big-expedition ethos. The British team included some of his most reliable climbing companions, including Peter Boardman and Joe Tasker. The Americans chose the striking North Couloir as their route, while the Brits were after the long, unclimbed Northeast Ridge. They were climbing without oxygen and knew that the major difficulties on the route would be high on the mountain between 7925 and 8382 meters.

The two teams enjoyed a festive evening together before heading their separate ways. Their next meeting would not be at all festive, as both teams experienced tragedy in the course of their climbs. While searching for a campsite at 8016 meters and while attached to a fixed line, American team member Marty Hoey inexplicably and without warning fell 1829 meters down the face. Her teammates were horrified to see that her harness and jumar were still attached to the fixed line, indicating some kind of buckle failure or human error. Much higher on the mountain, Boardman and Tasker were performing exceptionally well on the difficult terrain—as had been expected—and were poised for the summit. As the rest of the team watched through the telescope, they made steady progress, but after several missed radio calls and their disappearance around the corner, it was assumed that something had gone wrong. A search party was dispatched to the area where they were last seen, but to no avail. Bonington was forced to conclude that they had fallen, and it would be years before Peter Boardman's body was found lying alone on the ridge with no sign of his companion. Bonington later confided to Elizabeth that, although the trip had a tragic end and two of Britain's top Himalayan climbers were dead, it had been one of the happiest expeditions of his life. She was sympathetic, but he sensed a disapproving concern from Elizabeth for this clan of climbers she had adopted. Once again, people she knew and liked had gone off to the mountains and hadn't come back. Such deaths took their toll.

Can a climb be described as successful if one man does reach the summit but all four die in the descent?
—ELIZABETH HAWLEY

E lizabeth once characterized the 1980s as belonging to Reinhold Messner, the "supreme star of the Himalaya," and it was the spring of 1985 that truly belonged to him. He and his teammate, Hans Kammerlander, climbed a new route on the Northwest Face of Annapurna I in five days from base camp to summit, and then went on to climb Dhaulagiri I by its normal route in only three days. This brought his quest to summit all fourteen of the 8000-meter peaks to a total of twelve.

The previous winter Polish climber Jerzy Kukuczka had achieved an even greater feat with two 8000-meter summits in one month—in winter. The only person with more 8000-meter summits than Kukuczka was Messner, and so the "horse race" had begun. The phrase, first coined by Austrian climber Kurt Diemberger, became Elizabeth's preferred descriptor for the unofficial race between Messner and Kukuczka. Although they were two very different climbers, it appeared they had the same ambition.

Later in the winter climbing season of 1985, Elizabeth watched with great interest as other top Himalayan climbers put the pressure on Messner to be the first to climb all fourteen of the 8000-meter peaks. The Swiss climber Erhard Loretan, together with two partners, managed the first winter ascent of the East Face of Dhaulagiri I, bringing his total to nine. And in January 1986, Kukuczka and Krzysztof Wielicki completed an impressive winter, supplementary-oxygen-free ascent of Kangchenjunga, bringing Kukuczka's total to ten and Wielicki's to four.

One of Kurt Diemberger's favorite images of Elizabeth is in connection with the "horse race," which he describes in his book *Spirits of the Air*: "This charming lady, who you would be justified in calling a landmark of Kathmandu, and who knows really everything that's happened in the Himalaya, having painstakingly recorded it over many years—such as the 'horse race'... she keeps a table of all the mountaineers who have climbed 8000-meter peaks. You can see quite clearly how they are proceeding from year to year—this one has two, that one in the meantime has three, one has four ... And then there are two who have five each...."

Although there were important political elections in Nepal in the spring of 1986, the biggest race in town was not political; it was the mountaineering race that captured Elizabeth's imagination and dominated her reporting headlines. She wrote, "Himalayan mountaineering is not ordinarily considered to be a highly competitive sport. But last autumn's climbing season in the Nepalese Himalaya had much of the drama of the World Cup Final, when the race to be first to conquer all of the world's 8000-meter mountains was finally won by Italy's Reinhold Messner, by the relatively narrow margin of 14 to 11." By the end of that season, the runner-up, Jerzy Kukuczka of Poland, had moved his score from eleven to twelve, Swiss climber Marcel Rüedi scored ten and then died the next day on his descent, possibly from pulmonary or cerebral edema, and Swiss climber Erhard Loretan suffered the first failure of his career on what he had hoped would be his tenth 8000er.

Elizabeth believes that Messner did not conceive the idea as a race, but merely a personal challenge. However, it caught on, particularly with Kukuczka, making it hard for Messner to achieve his goal before anyone else. Together with his frequent partner, Hans Kammerlander, Messner topped out on Makalu on September 26, bringing his total to thirteen. Less than three weeks later, the two of them reached the top of Lhotse on a day when most climbers were pinned down in their camps by high winds. October 16 was the day that was the jewel in the crown of a distinguished Himalayan career that began in 1970 on Nanga Parbat, which he climbed with his brother Günther. That 8000-meter victory took a greater toll on Messner than all the others, as it was on Nanga Parbat that his brother died on the descent.

Messner, who never climbed with artificial oxygen, had shown an entire generation of climbers what was possible. Elizabeth thought he was a true inspiration to climbers to go beyond their normal scope of achievement. Others agreed with her. Erhard Loretan, who raced up and down Everest, said, "The reason we can now climb so quickly and easily is that Messner served as an example for us." And Chris Bonington was quoted in a *TIME* article saying, "There is a wall called 'impossible' that the great mass of people in any field face. Then one person who's got a kind of extra imaginative drive jumps that wall. That's Reinhold Messner." And how did Messner feel? "Now I am free!" he exclaimed, with joy and satisfaction. She pushed him: "Free to do what?" As it turned out, he had a lot of plans: to climb other interesting peaks—at any altitude anywhere in the world—to make films, to search for the yeti.

Loretan's lightning-fast Everest climb was similar in style and aesthetics to Messner's "by fair means" philosophy. Together with his frequent climbing partner, Jean Troillet, and the equally impressive Pierre Béghin, they approached the North Face of Everest in the monsoon season. At 10:00 P.M. on August 29, 1986, the three left advance base camp, climbed through the night, and stopped at 11:00 A.M. at 7800 meters. They rested in the warmth of daylight, starting off again at 9:00 P.M. that night. Béghin turned back at 8000 meters, but the other two continued until darkness made it impossible to continue past 8400 meters. At 4:00 A.M. they could see enough to continue, and were on the summit at 1:00 P.M. They took advantage of the warmest part of the day, resting a bit before flying down the entire face in a five-hour glissade. The whole climb took them less than two days. Their style was unique: they climbed unroped; they climbed at night; they used no oxygen; they carried only a small amount of food and light sleeping bags; and above 7800 meters they carried no pack. Polish climber Voytek Kurtyka described it as "night nakedness."

The following winter, in February 1987, Messner's closest competitor, Jerzy Kukuczka, accomplished an ascent in a style that made the Pole happy and elicited admiration from Elizabeth. She observed that most mountaineers who came to the Himalaya did not choose the bitterly cold months of winter, but one Pole, Kukuczka, didn't seem to mind it. Together with Artur Hajzer, he braved the cold and wind to climb Annapurna I, bringing his total to thirteen and his winter ascents to four, all without oxygen. This was a record that no other climber had achieved—not even Messner—and Elizabeth grasped the significance of the extra effort, stamina, and determination required to pull it off.

⸻

Unrest continued in Kathmandu during these years, and in June 1985 a terrorist bomb exploded at the royal palace. Elizabeth immediately went to find out what had happened. She discovered damage to two palace gates, as well as to a building that held the government newspaper offices and the Annapurna Hotel, a property owned by the royal family. She also learned from a trusted, highly placed source that a number of printed leaflets claiming responsibility for the bombing had been distributed. She returned to her office and reported what she had seen and learned. The royal family was outraged. It turned out that the palace press secretary hadn't known about the leaflets, so the palace learned from the press something the secretary should have informed them of. But Elizabeth's source was impeccable—the story was true. That's not how the palace saw it, however. The press secretary was enraged and claimed that she was "spreading untruths and horrific gossip." His professional humiliation demanded revenge.

Elizabeth's bomb report would haunt her for years to come. Shortly afterward, while on her annual trip to the United States, she heard from Jim Edwards of Tiger Tops that the palace was seriously angry with her. She delayed her return from the United States to Nepal for "health reasons" and sent a telex to Reuters in New Delhi mentioning the "advisability of dodging shoot-the-messenger syndrome strongly afflicting Nepalese authorities following coverage of June bombings." Later that year, when she applied for her press accreditation renewal, it wasn't granted. The authorities even banned her from going to the ministry building to collect the news. This was a major problem, and it appeared to be indefinite. They didn't interfere with her seasonal mountaineering reports, but it was impossible to get her accreditation renewed, even though Ad Carter of the American Alpine Club and other influential people tried to change the authorities' minds. This inadvertently made her a local hero, especially with the working journalists in the valley, who protested strongly against this apparent muzzling of free speech.

Eventually, Reuters had to find a replacement for her. His name was Gopal Sharma. The all-important telex machine was still in Elizabeth's office and her door was always open for Sharma—literally. She gave him a key to come and go as he pleased, and he did so, filing stories at will. He reciprocated by helping her evade criticism from the Ministry of Tourism, a not infrequent occurrence. Since she was still interviewing expeditions as they came through Kathmandu for her seasonal mountaineering reports, she often learned something newsworthy from her sources on a weekend. The ministry offices weren't open on weekends, so they wouldn't find out until the following Monday. Therefore, the information wouldn't become "official" until Monday. She would share her news tidbits with Sharma while they were still newsworthy—on the weekend. To keep her from getting into trouble, Sharma would report it and take the criticism for reporting "unofficial" news himself. Her name never came up. He is sure she was targeted in part because she represented a threat, and in part because of her sharp tongue. Sharma knew there were many who had felt the sting of Elizabeth's words and resented it. In fact, his colleagues at the Reuters bureau in Delhi had often asked him to intercede on their behalf. They didn't want to call her for fear of the verbal abuse they might receive, so they would ask him to act as intermediary. "She heats up fast, but she cools down just as fast," is Sharma's observation.

But on the subject of mountaineering, Sharma can't imagine the Ministry of Tourism getting along without her. "They use her as a reference," he explains. "If you go to them for information about a climb, they will suggest that you go see Liz Hawley." He worries about the situation in Nepal should she ever leave Kathmandu, as nobody else has the information or the knowledge that she has about mountaineering.

Personal tragedy struck the Hawley household when Elizabeth's dog, Tigger II, passed away on the night of April 9. Though the cause of death was unknown, it was attributed to some kind of internal problem. Earlier in the week he had been vomiting and hemorrhaging, and nothing the vet did could save him. The apartment was suddenly quiet.

Some good news arrived soon after, as June Mulgrew had found her a new apso puppy, just three months old. Sir Edmund delivered the dog to her, letting it perch on his lap during the Royal Nepal Airlines flight. She remembers it with delight: "This great tall man with a little puppy in his lap!" She decided to call him Mallory after the famous British mountaineer. She briefly considered calling him Hillary or Messner, but thought it might be embarrassing—or even confusing—for them if she were calling the dog when they were there. It was the last dog she would own—and her favorite.

Meanwhile, Elizabeth's mother's health was failing in the United States, and it looked as if she would no longer be able to live alone. Elizabeth was distressed by her mother's loss of independence, and frustrated by her inability to be there for her. Yet she also understood that there comes a time when independence is no longer practical, and that such a time had arrived for her mother. For Elizabeth, it was a period of serious consideration for the future. Would she ever return to the United States? Would it be to care for her aging mother? How would she make a living there, and—more importantly—how could she ever adjust to life in America again? The prospect was not a happy one.

Elizabeth had a network of friends in Kathmandu, friends who represented a wide and varied slice of humanity, from the travel industry, to diplomats, to that crazy "family" of mountaineers she had adopted. She relished the climbing seasons, when climbers from around the world trooped in, one expedition after another, giving her a chance to visit, learn of their latest plans, and catch up on mountaineering gossip. And there was often a change of government, a new cabinet, or some political goings-on that kept her interested. She couldn't imagine being anywhere else.

In addition to Elizabeth's numerous jobs, a new one popped up: screening prospective air hostesses for Royal Nepal Airlines. When she heard about this latest job, Florelle was baffled. What kind of expertise did her daughter have in this field? Elizabeth admitted that it was a little sketchy, but that she was part of a panel interviewing candidates and weeding out the unsuitable ones. Pressed by her mother as to how one does that, Elizabeth explained that they were rated "on looks, self-possession, intelligent responses, fluency in English, and so on." One can't help imagining the scene: the critical, perfectionist, intelligent, and impatient Elizabeth Hawley screening potential airline hostesses for looks and intelligence. It can't have been an easy time for them.

Elizabeth's importance as a journalist was made clear in the fall of 1987 when a Chinese CAAC flight landed in Kathmandu direct from Lhasa, Tibet. It was the first flight from Lhasa to anywhere outside China, and it offered her an unexpected opportunity when two passengers walked into her office carrying written reports and photos of the riots that had taken place in Lhasa two days before. She didn't know the people who had sent them to her, but they knew her, and they knew how to find her. She sent a telex to Reuters about the accounts of marching monks and fierce police, and that evening she sent the photos to the Reuters office in Delhi in a traveler's hand luggage. They were among the first reports and photos to come out of Lhasa, and were widely distributed by an appreciative Reuters. She had achieved another (unofficial) scoop. Because of her report, flights from Lhasa to Nepal abruptly ceased.

A momentous event occurred in the Hawley household in January 1988: Elizabeth purchased a computer. Day after day she went to the salesroom to observe demonstrations of three different word processors to choose the best one for her. Then came the installation. First arrived the electronics man, then an electrician, and then a carpenter. Finally there it was, standing majestically on her desk. Then came the lessons—"God help me!" she exclaimed to her mother. "This week is the time I enter the computer age." She would have many hours of work transferring all her mountaineering data onto the computer, but she was optimistic that she would be able to figure it out. "God knows it's a thing of logic and detail, and I think I can handle those attributes."

It was a slow process, but it began to produce results. By January 23 she could word process, and had grown particularly fond of the delete button. By the thirtieth, she could create a right margin as straight as the left, and even the date at the top of the page was properly aligned. Another happy discovery was the spell-check feature: "I've learned how to call into play a wonderful invention, an ability the computer has to check misspellings, let you know if you've typed the same word twice in a row, or done something else you didn't really want to do. Lovely!" She began to enjoy her new toy.

The winter mountaineering season wrapped up in February and, although she was still not accredited to report for Reuters, she was faithfully doing the reports for her archives and assisting Mike Cheney with his mountaineering reports. Then Mike Cheney died suddenly of a heart attack. Like her friend Boris the previous year, another Kathmandu regular was gone forever. And when Hillary returned from a work visit to the Solu Khumbu, he too was looking weak and unwell—not his cheerful self at all. He had done no trekking and was silent and withdrawn.

Finally, in the spring of 1988, Elizabeth's accreditation was restored. Everest that year was a study in contrasts, as a huge 283-member expedition costing seven million dollars sent fourteen climbers to the summit on two of the more common routes. At the same time, a team of four climbers who hardly knew each other put one climber on the top by a difficult new route on the gaping, gigantic East Face of the mountain. Elizabeth's report summed it up beautifully: "The big party got the television coverage and a series of gala victory celebrations in three nations' capitals, while the little group quietly went their separate ways home."

It was the little group that captured her attention. Four climbers from England, the United States, and Canada formed a loose team with an ambitious objective—an unclimbed buttress they called the Neverest Buttress, leading up to the South Col on the East Face.

Briton Stephen Venables recalls having breakfast at their hotel on the morning before they were to head out for the climb, when Elizabeth Hawley showed up. To him, it felt as if the headmistress wanted to see them, looking severe in her spectacles and prepared to grill them. The four climbers—Venables, Americans Ed Webster and Robert Anderson, and Canadian Paul Teare—hardly knew each other, causing her to be skeptical about their chances of success, especially on such an ambitious objective. She told them that the Chinese-Japanese-Nepalese Friendship Expedition and the Australian Bicentennial Everest expedition would both be on the mountain at the same time, exclaiming, "It's going to be a zoo."

The climbers carefully scanned the Tibet Guesthouse dining room to make sure it was safe to bring out their six photos of the route to show her—they didn't want their plans to leak out because they didn't want to be "scooped." They finally felt confident she was trustworthy, so Teare showed her their intended route. Elizabeth may have appeared disapproving, but in fact she was fascinated. What a welcome break from the big-expedition tradition she was used to, and somewhat tired of—a big new route tackled by four climbers. She was polite with them and asked them to look in on her when they returned. Venables was sure that she thought they wouldn't make it back. In *Snow in the Kingdom*, Webster writes, "Impressed either by our phenomenal daring or our obvious stupidity, Miss Hawley wished us sincere good luck. . . . "

Without oxygen and in deteriorating weather, the team became fractured on the mountain. One member turned back due to altitude sickness and two retreated in bad weather, but Venables plodded on, despite the knowledge that he had lost feeling in his toes. Venables made the summit, and eventually all four climbers managed to get down alive.

When Teare later came to Elizabeth's office to tell her about the climb, Messner was there and expressed respect for what they had accomplished, praising them with "you have done a very brave thing," and then adding "you are very lucky!" After getting all the details, Elizabeth mentioned she was going to an Australian expedition party, and asked Messner and Teare if they'd like to accompany her. It turned out that Messner couldn't go, but Teare could, and he brought Venables with him. They later joked about how disappointed she must have been to end up with the two of them on her arm instead of Messner.

In contrast to her very real concerns about the four climbers getting lost on their route, Elizabeth thought it would be impossible for any of the 283-member team to get lost. "There were too many camps and climbers and walkie-talkie radios and oxygen bottles and support staff" for that to happen. There were three national governments (China, Japan, and Nepal) involved with the expedition, with tri-national commanders in Beijing radioing instructions to the climbing leaders on the scene. Despite her admiration for the complex handling of logistics, she concluded: "It is a wonder that the whole enterprise did not collapse of its own weight." But collapse it did not, and they sent fourteen climbers to the top. And what did her friend Hillary think of it? Not much. "It's a massive undertaking and I personally think a singularly unattractive one," he said.

Although this massive expedition was at the far upper end of the spectrum in terms of cost, it was also becoming more expensive for smaller, less flamboyant teams to come to the Himalaya, and funding the expeditions was becoming a bigger part of the task. Peak permit costs were going up, and climbers sought sponsorship funding more often. As a result, the climbing focus was tending toward the really big peaks that were considered newsworthy, and toward what Elizabeth described as "stunts"—also newsworthy. Some of these escapades she considered to be fund-raising stunts more than mountaineering stunts.

It was in this category that she placed French climber Marc Batard's next climb. His intention was to leave his base camp at 5350 meters, climb to the 8848-meter summit of Everest, and return in less than twenty-four hours. To acclimatize, he first climbed Cho Oyu, then helicoptered into the Everest area. One week after summiting Cho Oyu, he was preparing his camp at the foot of Everest. He employed eight Nepali climbers to help break trail, but he eschewed the use of oxygen. He didn't get to the summit on his first try. On his third attempt, he did it—although not in the time he had wanted. He reached the top in twenty-two and a half hours. The descent took him eight and a half hours, and two hours after reaching base camp he left for Kathmandu and France. Still, he had achieved a speed record as well another record in climbing four 8000-meter peaks in less than ten months. She acknowledged his strength, determination, and abilities, but questioned his motives. In general, she thought speed climbing was "gimmicky."

Despite her opinion on this type of climbing, however, she still thought it was important to keep records on them—accurate records. It took seven years before Batard's record was broken and even then she wasn't sure it was really broken. Tyrolean climber Reinhard Patscheider climbed from advanced base camp on the north side of Everest to the summit in twenty-one hours. But, as she pointed out, although his ascent was faster, he started a thousand meters higher than Batard, so it wasn't really a record breaker. The comparison was further complicated by the fact that advanced base camp on the north side was actually the bottom of the mountain. But she insisted that these records did matter and that the fine points did need to be acknowledged.

The question of motives was at the heart of a tragedy that took place on the Southwest Face of Everest when a small team of Czechoslovakia's best climbers attempted the first alpine-style ascent of this face, first climbed in 1975 by the British team led by Chris Bonington. The Czechs did climb the face, but all four died on the descent. They had no fixed ropes, no oxygen, and no Sherpa support. They had many difficulties on the route and became exhausted, yet they "succeeded" in getting to the top. Elizabeth challenged their claim of success. "Can a climb be described as successful if one man does reach the summit but all four die in the descent?" She wondered about the pressure they must have felt from their government and fellow Czech climbers, as there were high expectations that they would make a notable mountaineering achievement and thereby pave the way for more government approval for future climbs.

These four deaths, combined with three additional Czech deaths in the Himalaya in the same month, created an uproar in Prague as messages went out to Czech climbers around the world instructing them to "stop immediately." Perhaps more chilling than the political response to this tragedy, was the comment of a fellow Czech alpinist who wondered aloud who he would climb with in the future, as the country had lost so many of its best climbers.

Elizabeth was always careful to ask detailed and pointed questions of climbers when they returned to Kathmandu, and she was vigilant about recording and reporting the truth. But it wasn't always easy, and she didn't always get it right. That may have been the case in the fall of 1988 when a climber came to report her ascent of Everest without oxygen. Lydia Bradey was a flamboyant young New Zealand climber who was climbing with a New Zealand team loosely associated with the tragic Czech group on the South West Face. She claimed to have reached the top illegally via the Southeast Ridge, by herself, without a watch to ascertain the time, and with a frozen camera making it impossible to record the event.

As Elizabeth remembers the event, the Czechs had the permit for the Southwest Face but to save money they shared the permit with New Zealand team leader Rob Hall, Bradey, and the other Kiwis. The Kiwis did not go onto the Southwest Face with the Czechs, but over to the West Pillar, which was at the extreme right edge of the Southwest Face. The Kiwis did not reach the summit, and so they descended and returned to Kathmandu. All except Lydia. Just before they left base camp, they heard that Bradey had gone back up and reached the summit via the South Col. They didn't have a permit for either the South Col or the West Pillar routes. So when they returned to Kathmandu, they issued a statement saying she could not have climbed the peak because they didn't have a permit for that route. Rob Hall, the leader of her party, flatly dismissed her claim, stating, "It is simply not possible that she made the summit."

Elizabeth saw that the Kiwis were upset and believed there were two reasons for it. The first had to do with an earlier climb in the Karakoram, where Lydia had also gone up a peak for which they had no permit. Part of their funding for the earlier climb was from the Hillary Foundation in New Zealand, so when they came back to Everest, having again secured backing from the Hillary Foundation, they swore she would behave herself. But she hadn't. That was the first reason. The second reason, according to Elizabeth, was simple: she had reached the summit and they had not. Elizabeth was sure that this was strictly macho sentiment on the part of Hall and Gary Ball. Their statement seemed a double blow since they denied all responsibility for the climb and then said she didn't do it anyway! But Hall may have had other motivations for making the announcement because, as the leader of a team in which someone climbed on a route without permission, he could be banned for climbing in Nepal for up to ten years—and he made his living as a guide in Nepal.

However, when Lydia returned to Kathmandu she pointed out that they too lacked a permit for the Southwest Pillar on which they had been climbing. They countered that it was part of the Southwest Face. Elizabeth clarified to them that the ministry considered the Southwest Pillar a separate route; so in fact they were also in the wrong.

She spoke with Lydia at length when she returned to Kathmandu. Elizabeth remembers that it was very unpleasant for Lydia to get "slapped" by Hall and Ball, and though she believed Lydia had made the summit, there was simply no conclusive evidence at the time. Lydia subsequently gave a written statement to the Nepalese government expressing "confusion" about whether or not she reached the summit, which she may have done to lessen the expected punishment. But away from the mountain, she maintained her claim. In her seasonal mountaineering report, Elizabeth expressed both Ball's opinion that the climb hadn't happened as well as Lydia's claim that it had.

As time passed, many in the mountaineering community came to believe Lydia's claim, and assumed political and economic pressures prevailed upon her to sign that statement about her "confusion." Several years later, Elizabeth received confirmation of Lydia's ascent from a Spanish climber who said he was on the same route on the same day. He hadn't climbed with her, but he was at the South Col when she came back. They descended to Camp III and, as she was a "great chatterbox," she talked about the climb in detail. He told Elizabeth that her description was detailed enough that he was sure she had reached the summit.

Many wonder why Elizabeth didn't disclaim the statements made by Hall and Ball. They wonder if Lydia's personality struck Elizabeth as peculiar or unlikable, or whether perhaps Lydia said something that made her skeptical. Lydia had a free-spirited, brash personality that might have been off-putting to Elizabeth. Lydia doesn't remember it that way at all, stating that she thought they got along just fine. Elizabeth remembers feeling sorry for her as she returned from an exhausting climb and tragedy on the mountain only to be faced with rejection by her teammates. She came back from Everest and walked into a "guilty until proven innocent" situation, which Elizabeth placed firmly on the shoulders of Hall and Ball—but which others placed squarely on Elizabeth's. If nothing else, the incident illustrates the weight of Elizabeth's opinion in the climbing world at that time.

Writer and climber Greg Child later wondered whether Elizabeth comprehended the potential scale of the controversy. He doubted that she did because when he went to her years later for information on what had happened, she was as helpful as she could be, giving him signed statements from Hall and Ball stating that Lydia was a liar. They denied they had ever said this. Child is convinced that Elizabeth initially sided with Hall and Ball because of her past relationship with them, and that it took an enormous amount of fact-finding and, finally, proof to convince her otherwise. In the meantime, the damage was done to Lydia's climbing career. In Child's opinion, a large part of the damage was due to Elizabeth's report, which cast some doubt on Lydia's claim.

Lydia is ambivalent about Elizabeth now. From her pre-Everest meeting, she recalls liking Elizabeth's character and "wicked" sense of humor. Elizabeth seemed "grounded and realistic," so she was surprised at her attitude at the post-climb meeting, which seemed to Lydia like a bad dream. But maybe it *was* a bad dream. After all, Lydia was exhausted and devastated by what had happened to her Czech friends on Everest. Perhaps she wasn't clear and firm with Elizabeth. She wasn't upset that Elizabeth had doubts about her climb, but she did regret that Elizabeth seemed to have developed them before speaking with her. She credits that to Rob Hall's singular focus and force of personality—"nobody, not even Elizabeth Hawley, could get in the way of Hall once he had an agenda," claimed Lydia.

Talking about this incident fifteen years later in her Kathmandu living room, Elizabeth's disdain is not directed at Lydia, but at Hall and Ball, whom she proclaims to be chauvinists: "They were nice people but they were men!"

Another dispute arose, although not immediately, with the dramatic solo climb of Jannu by the Slovenian Tomo Česen in the spring of 1989. The twenty-nine-year-old sports journalist from Kranj arrived at the 7710-meter Jannu with only a physician who doubled as a cameraman, and no Sherpa support. He acclimatized on a nearby mountain and then headed up alone on a new route on the North Face. Twenty-three hours later he was on the summit and he immediately descended the Northeast Ridge in howling winds. Perhaps it was his manner that made him so believable. When Elizabeth asked him how he felt about this achievement, he answered, "I am satisfied." Messner was more effusive. "He climbed the only safe line. It is a beautiful line. This was the best climb of the season." Česen professed to like climbing solo because it was quicker and there were fewer problems. And so this was reported, recorded, and accepted as a significant achievement by a new star in the Himalaya. Time would tell.

In contrast to Česen's solo experience, a formidable Soviet assault was taking place on Kangchenjunga. Between April 9 and May 3, twenty-seven Soviet climbers and one Nepali Sherpa made a total of eighty-five ascents of the four main summits of Kangchenjunga. Even more impressive were the simultaneous traverses by two parties in opposite directions over the long, exposed summit ridges. This was the first-ever traverse of this mountain's ridges. It was a logistical tour de force. And it was a remarkable display of talent by the climbers, one of whom was Anatoli Boukreev.

That autumn, one of the brightest stars fell—Jerzy Kukuczka, the quiet, determined electrician from Katowice, Poland. He arrived with the intention of achieving the first ascent of the vast, unclimbed South Face of Lhotse, and in fine style, lightweight and fast. He and his team were forced to compromise on style almost from the beginning, when bad snow conditions forced them into siege tactics. After six weeks, he was poised only 170 vertical meters from the summit. The weather had improved and he was perfectly acclimatized. Even the wind had died down. But something slipped, Kukuczka fell, and then his belay rope broke. He fell nearly 3000 meters down the face to his death.

Some speculated about the poor quality of the rope used by some Eastern European climbers. Others wondered what a successful ascent would have done for his reputation, as it would have secured him a record that even Messner didn't have—climbing all fourteen of the 8000-meter peaks by either a new route or in winter. But Elizabeth only commented that it was a great loss of an intelligent, soft-spoken, patient, modest, and well-liked man. It had not been a good decade for the Poles, as many of the best climbers had perished on ambitious and difficult routes. As Kukuczka's teammate noted after his death, "From the stock of best climbers, only a few are left in Poland...."

Elizabeth had met Kukuczka many times, and he was always patient with her. She appreciated that. He was doing interesting things and had been close to overtaking Messner in that "horse race." She also admired his patience on the mountain. On Manaslu he had waited for an entire month at the base of the mountain for the weather to clear and the avalanche danger to subside before he started. Most expeditions complained about having bad weather for four days—they got trapped in a time-frame mindset that was rigid and unrealistic. They might have to go back to work, or they worried about their girlfriends or their families, or they just got tired of it. In Elizabeth's opinion, they lacked motivation. She thought Kukuczka was different than the peak baggers. He had a stick-to-it attitude that Elizabeth liked, something her own mother said she had. Messner was much more communicative about why he did what he did, and it was more difficult to understand Kukuczka because of the language barrier, but Elizabeth felt she understood him instinctively.

The year that brought this tragedy to the climbing community ended with a bizarre event that even Elizabeth couldn't have predicted—a physical battle between two teams. It was probably inevitable, as the Nepalese authorities were granting more permits for the same mountain and even the same route. The incident happened on Cho Oyu, where Sherpas and members of a large South Korean team attacked members of a Belgian team with fists and sticks. The Koreans initially denied their part in the attack, but they admitted in the end that a Belgian did receive a head wound, that a rope was tied around his neck, and that his arms were pinned behind his back. The Belgian team told Elizabeth that "mountain climbing should never turn into a battlefield." Clearly, it had.

Elizabeth's mother, Florelle, celebrated her ninetieth birthday in the spring of 1984. The time had come for Elizabeth to address the issue of where her mother would live her last years. Florelle needed to leave her apartment in Palo Alto and was grasping for ideas on where to go. Elizabeth invited her to come to Kathmandu and stay with her, as it would be difficult for Elizabeth to return to the United States now and make a living. Florelle decided against this and instead moved back East to live next door to Elizabeth's cousin, Lee Kneerim.

But within four years her mother became too frail to stay with the Kneerims. She needed too much attention now. Florelle's choices were to either enter a nursing home or go and stay with Elizabeth. The prospect of this mentally alert and curious woman staying in a nursing home was too unattractive for the family to contemplate, so Elizabeth's nephew, Michael, and his wife, Meg, brought Florelle to Kathmandu in 1988 at the age of ninety-four. It was hard for her American relatives to say good-bye when she left for Kathmandu, because they all knew she wouldn't return.

Florelle was carried up the stairs of Elizabeth's apartment in a wheelchair, and within the first week she had a stroke. Her leg collapsed and she never walked again. She moved into the spare bedroom in Elizabeth's apartment and had three women looking after her round the clock. One was a Tibetan nurse, the second was a young, strong Sherpa woman who could easily handle the 94-pound Florelle, and the third was a woman from the Terai. Their care for Florelle was loving and complete. They kept her company and, for Elizabeth, it was a precious time when she and her mother spent many hours together.

As Elizabeth's home was also her office, interesting people were always passing through. Her mother, still mentally sharp, was endlessly entertained by these comings and goings. She would get up in the morning, eat breakfast with Elizabeth, and then read the papers, magazines, and books, listen in on the conversations, and take frequent naps. She had brought her favorite books with her, many of which were murder mysteries. She didn't go out much, as she hated the terrifying trip up and down the steep stairs in a wheelchair. Since Florelle couldn't get out and about, the world came to her. A hairdresser came on a regular basis, as did a dentist. Elizabeth and Florelle ate dinner at 5:30 P.M. each evening, but before dinner they would sit and have a relaxing cocktail. Elizabeth usually had a beer or whiskey, but Florelle was faithful to a particular combination—Canadian Club with unsweetened apple juice. She enjoyed that drink every night until three days before she died.

One morning in November of 1989, Elizabeth went into Florelle's bedroom to say good morning. Florelle announced that she wouldn't be getting up for breakfast that morning and could someone please bring it to her in bed. She never got up again. Shortly before she died she pleaded, "Elizabeth, please let me go." Two nights later she had a stroke in the middle of the night. She died at age ninety-five.

For the first time in her life, Elizabeth didn't know what to do. Ang Rita, who worked downstairs in the Trust office, remembers the morning he came upstairs to learn that Florelle had died. He asked Elizabeth what she wanted to do about the cremation and, uncharacteristically, she said she didn't know. After two days she told him she wanted a cremation in the Buddhist tradition, and asked if he would help her. Ang Rita and the other Himalayan Trust Sherpas were like brothers, helping her make arrangements, organizing a place for the body, lending a truck, and doing all the other things that needed to be done for Florelle's final, fiery end. They organized Buddhist lamas, prayer flags of five different colors, musicians, and offerings for the gods. Ang Rita was one of many Sherpas who had benefited from Elizabeth's care and attention through the Himalayan Trust, and he remembered her concerns for him when he first came to Kathmandu as a student. He was glad he could help her in this time of sorrow.

The cremation took place along the banks of the Bagmati River in the untouchables section. Traditionally, the eldest son would light the funeral pyre. But there was no eldest son; there was only Elizabeth. So when the time came, surrounded by her friends on a cold, wet day as the lamas chanted their traditional prayers, she stepped forward and lit the pyre on which her mother's body lay encased in a white cloth. It was the most difficult thing she had ever done.

Just days before she died, Florelle wrote in a shaky hand a birthday greeting to her daughter: "Happy Birthday dear Elizabeth, I am so grateful for the good care and interesting life you provide for me." Florelle had often told Elizabeth that it had been the right decision to come to Kathmandu, and Elizabeth agreed.

A month later Elizabeth carried her mother's ashes back to the United States in a beautiful antique bronze urn about twelve inches high. Lee and Will picked her up at the airport, where they found her in a more emotional state than they had ever seen her. They got out a bottle of Jack Daniels and settled in. Elizabeth talked and wept and talked some more—about how difficult life had been and how important a role model her mother had been. She expressed how important it had been for her, after all those years of separation, to be able to bring her mother to Nepal and care for her. She was honest about her regrets and the sorrows in her life. The loss of her mother, even though it was expected, was as difficult for her as the premature death of her brother years before.

The entire family assembled in Dorset, Vermont. They stayed in an inn next to the cemetery, which sloped steeply downward with a view of the mountains beyond. Florelle's ashes were buried in the same plot as her husband and son John. Elizabeth's cousin, Lee, sang Bach's "Come Sweet Death," others read or told stories about Florelle, and Elizabeth read from a letter she had written shortly after Florelle died, explaining how important an influence this remarkable woman had been.

In June of 1990 Elizabeth received an unusual offer from New Zealand. They wanted her to be their honorary consul in Nepal—honorary, because she wasn't a New Zealand citizen. It intrigued her and it was an honor. It also paid. She said yes. Her work fell into two categories: helping Nepalese citizens get to New Zealand for study or for pleasure, and helping New Zealand citizens do what they wanted to do in Nepal. This sometimes meant arranging permits or visas, but more often meant getting them out of whatever jam in which they'd landed themselves. Occasionally, it meant arranging for a body to be returned to New Zealand, and these were the jobs she dreaded.

The greatest volume of work came from Nepalis wanting to go to New Zealand. Elizabeth didn't issue visas in her office, however, as they were handled in New Delhi. But that didn't stop people from coming to see her or calling her in droves. Her Reuters replacement, Gopal Sharma, watched her in action many times when some unsuspecting person would wander into her office looking for information about a visa for New Zealand. If they were at all confused about what they wanted, she would pounce on them, demanding, "What exactly do you want?" "What is it that you need?" "What is it that you are here for?" When they finally collected themselves enough to tell her, she would calm down, walk them through the process, and send them on their way. Despite her brusque manner, she was sympathetic. "There are hundreds of thousands of people who want to go to New Zealand to study, or to disappear into the woodwork," she says. "So the New Zealand authorities watch carefully to ensure that each person has real intentions of coming back."

She has had two cases of New Zealanders dying in Nepal. One was on the north side of Everest. Fortunately for Elizabeth, her Kiwi friend and mountain guide, Russell Brice, was there. Although he had to dispose of the body on the mountain, he brought the deceased's belongings back to Elizabeth—including his passport. It was this that Elizabeth returned to his grieving family in New Zealand.

The second death was a young woman, age twenty-three, who had just qualified as a doctor and who had come to Nepal to do volunteer work at a hospital at Pokhara. When she finished her work stint, she went on a trek, but on the way back to Pokhara the bus stopped for a bathroom break, and she suddenly collapsed. Her two friends commandeered a taxi to transport her to the Pokhara hospital and they did what they could to keep her alive on the way, but she was dead on arrival. Upon their return to Kathmandu, they contacted Elizabeth. With the help of an Austrian man who ran both a trekking agency and an undertaking company, she managed to wade through the multitude of international regulations and return the woman's body to New Zealand.

Less gruesome, but more irritating, was the story of Kiwi Tony Paroli, who found himself in Nepal without a valid visa. Paroli's problem was that his visa was six or seven months out of date and when he went to the authorities to finally renew it, they said, "Certainly, but we will have to charge you double the fee." It was a Friday afternoon and he didn't have enough money, so they said, "Well then, come with us." To his surprise they took him to a jail, from which he immediately called Elizabeth. There was nothing she could do at that moment and, unluckily for him, it was a three-day weekend, so nothing could be done until Tuesday. She went to see him on Saturday morning for a little chat—it was no mean trick getting through all that barbed wire to visit him, as she ripped her clothes in the process.

By the next week, Paroli was ready to pay. Of course, he didn't have enough cash with him, but he did have an ATM card. The problem was that his maximum disbursement was only $250 a day—and he needed eight thousand dollars for his expensive new visa! He was facing a long, slow process. Elizabeth brought him to her office, where he phoned his father in New Zealand, asking for help. His father had some money, but not enough. He agreed to six thousand dollars and, in due course, Paroli went to Western Union to pick it up. After paying for his inflated visa, Paroli was eventually released in Elizabeth's custody. But the authorities made it clear he needed to leave the country, and it was now her job to get him on a plane. She booked a seat for him and delivered him directly to his hotel in Thamel, and he swore he would come to her place the next day. Much to her surprise, he did. What a relief when she finally delivered him to the airport, saw him through immigration, and safely onto the plane—out of Nepal. Imagine her surprise when he called her up again a couple of years later. This time he was in Pokhara—again without a visa.

Visas were not something to treat lightly in Nepal. There were two young New Zealand women who came to Nepal with legal visas, but when they needed to renew them, they entrusted them to their travel agent. They got the visas back, but, unfortunately, discovered the visa stickers, arranged for them by the travel agent, were counterfeit; the first time they presented them for inspection they were promptly slapped in jail. There were four jails in Kathmandu, and these women ended up in Dilli Bazaar jail, which was a dreadful place. Elizabeth went to visit them and brought them food, but their luck really changed when their New Zealand member of parliament came charging in to Kathmandu. He met with the prime minister's office, emphasized the women's innocence, and managed to get them freed in about three days.

Not all of Elizabeth's consulate clients were innocents however. One man traveling on a New Zealand passport on his way to Singapore was stopped at the airport, where they found that he was carrying six kilos of liquid hashish. He ended up in a jail even worse than Dilli Bazaar. Elizabeth attended his court appearance, translated to her by Kumar, and wasn't surprised that he was sentenced to two years in the central jail. At this point, the New Zealand government wanted his passport back, so Elizabeth, now familiar with the jail scene, went to retrieve it and discovered that he had two passports. Officials in Wellington, New Zealand, became curiouser and curiouser about these two passports and eventually sent them back with the news that they were both well-executed counterfeits. They implored her to "please stop that man!" Alas, he had just been let out of jail. She raced to the Interpol office in her Volkswagen Bug and explained the situation to them. They leapt into action and sped to the airport, where he was caught just before getting on an international flight. They stuck him in jail again. Elizabeth went to visit him and asked where he had obtained the passports. He explained that he'd bought them in Singapore for five hundred dollars each. He would take drugs out of Nepal and bring back cheap electronic goods. In fact, he was Polish. His real name was Krawetz Matlak. She was elated. She called up the Polish embassy and said, "Here, take this man off my hands!"

So this was the life of an honorary consul? She wondered if perhaps it was less complicated dealing with climbers.

*He wasn't in his room more than 30 minutes
when the phone rang; it was Elizabeth Hawley,
congratulating him and setting up a meeting.*

"A New Star Shines in the Himalayan Climbing World" was the title of Elizabeth's spring report for 1990. The star was Tomo Česen, who came through on his promise to climb the route that everyone had been eyeing and trying—the South Face of Lhotse. Climbing alone, with no well-stocked camps and no bottled oxygen, Tomo Česen stunned the mountaineering world with a daring solo ascent of this formidable face.

Messner had taken a good look at the face and determined back in 1977 that, if it was possible, it would be a problem for the twenty-first century. He took another look in 1989, and was prepared to fix 5000 meters of rope to get up the route, convinced that three fixed camps would be required to climb it. He couldn't have imagined the boldness of Česen's climb, alone, and in the amazing time of 45 hours and 20 minutes from bottom to top. In fact the entire expedition was a whirlwind. Česen was at his base camp for only fourteen days, acclimatizing and watching the face to determine the best line of ascent to avoid rockfall and avalanches.

According to Česen's report to Elizabeth, just after lunch on April 22, he headed up from base camp with a sleeping bag, extra gloves, a bivouac sack, some socks, goggles, 100 meters of 6 mm rope, eight rock pitons and ten ice screws, three kilos of food, and three thermos bottles of liquid. He had two ice axes, crampons, a helmet, a headlamp, a walkie-talkie, and a camera. He was meticulous in his report to Elizabeth—he told her exactly what time he started, where he climbed, when and where he stopped for his bivouacs, how many hours he slept, the weather, and his strategy. He described in detail the difficult section of 50 to 70 meters of vertical rock covered in unconsolidated snow near the top and the long exhausting summit ridge covered in deep snow. He explained how he had reached the summit at 2:20 P.M. in strong winds. By 7:00 A.M. the next day he was back at the base of the mountain. He told Elizabeth that he felt good, although mentally exhausted, particularly from the descent. Physical exhaustion did not hit him until a day later. He concluded that he was "satisfied with his achievement."

In her usual style she prodded for more details: What had he seen from the summit? What landmarks and terrain features could he describe? Was there any evidence of other climbing teams? His answers were convincing. She had been impressed with him formerly when he told her of his solo ascent of Jannu by a new and difficult route, and that added to his credibility on Lhotse. It wasn't just Elizabeth who was convinced.

Messner was stunned with the boldness, the speed, and the vision of this climb: "That he did it so fast above 8000 meters! I cannot imagine how fast he could climb." Everyone agreed that this was something truly futuristic. Later that autumn, a twenty-member Soviet team climbed the South Face, taking weeks to surmount the route, and using oxygen as well. They expressed wonder, and finally doubt, that Česen had done what he claimed.

Greg Child was in Kathmandu and remembers the Soviet team's press conference and their skepticism about Česen's climb. They were guarded in their statements. "If he did the route he claims," they suggested, "he must be some kind of superman." After the press conference, Child questioned Elizabeth about her interview with Česen, and was surprised that she didn't seem to have any detailed notes on the climb. He wasn't sure if she understood the scale of the potential controversy. Had she simply written down what Česen told her rather than subjecting him to her usual interrogation? When she heard about Child's surprise much later, she too was surprised because her Česen file is complete with photos, statements, descriptions, and notes. Either she hadn't understood what Child wanted, or she wasn't willing to show it to him, or one of them remembered it wrongly.

When Česen returned home, inconsistencies began to appear in his story. When asked by the French magazine *Vertical* for a summit photo, he produced one. Some time later it became known that it was not his own but that of fellow Slovenian Viktor Grošlej (who was not amused). One thing led to another, and Elizabeth, along with most in the mountaineering community including Messner, finally came to believe that Tomo Česen did not climb the South Face of Lhotse.

In retrospect, Elizabeth doesn't believe Česen was "confused" about his claim. He was explicit. He told her he was just a few meters below the summit and that it would not have been safe for him to stand on the summit because of the wind and lack of space. He thought he could "touch" it by raising his arm to its full length, thereby confirming his summit claim. She recalls the interview: "I believed him. He'd been to Jannu and he came into my office and told me about the climb meter by meter. He came prepared. I remember that he had very detailed, minute descriptions of where he had gone, including a diagram. I asked how it compared with Jannu and he said, 'Well it's not technically as difficult, but it's much bigger and much wider and you feel very, very small.' And then he blew it. I'm sorry not to believe him, but now I don't."

And then people started doubting Česen's solo ascent of Jannu. "It's a pity," she says, thinking that perhaps he came to believe in his stories himself. After Lhotse, she never saw him again.

Elizabeth received considerable criticism for her reporting of Česen's successes on Jannu and Lhotse because she didn't catch the errors. Some said that with her reputation for detail and scrutiny on the 8000-meter peaks, she should have picked up on the fabrications. They felt she was the first line of defense for the truth—and she had been too easily breached. Others were more generous, pointing out that virtually every mountain magazine editor in the world believed Česen, too—at least until he began making obvious mistakes.

Other Slovenian climbers were having a better time of it. Marija and Andrej Štremfelj became the first married couple to summit Everest together. Marija remembers the rigor of their post-expedition interview; in addition to all of the normal questions about camps, times, and distances, Elizabeth asked what clothes they wore on summit day and who was first—Andrej or herself. Marija thought the obsession with seemingly meaningless details was strange, but it made sense when Elizabeth explained her reasons. There were actually two couples on the mountain that day, each trying to be the first to the summit. The other couple, an American woman and her Russian husband, was close behind, so Elizabeth had to determine exactly who was first. She was cross-referencing the times and details told her by the Štremfeljs against those reported by other climbers. Marija had been completely unaware of the tight time frame.

Elizabeth knew Andrej well and was genuinely happy for them. Over the years, they had often talked about expeditions, his and others too. She liked Andrej and trusted his honesty and motivations. In her opinion, he demonstrated a true mountaineering spirit, as opposed to the 8000-meter wrangling she saw so often. She told Andrej he would probably be surprised at the number of well-known climbers who said they'd reached summits she was sure they had not. He remembers talking with her about the Tomo Česen debacle and why she initially believed Česen had summited the South Face of Lhotse. She said Česen had described some oxygen bottles where she was sure they had been left by an American team. It was a detail that helped cinch the story for her.

Because Andrej was so often in Nepal, he was also the recipient of her massive repository of information—something he used to good advantage. She was a valuable resource for many Slovenian climbers, assisting them in finding inexpensive accommodation in Kathmandu and helping them with logistics and permits. She recognized their needs and did what she could to help them. But he also sensed there was a lot that she didn't share—stories about politics, the royal family, and individual climbers. He was curious, but didn't ask.

That fall of 1990 was a big season, with seventy-eight expeditions and 553 foreign climbers in the Himalayan peaks. With a 30 percent increase of climbers from the previous year, Elizabeth was kept busy running back and forth between her house and the climbers' hotels. Despite the numbers, not much new was happening. As she puts it, "Pioneering new routes or exploring seldom-attempted peaks was apparently not of paramount interest to the majority." Many of the expeditions were on Everest, where thirty-one people summited in a four-day period of beautiful weather.

The Nepalese Ministry of Tourism, regulators of mountaineering in Nepal, began to receive negative feedback about the number of permits they were granting for a single season, particularly on Everest and other "commercial" peaks. Foreign climbers—and Elizabeth—warned the authorities about the dangers and conflicts, not to mention the environmental pollution, of such crowding. They replied that they had several reasons to continue in this way: more revenue for the government, more revenue for the private sector (guides, trekking companies, porters, suppliers), and more opportunity for alpinists to climb their chosen peaks. For the most part, things worked smoothly, but there were incidents. A Spaniard on Dhaulagiri scoffed at the Swiss who "sold" their route to other expeditions. And at times, teams that were fixing routes resented later teams ascending their ropes.

Some teams arrived with meager supplies, apparently assuming that better-supplied expeditions would be there for them if needed. Well-stocked teams found themselves functioning as restaurants and supply depots. This didn't make them happy, but what really rankled was how the less-equipped climbers boasted of how they were freeloading and getting up the mountain "alpine style," and yet were utilizing other teams' fixed ropes, tents, and food.

Amazing stories filtered back to Elizabeth: Russian climbers were helping themselves to other people's food and tents; an ailing, ill-equipped French climber asked a British climber to supply him with oxygen, a stretcher, and manpower to carry him down through the icefall; and so on. An Italian visitor to Everest base camp described it as a fairground and said it was difficult to move among the tents.

At the end of the season, a ministry official admitted there had been some problems and perhaps they should limit the number of permits. But Elizabeth doubted his superiors would see things in the same light, despite the warnings.

As commercial and guided climbing increased in frequency, Elizabeth maintained an open mind, though she was not terribly interested in these new climbing objectives. She clearly delineates the two: "All guided climbs are commercial climbs, but not all commercial climbs are guided." With some commercial climbs, she explains, the organizers' responsibility is to get the team to base camp or advance camp and provide them with everything to that point, and then leave them on their own to climb the mountain. A guide's responsibility is to take the client to the top of the mountain. She points out that guided expeditions tend to have "frightfully inexperienced" climbers, whereas climbers on commercial expeditions tend to have more experience, although not necessarily at high altitude: "They tend to hire the commercial organizer because they don't have time. They don't know how to get permits or organize expeditions. They only know how to climb."

She is convinced that, even though guided expeditions insist on a minimum level of client experience, there is a lot of conning going on in that regard, and the results can be disastrous. She has met many climbers on guided expeditions who made their decision to climb in Nepal based on what exotic vacation they should take in any particular year: "I'll go on a Mediterranean cruise or an East African safari or climb a Himalayan peak." And yet Elizabeth's impatience is not so much with the commercial climbing industry as it is with the experts and professional climbers who look down on commercial expeditions as getting in the way and cluttering up the mountains. She objects to this condescension, adding "Well, they don't own the mountain, do they!"

The Nepalese government took advantage of this growing cash infusion by steadily increasing peak fees. Authorities said the increases were for environmental conservation, but Elizabeth wasn't convinced. Their professed strategy was to reduce the number of climbers on Everest and other popular 8000-meter peaks and spread them around to the lesser peaks, where the fees were lower. She didn't buy this argument either. The increases were substantial and shocking to climbers who had been coming to Nepal for years. In one year, Dhaulagiri I leapt from a two-thousand-dollar fee to eight thousand dollars, plus eight hundred dollars for each additional member over a total of nine. When Italian climber Sergio Martini returned from his attempt on Kangchenjunga and went to the ministry to obtain the same permit for the following year, he learned that it would cost him four times as much.

Elizabeth doubted the government's strategy would actually reduce the number of expeditions. Instead, she thought it would change the nature and makeup of the expeditions from small, self-financed teams to large, commercial expeditions organized by adventure-travel agencies and mountaineering clubs. Yet to Elizabeth's way of thinking, the smaller teams that tended to try difficult and unclimbed routes—routes that weren't interesting to commercial operators—were essential for the ongoing development of Himalayan climbing. Some climbers told her they were changing their objectives to peaks in Pakistan, where the fees were lower. Others admitted they would climb without official permission, a practice she disapproved of.

That August Elizabeth went to Lhasa, but it wasn't the city itself that impressed her. Her flight skirted the edge of Everest, and she vividly remembers her first view of the East Face: she almost fell out of her seat. She had always thought that the Southwest Face was big, and that the North Face was big, but this face was huge! It was completely covered in snow, and its immense whiteness overwhelmed her. She enjoyed exploring Lhasa, but that experience was completely overshadowed by her first glimpse of the East Face of Everest. Despite her obvious glee at seeing this spectacular mountain face up close, the mystery remains as to why Elizabeth has never gone to Everest base camp herself. She has had many chances to go, and it would be logical for her to be curious about this place so familiar to her through her work. And yet she has never gone.

Stephen Venables was back in Kathmandu, this time for a new route on the 6369-meter Kusum Kanguru, a stunning peak near Everest. He and Elizabeth ran into each other through their mutual friend Lisa Choegyal. Venables described the new, quite difficult route they had just done, and apparently she responded by referring to it as just a "trekking peak," asking whether he'd done any real climbing lately. Venables was stunned. He had thought she had a good understanding of what constituted a "real climb," but her comment changed his opinion.

Elizabeth remembers it differently and is dismayed that he felt insulted, reluctantly admitting that she isn't known for her diplomatic skills. She explains that she didn't interview him because Kusum Kanguru really *is* a trekking peak, a designation created by the Ministry of Tourism for climbing peaks of lower elevation. She knows there are difficult routes on some of the trekking peaks, but for her, it is impossible to keep track of them all. The ministry gives out a multitude of permits for trekking peaks, many of which are not used because the costs are so low. For Elizabeth, the volume is too much, so she has no way of knowing what routes are being done on those peaks. Looking back, she thinks she was probably brusque with Venables because she was busy.

Though he was disappointed by her lack of interest in his climb, Venables still valued Elizabeth as a chronicler, at least as far as what she actually chronicled. As an author himself, he had often contacted her for information and was always impressed at the care she took with details. He thinks she has been a valuable resource for climbing writers like himself, as well as the mainstream media, because it would be all too easy for the media to get misinformation and never know the difference. With Elizabeth, they are sure to get the facts.

But was she missing something by reporting on commercial climbs and overlooking an important new trend on the lower peaks? There was an emerging group of top climbers who were more interested in challenging routes—not on the height of the peak.

Some climbers who sought credit for their hard new routes complained publicly about her lack of appreciation. But American climber Dave Hahn doesn't have much patience for those who whine about Elizabeth not being sufficiently interested in their hard, esoteric, and dangerous climbs: "They're going to have to get used to climbing their climbs for their own reasons—they are probably never going to get the kind of acclaim from the public that they feel they deserve." But they weren't necessarily interested in public acclaim. They wanted their peers—other climbers—to know about their climbs, and they said it was Elizabeth's job to keep them informed. Some climbers thought that a lot of important activity was going unrecorded and that it smacked of elitism.

In 1991 Elizabeth had the opportunity to be reacquainted with American climber Richard Salisbury. She had met him in 1984 when he was part of an Everest climb sponsored by the Nepal police. It began as an effort to remove garbage from the mountain, but ended up a confusing mess of invalid permits and an illegal attempt on the summit, where two Sherpas lost their lives. This time Salisbury was back in Nepal with a permit for Annapurna IV. His team didn't get very high on the mountain because it was a snowy spring, but it wasn't their climbing that interested Elizabeth. Before heading to Annapurna IV, Salisbury sat down with her for the requisite interview. She brought out all the information she had on previous expeditions to Annapurna IV; to her surprise, Salisbury pulled out a spreadsheet with similar information. He had taken everything he knew about previous expeditions—times, camps, and elevations—and plotted them on a spreadsheet so as to better plan the food supplies and general logistics of the trip. She was fascinated. She had accumulated copious notes on every Nepalese peak being climbed and was interested in creating a database of the information. Salisbury, who was a computer analyst specializing in databases back at the University of Michigan, her old alma mater, offered to help.

At the time, a Nepali graduate student was helping her with the project, so she declined Salisbury's offer. But later, when the student left Nepal to study in the United States, she got back in touch with Salisbury to see if he was still interested. He was. In fact, Salisbury was the perfect choice. He knew about climbing and he knew how to program a database. He had both the skills and a passion for organizing information about climbing.

So Salisbury hired a Nepali woman to go to Elizabeth's house each morning to do data entry. For the next eleven years, she entered all of Elizabeth's files into the program that Salisbury designed. Twice a year Elizabeth sent Salisbury updates; he would then go through the reports carefully, checking the facts against other sources. Once all the disputable issues were resolved, they synchronized their databases, working on the same project from two different continents. He worked with her for thirteen years building the database. He recalls their working relationship with, "She didn't terrorize me—she got impatient with me sometimes, but I just let it roll off. I knew it wasn't personal."

A statistic that Elizabeth entered into that database with sadness was the death of Wanda Rutkiewicz on Kangchenjunga in 1992. There weren't that many women who impressed Elizabeth, but Rutkiewicz was one of them. The Polish woman was the world's leading female Himalayan climber, and Kangchenjunga was her ninth 8000-meter peak. Elizabeth described her as a skillful, although slow, climber. Rutkiewicz had conceived an exceptionally ambitious plan to bag all fourteen of the 8000-meter peaks by the end of 1992, which meant six in one year, although she had since reconsidered and thought it might take until the following spring to finish the job.

She was last seen by the Mexican climber Carlos Carsolio at about 8250 meters in a snow hole where she was spending the night between camps. According to Carlos, she had been climbing even more slowly than usual. Carlos went to the summit and was descending when he met her in her snow hole. He told Elizabeth that it was a well-protected spot but he still urged her to go down. Wanda told him that she was cold because her old down suit wasn't warm enough any more. She was pitifully short of equipment; no sleeping bag, stove, fuel, or food. She had only a liter of water and a bivouac sac that she had wrapped around herself to keep warm. "She seemed tired," Carlos told Elizabeth.

And yet she was determined to continue up. "I think she felt this was her last chance to climb Kangchenjunga," he said. He told Wanda that he would go down to Camp IV for the night, then descend to Camp II and wait for her there, as there was no food or fuel at Camp IV. Their conversation lasted not more than ten minutes.

Carlos descended, and never saw her again. "It was difficult for us to leave the mountain," Carlos told Elizabeth, "but I'm sure that she cannot have survived because of the bad weather and because she was extremely tired and without drink." He continued, "It is a sad loss for all of us and for the mountaineering world . . . she was a safe climber but she was extremely slow." She had confided to Carlos that she had to finish all the 8000ers quickly before she became even slower.

Elizabeth wondered if this was a case of ambition outstripping physical abilities. She remembers Wanda as a charming, complicated woman, and "tense . . . wound up like a mechanical doll . . . she had determination. She just kept plugging away at these mountains until she could plug away no longer."

Another tragedy played itself out in the fall of 1992 when the two French climbers Pierre Béghin and Jean-Christophe Lafaille attempted the South Face of Annapurna I. Lafaille remembers meeting Elizabeth when they arrived. As it was his first time to the Himalaya, he was the junior team member. "It's my first trip in Himalaya, my first expedition. I discover the magic Nepal, I don't speak English, and I'm the young boy with my boss Pierre." His impression of Elizabeth was that she was very serious and "not so much friendly."

The two were attempting an alpine-style ascent of the great South Face by a new line. With Béghin's Himalayan experience and Lafaille's technical skills, they were a strong team. They had made good progress over difficult terrain to an elevation of 7400 meters; then the weather deteriorated and they had to descend. During a rappel, Béghin fell to his death. Lafaille was left alone on that terrible face and had a multi-day epic getting down in the storm. His arm was broken in the process, and his exhaustion was extreme. As Lafaille described it, "I was completely tired, broken physically and psychologically."

When Elizabeth interviewed him upon his return to Kathmandu, Lafaille described Béghin as "the best Himalayan climber from France." He described their partnership as a "good cocktail of his experience and my technique." Béghin had remained true to his ideals of small teams on difficult routes, writing about it in the 1992 *American Alpine Journal*: "A simple rope team for days and days without logistical support striving with incertitude toward a summit, a goal with real meaning. What is the purpose of setting out with ten or fifteen climbers on that kind of objective while uncoiling kilometers of fixed rope? Today, when our technology lets us explore space, the conquest of the great walls of our planet is interesting only if done by fair means. . . . "—the phrase Messner had brought to Himalayan climbing.

But there were successes too. Described by Chris Bonington as "one of the most beautiful and difficult peaks in the Himalaya," Menlungtse was a prize to be plucked, and two Slovenian climbers did just that in the fall of 1992. A British team had climbed a lower summit of the peak in 1987, and an American team with John Roskelley, Greg Child, and Jim Wickwire tried hard on the East Ridge in 1990, but neither team considered attempting the route taken by the Slovenians: the Southeast Face, which led directly to the main summit. Marko Prezelj and Andrej Štremfelj combined their experience, confidence, and speed to reach the top on October 23 via a dangerous and difficult face in pure alpine style, spending just over fifty-three hours on the face. Elizabeth was pleased: a beautiful mountain, an ambitious route, and a skillful team.

A tragic story unfolded in the spring of 1993 when Nepalese climber Pasang Lhamu Sherpa and her husband, the director of the Thamserku trekking agency, assembled a team to get her to the top of Everest before any Nepali women from the joint Indo-Nepali expedition, on the mountain at the same time, summited. Before Pasang left Kathmandu, she issued a statement saying that, no matter what, she was going to climb the mountain on behalf of Nepali women. The most cynical of her detractors said that she had too much encouragement from her husband, who saw profit to be made by making her famous as the first Nepali woman on the summit. It was well known that she was not an experienced climber and that she was also quite slow.

An Indian team spread a rumor that they were going to attempt the summit on an absurdly early date in late April. Pasang took the bait. She had to be on top first. New Zealander Rob Hall, who was leading another party, spoke to Elizabeth about Pasang's summit party, describing them as completely on their own, way ahead of everyone else, without proper communications equipment, and no support climbers to help them out in case of trouble—all in the name of a record. Other foreign climbers at base camp reported that Pasang's husband ordered her "in good Asian, husband-to-wife fashion" to go up. She was in tears, but, being an obedient wife, she did it.

Rumors flew down to Kathmandu that she took her oxygen via a long hose from a bottle carried by another climber. She was apparently moving extremely slowly as she went to the summit and had to be dragged down to the South Summit on the descent. She and another Sherpa,

Sonam Tshering, had to spend the night in an unplanned bivouac, while three stronger climbers went down to the South Col. It was the last time Pasang and Sonam were seen alive. Elizabeth unforgivingly categorized it as "involuntary manslaughter."

Pasang became a national hero overnight. Newspapers that hadn't paid any serious attention to mountaineering accomplishments since Tenzing Norgay in 1953 gave Pasang ample press. According to one news report, "Pasang has carved an enviable niche in the history of mountaineering where she will stay till eternity, commanding the adoration of all those who love dignity, courage, and bravery." The prime minister hosted a great celebration, and several Sherpas were ordered to go back up the mountain, hack her body out of the ice, and bring it back down, a practice completely contrary to the Sherpa tradition of leaving bodies on the mountain. Pasang's body was taken with great fanfare and procession to the stadium and put on display, where it lay in state for a day. Hundreds of people lined up to see her prior to her cremation. The prime minister and the king both sent condolences to her family. A street was named after her and a mountaineering institute was established in her name. Postage stamps with her picture were issued and the government provided ten thousand dollars for the education of her children. In a final show of respect, the king bestowed the Star of Nepal on her. Ten years later, Elizabeth explodes, "The exploitation was absolutely repulsive!"

By the mid-1990s, French climber Jean-Christophe Lafaille had completely succumbed to the magic of Nepal. He met Elizabeth in 1993 when he climbed Cho Oyu, in 1994 on his way to Shishapangma, and again on the tragic Annapurna expedition. He was well aware of her persistence in getting an interview, and he laughs that many climbers worried about getting their telephone call from her while they were in the bathroom. "Many times when you arrive after a long flight or a long expedition, you dream to wash yourself in a good bath and many times when you are in that bath, the phone rings!"

He recalls an amusing incident with Elizabeth that demonstrated the depth of her sleuthing abilities. Lafaille was doing a solo climb on a new route on the North Face of Shishapangma in 1994. He remained a long time in base camp because of bad weather. As a result, he ended up ascending the mountain on a French permit and descending on a British permit. It would have been difficult for anyone to track his movements because of this convoluted combination of permits, trekking agencies, and nationalities. He finally returned to Kathmandu during a national holiday. His trekking agency was closed for the day and as far as he knew, nobody knew he was back in town. But he wasn't in his room more than thirty minutes when the phone rang; it was Elizabeth Hawley, congratulating him and setting up a meeting.

Another climber who impressed Elizabeth was the British woman Alison Hargreaves. In 1995 she had the ambition to climb the three highest mountains in one year: Everest in the spring, K2 in the summer, and Kangchenjunga in the fall. She was tackling Everest from the north side, in Tibet, and wanted to climb as a self-contained unit of one. Her publicist in England was touting it as a solo climb, but Hargreaves and Elizabeth agreed that it was not solo, only self-contained. As Elizabeth observed, "How could she [climb it solo] when there were 182 other climbers . . . on the same route?" Elizabeth checked with other teams on the mountain to be sure that Hargreaves' claims were true, and the cross-checking revealed "Self-contained she claimed, and self-contained she was." She was so self-contained that she wouldn't even enter anyone's tent to have a cup of tea with them—or drink their tea at all. She carried her own loads, put up her own tent and took it down, cooked for herself, and climbed the mountain by herself. She didn't even use other people's ropes.

A claim that Hargreaves did not make was that of being the first woman to climb Everest without oxygen, and here Elizabeth's reporting contradicted what she'd said earlier about New Zealander Lydia Bradey. At the time of Bradey's climb, Elizabeth expressed some doubt about her claim to have summited; since Bradey had climbed without oxygen, hers would have been an important record. Elizabeth's report that year included Bradey's statement along with her doubtful teammates', casting a long shadow on Bradey's claim and effectively nullifying it. But now

Elizabeth seemed convinced: instead of crediting Hargreaves with the first oxygen-free ascent, she said, "That distinction belongs to a New Zealander, Miss Lydia Bradey."

Hargreaves succeeded—at least on Everest. She died a few months later on K2 when she was blown off the mountain by a horrific storm after reaching the summit. Italian climber Marco Bianchi described her as "a star of the Himalaya and a remarkable climber." But Elizabeth added, "Unfortunately the star of the Himalaya shone a very short time." She saw Alison as an ambitious, talented climber whose ambitions more or less matched her abilities and who climbed to support her children. She liked and admired her, and was genuinely saddened by her death on K2.

The 8000-meter-peak bagging continued, and one climber whose face was becoming familiar was the friendly, efficient, and talented American Ed Viesturs. Viesturs, together with New Zealander Rob Hall and Finn Veikka Gustafsson, achieved the fastest ascent to date on Makalu in the spring of 1995. They accomplished it without oxygen or Sherpa support. They could do it because of their high degree of acclimatization, having helicoptered over from the Everest region where they had been high on Everest and Lhotse. Viesturs was clearly headed for all fourteen of the 8000-meter peaks which he completed in the spring of 2005.

Elizabeth knew him well enough to keep him honest about his claims. He remembers being chastised for not having gone to the top of Shishapangma: "You know, Ed, if you want to do all fourteen, you have to go back to Shishapangma." So he did. He was always honest with her about his summits, but is convinced she would have known even if he hadn't been. He describes her as a kind of taskmaster—but a caring one. In her parting comments to Ed before each expedition, she always urges him to "be as careful as you've always been, I want to see you come back."

And the soft-spoken Mexican climber Carlos Carsolio was back with two more 8000-meter summits to add to his list—Annapurna I, followed swiftly by Dhaulagiri I. His superb acclimatization achieved on Annapurna allowed him to climb Dhaulagiri during the night, alone, and to reach the summit at 10:00 A.M. on May 15. She interviewed him in Kathmandu and heard the seemingly easygoing Carsolio say, "I am not in a hurry ... but I would like to climb them all."

Elizabeth had little patience with climbers who she thought made false claims. If she sensed exaggeration, she was like a bloodhound on a fresh trail, hunting down the truth. One of these cases was the French climber Benoit Chamoux, who died on Kangchenjunga in the fall of 1995. She had met him many times in Kathmandu, as he was the leader of a professional team of climbers named *l'Esprit d'Equipe*, fully sponsored by the French computer company Bull. His publicists claimed that Kangchenjunga would be his fourteenth 8000-meter peak. Before he headed off, she interviewed him and challenged his claim, since he had previously told her that he had not reached the highest of the summits on Shishapangma, another 8000-meter peak. He agreed his earlier statement was correct, but that he had gone to *a* summit of Shishapangma that is over 8000 meters. Elizabeth's response offered no compromise: "That's fine but it's *a* summit, not *the* summit. People who reach the South Summit of Everest don't claim that they reached the top of Everest, even though the South Summit is well over 8000 meters, too." He conceded that perhaps he would have to go back to Shishapangma sometime and climb *the* summit.

But it wasn't just Shishapangma that gave her problems with Chamoux. His claims on Dhaulagiri were also in question, according to Elizabeth. Normally, proof of a summit climb was a description or, better yet, photographs of the flags, prayer flags, and *katas* that are the normal summit decorations on Himalayan peaks. But Dhaulagiri was a trick summit and she had caught a number of false claimants due to her knowledge of the peak. She explained that on Dhaulagiri there are flagpoles, prayer flags, and *katas*—but not at the highest point. To get to the highest point from these flags, one must go down a bit and then traverse. She was impressed with the integrity of the Basque climber Juanito Oiarzabal when he learned that he hadn't gone to the true summit. He went back later in the same season and climbed it again, this time going the entire distance.

In fact, she thought Chamoux was a man of multiple false claims. Although she didn't challenge him at the time, she later disbelieved his claim of Cho Oyu because several years later someone from his team told her that Chamoux and British climber Alan Hinkes didn't go to the summit; they'd stopped on the summit plateau because of deteriorating weather. She mentioned the discrepancy to Hinkes, and he denied it: "I thought we did, although we couldn't see very well, but I'm sure we got it." Many people stop at the lower summit, she says—some claim it as the summit and others do not. Elizabeth does not consider the summit plateau to be the summit of Cho Oyu, as it is not the highest point.

One of her favorite questions for climbers coming back from Cho Oyu is what they saw from the summit. If they say they saw a lot of mountain peaks, she nails them: "Forget it! They didn't reach the summit, because only from the highest point or just a few meters away from it, can you see Everest and Lhotse and even Makalu in clear weather." So if they haven't seen Everest and Lhotse, they weren't there. She has other questions for those who supposedly reached their summits in bad visibility. She asks for details of the terrain and whether there were any particular landmarks, and she waits to see if they volunteer those details. If possible, she checks with other expeditions. She does what she can, depending on the situation.

In the end, Elizabeth credited Benoit Chamoux with only ten of his thirteen claims. False claims included Shishapangma, Cho Oyu, and Makalu. In her archival mountaineering database, she adjusted her notes to say claims were unsubstantiated if she wasn't sure. In Chamoux's case, she thought she understood the problem. He was under pressure from Bull, the computer company, to succeed. To keep the sponsorship, he needed to succeed, and succeed, and succeed again. She thought that the pressure to produce results was too much for him, and so he lied.

She was convinced that Chamoux's death on Kangchenjunga was linked to the 8000-meter race. On the mountain at the same time were the Swiss Erhard Loretan, who was going for his fourteenth 8000-meter peak, and Sergio Martini, an Italian who was going for his eleventh. Loretan climbed Kangchenjunga, efficiently as always, with his frequent climbing partner Jean Troillet. Elizabeth pressed him for details of the climb, and tried to learn more about the Chamoux situation. He replied that when he and Troillet reached the bottom of the West Ridge at 4:00 P.M. on their descent, they encountered Chamoux and his partner Bernard Royer moving up. About thirty minutes later, Royer radioed that he was abandoning his summit bid because of fatigue. About an hour after that, at 5:30 P.M., Chamoux also radioed that he was too tired to continue and that he was unable to find his way down the ridge. He stayed that night a few meters above the col and got back on the radio at 8:10 A.M. the morning of October 6. He was seen reaching the col, but then went out of sight on the north side of the mountain. Neither Chamoux nor Royer was seen again. As a footnote, their Sherpas did not try to mount a rescue or even search for the French climbers, because earlier in the expedition the two had done nothing to help one of them when he fell. A few days later, Sergio Martini summited, making it eleven 8000ers for him.

There was much discussion in the mountaineering press about the presence of three world-class mountaineers—all racing for the 8000-meter prize—climbing on Kangchenjunga at the same time. Did they create a dangerously competitive situation on the mountain? An American climber put it bluntly: "It was a fatal challenge for Chamoux. The Swiss were much faster. Loretan is the best.... The French were not well acclimatized. They tried to keep up with the Swiss, and they killed themselves." From her observations, Elizabeth was inclined to agree.

When Loretan returned to Kathmandu, she asked him how he felt about the accomplishment. He said only, "It is something done." He told her that the 8000-meter goal had not been a burden to him, and, therefore, having achieved it, he didn't feel any great sense of relief. She pressed him more on his dreams for the future, wondering if he would continue to climb in the Himalaya. He responded with other mountaineering projects—ambitious, steep climbs such as the unclimbed West Face of Makalu. She was certain she would see more of Erhard Loretan.

Although she wasn't fond of the 8000-meter obsession in general, she hesitated to lump all of the aspirants into the same pot. Messner had been the first and, for that reason, she thought he stood alone. For Messner, it was an idea—an original idea—and she was convinced he did it for the fulfillment of that idea, not for the glory. She felt

Kukuczka took it to another level by doing so many of the climbs in winter. He was a true mountaineer. Loretan she saw as an incredibly talented and efficient climber and a real mountaineer as well. Krzysztof Wielicki was a serious climber, and not afraid of winter. But on the topic of Alan Hinkes, she became critical. She was convinced that he was opportunistic, that he timed his climbs so that the other teams on the mountain had already set up the fixed ropes. He would then show up with one Sherpa and off he would go. And Chamoux—she saw him as a tragic figure.

Elizabeth had a welcome respite from all the peak bagging when she was invited to Tokyo by the first woman to climb Everest, Junko Tabei. It was the twentieth anniversary of Tabei's ascent and she had invited ten of the twenty-six living women Everest summiteers to Tokyo for an international symposium and a celebratory climb of Mount Fuji. Among the ten invitees was the Chinese climber who summited just two days after Tabei's historic climb. Elizabeth gracefully declined the Fuji climb, joining the others at a nearby hot springs resort. She was initially confused about why she was invited, and speculated that she had been "tacked on as an observer." In fact, she was invited because of her knowledge of the history of women climbers in Nepal, and so was asked to give a speech after the Everest summiteers had been honored.

In her speech, Elizabeth was typically blunt, expressing a certain amount of disappointment. With few exceptions, she felt that women were following in footsteps that had been made by men before them. She pointed out that thirty-one years had lapsed between the time that the first men came to climb in the Nepal Himalaya and time that the first woman, Hettie Dyhrenfurth, came and climbed on Kangchenjunga in 1930. Women tended to use standard routes in standard seasons. Not many had been leaders, and not many had done all-women expeditions. "They just haven't progressed a whole lot in terms of coming to the forefront of mountaineering in Nepal," she said.

Using example after example, she pointed out that women were not opening new routes or advancing the standards set by men. "Women have yet to prove their ability to lead the way in change and innovation."

She wondered if it was because female alpinists were a smaller group from which to draw. She was sure it was not a physical disadvantage because, as she pointed out, some of the best Himalayan climbers were very small men. Finally, she challenged them to attempt some of the last big Himalayan prizes, such as the Horseshoe Traverse. "Are there women who can find the financing, calculate the logistics, and enlist the highly talented climbers needed to accomplish such a feat?" Her standards were high for men—and for women.

*"I've got to go back—Elizabeth says
I didn't really climb it."*
—ANATOLI BOUKREEV

Having been an observer of the mountaineering scene in Nepal for almost forty years, Elizabeth was beginning to see developments that disturbed her. First was the increasing number of sloppy (and sometimes incorrect) reports coming out of Nepal regarding expedition successes, failures, and, most seriously, fatal accidents. Much of the misinformation emanated from the Internet. One report indicated that five Kazakhs died in a storm when they were actually three Russians. Another report suggested that seven New Zealanders died—but there weren't seven New Zealanders among all the climbers on the mountain at the time, and none of them had been involved in an accident. She thought this "instant kind of reporting" was unreliable and sometimes irresponsible. It wasn't subjected to the rigorous cross-checking for accuracy that she practiced. There were apologies and retractions about the errors, but she knew the families of these climbers must have been distressed—and for no reason other than sloppiness.

She also wondered what kind of impact satellite phones and other forms of instant communication would have on an expedition's concentration level. She cautioned a Polish team attempting a difficult winter ascent of Makalu to consider leaving their phones behind. She believed they needed to concentrate on the task at hand, not their families, their kids' school problems, and so on. But ever the journalist, she added, "But don't forget to call me when you get back to Kathmandu."

She saw another disturbing trend within the guiding business. As it became more profitable, it was inevitable that some questionable players would enter the arena. In 1996, the peak fees alone earned the Nepalese government around $1.8 million. Elizabeth was painfully aware of guiding inconsistencies because she heard the stories firsthand. Some commercial guiding companies were highly reputable, providing excellent services, experienced guides, plenty of oxygen, and other important equipment. Others did not, and some were outright illegal. One German company accepted payments from thirty to forty clients for expeditions to Everest, Cho Oyu, or Shishapangma, but failed to forward any payment to Kathmandu agents for their transport to base camp, or to Kathmandu staff to prepare their food and arrange logistics. When the unsuspecting clients arrived in Kathmandu, they were shocked to learn that the agent wouldn't do anything for them unless they paid him directly—and immediately. The German company was already so indebted to him that he refused to grant any credit to the company's clients. Some went home disappointed, while others stayed and paid—a second time.

But Elizabeth's most fundamental disappointment was with the climbers themselves. She categorized them into three major types: pioneers who attempted unclimbed mountains or routes; peak baggers who attempted as many 8000-meter peaks as possible; and fee-paying clients and their guides.

One of the few climbers she placed in her "preferred" category—the pioneers—was the Slovenian Tomaž Humar. In the fall of 1997 Humar had made a brief appearance in Nepal with climbing partner Janez Jeglič to climb an impressive direct line up the previously unattempted West Face of 7742-meter Nuptse. The two completed the route, but Jeglič fell to his death. They needed three bivouacs on their ascent and solo climbed with no belays and no fixed lines. Humar described the face as wracked with avalanches and falling seracs. Although they climbed together during the ascent, they became separated and summited separately, Jeglič about 15 minutes before Humar. When Humar arrived on the summit, all he saw were his partner's footprints in the snow leading toward the south side of the mountain. He surmised that Jeglič had gone beyond the summit by mistake and been blown down the South Face by the strong, gusting winds. Humar then had the long, complex, and dangerous descent to do alone. He explained to Elizabeth: "If you are pushed and you want to survive, everything is possible." She queried his ambitions to climb such dangerous routes and he explained that steep Himalayan faces roused his mountaineering passion—he couldn't explain why. As they looked at photographs of other unclimbed faces in the Himalaya, he referred to Nuptse's West Face as "gorgeous" and talked at length about his dreams of other faces. This was the kind of conversation that Elizabeth loved—reminding her of the old days discussing new routes with Messner and other Himalayan pioneers.

In the second category—the peak baggers—Elizabeth's interest was primarily statistical. There were certainly a lot of them to keep track of in 1997. Basque climber Juanito Oiarzabal knocked off his twelfth 8000er with Manaslu, and South Korean Park Young-Seok claimed an unprecedented five 8000-meter summits in six months. Two Spanish brothers, Jesús and José Antonio Martinez, set themselves the ambitious goal of climbing all the 8000ers within a year of their first success, all without oxygen or Sherpa support. They were now up to three. Elizabeth grilled them about their plan, asking whether they ever tired from such an ambitious schedule. Antonio replied, "Three days' stay here in Kathmandu . . . is enough to recover from a climb." She asked if they ate anything special to help them succeed. "Aspirin," he said.

Italians Sergio Martini and Fausto De Stefani made it to twelve successful 8000-meter summits, if you count a confusing account of their ascent of Lhotse. At first they told Elizabeth they had summited, but when pressed for details, they clarified they had been so near the top they felt they could rightly claim it, though they weren't sure just how close they had been because they couldn't see a thing. Then Young-Seok, who summited three days later, followed the Italians' crusted footsteps in the snow and said they ended at least 150 vertical meters below the summit.

When Martini summited Everest in 1999, he called it his fourteenth. But that included his "almost" summit of Lhotse, which Elizabeth didn't count. However, he did tell her that he might return and climb Lhotse again.

Martini allegedly refused to talk to Elizabeth for two years because of her report on Lhotse, but she insists she used their words, verbatim:

"We think that we did."

"How high did you get?"

"We think that we got very, very close."

"How close?"

"Maybe 50 meters."

So she reported what he said, rather than saying they had definitely reached the summit. They were unhappy about that, but they subsequently went back to Lhotse and climbed it, making sure to get pictures.

Also in 1999, Oiarzabal summited Annapurna as his fourteenth. Oiarzabal told Elizabeth that he would probably return and do some of the 8000ers again. She wryly observes, "It seems to be extremely difficult for climbers to stop climbing."

Another 8000-meter man, Alan Hinkes, had a plan of adding a few more 8000ers to his list in short succession, but it was thwarted by a bizarre mishap. While at base camp for Nanga Parbat in 1998, he inhaled the flour coating on the chapati he was eating, causing a violent sneezing fit that injured his back so badly that he was unable to move because of the pain. He was rescued by helicopter and was eventually hospitalized in Britain. Elizabeth found this amusing, as did Hinkes, since he told the story in all of his lectures, to the delight of his audiences.

And in the third category, the guided clients were just too numerous to talk about, in Elizabeth's opinion. But one season, guided climbs in particular dominated Elizabeth's journalistic reports: 1996 and the much-written-about Everest disaster that killed a total of eleven people. She interviewed many people and did her own analysis of what happened and why. She became convinced that the real fault for the disaster lay with the rivalry between the leaders of two commercial expeditions—Rob Hall, a New Zealand guide and owner of Adventure Consultants, and American Scott Fischer, head of Mountain Madness. Fischer was just getting into the business and, in her opinion, was "elbowing his way in." On the other hand, Hall was a well-established Everest guide who had not succeeded in guiding anyone to the summit the previous year. He had firm rules for himself and his clients about turning back if they hadn't reached the South Summit by 1:30 P.M. He followed his own rules in 1995; as a result, nobody reached the summit, but everyone returned home alive. That was not the case in 1996 when four of his team, including Hall, and five more from other expeditions, perished on their descent in a terrible storm.

Elizabeth believed the tension on the mountain was created by two very different styles of leaders, each with a huge amount at stake. They were on a collision course, with both teams scheduled to summit on the same day. She described Anatoli Boukreev, Fischer's talented Russian guide, as being sadly miscast as a guide. In his book *The Climb*, Boukreev explained that he didn't see himself as a hand-holding kind of guide, but rather a route fixer who would go ahead and prepare the route for the clients to follow. Elizabeth thought this strategy might have worked, except that Fischer was sick that summit day and not in a position to do the hand-holding that clearly needed to be done to get all the clients down safely.

She thought that both Fischer and Hall also may have felt pressure to succeed from organizers of other, less-expensive commercial guide companies, who charged clients around twenty thousand dollars rather than their pricier sixty-thousand-dollar fee. Although the cheaper expeditions provided fewer Sherpa helpers, less bottled oxygen, and virtually no professional guides, there were occasional success stories, and this could have been perceived as a threat.

Elizabeth knew them both well, and she wondered about the adage that familiarity breeds contempt, or at least that familiarity can foster a more blasé attitude about danger. Experienced climbers who later found their bodies on the mountain were surprised that both Hall and Fischer were clad in relatively lightweight clothing and nothing with down. She wondered if their strong track records led them to be overly confident in their abilities at high altitude.

Two weeks later, another tragedy occurred with a team from South Africa claiming Nelson Mandela as its patron. The expedition was plagued with internal distress from the start. Led by expatriate Briton Ian Woodall, it included black South African climber Ed February, who resigned along with two others on the team. Woodall refused to comment when Elizabeth questioned him about the incident. Back home in South Africa, the press went wild and built a story around Woodall's authoritarian leadership style. The three remaining high-altitude climbers, Woodall, Cathy O'Dowd, and Bruce Herrod, made it to the summit on May 25. But this is where the real trouble began because Herrod was slower than the others, perhaps due to his role as a professional photographer. He radioed from the top at 5:00 P.M. but failed to make contact at the scheduled 6:00 P.M. call. His teammates below him in Camp IV did not mount a search for him that night, or the next morning. O'Dowd and three Sherpas continued descending, and Woodall waited till midafternoon, at which time his bottled oxygen ran out and he too descended. Woodall speculated that Herrod must have fallen somewhere above the South Summit.

In the wake of all the Everest activity that season, Elizabeth was sickened by the numbers: eleven deaths out of eighty-seven summiteers. She tried to determine the major causes. Certainly high altitude and unpredictable storms were factors. But she wondered about the number of people on the mountain. In the past, the Nepalese authorities had controlled the number of permits on the Nepalese side, but this season, due to pressure from Nepalese citizens earning a living from expeditions, they opened it up—there were no limits. There was congestion at the Hillary Step as a result, and delays were a serious problem. This reduced the time available to descend before the weather turned.

Elizabeth, like many others, also doubted the skills and strength of many of the climbers on the mountain. American guide Ed Viesturs says there were probably quite a few climbers who shouldn't have been there. As he puts it, "They're competent mountaineers, but Everest is another ballgame."

Her comprehensive reports on the Everest disasters elicited conflicting responses. Some said that by reporting excessively on the expeditions that drew the most public attention, especially disasters involving guided clients, she was distorting history. By reporting on these large-scale disasters that had no serious place in the history of mountaineering, was she missing more important climbs being done at the same time? Some felt that by focusing on these commercial disasters, she stooped to the level of journalistic sensationalism, and fed public misconception about the majority of climbing exploits in the Nepal Himalaya.

Despite the great attention given to Everest, Elizabeth did report on other important mountaineering achievements that season. On Manaslu, the Mexican climber Carlos Carsolio became the fourth person to climb all fourteen of the 8000-meter peaks. His summit day was May 12 and probably would have drawn much more attention had it not been overshadowed by the tragedies on Everest. At age thirty-three, Carlos was the youngest to do all fourteen, and the first to reach the top of four 8000ers in one year: Annapurna I, Dhaulagiri I, and Gasherbrums I and II, all in 1995.

Another climber on the trail of the 8000ers was also on Manaslu. French climber Chantal Mauduit, having summited Pumori and Lhotse on April 28 and May 10, helicoptered to the foot of Manaslu with one Sherpa, Ang Tshering. There was already some doubt about her claim earlier that year to have summited Lhotse. Climbers on the mountain saw her disappear from sight while climbing slowly in the couloir just below the summit and later told Elizabeth that she reemerged from it on her descent rather quickly. They doubted that she could have reached the summit in such a short time. On Manaslu, however, she reported seeing prayer flags on the summit, so Elizabeth did not question her claim. But could Mauduit have obtained this information from other climbers? Was Elizabeth too ready to accept "facts" from climbers?

Mauduit had climbed six 8000-meter peaks by the time she died in the spring of 1998 on Dhaulagiri. When she was climbing up to what would be her fatal camp, other teams were coming down because of deteriorating conditions. But Mauduit stayed on. She had a flamboyance about her—in the colorful things she wore and in the naming of each of her expeditions after a flower. Her Dhaulagiri expedition was called "Sunflower," with sunflowers painted all over her tent. She and Sherpa Ang Tshering were eventually found in that sunflower-painted tent. After an initial assumption that they had both been asphyxiated or suffocated, it was discovered in a post-mortem that Mauduit's neck was broken. As there had been a lot of avalanche debris piled on one side of the tent, it was unclear whether her neck was broken before or after death. Elizabeth thought that Mauduit may have been overly ambitious for her skills, and remembered reports from others that she was a slow climber. But Elizabeth had enjoyed her company, appreciated her charm, and genuinely admired her combination of ambition and determination. She was disappointed it had to end so tragically.

————— ⚬ —————

In the fall of 1996, Dutch climber Bart Vos claimed to have reached the summit of Dhaulagiri I by the seldom-climbed East Face, a route climbed in 1982 by a strong team who then turned back because of extremely dangerous snow on the summit pyramid. Elizabeth doubted Vos; he had lost credibility in 1984 when he made a false claim on Everest. He produced a Dhaulagiri summit photograph, but Elizabeth laughed—it was a night shot with him standing in the snow. It could easily have been taken in the Alps or lower on the mountain—it didn't prove anything about being on the summit of Dhaulagiri, she said. In fact, in her opinion, it didn't even look like a summit shot, just a snow shot. Along with Elizabeth, Dutch reporter Milja de Zwart did some investigative interviewing of other teams on the mountain. Zwart wrote a disparaging article about Vos's claim and was subsequently sued for libel. Vos lost the case. Elizabeth describes him as "a complicated man, as so many climbers are, and I have the feeling that he really believes his claims. I really think he is a Walter Mitty type. He lives in a world of fantasy and he believes he was successful."

In Vos's case, as with other doubtful claims, Elizabeth cross-checked with other expeditions who were on the mountain at the same time. As the inconsistencies grew, she dug deeper. She learned from members of the Dutch expedition that, while still on the mountain, they had promised each other that they would not dispute Vos's summit claim. When they returned to Kathmandu and were interviewed by Elizabeth, they stuck with the agreed-upon line. But following the court ruling in favor of Zwart's article, Vos had three months to appeal the decision against him, and he did not. In Elizabeth's seasonal mountaineering report and statistics, she revised her findings on Vos to state that the claim was almost surely not true. From a mountaineering "interest" point of view, she realized that Vos's claims were not that important, but from the perspective of accuracy, they were. Elizabeth wanted her records to be accurate.

That summer brought a welcome respite from climbing via an invitation from the governor general of New Zealand. July 20 was Hillary's eightieth birthday and she was invited to the party. The festivities included a gala black-tie dinner in his honor. As she flew to Wellington with the Hillarys, each and every passenger who saw Sir Edmund stopped to say happy birthday. After several of these congratulations, he muttered to Elizabeth, "This is getting embarrassing." She was struck once again by his modesty: "What world-famous person would be embarrassed by this!"

That evening they dressed in tuxes and ball gowns and headed to the banquet hall of the governor general's residence, where elegantly decorated tables were placed around the room. Elizabeth wore a deep red, floor-length, Thai silk gown with golden slippers and a matching gold purse. She met a fascinating mélange of New Zealanders: opera singers, sports heroes, business tycoons, politicians, a chief justice of the Supreme Court, and a Maori queen. Among the many greetings and congratulations from around the world, there was a formal message from the queen of England. And then it was time to cut the cake. Much to Hillary's delight, the icing read, "We knocked the bastard off." It was a magnificent evening.

Back in Nepal, high-performance athletes brought some ambitious schemes to the Himalaya in 1997, but perhaps they were too ambitious. Britain's Alan Hinkes planned to add three more 8000ers to his list this season alone: Lhotse, Makalu, and Kangchenjunga. Bringing publicity material that described him as "the most successful high-altitude mountaineer in Britain," he planned to break a one-year record by climbing six of the giants. After those first three, he planned to go on to Nanga Parbat, Dhaulagiri, and Annapurna I in the fall. But bad weather so greatly delayed his ascent of the first one that he was unable to reach the top of the second and he never attempted the third.

A complex plan hatched by Anatoli Boukreev also fell apart. He summited Everest while leading an Indonesian expedition and subsequently summited Lhotse, but his goal to traverse from the top of Lhotse over to Everest and then descend Everest's northern side was not achieved.

His complicated plan required three permits: a British team's Nepalese permit for the south side of Everest, a Kazakh permit for the north side of Everest, and a Russian permit for Lhotse. Everything was in place, but Boukreev made the fatal error of coming back to Kathmandu after Everest with the Indonesians. A week later he returned to the mountains and climbed Lhotse, but he had picked up a lung infection in Kathmandu and was unable to continue his traverse. It was a bitter disappointment.

A happier occasion in the spring of 1997 was the ascent of Everest by Tashi Tenzing, grandson of Tenzing Norgay. A devout Buddhist, he carried a six-inch bronze statue of Buddha to the summit as a message of peace and compassion to the world. With boyish enthusiasm, he told Elizabeth what he saw from the top: "Two great orange balloons in the sky—the setting full moon and the rising sun."

Elizabeth queried him about his reasons for climbing Everest and he explained that it wasn't the same reason as many of his fellow Sherpas—to make a living. He was paying his respects to his grandfather. She liked his answer since she was a fervent admirer of Tenzing Norgay, whom she thought was the greatest Sherpa in the history of climbing. She concluded that Tashi was climbing for the right reason—for passion. Even though Elizabeth claims to have "never been passionate about a single thing," she recognizes it in others, and she approves.

On Christmas Day, 1997, Anatoli Boukreev was killed by an avalanche. He and the Italian Simone Moro had come to climb the South Face of Annapurna I. When they arrived, the snow conditions were too dangerous for the face, so they opted for an alternative ridge route. Moro was in the lead when a cornice fell off, broke into pieces and created a large ice and snow avalanche. He saw it just before Boukreev did and shouted a warning, but neither Boukreev nor their cameraman, Dmitri Sobolev, was seen again. In his subsequent interviews with Elizabeth, Moro said of Boukreev, "I never saw another person with such instinct for mountains. . . . His death is a big loss for the mountaineering world."

American Conrad Anker remembers a more amusing connection between the Russian überclimber and Elizabeth. Boukreev, like Ed Viesturs and Erhard Loretan, had climbed the secondary summit of Shishapangma and had been "bullied" by Elizabeth into going back and getting the real summit. Boukreev had confided to Anker, "I've got to go back—Elizabeth says I didn't really climb it."

Frustration and disappointment permeated Elizabeth's 1998 spring climbing report. Some of the best climbers died in the mountains, and others, she felt, exaggerated their achievements. She described the season as one "marred by false claims of success, a pile-up of frustrated would-be Everest climbers at its South Summit, and several deaths on Everest and Cho Oyu due to ambitions beyond the strengths of unsupported and mostly insufficiently skilled climbers."

In 1998, two Everest hopefuls, the Russian Sergei Arsentiev and his American wife, Francys, were part of a twenty-two-member expedition, of which many were Russians. By the time the Arsentievs went to the summit without oxygen on May 22, all of their teammates had already descended to lower camps. They summited at around 6:00 P.M. and then bivouacked. They survived the night, and the next day were met by another Uzbekistani team on their way to the top. Francys was seen at the First Step at about 8600 meters, standing motionless and not speaking. They gave her some oxygen, sat her down in a comfortable position, and received no response from her, so continued on to the summit. They explained to Elizabeth that they had met her husband just 100 meters below, and he seemed to be okay, so they assumed he was going for help for his wife. Because the Arsentievs had no radios, they couldn't call for help, which would have been readily available if they'd only had the means to ask.

Elizabeth learned that Arsentiev reached camp and turned around to start back up with oxygen, medicine, food, and drink for his wife. He was not seen again. But his wife stayed where she was. On the following day, a South African party came upon her early in the morning, moaning and spasming and saying over and over again, "Don't leave me alone . . . why are you doing this to me . . . I am an American." They too spent some time with her, making her more comfortable and giving her something to drink, but concluded that nothing could be done to save her. The two South Africans, Cathy O'Dowd and Ian Woodall, turned around and descended with one Sherpa while two other Sherpas continued to the summit. By the time the two Sherpas descended, Francys had died. Elizabeth refused to be judgmental in her official report—or in private—as she admitted she didn't know what it was like up there: "That's a judgment that only a person who was there can make."

In the fall of 1998, Sherpa Kaji claimed a controversial speed ascent of Everest, saying that he had raced from base camp on the Nepalese side to the top of the world in 20 hours and 24 minutes, cutting 2 hours and 5 minutes from French climber Marc Batard's record. But Elizabeth thought that Kaji's methods weren't as sporting as Batard's. Kaji had five teammates with him to break trail on parts of the ascent and they all used oxygen (he on the descent). Japanese climber Norichika Matsumoto flatly discounted the account, and explained why to Elizabeth. He had caught Kaji in untruths in a number of instances, and, when he asked for photographic proof, he pointed out that Kaji's photo looked suspiciously like one taken of him on the summit in 1993. Kaji denied it, saying that he always wore the same suit and belt and cap. "More wrangling over silly records," was Elizabeth's comment.

In addition to being sucked into the vortex of these climbing controversies, Elizabeth continued to berate and cajole the climbers she knew to be their very best. American Himalayan guide Dave Hahn remembers a post-climb interview after guiding a trip on the North Ridge of Everest in 1998. She asked him at what altitude they had turned on their oxygen. Hahn replied that his client had been ill for most of the trip and, since the summit was going to be a long shot for him, they had turned on the oxygen at 24,000 feet. Her response to Hahn was blunt: "Huh, bringing the mountain down to your size, I see. . . ." Initially irritated, he asked her if she had ever hiked or skied or climbed herself. She answered, "No, I wouldn't think of it."

On another occasion, Hahn led a women's expedition on Everest and Elizabeth disputed the claim that it was a women's expedition at all, pointing out that Hahn was clearly a man. He recalls that she was particularly hard on a number of the women on the trip because there had been so much media hype about it being a women's expedition. Elizabeth wasn't having any of it.

Sitting in on that interview was a young woman from Washington State, Heather Macdonald. Heather was a climber and had just returned from what she suspected would be her last attempt to climb Everest. She had met Elizabeth before and had observed how overworked she was. She saw her humor and wit and liked her immediately. She jokingly suggested that Elizabeth needed an assistant—why not her? Much to her surprise, Elizabeth accepted the offer.

At their first work meeting, Elizabeth sat Heather down next to her big oak desk and, with little preliminary small talk, began to explain her system of interviewing Himalayan expeditions and climbers. She outlined Heather's role in collecting data and writing up narrative reports to be sent as news to the wire services. Heather agreed to work for two seasons.

The pace was frantic. She was up at 5:00 A.M. writing reports, and making phone calls and running around to hotels to do climbing interviews during the day. As a climber who had previously been interviewed by Elizabeth, Heather found it strange to be on the other side of the fence. Now she was on the side of history, of facts being recorded, of stories getting told. But there was a difference between Elizabeth and Heather: Heather had been there—she had breathed the thin, lifeless air, twisted ice screws, and seen the sunrises and the curvature of the earth from airy bivouacs. Elizabeth hadn't.

The learning curve was steep, but Heather had a good teacher. She watched Elizabeth's direct approach to acquiring information, witnessed questioning so relentless that even the strongest climbers would collapse with their head in their hands, pleading, "I don't know! I can't remember! Your questions are too hard!" And if Elizabeth thought someone was lying about reaching the summit, Heather watched the equivalent of a "seventy-year-old firing squad with pink lipstick, glasses on the end of her nose, and clutching a clipboard."

Sometimes they did the interviews together, but as Heather became more confident, she collected the data alone. Heather sometimes became distracted in ways that Elizabeth never could—for example, she would meet with the Bulgarian Annapurna team, do an interview, and end up spending the rest of the day drinking vodka and exchanging war stories about everything from frozen pee bottles to the age-old question, "How high have you had sex?"

When collecting information, Heather tried to place the climbs and climbers within the larger Himalayan mountaineering perspective.

Together with Elizabeth, she also collected overlapping reports from the disparate teams, carefully interviewing each team and cross-referencing their findings. This was the only way to learn conclusively what had happened, something that was important in the case of fatalities. Grieving families often turned to Elizabeth to find out the truth. Heather and Elizabeth unearthed difficult information from time to time, and had to handle it delicately.

When they weren't interviewing climbers or writing reports, they attended parties together. At one formal reception, Heather arrived a little "fuzzy" from a strong painkiller she had taken, embarrassing Elizabeth. When Heather met U.S. ambassador Ralph Frank that evening, she proceeded to call him Ralph when she was unable to remember his last name. Elizabeth pulled her aside and said, "What the hell is wrong with you? That is Mr. Frank to you, young lady." Elizabeth introduced her to an endless procession of "diplomats, ambassadors, big-name, kingpin climbers." Elizabeth was in her element, surrounded by climbers and commanding their attention. "She could hold court," Heather concludes.

Elizabeth shared her opinions freely with Heather. "She loves Reinhold Messner," Heather says. And "she's also fond of Tomaž Humar." But there were others whom she decidedly did not like, and these she sent Heather to interview. British climber Alan Hinkes was one of them. As Heather explains, "There is only a certain amount of arrogance any one person can tolerate, because she's seen it all. . . . When climbers try and tell her how great they are, she knows what greatness is in a climber!"

They had some amusing experiences as well, such as an interview they did together in the Hotel Gauri Shankar with a man who had just survived an "epic" on Everest. He wanted Heather to videotape the interview but was somewhat of a wreck: his glasses were duct-taped together, his fingers were frostbitten, and his brain seemed addled by his high-altitude experience. He sat next to Elizabeth on the couch while Heather dutifully recorded the event on camera. Suddenly, she noticed his fly was open. What's more, he wasn't wearing any underwear. What to do? She decided to keep mum and continue—he could do the necessary edit when he returned home—rather than ask him to adjust his clothing then and there. She told Elizabeth about it later, and remembers "she was in stitches!"

CHRONICLER OR HISTORIAN? 15

Organizing the media on this one will be like
organizing a goat rodeo.
—Elizabeth Hawley

The biggest news out of Nepal in years was the discovery of George Mallory's body high on the slopes of Everest in 1999. It captured the world's news media like no other story since the 1996 disaster on Everest. The drama and mystery of the disappearance of George Mallory and Andrew Irvine in June 1924 had lived on in people's imaginations because it was not known whether they had reached the summit. If they did, they would have been the first by more than two decades before Hillary and Norgay. They were last seen by their teammate Noel Odell on June 8, 1924, "going strong for the top" high on the North Ridge.

Numerous expeditions had set out to find the men's remains over the years, to no avail. But in 1999 a predominantly American team led by Eric Simonson arrived well prepared for their mission to find the bodies and, perhaps, Mallory's camera. It was thought that the camera could determine once and for all whether they had reached the summit. The searchers faced a lot of skepticism regarding their quest to find "a needle in a haystack," but they had the help of historian Jochen Hemmleb, who had studied the fateful climb extensively and thought he knew where the search should be concentrated. He was right. They were successful on the first day, when Conrad Anker came upon Mallory's body at 8230 meters on a 30-degree slope not far above the site of Mallory's Camp VI.

Expedition leader Simonson was a good friend of Heather Macdonald, who still worked as Elizabeth's assistant. After the discovery, but before the news had been released, Heather received a note from him: "Heather, I am sending this barrel with Schelleen to give to you. Guard it with your life. Very important. Eric." The precious barrel contained old letters by Mallory and his wife, his boot, clothes, goggles, altimeter, and pocketknife, and some rope, but no camera.

Of course, Heather had to tell Elizabeth, and Elizabeth could not believe it. She needed proof. But once she got it, Heather laughingly recalls, "I thought she would need rescue breathing, she was so excited." Elizabeth remembers the day, too: "Of course, I got excited—I'm an historian, damn it!"

But "historian" is not the title Elizabeth typically applies to herself. Usually, she is adamant about being a "chronicler" and not an historian because, she says, her lack of experience in the mountains precludes having a true historian's perspective.

So which is it? Chronicler or historian? Is it really a lack of mountaineering experience that holds her back from the larger role of mountaineering historian? Or is it the responsibility such a role would demand?

The media frenzy in Kathmandu following the discovery of the body was incredible. Elizabeth had the inside track as she was one of the few people qualified to comment on the find. When she regained her composure from the initial excitement, she pronounced, "Organizing the media on this one will be like organizing a goat rodeo." She interviewed Simonson and other members of the team, including Conrad Anker.

Dave Hahn, also on the expedition, remembers that when Elizabeth finished the formal interview regarding the expedition, she asked Hahn and Simonson to remain a bit longer. With the others gone, she lost all semblance of formality and wanted to know every detail of the discovery. Hahn was captivated by her obviously genuine fascination with high, cold places and the people who made history there.

Also very interested in the discovery of Mallory's body was British mountaineering historian, author, and Everest expert Audrey Salkeld. Many at the heart of the mountaineering community compared Elizabeth and Salkeld, with some suggesting that Audrey was far more learned about mountaineering. She'd been into the mountains and often explored the nuances and motivations of climbing—with fellow climbers. Others maintained that Elizabeth didn't examine the fine details of climbing the way Salkeld did, which they thought precluded Elizabeth from understanding the motivations behind the climb rather than just the facts. They believed her job of delivering "one-liners" for Reuters more or less predetermined that the content would be somewhat superficial, regardless of the real depth of her interest. But comparing the two women may have been unfair because their jobs were very different. As a reporter, Elizabeth had to produce stories and information on a regular basis for a wide variety of publications under tight time frames, while Audrey focused on larger writing projects that allowed her much more time for research into the nuances of climbing.

According to British filmmaker Leo Dickinson, both Elizabeth and Salkeld were acknowledged authorities on Everest, so he thought it was odd that the two women didn't know each other well or have some kind of a relationship based on their mutual interest. He says Salkeld's personality lacked the hard, journalistic shell that Elizabeth had developed, suggesting that Salkeld's lighter touch produced better stories. But on the other hand, Salkeld wasn't a journalist. Dickinson recognizes that Elizabeth's authority evolved naturally as she acquired her knowledge base over time: "I doubt that she set out to be queen of Everest at the beginning."

Salkeld herself felt somewhat wary of Elizabeth. She had met her socially a number of times in Kathmandu when she was there in connection with projects such as the IMAX Everest film. She had found Elizabeth guarded, and thought Elizabeth was trying to catch her making mistakes. But Salkeld concedes that many referred to her as Elizabeth's "British counterpart," and that this comparison probably irritated Elizabeth. Salkeld acknowledges Elizabeth's vast network of climbing friends and doubts there is a person alive who knows more climbers than Elizabeth. However, she believes that doors opened more easily for Elizabeth because of her connection with Hillary.

Despite the discussions and disagreement about her role, one Kathmandu institution did view Elizabeth as the ultimate historical authority on their particular tradition. The popular Rum Doodle bar and restaurant had large plywood boards on which successful Everest climbers could sign their names, entitling them to free meals from that time onward. But before the restaurant allowed the climber to sign on, they always called Elizabeth for verification. One May evening she received a call from Rum Doodle asking her to verify the names of three Poles who had been to the summit not long before. She agreed on Pawlowski and Maselko, but the third name was Kudelski. She was horrified! Kudelski had summited but died during the descent. Someone had decided to impersonate him and be eligible for free meals for the rest of his life.

The Sherpa climbers were a group that Elizabeth kept a particularly close eye on. In 1999, a new record was created by Babu Tshering, also known as Ang Babu, when he spent twenty-one hours and fifteen minutes on the summit of Everest cozied up in a small tent with a mattress, sleeping bag, and walkie-talkie. Prior to this stunt, in 1995 he became the first person to do two round-trips from the base to the top within a time span of ten days. Then, in the spring of 2000, he broke another record by going from base camp to the summit in sixteen hours and fifty-six minutes. She spoke with him back in Kathmandu and learned that his goal had been to climb it faster, but bad weather and tough trail-breaking conditions had slowed him down. She asked him about his future goals, but he was coy, evading her (usually successful) prodding. This brought his Everest ascent record to ten.

Another well-known climbing Sherpa was Sungdare Sherpa, who was the first Sherpa to climb Everest five times and who later became an alcoholic. Elizabeth is pragmatic about this weakness: "It's cold up in Khumbu where they grow up and they have lots of nice warm parties where they drink rakshi. The way the Sherpas drink is that you never finish the glass before it's filled up again." She explains that when Sungdare succumbed to alcohol, people didn't want to climb with him anymore. He spent all of his money on booze and finally committed suicide because he could not support both his family and his drinking. Climber Ang Rita was also dependent on alcohol. An exception to this pattern was Apa Sherpa who, by spring 2004, had been up Everest fourteen times. Apa's motivation appeared to be less for fame or records than "to add to the family wealth." He also said he hoped his children would find careers in fields other than mountaineering because of the huge risks. When she asked him when he was going to retire, he said not until he turned fifty-five. In Elizabeth's estimation, "He's no boozer. He's a clever fellow."

Elizabeth knew the climbing Sherpas well and felt that some foreign climbers treated them badly. She was certain the Sherpas resented the fact that foreigners got all the publicity overseas. They were well aware that their names appeared at the bottom of climbing reports, if at all. When Elizabeth interviewed some expeditions, she would be told the names of the summit climbers, and then would have to ask, "What about Sherpas?"

"Oh yes, there were two Sherpas there."

"Who were they?"

"Oh, I don't know . . . one was Mingma, one was Dawa."

"What were their second names? Most Sherpas have two names."

"I don't know. We just called him Mingma."

Frustrated, she found that only a few climbers were concerned about these details; most just didn't care about the Sherpas.

And on the mountains, conflicts again arose between the commercial expeditions and individual climbers. Russell Brice, an experienced New Zealand commercial expedition leader, was increasingly frustrated by the time, expertise, and supplies he was expending each year to rescue people who weren't part of his teams but who were on the mountain at the same time. As he saw it, climbers were coming in with enough energy and expertise to do their climbs successfully—as long as everything went well and the weather cooperated. But they weren't strong enough to deal with the unknown and, as a result, he was frequently asked to assist.

Someone who didn't appear to need any assistance was Tomaž Humar. Elizabeth watched his career with keen interest, and in the fall of 1999 he succeeded on the South Face of Dhaulagiri. In Elizabeth's estimation, it was a remarkable achievement for several reasons: even though he hadn't reached the summit, he climbed a route that was terribly steep and dangerous, and he did it entirely solo. Reinhold Messner was said to have taken a look at the face in the seventies and turned around without making an attempt. Humar went straight up the middle, reaching 7900 meters before he veered off to the ridge. As he told Elizabeth, "I knew if I went higher, I would die." All of this was observed through long lenses by his nonclimbing support team, so there would be no confusion or doubt about his success, as had been the case with his countryman Tomo Česen. No fixed camps, no bottled oxygen, no partner—Elizabeth was impressed.

But at least one respected climber, fellow Slovenian Andrej Štremfelj, had some words of caution about Humar's achievement. He pointed out that Humar was claiming his route as the first ascent of the face, but in fact the first ascent had happened almost eighteen years earlier in 1981 by Humar's own Himalayan mentor, Stane Belak. He added that both routes ended at the same spot, which is where both climbers decided to descend, relinquishing the summit in exchange for their lives. In addition, Štremfelj wondered aloud about the possibility that Humar chose this dangerous route because it had "sensational" value and therefore would add to his reputation, his career, and his sponsorships. Elizabeth thought this was a little unfair because she felt that Štremfelj himself participated in highly dangerous and "sensational" climbs.

As to the similarity of Humar's and Belak's routes, she hauled out the two files filled with supporting documentation, detailed descriptions, and photos. The 1981 file had a photo with both the intended route and the actual route carefully drawn in. Humar's file also had a photo with the intended line and the actual line. She pointed out that the 1981 actual line was substantially to the right of Humar's line. She described Humar's climb as the "middle" of the South Face, while she phrased the 1981 climb as the "right side" of the South Face. It was a matter of interpretation, but she was adamant that the routes were different. She added that part of the value of a "landmark" climb was the influence it had on the next generation of climbers: "Surely, Humar's climb did that."

As the century drew to a close and Elizabeth entered her seventy-sixth year, she was at the height of her reporting career. American climber Carlos Buhler remembers watching her take notes from a Russian expedition attempting the North Face of Jannu. It was a small, dank room, not clean by Western standards, and there she was, looking prim and proper, chasing down the news in her methodical way. She tried to clarify points that were difficult to understand, and to put them into a formula that others could not only understand but would be able to use in the future.

Buhler watched with admiration as she probed for all the information, getting the dates, the altitudes, and the reasons for this and that just right. He had the impression that she wasn't doing it for her own use or enjoyment, but for others to use—all they had to do was ask. He could imagine a climber from Spain or the United States showing up at her house sometime in the future, asking for information. She would offer up some facts, a photograph, and some specific tidbits of information about why the Russians used a camp at this altitude and why it gave them problems. Or perhaps she would suggest it would be better to try a little lower or a different spot. "I think she wanted to truthfully further the sport," he says.

Many climbers agreed that she was at the top of her game. She had a tremendous grasp of Himalayan climbing that few other individuals could muster because she'd talked with literally hundreds of climbers coming through town. She'd seen all the character types: the amazing athletes, the wizened old guys, the young hot shots. She'd spoken with them when they were fresh and fired up going off to their climbs, and again when they were exhausted and either triumphant or defeated on their way out.

She'd interviewed people about style and controversies and issues concerning Himalayan climbing at a level that would leave most people, and even some climbers, oblivious to the content and context. But her long career in Nepal and focus on only Himalayan climbs worked against her, according to some. She hadn't lived outside Nepal in such a long time that some thought she failed to grasp where climbing was at in the global context; she only understood it from the perspective of the climbers who came to Nepal. These critics were sure she could not perceive what rock climbing in Yosemite was all about, or how Alaskan climbers transferred their knowledge to the big walls in the Himalaya. Elizabeth agrees. Not only does she admit to making no attempt to educate herself about climbing in other parts of the world, she adds that she has no interest.

The most persistent criticism was that she could never possess a comprehensive understanding of climbing because she hadn't done it. She didn't know what it felt like to go outside in frozen boots to chop ice to make water. Every bit of information she had was secondhand.

Elizabeth's critics insisted that firsthand experience was essential for a true, deep understanding of climbing. Even though she had access to all of the climbers, it was in an urban setting. People were different when they were showered and dressed and in Kathmandu, even after a long trip. When they sat down with the official chronicler of Himalayan climbing, they were on their best behavior. A lot played out in those moments of the interview, and it would be hard for her to understand all the nuances of truths and untruths, as their egos were so much on the line. Some believed she needed to see the climbers in their element—the mountain—to reach this true understanding of what they were saying and why they said it.

But most within the mountaineering community agree that she is a powerful individual. The facts and statistics she gathers might be of little importance to most people in the world, but they are important to mountaineers. Some climbers worry that her word is considered gospel—they think it is dangerous to put so much power in one person's hands and they are wary of taking her opinions as blanket truths. They are equally wary of saying these things in public. Why? Because they love her, they respect her, and they are afraid of her. "She is making a mosaic of all the climbs," Messner says. He believes Elizabeth's power lies precisely in her ability to synthesize so many facts. Though she makes the odd mistake, she is only human, he says. When she makes a mistake, she corrects it. "She's a first-class journalist!"

She is also a tough journalist. American filmmaker Michael Brown recalls an interview that she did with Jim Nowak, climbing leader of the 1998 Pumori expedition, where she appeared to be passing judgment. Nowak was making some observations about the receding ice, changing climate, and the fact that the route, as well as climbing in the Himalaya in general, was getting harder. She responded that perhaps it was the standard of climbing that was getting lower. "I'll never forget the stunned look on his face," Michael says.

Austrian climber Kurt Diemberger is more magnanimous in his praise. He has been coming to the Himalaya for decades and has a long-standing friendship with Elizabeth. His image is of a woman who is at the very epicenter of some of the most exciting climbing—and discussions about climbing—on the planet. He calls her simply "the living archive."

Then the inconceivable happened.

As an increasing number of commercial expeditions came to climb peaks that had "commercial" interest, Elizabeth spent more and more time reporting and recording Everest climbs, many of which held little interest for her due to the repetitive nature of the routes, the use of oxygen at low altitudes, and the general sameness of it all. But there were still a few climbers coming to the Himalaya to do things that interested her.

The Frenchman Jean-Christophe Lafaille was one of these. In the spring of 2000 he soloed a direct line up the Northeast Face of Manaslu, summiting on May 5. Another was the talented and persistent Russian Valeri Babanov, who established a new line on the 6799-meter Kangtega, a peak southeast of Everest.

But on Everest, the crowds were huge, and climbers were continuing to get on each other's nerves. An incident occurred between an American Discovery Channel correspondent, Finn Olaf Jones, and Briton Henry Todd. Jones was filing Internet reports from base camp that so irritated Todd he threatened to kill Jones. Elizabeth heard several versions of the goings-on; one was that Todd beat Jones up. Todd denied that he even touched Jones and only shook his fist at him. Whatever the truth, Jones fled—and in the act of doing so, he fell and injured himself on a boulder. Threats of legal action flew back and forth, and Jones was finally whisked away by helicopter. Elizabeth was disgusted.

The death of Babu Chhiri at the end of April 2001 stunned the climbing world and all of Nepal. Elizabeth heard that he had left Camp II to take some photos, and when he had not returned five hours later, his brother Dawa went out to search for him. At midnight they found footsteps in the snow that ended at a crevasse, where they found his body. A media frenzy ensued with reports around the world. His body was brought to Kathmandu and displayed at the Sherpa Center, where it was covered with flowers and ceremonial scarves. Many dignitaries, including the prime minister, came to pay their respects. Tributes poured in—even King Birendra sent a condolence message to his family: "Babu's demise has caused irreparable loss to the nation and to the mountaineering fraternity."

Elizabeth was saddened by the death of this charming man. He had wanted to build a school for the children of his home village, Taksindu, which was still without a school. And he had finally told her that his next great project was going to be a traverse of Everest from the northern slopes to the top, down the southern side to base camp, and then an immediate reversal from south to north—an itinerary that Elizabeth described as "a plan that only Babu Chhiri could even contemplate."

Elizabeth had seen many climbers die over the years. Most often she was not emotionally involved with their lives, but every now and then she grieved, such as when German climber Robert Rockoff died in the fall of 2003 while leading an expedition on Ama Dablam. He had gone ahead of the rest of his team to inspect some old fixed ropes and must have lost his balance and reached for a rope that either came out or was rotten. He fell the entire distance of the route and was found dead at the bottom of the mountain. She remembered him as a man full of energy, someone who was patient and kind. A year later she could not speak about him without her voice breaking.

Another death that distressed her was of the French snowboarder Marco Siffredi. She first met him in 2001 when he climbed and snowboarded Everest. In 2002, he returned to attempt a snowboard descent of the much more direct Hornbein and Japanese couloirs on the North Face. He came to see her before he went and she recalls that he was "very nice, interesting, and so very, very young—twenty-three years old. He was doing remarkable things and he was excited about his opportunities—his life was in front of him. He just disappeared!" His parents came to Nepal a few months later and explained that they had had two sons; one died in a climbing accident in the Alps, and the second in Nepal. "That one really did sadden me," she says. "He was so full of life and had tremendous enthusiasm. It was a wonderful world for him and it just went up in smoke!"

On the subject of disabled climbers, Elizabeth was impatient at best, seeing them as stunt climbers. Her reaction to the blind American climber Erik Weihenmayer's plans to climb Everest after his Ama Dablam ascent in 2000 was classic: "I hope for his sake that he doesn't come back." Despite her comment, he did come back in the spring of 2001—and he succeeded in his quest. He told her that he had spent two and a half months from his arrival at base camp, had worked incredibly hard along with a devoted team, and had taken it day by day. He explained to her that one of the biggest challenges was negotiating the complex ladder system in the Khumbu Icefall. Jumping crevasses was difficult because he couldn't see how far to jump. She asked him why he would want to go to Everest when he couldn't even see the view. Erik responded that he experienced great pleasure from the wind and sun on his face and the feeling of rock and snow under his feet. An enormous amount of vicious cynicism and black humor had accompanied Erik up the mountain, with one climber commenting that he hoped to "get the first picture of the dead blind guy." But it didn't faze Erik. Guided by a bell on his teammate's rucksack and his own determination, he stood on the summit on May 25. Although she may have been cynical initially, Elizabeth was professional with Weihenmayer. American filmmaker Michael Brown, who created an award-winning film about the climb, remembers her interview with Weihenmayer as respectful: "She didn't pass judgment—she was classy."

Another event that many considered a stunt—a ski descent of Everest—captured Elizabeth's imagination and admiration. Slovenian skier Davo Karničar made what she considered to be the first honest-to-goodness, top-to-bottom ski descent of the mountain. He used oxygen for his climb but not on the descent. As Elizabeth observed, "What for? He was going too fast." For the steepest sections of the descent, he sidestepped with his skis down the slopes. When she inquired about his method of avoiding avalanches, he replied, "I go very fast." At less than five hours, his descent was actually faster than he expected. Elizabeth thought this was "quite an accomplishment."

Elizabeth is hard to pigeonhole. She didn't consider the ski descent to be a stunt, yet a blind climber attempting Everest, or a speed climber was. Who created these rules of engagement on the mountain? Did she come to these conclusions individually, based on her like or dislike of someone's personality? Did she have some kind of guideline for what she considered admirable? Who influenced her opinions?

Sometimes her opinions were influenced by reports she heard from the climbers she trusted, including Italian climber Simone Moro. Such was the case on Lhotse in 2001. Nineteen-year-old British climber Thomas Moores was on a U.S.-led commercial expedition and fell at about 8300 meters. Moro was in his tent at 7950 meters at the time, preparing for his summit bid the next day. As soon as he heard shouts about the fall, he left his tent and proceeded to try to rescue Moores. He was the only one who did. Everyone else at the same camp apparently refused to help. Elizabeth was sure it was because they didn't want to jeopardize their chances of reaching the summit the next day. Moro found Moores at 7:00 P.M., picked him up, and carried him to his tent, where he gave him water and administered first aid. Moro arranged for some Sherpas to carry him down the next day and then realized that he was too tired to try for his own summit bid. Other climbers on the mountain said that Moores was inadequately prepared with backup support and, when things went badly for him, it meant that another team (in this case—another individual) had to cover for him.

She heard of more antics on the French Annapurna I expedition commemorating the original 1951 climb, on which Lionel Terray had played an important role. Nicolas Terray, son of the famous climber, was the leader of the 2001 climb. The team, which included Christophe Profit, didn't get far on the mountain. Profit came back earlier than the rest of the team and contacted Elizabeth because he wanted to talk. He told her that he was upset because when the leader decided to retreat, he (Profit) asked to continue, believing he had found a safe alternative. He wanted to try it alone with two Sherpas. They made a stab at it and Profit actually got quite high, but one of the Sherpas was worried about frostbite and had to descend. Profit was sure it was worth another try, but when he got down to base camp the decision had been made to abandon the mountain. The expedition was declared over. Profit was forbidden to stay back and try again. He was infuriated, and wanted Elizabeth to know.

When Elizabeth met the leader, Nicolas Terray, a few days later, she asked him why he hadn't allowed Profit to stay on longer to try to finish the route. Startled by her question, Terray was irritated and abrupt with her. About two weeks later she received a fax from him: "I think you are not allowed to judge it. It's not your problem even if you think it . . . I have been a little bit disappointed by your attitude." She wrote and rewrote her response letter, communicating in what she considered to be her most diplomatic style: "I don't know about my being allowed to judge that decision, but you must be aware that I try to learn and understand as much as possible about any climb and the reasons for putting an end to them before a summit has been reached. Furthermore, I also understood that in the case of your expedition the decision to stop was not unanimous, and I wanted to learn your point of view. . . . Please accept my apology if my questioning was too sharp."

But despite her attempts to understand the nuances of the members of this particular expedition, she sometimes questioned the motivations of climbers and their obsessions with peaks, routes, and records. She tried to put it into a bigger context—just how important were these climbs?

In the larger arena of Nepal, the political situation was beginning to affect climbers and trekkers, and Elizabeth heard more frightening stories all the time. In the fall of 2001 six young Spanish students intent on climbing Manaslu were camped at a village named Soti when about two hundred terrorists, later identified as Maoists, surrounded them. They were forced to give up every rupee they had. The Maoists injured one of the porters and confined the climbers to their tents all night. After this incident, the climbers flew by helicopter to Kathmandu to flee the area, as well as to get more money from home to continue the expedition. They expected the Nepalese government to cover the cost of the helicopter, but the government said no. To add insult to injury, they returned to the area, having been promised police protection, but found none.

Another team approaching Shringi Himal, a 7187-meter mountain northeast of Manaslu and not far south of the Tibetan border, was turned back by a group of Buddhist monks who said they could not continue up the Shringi River because the gods living on Shringi's west side would bring violence to them if they did. Despite considerable discussion, the monks wouldn't back down, so the team changed their objective and went to a different side of the mountain—one the monks didn't object to. After some time and effort, they abandoned their climb only to find that local villagers had stolen about five thousand dollars' worth of belongings from their advance base camp.

Along with the rise in crime, Elizabeth continued to be concerned about the growing number of permits issued for expeditions. Especially in the spring season, when the weather was supposedly a bit more favorable, the numbers kept increasing. According to her, the Nepalese authorities briefly tried to limit the number of permits, but they received resistance from trekking agents and Sherpas who made their living from expeditions. Ama Dablam was a typical example of this. As Elizabeth explained, it was a beautiful mountain and not difficult, so everyone wanted to climb it. As a result, there were often too many expeditions on the peak at the same time, causing long waits on certain parts of the ridge. There was also overcrowding at the camps; people were sometimes forced to skip camps and go up the mountain too quickly, which caused physiological problems and accidents.

There were a lot of complaints to the ministry from teams returning from the mountain, but "it goes in one ear and right out the other," Elizabeth said. Foreign exchange was a highly prized commodity in Nepal, and mountaineering was an important foreign exchange earner.

Then the inconceivable happened. At 4:00 A.M. on the morning of June 2, 2001, Elizabeth received a telephone call from Lady Hillary in Auckland, asking her if it was true that the royal family had been massacred. New Zealand reporters had called Sir Edmund for comments. Elizabeth immediately called the Reuters correspondent in Kathmandu, who confirmed the news. An army source had informed him just hours before.

On the evening of June 1, at the regular royal family dinner gathering at the palace, Crown Prince Dipendra took up his personal weaponry and proceeded to slaughter his parents, two siblings, two aunts, two uncles, a cousin, and finally himself. The house of Shah was finished. In one fell swoop, a dynasty that had ruled Nepal for ten generations was wiped out.

Pandemonium broke out as news of the massacre spread like wildfire throughout Kathmandu and the world. Meanwhile, what remained of the royal family was in a state of shock and upheaval. The problem was that the crown prince, successor to the throne, did not die immediately of his self-inflicted wounds. Would tradition require them to crown a known murderer? In the end, they did just that, and an unconscious Dipendra was declared king, while the former king's brother, Gyanendra, was appointed regent until the new King Dipendra could carry out his duties. Dipendra died two days later and Gyanendra became king. The people of Nepal had had three kings in four days.

In those four days, no explanation for the massacre was forthcoming from the palace. Like the rest of Kathmandu, Elizabeth wondered why they didn't immediately issue a statement to stop the rampant speculation and fear-mongering that swept the city. But when she realized what they had faced with the delayed death of Dipendra, she understood their hesitation. In the meantime, massive conspiracy theories floated about: the Maoists, Gyanendra, or the queen mother was behind it. Elizabeth knew the physician who was taking care of the royal family, and was convinced that the official version—that it had been Dipendra—was the truth.

As the story came out, it became known that the prince had developed a serious drug and alcohol dependency and was angry with his family because they had used every argument they could muster, including talk of revoking his right of succession, if he persisted in marrying the woman he had chosen. This unstable man had also accumulated an arsenal of weapons that included an M16 assault rifle capable of firing up to a thousand rounds a minute, a 9 mm submachine gun with 900-rounds-per-minute capacity, a single-barrel shotgun, and a 9 mm pistol. The public was shocked to learn that the palace had allowed such a situation to develop—an unstable prince with unlimited access to drugs, booze, and weapons, and a seemingly unresolvable conflict with his family over the woman he loved. Escaping the slaughter was Queen Mother Ratna, the woman chosen by Crown Prince Mahendra against his father's wishes fifty years earlier. She had been in another part of the palace when the bullets flew.

There was considerable instability in Nepal following the massacre, some of which was caused by the palace's delay in telling the truth. Political leaders hoping to gain some headway fueled the conspiracy theories, as did the Maoists, who hoped to further their own cause. In Kathmandu, a curfew was imposed from 3:30 P.M. to 5:00 A.M. Outside Elizabeth's door, demonstrators taunted and threw stones at police, burned tires and effigies in the road, and demanded an investigation. The funeral procession carrying the bodies to the royal cremation site at Aryaghat was lined with demonstrators shouting and throwing stones, and condemning Birendra's murder. These demonstrations confirmed the affection the population had for Birendra and the queen. Elizabeth found this confusing, as just ten years earlier huge crowds had protested against the royal couple, calling the king a thief and the queen a whore.

Once again, Elizabeth was witness to a royal cremation at Pashupatinath Aryaghat, the site reserved for royals. Only this time it wasn't just the king. It was the king, queen, princesses, and princes, all aflame at once. Elizabeth, and others gathered on the far side of the Bagmati River, watched a complete dynasty go up in smoke.

On June 4, fifty-three-year-old King Gyanendra was crowned, for the second time in his life. In 1950, Gyanendra, then four, had been crowned after King Tribhuvan fled Nepal for India and left him behind. The last of the Rana prime ministers had crowned the child, but there was no international recognition of this boy king. Now crowned king of Nepal for the second time, Gyanendra named his wife, Komal, queen. She had been seriously injured in the bloodbath, with a bullet missing her heart by millimeters. The citizens of Kathmandu were exhausted. In one week they had witnessed ten funerals.

By fall, the numbers of climbers coming to Nepal had fallen drastically. Elizabeth attributed this to several factors: the massacre, fear of terrorism in Nepal, fear of aviation safety following the September 11 tragedy in the United States, and downturns in the economies of

Western Europe, North America, and Japan. In Nepal, the Maoists and the security forces had agreed on a ceasefire, but the Maoists broke it in November and a number of villages across the country—even in a remote part of the Kathmandu valley—experienced violence. The death toll continued to rise. The king declared a state of emergency, allowing the Royal Nepal Army to be unleashed on the Maoists. Two platoons of soldiers were flown by helicopter to Namche Bazaar, and the army was active around the country trying to flush out the Maoist fighters. Elizabeth acknowledged that it was no longer safe to travel about the country.

But the climbers who were still in the country needed to travel through the valleys to get to their peaks, and Elizabeth heard many frightening stories about Maoist attacks. In some cases, it was impossible to determine whether the bandits were Maoists or just Nepalis posing as rebels, but climbing teams were regularly stopped by armed men demanding money and cameras. Near the village of Tashigaon on the way to Makalu, a six-member Spanish team led by Edurne Pasaban encountered a group of men and boys armed with rifles, pistols, and grenades. The team was relieved of about 5000 rupees and several cameras. A Swiss team in the same area was stopped by Nepalis carrying rifles but not wearing Maoist uniforms, who demanded 10,000 rupees and one camera. In the Solu Khumbu, two days of incidents at the Lukla Airport damaged the airport tower, and a bank was robbed. The number of trekkers dropped, business was down, and Elizabeth's Tiger Tops earnings suffered as a result.

Elizabeth had frequent reminders from her nephew Michael that she could, at any time, return to the United States and live with him and his family. In light of the deteriorating situation in Nepal, she appreciated the offer, but she declined. She tried to assuage his fears by telling him that Kathmandu itself had a noticeable presence of security forces: armed soldiers and police were on patrol and manning checkpoints. She added the reassuring news that "only a few small bombs" had caused damage, and they were not in central areas. She felt secure going out in her Volkswagen Beetle with her driver, and she stayed home at night.

The climb that captured Elizabeth's attention in the spring of 2002 was by Jean-Christophe Lafaille and the equally talented Basque climber Alberto Iñurrategi. They succeeded in a traverse of Annapurna I's long summit ridge, starting from Glacier Dome in the east and crossing to Roc Noir and Annapurna's three summits—each more than 8000 meters—and then back again. They did it with no bottled oxygen or Sherpa support. They spent five exhausting days at high altitude, negotiating avalanche-prone slopes, technical climbing, steep rock, cold bivouacs, and the ever-debilitating thin air.

Lafaille met with Elizabeth after this expedition, and noticed that she preserved all the most important pieces of information, for historical purposes and for future climbers. She diligently probed for information on camps, oxygen, fixed ropes, distances, and times. They poured over photographs and agonized over the details. Lafaille, knowing the significance of this climb within the context of the history of Himalayan climbing, was happy to accommodate her. He wanted the story to be correct. They talked at length about changes in the style of climbing in the Himalaya, and about the style Lafaille and Iñurrategi had employed.

She also saved him a lot of money by mediating in some bureaucratic wrangling. The Nepalese authorities wanted the expedition to pay multiple fees because of the number of subpeaks on the summit ridge, but she talked them out of it and the fee was limited to one summit. He believes they became friends through this post-climb meeting; however, "She stayed Miss Hawley for me and not Elizabeth."

Another climber undeterred by the turmoil in Nepal was the Russian Valeri Babanov, who was making a solo attempt on a pillar on the South Face of Nuptse. He would have to climb about 2500 meters, much of it highly technical, with huge snow mushrooms to overcome at the top. He reached 6300 meters four weeks after his arrival, but then ran out of fixed rope, time, and energy. He told her he hoped to return the following year to finish it. The famous South Tyrolean climber Hans Kammerlander, who had climbed seven 8000-meter peaks with Messner, was on a route nearby and told Elizabeth that he, too, wanted to return, perhaps to combine forces with Babanov. But Babanov wasn't interested. Although Babanov's climb was an impressive effort, she pointed out that it wasn't alpine-style climbing, which was generally defined as climbing a route in a single, continuous push without external help, without preplaced fixed rope, camps, or caches of supplies, and without reconnoitering the route.

In her seasonal mountaineering report, Elizabeth didn't express an opinion on either climb, simply stating the facts. She didn't evaluate which climb was more important because she didn't think it was her place to do so. She continued to call herself a mountaineering chronicler, not an historian, explaining the difference: "A historian is someone who goes beyond the facts and looks at the context, and then comments on that context." She stuck with the formula that worked for her, and kept to the facts in her interviews, believing that they spoke volumes. She thought the reader should decide which climbs had greater significance.

Not everyone agreed. Christian Beckwith, former editor of the *American Alpine Journal*, reflects that as he tried to move the *AAJ* from a journal of record to a journal of significance, he found Elizabeth moving in the opposite direction: "She has chosen to be a record keeper of record rather than significance." In his view, her reports were written for a wide audience and although she interviewed Babanov, she reported on Kammerlander because of his star power. She defends herself, stating that her reports for fall 2002, spring 2003, and fall 2003 record Babanov's climbs as well as Kammerlander's. It was on the third attempt that Babanov and Vladimir Suviga succeeded. Her report on their climb comprised a comparatively extensive eight paragraphs, providing detailed commentary on the difficult and technical climb as described to her by Babanov. Comments from other climbers were included; according to Tomaž Humar: "The future of climbing belongs to the new Russian teams around Valeri Babanov." But she pointed out that admiration for Babanov was not universal—at least one unnamed American climber remarked disparagingly that Babanov used bolts on his climb. Elizabeth didn't comment either way.

But journalists continued to find fault. British journalist Lindsay Griffin corroborates Beckwith's opinion that Babanov's climb on Nuptse was the most significant climb of the season, and Elizabeth's report didn't acknowledge this. He says there have been other occasions where she missed important climbs because they've been outshone by ascents on a bigger peak or by a better-known person. Others agree that there have been many fine climbs in the Himalaya during her tenure that did not register on her radar. They argue that she focuses too much on well-known routes, well-known peaks, and well-known people.

Robin Houston disagrees, maintaining that Elizabeth has always been fair and objective in her reporting, not aggrandizing famous climbers more than unknown climbers, not focusing on an expedition just because of the height of the mountain, and not stooping to the level of gossip. Elizabeth was completely unaware that such discussions and evaluations of her work were taking place.

Let's face it—Liz is an icon!
—John Roskelley

I n 2003, Elizabeth's attention was focused on Everest. In fact, the
entire world was captivated by the fiftieth anniversary of the first
ascent of Everest—and Kathmandu was the center of that attention. And it wasn't just climbing magazines that focused on the story:
mainstream magazines published lengthy pieces, other media ran major
stories, and numerous books were written. The Nepalese government and
other organizations sponsored a series of events in Kathmandu that kept
Elizabeth busy. All the important Everest climbers were in town: Hillary,
Messner, Junko Tabei, Apa Sherpa, and many others were driven around
the streets of Kathmandu in horse-drawn carriages. They were received
by King Gyanendra and Crown Prince Paras. In a grand gesture, the king
conferred honorary Nepalese citizenship on Hillary in recognition of
his historic climb, as well as his work in the ensuing decades bettering
the lives of people living in the Everest regions by building schools and
hospitals and restoring monasteries.

For Elizabeth the timing of this big celebration couldn't have been
worse. It was May 29; expeditions were pouring back from the mountains and she had a mountaineering report to write. Yet the Hillarys
were staying downstairs and there were innumerable events to attend.
In each twenty-four-hour period, she felt she had at least twenty hours
of work to do. Frankly, the whole thing made her grumpy.

It started badly for the Hillarys, too. Just prior to the celebrations in
Kathmandu, Hillary had been in Delhi, where it was frightfully hot. The

Indian government had staged a number of elaborate events, including the inauguration of Sir Edmund Hillary Marg and Tenzing Norgay
Marg, two streets near the New Zealand embassy. With temperatures of
42 degrees Celsius, the heat made Hillary ill and he was not fully recovered when he arrived in Kathmandu for the celebrations. To Elizabeth's
alarm, when he and Lady Hillary came off the plane, Sir Edmund was in
a wheelchair! The press was there in full force, but he looked terrible, so
Elizabeth whisked them away to her house and put him immediately to
bed. Lady Hillary laughingly recalls that neither Elizabeth nor Ed lasted
much longer than two or three hours at a time at any of the events that
week. "They're quite united in that," she says, "they get tired." And when
that happens, "She gets testy."

The celebration went on for several days. Another important climber
at the 2003 celebrations was, of course, Messner. Elizabeth marveled
at the change from when she first met him in 1972. "He looked like a
country bumpkin. . . . Now his English is so much better, his style of
dress is the latest, his hair is the latest, he lives in a small castle, he is a
member of parliament, and when he came to Kathmandu for the Everest
celebrations, he was given absolutely VIP treatment."

One of the more memorable Everest events was a cultural performance presented by the Himalayan Trust Sherpas. The defining moment
was the presentation of a bottle of Chivas Regal, bottled in May 1953. A
Scotsman, dressed in a kilt and playing bagpipes, marched up the aisle
to deliver the bottle. Elizabeth enthused: "A Scotsman marching in a
kilt—there's something about his leg action, his knee action that's just
frightfully impressive!" Along with the bottle, he brought some rather
large checks from Chivas Regal for the Himalayan Trust. Later that evening, the Hillarys and Elizabeth admired the checks and just managed
to resist opening the Chivas.

On the highest mountain itself, climbers crowded in with thirty-five
teams on the Nepal side and thirty-four on the Tibet side. All but two
expeditions were climbing standard routes via the South Col from Nepal
and the North Col from Tibet. One of the two was an attempt to climb a
totally new route on the East Face in Tibet. Briton Ian Woodall and his
South African wife, Cathy O'Dowd, both previous Everest summiteers,

were turned back from their preferred route, so they went on to tackle the difficult, unclimbed East Ridge. They were turned back from this as well, but Elizabeth lauded their attempts to try something new while the majority crowded the standard routes.

And crowds there were. At base camp on the Nepal side, a sizeable village of tents sprang up, housing 441 climbers plus their base camp staff and Sherpas, as well as climbers for Lhotse and Nuptse—totaling at least 600 people. There were satellite communications tents, cafés, a medical clinic, a massage parlor, and tee shirt shops. Including the trekkers in the area, Elizabeth estimated the population probably equaled or exceeded that of the area's largest village, Namche Bazaar, at 850. Messner paid a visit to base camp and reported back to Elizabeth that he was horrified at what he saw. Expedition leaders told her that they felt the skill level of guided climbers was lower that year than ever.

The hullabaloo and crowding elicited strong statements from some of the veterans as they reminisced about the good old days. Hillary and Messner both voiced emphatic views that the numbers of permits for Everest should be restricted for reasons of safety and pollution. Others thought that climbers should be required to have summited at least one 8000-meter peak to qualify for an Everest permit. Elizabeth listened to these opinions, but was struck by something she read in *TIME* magazine, written by a man she had originally urged not to return to Everest—the blind American climber, Erik Weihenmayer. He wrote: "Many climbers argue that Everest is no longer an epochal achievement and that the conga lines of climbers waiting for a shot at the summit are degrading a once pristine environment... the door to Everest's slopes has been blown wide open, and some critics speak of the death of great adventures ... but Everest's history is the modern world's history with all its challenges and abuses, and the unparalleled opportunities for human endeavor ... we cannot step back and close the mountain, for retreat would annihilate the modern age's greatest gift to humanity: the freedom of an individual to choose his own path. ... " Elizabeth admitted that he had a point.

Two of those choosing their own paths were young Sherpa climbers Pemba Dorje and Lhakpa Gelu, who were challenging the speed record for an Everest ascent from the Nepal side set by deceased Sherpa Babu

Chhiri in 2000 when he climbed it in sixteen hours and fifty-six minutes. Pemba Dorje claimed an ascent of twelve hours and forty-five minutes, and then Lhakpa Gelu topped that with ten hours and fifty-six minutes. But all was not well in Sherpa land. Pemba charged Lhakpa with lying. Lhakpa countered with supporting documents from the government liaison officer posted at base camp. Their competition would continue the following year.

John Roskelley returned to the mountains, this time with his twenty-year-old son, Jess. Elizabeth knew and respected Roskelley from previous expeditions, but that didn't blunt her sharp response to his current objective—Everest by the South Col with oxygen. She wanted to know what they were doing that was different. Jess explained that he was trying to be the youngest American to climb Everest. She responded, "So what? Are you going to do a new route without oxygen?" John didn't take it personally, but his son was taken aback. Roskelley explained to Jess, "Nothing impresses her. She interviews the greatest climbers in the world and they don't tell her what they *intend* to do, they just *do* it." In fact, when Jess returned, having climbed it, she did show a somewhat more appreciative attitude regarding his achievement, and they got along just fine.

Roskelley wonders whether Elizabeth became jaded by working with some of "greatest climbers in the world." He knows she had a strong interest in them, but adds, "They're human beings, and highly focused human beings at that—some could say egotistical." He suspects part of her cynicism came from personal disappointments with some of the prominent personalities and emphasizes, "Anybody who has done what she has done for years, dealing with prima donnas and putting them in their place, deserves respect." He maintains that Elizabeth knows "ten times more about climbing than all these other climbers." His final analysis is, "Let's face it—Liz is an icon!"

Although Elizabeth's compound remained an oasis of calm, Nepal seethed with unrest. In March 2003, a serious incident took place at Beni Bazaar, a town of five thousand situated astride the main trail to the Annapurna trekking area. Thousands of Maoists descended from the hills to launch a sudden attack on the army post, the district police post, the jail, and the bank. Mortars and other weapons filled the night. Many of those fighting on the Maoist side were adolescents who had been kidnapped and forced into battle. The casualties were in the hundreds.

As the political situation in Nepal continued its downward slide, the threat of external forces intensified. Nepal became vulnerable to influences from China, India, the United States, and others. The Chinese, for the time being, remained silent, but the Americans did not. A statement from the American government urged action: "The palace and the parties must unify—urgently—under an all-party government as the first step to restoring democracy and presenting a unified front against the terrorist insurgents."

There was an enormous amount of distrust and paranoia within the country. According to *Nepali Times* editor Kunda Dixit in his April 2 editorial, "The Maoists, the parties, and the palace are each suspicious of the other two ganging up." He observed that while the king was off hugging babies in the districts, the political parties were marching on the palace. A new low was reached in May when Prime Minister Thapa resigned after just eleven months in office. It was generally thought that the king had asked him to resign because of his inability to advance the peace talks between the Maoist leaders and other party leaders.

Street protests increased and injuries were commonplace. Party leaders were arrested and the Maoists continued to wreak havoc in the districts. The king appointed Sher Bahadur Deuba to succeed Thapa and charged him with the same task he had given Thapa—get the party leaders and Maoists talking seriously about peace. Public morale dropped still further in response to this news, as the king had dismissed Deuba from the same job just two years earlier due to "incompetence in not being able to conduct the general elections on the stipulated date."

The Maoist insurrection increased its intensity, not just against the security forces but also against civilians. They kidnapped children, extorted officials and trekkers, blocked roads, destroyed property, beat and maimed farmers who didn't cooperate, forcibly recruited men, women, and children into their militia, and used weapons, land mines, and bombs to maim and kill. Local citizens' resistance groups formed in some villages, but members were at risk of violent retaliation. "Disappearances" increased sharply. Nepal was once again on the international radar screen as groups like Amnesty International and the United Nations expressed concern. Aid agencies from around the world pulled out of rural regions because of inadequate security for their staffs. The World Bank stopped releasing funds to complete the construction of a highway.

Elizabeth, who wasn't directly affected by the instability, couldn't avoid it completely. Demonstrators marched in the street outside her door. She read fresh horror stories in the two local newspapers each morning. She heard disturbing reports from the Himalayan Trust staff and others in the remote districts. But still she stayed in Kathmandu.

*She is like the last of the Mohicans; after the last
has gone home she is still out there on her own.*

There is only one Miss Hawley, but with a personality as complex as hers, she has inspired many different impressions and conflicting opinions, mostly from men. They respect her, fear her, care about her, criticize her, and vie for her attention. In conversation, Elizabeth occasionally reveals intimate details and private opinions, often in stark contrast to the opinions of others. But what does she hold back? And there are so many inconsistencies—for example, many people call attention to her modesty, yet there is a note of pride as she talks about famous friends and points out the many awards and medals decorating her home.

The first of those awards came in 1990 as a special citation from Reuters. To make the presentation, Reuters brought in a couple of correspondents who became increasingly flustered as she kept interrupting their speech with corrections. In her undiplomatic style—hilarious to those who know her well—she hollered out dates, places, and people that they had incorrect. The correspondents got through the ordeal somehow, and she took home a brass plate for her efforts.

In 1994, the American Alpine Club honored Elizabeth with their prestigious Literary Award. She's modest about this one, saying it was likely Ad Carter's doing. Carter was the long-time editor of the *American Alpine Journal*, a close friend of Elizabeth, and recipient of her seasonal mountaineering reports for many years. The two friends were similar in their attention to detail. If he was responsible for her award, it was a case of one meticulous record keeper honoring another.

On April 8, 1998, she received a letter from the Swiss-based King Albert I Memorial Foundation offering her a medal for "outstanding services to the mountaineering world." The letter went on to list a few previous recipients: Lord Hunt of Britain, Brad Washburn and Dr. Charles Houston of the United States, Wanda Rutkiewicz of Poland, and Erhard Loretan of Switzerland. "I am deeply honored and frankly astonished. . . . " she began in her acceptance letter, which ended with "I accept this distinction with great pleasure, however underserved it may be." And so she went to Switzerland to bring back a sizeable chunk of gold. While sightseeing in the Alps, she was surprised that her mountain perspective had changed. The Alps were "gorgeous, but they sure looked small."

The summer of 2003 brought yet another award, this one from Nepal itself. The Sagarmatha National Award from the Ministry of Tourism was given to her for her contribution and efforts in promoting Nepal's mountains and adventure tourism to the world for forty-three years. In her acceptance speech, she spoke less of her own work than her dreams for the future of climbing in Nepal, particularly for the Sherpas.

In 2004 Elizabeth was presented with the Honorary Queen's Service Medal for Public Services in recognition of her years of work with the Himalayan Trust and as honorary consul for New Zealand. The ceremony took place in the elegant Dynasty Room in the Yak and Yeti Hotel in Kathmandu. The room was filled with finely laid tables, a seating area for guests, and a small stage for the actual medal ceremony. She was surrounded by her closest friends.

Caroline McDonald, the New Zealand ambassador to Nepal, thanked Elizabeth, saying, "The help Miss Hawley has extended to New Zealanders in difficulty in Nepal, often under tragic and difficult circumstances . . . is greatly appreciated." Several of the guests spoke about Elizabeth's positive impact on their lives as a mentor or a colleague. Kathmandu publisher Kunda Dixit explained how she had been an important influence in his career as a journalist, and for all journalists in Nepal—Elizabeth had given him valuable experience filling in on her Reuters beat when she was away.

But it was the words of Sir Edmund Hillary that meant the most to her that day: "Elizabeth Hawley is a most remarkable person and a woman of great courage and determination . . . I know of no person who is more highly respected in the diplomatic or public community in Nepal and I can think of no one who more highly deserves consideration for a New Zealand Royal Honor."

Elizabeth was thrilled. Her diplomatic skills being more finely honed than when the hapless Reuters staff presented their award fourteen years earlier, she accepted graciously. She regaled those in the room with a few stories—some of sad or frustrating experiences, but also some that made for happy memories. In the end, she looked around the room and thanked her friends who had helped her "every step of the way"—a woman of pride, and modesty.

Even as Elizabeth was being recognized for her many contributions in Nepal, her biggest reputation was still in the mountaineering world. As she reflected on the many great, and not so great, climbs she had been privy to over the previous forty years, a few stood out as having "raised the bar." To her mind, the outstanding Everest events were: Mallory in 1922 and 1924, Hillary and Tenzing in 1953, the Americans in 1963, Messner and Habeler without oxygen in 1978, Bonington and the South West Face in 1975, Messner solo in 1980, the Kangshung Face in 1983, the first woman's ascent in 1975, and the first winter ascent in 1980. She said another bar would be raised when the East Ridge is finally climbed. But it wasn't just Everest climbs that impressed her; she also cited Tomaž Humar in the far west of Nepal on Bobaye and again on Dhaulagiri, and she singled out the first ascent of the West Face of Nuptse: "Babanov has done some pretty good stuff."

The Sherpas' climbing goals were a source of frustration for her. In her speech at the Sagarmatha Award ceremony, she had encouraged them to go for lower peaks and unclimbed routes because that's where she saw the future of climbing in Nepal. But she was doubtful it would happen since most Sherpas were not that technically skilled and would not go on a high mountain without fixed ropes: "They are perfectly willing to fix the ropes but they don't want to be on a mountain where there is no escape route." She pointed out that foreign climbers on technical routes didn't take Sherpas as a rule, citing Babanov as an example. She thought there were only one or two Sherpas who were highly skilled, although many were very fast. For most of them, it was a job.

Even among foreign climbers, the lesser-known peaks were rarely attempted, and this also concerned her. For the most part, these climbers went for Ama Dablam, Everest, and Cho Oyu: Ama Dablam because it is visible from the valley, Cho Oyu because it is the easiest of the 8000ers and climbers can thereby bag an 8000er, and Everest because they want to be a hero. She found these predictable objectives discouraging.

As to future great projects in the Nepal Himalaya, Elizabeth is reluctant to engage in this discussion at first, but eventually she grows animated imagining the possibilities. The great event, in her opinion, will be the Horseshoe Traverse—up Nuptse, across Lhotse, and then up Everest. She explains there are two critical issues: technical proficiency and high altitude. She thinks the elegant way to do it is not the way the Soviets did Kangchenjunga with pre-placed high camps, but with one continuous push. Who can do it? Who are the great ridge climbers? She thinks Boukreev probably could have done it; he was good at high altitude, strong as an ox, and fast. In his younger years, Messner probably could have done it. She settles on Jean-Christophe Lafaille and Alberto Iñurrategi as possibilities; maybe they could do it together. Being able to function without oxygen for extended periods will be important, since the Horseshoe Traverse will take days to do. She enjoys imagining these great projects paired with great climbers.

She thinks the East Ridge of Everest is another big objective. A Japanese team attempted the route and found it to be a long, difficult, dangerous ridge. An Indian woman, Santosh Yadav, also attempted it, as did Cathy O'Dowd's team. Other good projects, in Elizabeth's opinion, although far less difficult technically, will be the traverse of the whole ridge of Annapurna and a grand traverse of Kangchenjunga—without the use of support camps.

Concerning face climbs of the future, she thinks the enormous East Face of Everest surely contains some challenging—perhaps actually unclimbable—lines. There is still the top part of the middle of the South Face of Dhaulagiri—the part that Humar didn't do—as well as the North Face of Makalu. Some very good climbers have taken a look at it and a few are inching toward it, but it is still there for the taking. And there are many wonderful routes on the smaller peaks. As for the strongest face climbers, she names Humar and Babanov.

Reflecting on her own life and career, Elizabeth seems unable to identify any particular moments or periods that stand out. "I've never been passionate about a single thing!" she exclaims. She doesn't think she had a "golden age"; it was all golden to her. At least there were interesting moments throughout. Of course, there were dull periods too, but she thinks her patience paid off. Even though she had to report endless ascents of Ama Dablam, occasionally someone came through her door with something special.

Pushed a little, she finally relents and picks out a few high points: the two years of solo travel were memorable because she could go where and when she wanted, she met interesting people along the way, and she saw places she wanted to see. Her studies in modern European history were good preparation for these travels, and her natural curiosity ensured many interesting adventures. She'd also been intrigued by the politics of the time: Israel was just being created, there were Marines on the beaches of Beirut, and mobs had just torn apart Faisal and his prime minister in Baghdad. She also fondly recalls favorite verandas she encountered on her way: Isak Dinesen's veranda outside of Nairobi, the St. George Hotel veranda in Beirut, where gossip and intrigue exchanged hands each day before lunch, and the veranda in Khartoum where she enjoyed languid conversation and whiskey with Mamoun El Amin.

Asked again whether there has been any one thing in her life experience thus far that really excites her, she snorts, "Nothing!" But then she admits that she has been interested in climbing statistics and the comparative analysis of success rates among nationalities, seasons, ages, sexes, and Sherpa vs. non-Sherpa support, as well as the average death rate per season. She and Richard Salisbury worked together to amalgamate all of her files, notes, and letters into one massive database that contains the details of more than four thousand expeditions, thirty-six thousand climber biographies, and extensive analysis of trends. Published in October 2004 by the American Alpine Club as *The Himalayan*

Database: The Expedition Archives of Elizabeth Hawley, her life's work is now a lasting legacy.

At age eighty, Elizabeth doesn't foresee any changes in her situation, as long as her health holds out. Although she has handed over some of the Himalayan Trust work to Ang Rita Sherpa, she continues to oversee it. And the mountaineering reporting still dominates her time. The most pressing problem for the future is that she hasn't groomed anyone to replace her.

Eventually, her collection of files and books on mountaineering will go to the American Alpine Club; their future value is hard to fathom. They'll be used by climbers researching new routes and writers researching mountaineering books. She points out that the files contain a wealth of stories. For the present, people have been mostly interested in her lists and statistics contained in the database, but she maintains the real value is in the files.

Messner worries about the future of her work because he doesn't see anyone stepping in to help her. He can see she is aging and won't be able to continue indefinitely. It already takes her longer to do things and she is more forgetful, but she wants to continue. Sometimes she wishes there were eight days in the week.

There are some who speculate that self-reporting via the Internet will replace her work, and Elizabeth herself doubts there will be a need for someone like her in the future. But she knows that self-reporting is not the same thing as the diligent fact-finding she has practiced. British journalist Lindsay Griffin agrees that self-reporting won't provide a complete overview.

Elizabeth sounds a little sad as she projects the future of the chronicling of Himalayan climbing. She is sorry to see the passing of objective journalism and the approach of the end of her career.

She has had discussions with magazine editors about a succession plan, but it has proven elusive so far: the person who succeeds her ideally should have a good knowledge of the history of climbing in Nepal, have access to the Ministry of Tourism, know the dozens of trekking agents, be familiar with the city of Kathmandu, speak English, and, most importantly, be able to obtain a work visa for Nepal. She points out that mountaineering reporting is not enough to be granted a visa; some other valid work in Nepal will also be necessary. There is probably no one person who can replace her. It will take a team. Some who know her worry that she might have a case of "founder's syndrome," and might be reluctant to trust someone else to take over her life's work. Under someone else's guidance, the work will almost certainly not be done the way she does it. She knows that she needs to begin grooming someone immediately. In a letter to Christian Beckwith, she confirmed, "I certainly want to do whatever I can to make it possible for someone to succeed me." But she knows it will not be an easy problem to solve. She evolved into her position over almost five decades, whereas her replacement will have to be proficient in the job immediately.

Despite her acknowledgement of the importance of her moun-taineering work and the almost impossible task of replacing her, she is modest about her contribution to the climbing community, saying, "I've been on the fringe and they let me in from time to time." Her main con-tribution, she thinks, is some "good, accurate records." Apart from a few exceptions, she seems ambivalent about being considered a "friend" of climbers and doesn't see herself as a friend of the climbing community. In fact, she doesn't believe there *is* a climbing community. She sees such great diversity in climbers' backgrounds, motivations, and skills that they don't form a cohesive group in her mind. Her consistently high standards force her to ask, "Who is included in the group? Is it the dilettantes? The peak baggers? The explorers?" She challenges anyone to lump Sandy Hill Pittman and Anatoli Boukreev into the same community.

But others think there *is* a climbing community, and they see Eliza-beth at its center—at least in Kathmandu. David Breashears concludes that Kathmandu without Elizabeth Hawley just wouldn't be the same. He remembers how it changed when Jimmy Roberts was no longer there, and again when Boris died, pointing out that Elizabeth has endured through it all: "The Ministry of Tourism changed, the pilots came and went, the trekking agencies changed from one to 150, but the one consis-tent force that never wavered is Liz." She is like the last of the Mohicans; after the last has gone home she is still out there on her own.

Though she may distance herself from climbing friends, they speak warmly of her. Breashears maintains that Elizabeth is one of those people for whom it is worth being tolerant of their eccentricities: "We are tolerant because we really love her, and we love her because she never gave up on us in a way—she carried the flag and there's something about the gravity that she created for the climbing community. She gave the disparate groups—the Czechs, the Japanese, the Poles, the Bulgarians—a dialogue."

He explains that climbers have a unique kind of camaraderie and they travel in the same circle. Over time, Elizabeth became part of that circle; it was her extended family, passing through Kathmandu. She has seen them come and go, and a great many of them have died. What has it been like for her to watch the planes take off for Lukla, wondering whether the climbers on board will return? Perhaps the detachment she maintains is part of her emotional survival strategy. It may help to distance herself from people whose life expectancy is always in question.

Climbers have expressed their affection for her in different ways. Bill Crouse bought a gas-powered heater for her car so that she'd be warm when she drove around Kathmandu. He says he did it because he wanted to take care of her. Breashears thinks a lot of people would love to help take care of her, but her brusque manner discourages it. Carlos Buhler ruminates, "The great beauty of surviving all these years is getting back to see your friends—and I would count her as one of my friends." But it has always been on Elizabeth's terms. He has never been to her house, never had dinner with her, never gone to a monastery with her. His only interaction with her has been over climbing, and he regrets that.

Tomaž Humar fairly explodes with affection for her: "She's the one for me . . . she is the most important person, maybe even more than Hillary . . . she knows everything about anyone in the mountains." In his rapid-fire, nonnative English, he expounds: "She has rich stories . . . she has the opportunity to meet the most remarkable people in the history of alpinism . . . I think nobody on the planet has the same chance like she has." If Tomaž had a chance at another life, he says, he would want to spend it as she has—to be present with all the mountaineering legends. "She is like a Nepal ritual for me—one cup of tea is enough for my soul."

Humar showed his regard by getting in touch with Elizabeth shortly after he experienced a crippling accident at home in Slovenia, where he fell off his roof into a trench, breaking several bones and crushing his heel. From his hospital bed, he arranged for a friend to call her on her birthday, November 9, to wish her a happy day and let her know about his accident. This act of kindness touched Elizabeth, although she downplays it in her typical fashion: "Now of course this is charming for me, but why he bothers I just don't understand. . . . Maybe he runs out of people to talk to, so he calls up Kathmandu. Nice guy, I like him!"

Despite her obvious independent streak, many people have wondered about her life alone in Nepal. Was she lonely—or simply alone? Was she strong—or vulnerable? Frances Klatzel once asked her why she chose to stay in Kathmandu. Elizabeth answered it was because she learned something every day—the answer of a true journalist. Frances thinks she is someone who is content and happy with her own company. Elizabeth agrees, insisting that she enjoys her own company immensely and is certainly never lonely. But a good friend, Mal Clarbrough, remembers stopping by her apartment one Christmas to find her quietly weeping at the dining room table, alone. It broke his heart to see her.

British author Ed Douglas sees Elizabeth as a sad personality—someone quite alone in the world. He remembers a visit when she answered the door demanding, "What do you want? Everybody wants something from me." When he told her he had just come by for a visit, she seemed surprised and delighted to share a cup of tea with him. He believes she safeguards her privacy in a hard shell—a protective covering for something vulnerable inside.

Mary Lowe, wife of Everester George Lowe, doesn't see Elizabeth as lonely, but rather as a "lone" person. She thinks that many people probably think of her as a romantic personality, someone living a romantic life in a romantic place filled with romantic people. Mary doesn't think Elizabeth would actually count many of these romantic personalities as her friends. In fact, even though she has known Elizabeth for twenty years and regards her as a friend, Mary remains guarded: "How she regards us is a different matter. She receives us with warmth, if it is convenient to her. Otherwise, we have to wait." Messner emphatically counts her as a friend, and a friend of his family, saying, "She is a really good woman."

Many people consider Elizabeth Hawley to be their friend, yet she doesn't reciprocate, stating categorically that, apart from two or three climbers with whom she is close, the rest are acquaintances. Could this be true? Could all those people be mistaken? Breashears, Humar, Buhler and Lowe—is it just wishful thinking on their parts? Is Mary Lowe correct in thinking that any kind of relationship must be on Elizabeth's terms? Or is Ed Douglas's speculation closer to the truth—that by opening up to friendship she might expose a soft underbelly?

Heather Macdonald felt reasonably close to Elizabeth when they worked together, but she admits there was always a wall she could not penetrate. However, as Heather grew closer to her, working together day in and day out, she stopped seeing Elizabeth as a "famous Himalayan reporter" and began to relate to her as a friend—someone who could be complimented on her earrings or who would commiserate over computer frustrations: "Her computer would drive her nuts!" Heather thinks Elizabeth is selective about who she lets in, and she's also convinced that her heart was broken at some point, perhaps by Jimmy Roberts or Edmund Hillary, and that she subsequently "closed down emotionally."

Elizabeth admits she does have strong feelings for Hillary: "Ed is one of my oldest friends and I am one of his greatest admirers. I guess it's mutual!" But she takes care to provide historical context, noting that they have worked together since the mid-1960s, dispensing funds for hospitals, bridges, schools, and so on for the people of the Solu Khumbu. They have been through a lot together: "Good times, such as the recent fiftieth anniversary of the first ascent of Mount Everest celebrations . . . and tragic times, such as when I flew by helicopter to tell him that his wife and daughter had been killed in a plane crash. Sir Edmund Hillary is the finest person I ever met."

He is effusive about her, too: "I think Liz is a special person . . . always exceptional. We relied on her. She is a remarkable woman. I have a great respect for Liz and I'm very fond of her."

Yes, but what of the famous rumored affair? Elizabeth laughs at the question: "I'm sorry to disabuse anybody—and I'm telling the truth—but we didn't." She knows the rumor has been out there for years and she thinks it stems from the fact that he has often been a guest in her apartment and her companion at so many parties. But, she insists: "Believe me, we didn't." After his first wife was killed, she admits there was a brief period when she speculated about what his next move would be. Nonetheless, she confesses, "I'm not the marrying type and I couldn't have fulfilled the role of diplomat's wife as beautifully as June has."

As Elizabeth looks back at her alleged—and real—love life, the only men she'll admit to having considered settling down with are Micky Weatherall and Mamoun El Amin. The rest of the rumors—Jimmy Roberts, Eric Shipton, General Mrigendra, Andrzej Zawada, Don Whillans—"It's a resounding no! There's nobody else except the ones that I confessed to . . . oh, well there's Krishna Bhadurai, who used to drive me home sometimes." With Elizabeth Hawley there is always more to the story.

With thirty-some years of educating herself and apprenticing as a world traveler and curious observer, Elizabeth had prepared herself well for the adventure that awaited her in Nepal. When she flew into Nepal for that first election, she was purposeful about it. She wasn't going there just to take a look, but to experience an important moment in world history. What she saw was something special; she saw that she could create a life for herself in Nepal that would be unique. She could avoid a life of sameness and obscurity in New York, and become someone special and important—and needed.

During more than forty years in Kathmandu, Elizabeth created that unique life. Beginning with her interest in politics, she evolved into a major player in a new kind of travel industry. Her insatiable curiosity brought her into the world of mountaineering, where she became an expert. And through her highly placed contacts and hard work, she greatly influenced the work of the Hillary Trust. By leaving New York, she became part of a circle that included royalty, prime ministers, and explorers. She learned about, and became an important personality in, a global mountaineering community, despite her reluctance to acknowledge its existence. In Nepal, she could afford a life of comfort, with a personal staff to attend to all her basic needs. She could entertain lavishly. As Heather Macdonald says, "I couldn't even dream her life." All of this took courage; she went to a place in the world at a time when it wasn't easy for a single woman to make her way. She went with no steady job and no contacts. Like many of the mountaineers she admires, she was a pioneer.

Elizabeth plans to stay in Kathmandu. There are people there who care for her. The next generation is there to support her. There is respect and reverence for the elderly in Nepal, and Elizabeth is now one of those people.

She won't leave Nepal because she has a purpose there; she has work to do and she's making a difference. This is what keeps her alive. Her nephew suggests there are many ways of evaluating a life—some people make money, and some people make a difference: Elizabeth has made a difference. He adds, "I would put her on my list of heroes, and it's a very short list."

Always pragmatic, Elizabeth concedes that she would leave if the Maoist regime became too difficult or in the extreme event of the city being destroyed by a natural catastrophe, but she asks, "What would I do? As long as my health lets me stay on, I want to stay. I want to live independently. I am useless in someone else's house. I can't cook. I suppose I could set the table and I do know how to make drinks. I'd just be in the way." Then, looking at me with dark, steady eyes, she states, "The jobs I do couldn't be done anywhere else—it's Nepal."

And in that statement I suddenly understood the depth of her love for her adopted country, and for the life's work she has created—and for which she will always be remembered.

BIBLIOGRAPHY

Periodicals and Newspapers

Outside Online, December 23, 2003

Rock & Ice, November/December 1994

———September 2004

Gripped, Summer 2004

American Alpine Journal, 1970, 1992

Bangkok World, August 17, 1970

Kuala Lumpur Straits Times, August 25, 1970

The Sunday Times, May 28, 1972

Daily Telegraph, London North Edition, November 16, 1972

San Jose Mercury News, August 19, 1973

The New York Times, October 6, 1979

Peninsula Times Tribune, August 3, 1983

Alpin Nr. 9

TIME, October 27, 1986

Nepali Times, April 12, 2003

General

Band, George. *Everest: 50 Years on Top of the World*. London: Harper-Collins Publishers Ltd., 2003.

Bernstein, Jeremy. *The Wildest Dreams of Kew: A Profile of Nepal*. New Delhi: Book Faith India, 1998.

Bista, Dor Bahadur. *Fatalism and Development: Nepal's Struggle for Modernization*. Calcutta: Orient Longman Ltd., 2001.

Bonington, Chris. *Everest the Hard Way*. London: Hodder & Stoughton, 1976.

———. *The Everest Years: A Climber's Life*. London: Hodder & Stoughton, 1986.

Boukreev, Anatoli, and G. Weston DeWalt. *The Climb: Tragic Ambitions on Everest*. New York: St. Martin's Griffin, 1997.

Curran, Jim. *High Achiever: The Life and Climbs of Chris Bonington*. London: Constable & Company Ltd., 1999.

Diemberger, Kurt. *Spirits of the Air*. London: Hodder & Stoughton, 1991.

Douglas, Ed. *Chomolungma Sings the Blues*. London: Constable & Company Ltd., 1997.

Douglas, Ed, and David Rose. *Regions of the Heart: The Triumph and Tragedy of Alison Hargreaves*. London: Penguin Books, 1999.

Fanshawe, Andy, and Stephen Venables. *Himalaya Alpine-Style*. London: Hodder & Stoughton, 1995.

Gregson, Jonathan. *Blood Against the Snows: The Tragic Story of Nepal's Royal Dynasty*. London: Fourth Estate, 2002.

Hawley, Elizabeth, and Richard Salisbury. *The Himalayan Database: The Expedition Archives of Elizabeth Hawley*. Golden, CO: The American Alpine Club, 2004.

Hemmleb, Jochen, Larry Johnson, and Eric Simonson. *Ghosts of Everest*. Seattle: The Mountaineers Books, 1999.

Hillary, Edmund. *View From the Summit*. New York: Simon & Schuster Inc., 1999.

Hillary, Louise. *A Yak for Christmas*. New York: Doubleday & Company Inc., 1969.

Humar, Tomaž. *No Impossible Ways*. Ljubljana: Mobitel, 2001.

Iyer, Pico. *Video Night in Kathmandu And Other Reports From the Not-So-Far East*. New York: Knopf, 1988.

Krakauer, Jon. *Into Thin Air*. New York: Villard, 1997.

Leuchtag, Erica. *Erika and the King*. New York: Coward-McCann Inc., 1958.

Peissel, Michel. *Tiger for Breakfast*. London: Hodder & Stoughton, 1966.

Roskelley, John. *Stories Off the Wall*. Seattle: The Mountaineers Books, 1993.

Simpson, Colin. *Kathmandu*. New Delhi: Vikas Publishing House, 1976.

Suyin, Han. *The Mountain Is Young*. London: Jonathan Cape Ltd., 1958.

Tenzing, Tashi. *Tenzing Norgay and the Sherpas of Everest*. Camden, ME: Ragged Mountain Press, 2001.

Venables, Stephen. *Everest: Kangshung Face*. London: Hodder & Stoughton, 1989.

———. *Everest: Summit of Achievement*. New York: Simon & Schuster Inc., 2003.

Webster, Ed. *Snow in the Kingdom: My Storm Years on Everest.* South
     Freeport, ME: Mountain Imagery, 2000.
Wielicki, Krzysztof. *Crown of the Himalaya: 14 X 8000.* Krakow:
     Wydawnictwo, 1997.

INDEX

ABOUT THE AUTHOR

Bernadette McDonald is Vice President, Mountain Culture at The Banff Centre, Director of the Banff Mountain Film Festival, now in its 30th year, and founding Director of the Banff Mountain Book Festival. She is a founding member of the International Alliance for Mountain Film and was an invited speaker at the General Assembly of the United Nations in 2001 to launch International Year of Mountains.

Bernadette is the co-editor of *Voices From the Summit: The World's Great Mountaineers on the Future of Climbing*, editor of *Extreme Landscape*, and co-editor of *Whose Water Is It*. She is author of *Ritratti dalle vette, alpinisti fotografati da Craig Richards*, published in Italian in 2003.

Photo by Donald Lee, The Banff Center

Bernadette is an avid climber, hiker, and skier and travels the world in search of warm rock and deep snow.

THE MOUNTAINEERS, founded in 1906, is a nonprofit outdoor activity and conservation club, whose mission is "to explore, study, preserve, and enjoy the natural beauty of the outdoors...." Based in Seattle, Washington, the club is now the third-largest such organization in the United States, with seven branches throughout Washington State.

The Mountaineers sponsors both classes and year-round outdoor activities in the Pacific Northwest, which include hiking, mountain climbing, ski-touring, snowshoeing, bicycling, camping, kayaking, nature study, sailing, and adventure travel. The club's conservation division supports environmental causes through educational activities, sponsoring legislation, and presenting informational programs.

All club activities are led by skilled, experienced instructors, who are dedicated to promoting safe and responsible enjoyment and preservation of the outdoors.

If you would like to participate in these organized outdoor activities or the club's programs, consider a membership in The Mountaineers. For information and an application, write or call The Mountaineers, Club Headquarters, 300 Third Avenue West, Seattle, WA 98119; 206-284-6310. You can also visit the club's website at www.mountaineers.org or contact The Mountaineers via email at clubmail@mountaineers.org.

The Mountaineers Books, an active, nonprofit publishing program of the club, produces guidebooks, instructional texts, historical works, natural history guides, and works on environmental conservation. All books produced by The Mountaineers Books fulfill the club's mission.

Send or call for our catalog of more than 500 outdoor titles:

The Mountaineers Books
1001 SW Klickitat Way, Suite 201
Seattle, WA 98134
800-553-4453
mbooks@mountaineersbooks.org
www.mountaineersbooks.org

The Mountaineers Books is proud to be a corporate sponsor of The Leave No Trace Center for Outdoor Ethics, whose mission is to promote and inspire responsible outdoor recreation through education, research, and partnerships. The Leave No Trace program is focused specifically on human-powered (non-motorized) recreation.

Leave No Trace strives to educate visitors about the nature of their recreational impacts, as well as offer techniques to prevent and minimize such impacts. Leave No Trace is best understood as an educational and ethical program, not as a set of rules and regulations.

For more information, visit *www.LNT.org,* or call 800-332-4100.

MORE ADVENTURE READING FROM
THE MOUNTAINEERS BOOKS

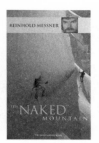

The Naked Mountain, Reinhold Messner
The legendary Messner writes about the most tragic event in his career—the death of this brother on Nanga Parbat.

The Beckoning Silence, Joe Simpson
Brash and colorful, Simpson has never been more entertaining.

The Villain: A Portrait of Don Whillans, Jim Perrin
Brawling, hard-drinking hellman—Don Whillans' reputation was as wide as the Yosemite walls and as high as the Himalayan peaks he risked his life to scale.

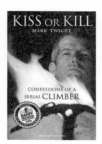

Everest: The West Ridge
Tom Hornbein
The classic, gripping mountaineering saga of the first ascent of Everest's West Ridge.

Kiss or Kill: Confessions of a Serial Climber, Mark Twight
"This is literature about the soul of alpinism." —*Rock & Ice* magazine

The Himalayan Database: The Expedition Archives of Elizabeth Hawley, Elizabeth Hawley; Richard Salisbury, database developer
More than 40 years of Himalayan expedition information is easily accessed on this searchable CD.

Available at fine bookstores and outdoor stores, by phone at 800-553-4453, or on the web at *www.mountaineersbooks.org*

THE MOUNTAINEERS BOOKS